HTML & XHTML

Creating Web Pages

AGAINST THE CLOCK
PERFORMANCE SUPPORT & TRAINING SYSTEMS

Prentice
Hall

Upper Saddle River, NJ 07458

Library of Congress Cataloging-in-Publication Data

HTML & XHTML: Creating Web Pages/Against The Clock
      p. cm.
Includes Index
ISBN 0-13-031054-9
1. HTML (Document Markup Language) 2. XHTML (Document Markup
Language). I. Title: HTML and XHTML. II. Against The Clock (Firm)

QA76.76.H94H75 2002
005.7'2—dc21

              2001054899

Editor-in-Chief: Stephen Helba
Director of Production and Manufacturing: Bruce Johnson
Executive Editor: Elizabeth Sugg
Managing Editor-Editorial: Judy Casillo
Editorial Assistant: Anita Rhodes
Managing Editor-Production: Mary Carnis
Production Editor: Denise Brown
Composition: Against The Clock, Inc.
Design Director: Cheryl Asherman
Senior Design Coordinator: Miguel Ortiz
Cover Design: LaFortezza Design Group, Inc.
Icon Design: James Braun
Prepress: Photoengraving, Inc.
Printer/Binder: Press of Ohio

A portion of the images supplied in this book are Copyright © PhotoDisc, Inc., 201 Fourth Ave., Seattle, WA 98121. These images are the sole property of PhotoDisc and are used by Against The Clock with the permission of the owners. They may not be distributed, copied, transferred, or reproduced by any means whatsoever, other than for the completion of the exercises and projects contained in this Against The Clock training material.

Against The Clock and the Against The Clock logo are trademarks of Against The Clock, Inc., registered in the United States and elsewhere. References to and instructional materials provided for any particular application program, operating system, hardware platform, or other commercially available product or products do not represent an endorsement of such product or products by Against The Clock, Inc. or Prentice Hall, Inc.

Acrobat, Adobe Type Manager, Illustrator, InDesign, PageMaker, Photoshop, PostScript and Premiere are trademarks of Adobe Systems Incorporated. Macintosh is a trademark of Apple Computer, Inc. CorelDRAW! and Painter are trademarks of Corel Corporation. Director, Dreamweaver, FireWorks, Macromedia Flash, FreeHand and Generator are registered trademarks of Macromedia, Inc. FrontPage, Publisher, PowerPoint, Word, Excel, Office, Microsoft, MS-DOS, Windows, and Windows NT are either registered trademarks or trademarks of Microsoft Corporation. QuarkXPress is a registered trademark of Quark, Inc. RealNetworks, Real.com, RealAudio, RealVideo, RealSystem, RealPlayer, RealJukebox and RealMedia are trademarks or registered trademarks of RealNetworks, Inc. TrapWise and PressWise are registered trademarks of ScenicSoft.

Other products and company names mentioned herein may be the trademarks of their respective owners.

Pearson Education LTD.
Pearson Education Australia PTY, Limited
Pearson Education Singapore, Pte. Ltd
Pearson Education North Asia Ltd
Pearson Education Canada, Ltd.
Pearson Educación de Mexico, S.A. de C.V.
Pearson Education -- Japan
Pearson Education Malaysia, Pte. Ltd
Pearson Education, Upper Saddle River, New Jersey

10 9 8 7 6 5 4 3

ISBN 0-13-031054-9

Contents

Purpose

The Against The Clock series has been developed specifically for those involved in the field of computer arts and now — animation, video and multimedia production. Many of our readers are already involved in the industry in advertising and printing, television production, multimedia and Web design. Others are just now preparing for a career within these professions.

This series will provide you with the necessary skills to work in these fast-paced, exciting and rapidly expanding fields. While many people feel that they can simply purchase a computer and the appropriate software and begin designing and producing quality presentations, the real world of high-quality printed and Web communications requires a far more serious commitment.

The Series

The applications presented in the Against The Clock series stand out as the programs of choice in professional computer arts environments.

We've used a modular design for the Against The Clock series, allowing you to mix and match the drawing, imaging, multimedia and page-layout applications that exactly suit your specific needs.

Titles available in the Against The Clock series include:

Macintosh: Basic Operations
Windows: Basic Operations
Adobe Illustrator: Introduction and Advanced Digital Illustration
Macromedia FreeHand: Digital Illustration
Adobe InDesign: Introduction and Advanced Electronic Mechanicals
Adobe PageMaker: Introduction and Advanced Electronic Mechanicals
QuarkXPress: Introduction and Advanced Electronic Mechanicals
Microsoft Publisher: Creating Electronic Mechanicals
Microsoft PowerPoint: Presentation Graphics with Impact
Microsoft FrontPage: Creating and Managing Web Sites
HTML & XHTML: Creating Web Pages
procreate Painter: A Digital Approach to Natural Art Media
Adobe Photoshop: Introduction and Advanced Digital Images
Adobe Premiere: Digital Video Editing
Macromedia Director: Creating Powerful Multimedia
Macromedia Flash: Animating for the Web
Macromedia Dreamweaver: Creating Web Pages
Preflight and File Preparation
TrapWise and PressWise: Digital Trapping and Imposition

There are a number of standard icons that you will see in the sidebars. Each has a standard meaning. Pay close attention to the sidebar notes as you will find valuable comments that will help you throughout this book and in your everyday use of your computer. The standard icons are:

The **Pencil** icon indicates a comment from an experienced operator or instructor. Whenever you see the pencil icon, you'll find corresponding sidebar text that augments or builds upon the subject being discussed at the time.

The **Bomb** or **Pitfalls** icon indicates a potential problem or difficulty. For instance, a certain technique might lead to pages that prove difficult to output. In other cases, there might be something that a program cannot easily accomplish, so we might present a workaround.

The **Pointing Finger** icon indicates a hands-on activity — whether a short exercise or a complete project. Note that sometimes this icon will direct you to the back of the book to complete a project.

The **Key** icon is used to point out that there is a keyboard equivalent to a menu or dialog-box option. Key commands are often faster than using the mouse to select a menu option. Experienced operators often mix the use of keyboard equivalents and menu/dialog box selections to arrive at their optimum speed of execution.

Support Materials

For the Reader

A variety of resource files are included. These files, necessary to complete both the exercises and projects, may be found on the CD-ROM within the RF_HTML folder.

A glossary for this book is included in PDF format on the CD-ROM. The appendix, also available on the CD-ROM in PDF format, includes charts of elements, attributes and CSS properties.

For the Instructor

The Instructor's CD-ROM includes various testing and presentation materials in addition to the files that are supplied with this book.

- **Overhead Presentation Materials** are provided and follow along with the book. These presentations are prepared using Microsoft PowerPoint, and are provided in both native PowerPoint format and Acrobat Portable Document Format (PDF).

- **Extra Projects** are provided along with the data files required for completion. These projects may be used to extend the training session, or they may be used to test the reader's progress.

- **Test Questions and Answers** are included on the Instructor's CD-ROM. These questions may be modified and/or reorganized.

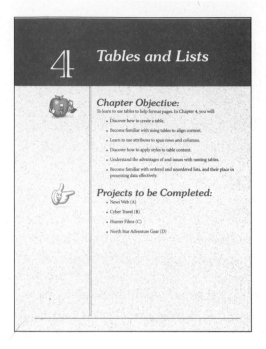

Chapter openers provide
the reader with specific objectives.

Sidebars and *hands-on
activities* supplement concepts
presented in the material.

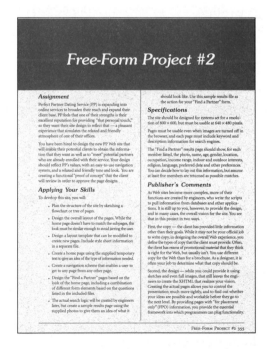

Free-form projects allow you to use
your imagination and your new skills
to satisfy a client's needs.

A *Glossary* and an *Appendix of
Charts* in PDF format, is
included on the CD-ROM that
accompanies this book.

In addition to explanatory text and illustrations, Against The Clock books have been constructed with two primary building blocks: exercises and projects. Projects always result in a finished piece of work — digital imagery built from the ground up, utilizing images and copy from the library supplied on your CD-ROM.

This book, *HTML & XHTML: Creating Web Pages*, uses step-by-step projects on which you will work during your learning sessions. There are also free-form projects immediately preceding the two reviews. You will find images of the step-by-step projects you will complete displayed on the inside front and back covers of the book. Here's a brief overview of each:

Project A: News Web

A local newspaper is moving into online content as well as print publications. You are working on the front page of their new Web site, News Web. You will give their home page a clean layout to facilitate easy use. Starting from the client-approved sketch, you will use the skills learned so far to determine the best way to structure and format the content. In this project, you will create the page and structure it to match the sketch using complex (nested) XHTML tables. You will document the table, and then add text, images and hyperlinks. In addition to tables, you will use Cascading Style Sheets to format the content of the News Web online news agency.

Project B: Cyber Travel

It would be virtually impossible to take orders over the Web without the use of XHTML forms for the user to fill out. Cyber Travel, a travel agency, has decided to make their existing Web site more interactive by adding just such a form to encourage potential customers to submit travel questions, plans and desires as well as contact information. In this project, you will create a user survey for Cyber Travel. After you build the basic form and a series of subforms, you will add different types of form elements including text boxes, checkboxes, radio buttons, select boxes, a submit button and more. Finally, you will use tables to enhance the appearance of the form.

Project C: Hunter Films

Your company, Hunter Films, needs a Web site to feature your products — movies. This multimedia site should feature some of the bells and whistles of Web design to suit the company's products. You will build the home page for hunterfilm.com with thumbnails of the three featured films. Clicking a thumbnail will open a new window that will play the selected movie. In this project, you will create the layout of the page using tables and divs. You will create the individual movie pages, embed the movies and add controls. You will also use JavaScript to create those pop-up windows that display the provided video files.

Project D: North Star Adventure Gear

Creating a Web site is more than just bells and whistles. A business must plan for its content to be available in many different forms, meeting a variety of different needs, whether accommodations of disabilities or alternate formats to suit browsers for PDAs, cell phones and more. In this project, you will take the existing North Star Adventure Gear Web page and determine areas where accessibility and usability can be improved. You will redesign the site, using CSS, divs, alternative text navigation, tables, alt text, summaries, an altered color scheme and more. You will also add <meta /> tags to improve the site's performance on search engines.

Acknowledgments

I would like to give special thanks to the writers, illustrators, editors, and others who have worked long and hard to complete the Against The Clock series.

Thanks to the dedicated teaching professionals whose comments and expertise contributed to the success of these products, including Doris Anton of Wichita Area Technical College and Jamey Weare of Santa Fe Community College.

Thanks to Terry Sisk Graybill, senior copy editor, and final link in the chain of production, for her tremendous help in making sure that we all said what we meant to say.

A big thanks to Denise Brown and Kerry Reardon, for their guidance, patience, and attention to detail.

— Ellenn Behoriam, October 2001

About Against The Clock and the Author

Our History

Against The Clock (ATC) was founded in 1990 as a part of Lanman Systems Group, one of the nation's leading systems integration and training firms. The company specialized in developing custom training materials for such clients as L.L. Bean, *The New England Journal of Medicine*, the Smithsonian, the National Education Association, *Air & Space Magazine*, Publishers Clearing House, the National Wildlife Society, Home Shopping Network and many others. The integration firm was among the most highly respected in the graphic arts industry.

To a great degree, the success of Lanman Systems Group can be attributed to the thousands of pages of course materials developed at the company's demanding client sites. Throughout the rapid growth of Lanman Systems Group, founder and general manager Ellenn Behoriam developed the expertise necessary to manage technical experts, content providers, writers, editors, illustrators, designers, layout artists, proofreaders and the rest of the chain of professionals required to develop structured and highly effective training materials.

Following the sale of the Lanman Companies to World Color, one of the nation's largest commercial printers, Ellenn embarked on a project to develop a new library of hands-on training materials engineered specifically for the professional graphic artist. A large part of this effort is finding and working with talented professional artists, authors and educators from around the country.

The result is the ATC training library.

About the Authors

Nicholas Chase has been involved in Web-site development for companies including Lucent Technologies, Sun Microsystems, Oracle Corporation and the Tampa Bay Buccaneers. Nick has been a high school physics teacher, a low-level radioactive-waste facility manager, an online science fiction magazine editor, a multimedia engineer and an Oracle instructor. More recently, he was the Chief Technology Officer of an interactive communications agency in Clearwater, Florida, and is the author of several books on Web development. He currently lives in Florida with his beautiful wife Sarah and their teenage son, Sean.

Jamey Weare has been an instructor at Santa Fe Community College in the Information Technology Education department for two years. Prior to teaching at the college, he worked in a number of academic support roles including Web designer and network technician. Jamey holds an associate degree in Computer Systems Analysis, an associate degree in Business, and is currently working towards a bachelor degree in Decision Information Science.

Getting Started

Platform

This book covers the creation of Web pages that work with all traditional browsers, whether they are running on a Macintosh, Windows-based PC, or Linux or other UNIX-based operating system. Both Netscape Navigator 4.x and above and Microsoft Internet Explorer 5.x and above are covered.

Naming Conventions

In the early days of the PC, the Windows operating system placed several restrictions on naming files. All file names consisted of two parts: a name, which could contain no more than eight alphanumeric characters, and a three-character suffix. The suffix defined the nature of the file. Applications generally ended with the .exe (for executable) suffix, while documents used suffixes like .doc (document), .txt (text file), .wav (wave, a sound format), .htm (HTML format) and many others.

For at least the past five years, Windows systems no longer restrict you to eight characters for the name; you can use 256 characters. Every application appends a three-character suffix to its files. You might not see these extensions, however. By default, the Windows operating system hides extensions for "known" file types. These known file types include just about every file you're will use in this book.

To configure your system so that file extensions are visible, click the Start button (in the lower-left part of your screen), and select Settings>Folder Options from the pop-up menu. Select the View tab, and uncheck the Hide File Extensions for Known File Types.

The CD-ROM and Initial Setup Considerations

Before you begin using your Against The Clock book, you must set up your system to allow access to the various files and tools to complete your lessons.

Resource Files

This book comes complete with a collection of resource files. These files are an integral part of the learning experience. They're used throughout the book to help you construct increasingly complex elements. Having these building blocks available to you for practice and study sessions will ensure that you will be able to experience the exercises and complete the project assignments smoothly, spending a minimum of time looking for the various required components.

Locate the RF_HTML folder and drag its icon onto your hard disk drive. If you have limited disk space, you may want to copy only the files for one or two lessons at a time.

Creating a Project Folder

Throughout the exercises and projects, you'll be required to save your work. Since the CD-ROM is read-only, you cannot write information to it. Create a "Work in Progress" folder on your hard disk, and use it to store your work. Create the folder at the highest level of your system, where it will always be easy to find. Name this folder "WIP".

System Requirements

There are no specific system requirements necessary for this book, with the exception of an available browser. Examples are shown using Microsoft Internet Explorer 5, downloadable from the Microsoft site:

Macintosh: http://www.microsoft.com/mac/download/ie/ie50.asp

Windows: http://www.microsoft.com/windows/ie/downloads/archive/default.asp

The examples in this book can also be used with Netscape Navigator version 4.7 and above. Navigator can be downloaded from the Netscape site at http://home.netscape.com/computing/download/index.html.

A CD-ROM drive is also required.

Prerequisites

This book assumes that you have a basic understanding of how to use your system. You should know how to use your mouse to point and click, and how to drag items around the screen. You should know how to resize a window, and how to arrange windows on your desktop to maximize available space. You should know how to access pull-down menus, and how checkboxes and radio buttons work. Lastly, you should know how to create, open and save files.

If you're familiar with these fundamental skills, then you know all that's necessary to utilize the Against The Clock library.

Introduction

Introduction

The World Wide Web (the Web) is so visible and accepted today that it's safe to say that if you're picking up this book, you've already had experience using the Web. Perhaps you've just surfed around, admiring other people's work, or perhaps you've already tried your hand at building a Web page. In either case, now you're thinking about getting more involved and learning HTML, the language of the Web. This book will show you what you need to know, guiding you through the basics and into the bells and whistles that make a designer's job so much fun.

If you've never tried to build a page before, don't worry — we'll get you started. If you have built pages in HTML before, hang on, because there's still more to learn. We'll discuss the basic principles behind both HTML and its latest incarnation, XHTML.

HTML and XHTML have come a long way since they were developed as an application of Standard Generalized Markup Language, or SGML. Designed to allow users with different software programs to view the same content, early versions came with major limitations. Now designers have almost complete freedom as far as what appears where, why and how, just by getting into the actual code.

Aren't There Editors for This?

Right about now, particularly if you're a designer, you're probably asking yourself why you would even want to code by hand. After all, these days you can't turn around without running into a program (editor) for designing Web pages. The first editors focused on the code itself, making it easier to see tags, or inserting them at the click of a button. Then along came several editors of a new sort.

WYSIWYG — What You See Is What You Get

Once designers started working on Web pages, a whole new crop of editors hit the market. Most of these programs fall under the category of *WYSIWYG*, or What-You-See-Is-What-You-Get editors. These are programs, such as Macromedia Dreamweaver and Microsoft FrontPage, which enable users to create a Web page in much the same way that they might create a document in Microsoft Word or QuarkXPress — by moving elements around, applying styles to them and then saving the page in properly formatted HTML.

The effectiveness of these programs has ranged from very good (as in the latest versions of Dreamweaver) to downright awful (as in any of the early applications).

The Limitations of WYSIWYG

So if there are very good WYSIWYG programs out there, why bother to learn the code? There are several reasons.

First, no matter how good a WYSIWYG program is right now, eventually it will be out of date, and if you want to add the latest XHTML abilities to your page, you'll have to do so by hand-coding.

Second, while WYSIWYG editors may be very good at creating static HTML pages, the Web is gradually moving away from static content in favor of dynamically generated content, such as that coming from a database. WYSIWYG editors can't always help you here; you're going to have to be able to get in there and work the pages "with your bare hands."

Third, and most important, understanding how the code works enables you to be more creative. The programmers of your editor have tried to think of all the possibilities, but as the designer, it's your job to come up with the new and different. Understanding how code works gives you the freedom to create pages a group of programmers never would have planned, so didn't build into the editor.

And the name of the game is creativity, isn't it?

In this book, we'll look at both the basics of XHTML and ways for you to take it even farther, such as with Cascading Style Sheets and scripting. We'll cover all of the important tags, but, more important than memorizing a series of tags that you can look up, in any case, we'll give you a grounding in how they actually work, to help you take your site to the next level.

1 HTML and XHTML — The Basics

Chapter Objective:

To learn how to create a simple XHTML page using the basics common to all World Wide Web content. In Chapter 1, you will:

- Discover some key differences between HTML and XHTML.

- Learn about the three types of XHTML and how to validate pages created in each.

- Become familiar with some of the history of browsers, text editors and coding.

- Discover how to create a Web page using just a text editor.

- Become familiar with tags, elements and attributes.

- Learn how to format text on the page.

- Become familiar with controlling white space.

- Discover how to add images to a Web page and align them properly.

Projects to be Completed:

- News Web (A)

- Cyber Travel (B)

- Hunter Films (C)

- North Star Adventure Gear (D)

XHTML and HTML — The Basics

HyperText Markup Language, or HTML, has come a long way since it was first standardized in the early 1990s. It began as a way for people with different programs and operating systems to exchange information without worrying about having the same programs and file formats. No matter what program the recipient used to view the information, it always looked (just about) the same. This ability to exchange information grew out of an idea.

Origin of the Browser

The idea of modern hyptertext is thought to have originated in a 1945 article by Vannevar Bush titled "As We May Think." Bush described the memex, a vast collection of information in which users left "trails" that others could follow, or even supplement. The memex was a photo-electrical-mechanical device that linked documents on microfiche.

Vannevar Bush was concerned about the growing amount of information with which humans were forced to deal back in 1945. Who says information overload is a new problem?

The term "hypertext," however, was coined in 1965 by Ted Nelson, who described a system called "Xanadu," in which every piece of information was identified by a unique number. In Xanadu, an author could make a virtual copy of existing text and include it in a new work, but the original would always be linked to this copy. Nelson also described hypermaps and hypermedia, such as a movie that had different optional directions, shown at the Czechoslovakian Pavilion at Expo '67.

Although Xanadu never materialized, others, such as Doug Engelbart, Andries Van Dam and Bill Atkinson, the creator of HyperCard, pursued similar ideas, and much of the Xanadu concept was eventually incorporated into the World Wide Web.

In 1989, Tim Berners-Lee was working at the European Particle Physics Laboratory (CERN) on developing the ability for people to link information on different systems using a single addressing method, which became today's Uniform Resource Locator (URL), or Web address. He wanted his system to enable users to make their own information readable on another user's machine with a minimum of effort, as well.

Before this approach, if someone had a document written in Microsoft Word, for example, only individuals with Microsoft Word on their computers could read it. Other hypertext systems had already been created, but all of them required authors to possess programming skills, to greater and lesser extents.

Berners-Lee's idea was simple: design a standard way of creating content, so that it would be simple to write a program to read this content. In fact, this standard way of creating content was already being done with a formatting language called "Standard Generalized Markup Language," or "SGML." SGML, however, can be difficult to use, and that complexity was not required for what Berners-Lee planned to do.

The idea, however, was just what he needed. HTML would use SGML's method of "tagging" content, or surrounding it with tags, as in:

Don't forget to check out our **<b>**new**</b>** listings!

HTML would become the standard way to present content, and the program to read it was called a "browser."

HTML Tags

An *HTML tag* is a character or set or characters enclosed in less-than (<) and greater-than (>) signs, as in:

- <b> (for bold)
- <i> (for italics)
- <h1> (for one of a number of heading types)

Tags generally come in pairs, with an opening and closing tag. The *opening tag* indicates the start of a section, and the *closing tag* indicates the end of it. A closing tag is designated by a /, as in </b>. So in our example above, the word new would be bold, but the rest of the sentence wouldn't, as we can see here.

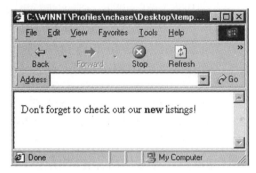

HTML also allows us to use nested tags. A *nested tag* is one that is contained within another tag. For instance, we could italicize our entire sentence using:

<i>Don't forget to check out our <b>new</b> listings!</i>

In this example, the entire sentence would be italic, and the word new would be both italic and bold.

Of course, none of this does us any good without a *browser*, the program that interprets the HTML.

The First Graphical Browsers

Berners-Lee began serious work on his browser (then called "WorldWideWeb") in 1990, but the very first graphical browser to significantly penetrate the market was Mosaic, developed by the National Center for Supercomputing Applications (NCSA). Mosaic was primitive by today's standards. The first version, in fact, couldn't even display graphics on the same line as text!

When Marc Andreessen, of the Mosaic team, decided to leave NCSA and start his own company, he brought Mosaic with him and renamed it Netscape Navigator.

The more things change, the more they stay the same. In the early days, Web-page authors had to insert line breaks into their tables to compensate for earlier browsers that didn't support them. Now authors have to worry about whether older browsers will understand their pages at all!

The State of Browsers Today

Netscape Navigator started a trend that has continued into the last few years by beginning to add its own capabilities. For instance, the early versions of Mosaic didn't understand tables, which are used to format information into rows and columns. If you built your page using them and someone with an older, less capable browser visited your site, the result was often a jumbled mess.

Netscape was not the only company guilty of adding features. When Microsoft decided the World Wide Web was not going to go away, it put out its own browser, Microsoft Internet Explorer (IE). IE also added its own new features, such as a scrolling marquee, which could not be seen by Netscape Navigator users.

These examples are only a tiny taste of what occurred in the late 1990s during the so-called "browser wars," when Netscape and Microsoft tried to outdo each other with every new release of their browsers.

The result was a veritable explosion of new features making their way into HTML. While the first browsers seemed a marvel because you could put an image on the page, Web designers now can not only designate precisely where on the page that image should go, but also direct the page to change that image when the user's mouse rolls over it and much more. Interactivity, once reserved for complex programs, can now be implemented by non-programmers.

HTML 4.01 and XHTML 1.0

The reason that the Web took off so quickly is that virtually anybody could build a Web page. It didn't require complicated software or mechanics that would be difficult for non-programmers to understand.

One example of this simplicity in action is the following basic Web page created to announce the birth of a friend's baby.

*Note: you will use two types of programs to work on your Web files throughout this course. One is a **text editor**, a program that lets you add or change text, add or change code, and generally work on the underlying structure of the page. The other type of program you will use is a browser that lets you see the page as it is rendered from the code. Each one serves its function without overlapping the other's purpose. Our instructions will frequently alternate, having you alter or add material in the text editor and then refresh the browser so that you can see the results of your work.*

To create this page, we didn't have to learn or buy a $900 page-layout program. Instead, we merely opened a text editor, such as SimpleText on the Macintosh or Notepad on the PC, and created a file with the following text:

```
<html>
<head>
   <title>It's a boy!</title>
</head>
<body>

<font size="+3"><b>It's A Boy!</b></font>

<p>Renee and Christopher would like to announce the birth of their son, Mark.</p>
<center>
   <img src="mark.jpg">
   <p><b>Mark Christopher Volkers</b></p>
   <p>Born April 18, 2001 at 4:35am</p>
   <p>17 inches</p>
   <p>8 lbs, 12 oz.</p>
</center>
</body>
</html>
```

We'll look at code in much greater detail later, but those of you who have experience with some older programs, such as early WordPerfect, or with typesetting code, may recognize the technique. It's called "markup" — tagging a specific section of text to tell the program what to do with it. We wanted the birth information centered, so we put a center tag around it.

Users also quickly discovered that if they liked the way a page that they visited looked, the browser could show them the page as text, called the "source." Doing so enabled them to examine the source and learn how to write it themselves. No specialized programs or training were required.

HTML 4.01 is the most recent (and likely final) version of HTML to be recommended by the World Wide Web Consortium. *The World Wide Web Consortium*, or *W3C*, is an organization that was brought together in 1994 to an industry that was changing rapidly. The de facto standards body of the Web, it issues the recommendations that companies (theoretically) live by. HTML 4.01 lists all of the "official" tags, which range from simple formatting tags like the ones above to those that allow complicated page layout and interactive scripting.

Then What Is XHTML?

One aspect of the browser wars was both companies' attempts to implement their own features to make life easier for Web-page authors, hoping that these authors would be more likely to code for one specific browser. The problem with that approach was that standards often fell by the wayside. For instance, HTML 4.01 designates a paragraph, or <p></p> tag, that goes around a block of text to set it off from the text around it, as it does in the example above. Both major browsers, however, allow users to leave off the </p>, effectively using the <p> tag as just a double line break. That's not so bad, but IE actually allows authors to leave off the end of a table, as well. Unfortunately, not all browsers are so flexible. It is not uncommon for a page that looks fine in IE to be completely blank in Netscape.

The result is that it's estimated that 50% of the programming that goes into a browser today is there simply to allow for errors, or deviations from the standard, on the part of the Web-page author. No wonder it takes so long to download IE 5.5!

Another difficulty stemmed from the way in which new capabilities were added. Deciding on a new tag and trying to get authors to adopt it was clearly not the most efficient way.

To fill this need, the W3C created *XHTML 1.0*, or Extensible Hypertext Markup Language, which is described as "a reformulation of HTML 4.01 into XML."

XML + HTML = XHTML

XML is also a tagging language, but is more general than HTML. Where HTML is comprised of a specific set of tags, XML is a method for specifying any tag you want, as long as it makes sense to you. Away from the Web, XML is used for storing data, moving it from place to place, and as a standard way for different companies or programs to communicate with each other.

Of course, that doesn't mean that we can just make up tags and expect the browser to display them, necessarily. After all, if we created a <sectionheading></sectionheading> tag, how would the browser know what to do with it?

Content vs. Presentation

One reason we might want to create a <sectionheading></sectionheading> tag might be for other media. While right now we're building pages for a browser on a computer, eventually we're going to want to display this same information on other media, such as mobile phones, PDAs or even other media we haven't thought of yet!

That flexibility would be difficult with our simple page. For instance, we might decide that on a mobile phone, we would only want to display the key information: Mark's name, birth date and weight. Unfortunately, while it's easy for a person to tell the difference between his name and our announcement ("It's a boy!"), a computer couldn't distinguish between them because it only recognizes that they're both bold.

On the other hand, if we could rewrite the page as:

```
<html>
<head>
   <title>It's a boy!</title>
</head>
<body>

<h1>It's A Boy!</h1>

<p>Renee and Christopher would like to announce the birth of their son, Mark.</p>
<center>
   <img src="mark.jpg" />
   <p><b>Mark Christopher Volkers</b></p>
   <p>Born April 18, 2001 at 4:35am</p>
   <p>17 inches</p>
   <p>8 lbs, 12 oz.</p>
</center>
</body>
</html>
```

In this case, the display will look the same, but we've set the announcement as a heading (<h1></h1>), which tells the browser to render it large and bold. This way, we can see the difference, and direct a mobile phone to display just the key information, which is between <p> tags.

This process is called "separating content from presentation" and will become more important as content is reused in different formats. It's already important to search engines, such as Altavista or Lycos, and to a much lesser extent, Yahoo!, which attempt to identify the most important information on a page to determine what searches (by what key words) will bring up that Web page. There are other tags besides headings that could be used to make the content look important to a human, but the search engine wouldn't understand that form of emphasis.

The Reformulation of HTML 4.01 into XHTML 1.0

So there are three basic purposes behind XHTML, or Extensible Hypertext Markup Language:

- Clean up sloppy HTML by requiring that Web-page authors follow the W3C standards.
- Allow for easier ways to extend the language and add new features.
- Separate content from presentation.

These are worthwhile goals, but the authors of the XHTML specification realized that there are millions (by some account, billions) of Web pages already out there, and millions of people used to the old, less stringent rules. So they decided to ease into these goals slowly, giving authors and software vendors time to catch up.

They did this by creating three different "flavors" of XHTML 1.0. These are individual recommendations that Web authors can choose to follow. Browsers don't force any particular set of tags on an author, but as we will see, there are ways to determine whether we've strayed from the standard. They are:

We don't need to worry about creating a DTD, because each flavor of XHTML has a standard DTD to which we will refer.

- **Strict.** In order to be in compliance with this recommendation, we must not only follow the XML rules that prevent us from creating sloppy code, but also remove any HTML that is focused on presentation, relying instead on Cascading Style Sheets (CSS), which we will cover in Chapter 3, to determine the appearance of the page. This is also the version closest to XHTML 1.1.

- **Transitional.** Transitional XHTML 1.0 is literally a reformulation of HTML 4.01. Virtually every tag is reproduced in its entirety, but all of the loopholes for which browsers have been compensating have been removed. That means that while some pages will have to be tweaked to conform to the new rules and remove some features that have been *deprecated*, or marked for extinction, any page that's been written properly will need very little work to conform to this standard. Transitional XHTML is closest to the vast majority of Web pages that already exist, and is sometimes needed to compensate for browsers that don't fully support CSS. (This is the version of XHTML that we will use and discuss throughout this book, with a few exceptions.)

- **Frameset.** HTML frames enable us to create a type of window-in-a-window effect on a Web page. We will deal with frames more fully in Chapter 6.

Each of these versions of XHTML is described by a Document Type Definition, or DTD. We can use this DTD to make sure that we haven't made any structural or typing mistakes in a page. This process of verifying the page is called "validation." Before we worry about validation, however, we need to create a page to validate.

The Basic Web Page

When you really come down to it, a Web page is just a text file that refers to other files, such as images. The browser knows how to interpret this file because it understands the system of tags that describes the content. Each string of text is described by tags, whether it represents a headline, an image, someone's name rendered in bold or the overall body of content. Every page uses a standard structure.

Creating a Web page involves a series of steps:

- **Create a folder in which all of our files will live.** Remember that a Web site can have hundreds of individual pieces, such as images, so it's a good idea to organize the images in a separate folder, as much as possible. For now, however, we will create a single folder in your WIP folder.

  In a production environment, our files would be on the Web server, but we won't need to do that for now.

- **Create the text of the Web page.** Once the folder(s) exist, we create the text of the page in a text editor such as SimpleText or Notepad. In some cases, you may be using an application such as Macromedia Dreamweaver, which enables you to move items around on the page, but at the end of the day, Dreamweaver just saves a text file.

- **Review the page in a browser.** Once the text file is created, we can look at the results by opening the page in a browser such as Netscape Navigator or Microsoft Internet Explorer. Browsers only allow us to view the page; we can't edit it from within the browser. To do that, we need to go back to the text editor.

Exercise Setup

Enough theory, let's get our hands dirty. We're going to create the beginning of a Web site for "Ask Dr. Know-It-All." We'll begin by creating the folder on our local hard drive and naming the folder "WIP" ("Work In Progress"). We will also create a text file within that folder for our first page.

Create the Basic File

1. If you haven't already done so, create a new folder on your desktop called "WIP". Inside this folder, create another new folder called "basics".

2. Open a simple text editor, such as SimpleText or Notepad.

3. Create a new document by selecting File>New.

4. Type "Hello World!" (without the quotes) on the first line of the document.

5. Save the document as "hello.html" to the **WIP>basics** folder.

6. Start your browser. We will use Microsoft Internet Explorer (IE) for the illustrations in this book. (You can use any browser that you want to work on the exercises, but there may be slight differences in button names or in the way that the page is rendered.)

The production environment is where your finished Web site lives. You should work directly on production files.

You'll want to make sure that you're using a text editor, and not a word processor, such as Microsoft Word or Corel WordPerfect. MS Word, in particular, can add to our text in an attempt to be "helpful."

While we want the file to be text, we want it to have an .html extension instead of .txt. Occasionally, Windows adds .txt to the filename, making our file hello.html.txt. If so, change the file name and reopen it. This time Windows will leave the name alone.

Different browsers sometimes use slightly different terms. For instance, some browsers might say Open File or Open Page. Don't be alarmed if your browser varies the phrases.

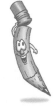

The fact that old browsers ignore tags that they doesn't understand is no guarantee that a page that uses new tags will be readable on an old browser, At least there won't be any errors!

7. Choose File>Open (or Open File) in the IE window.

8. Navigate to the file by selecting Browse>**WIP>basics>hello.html** (or Locate File>**WIP>basics>hello.html**).

9. Double-click the file.

10. Click OK. Congratulations! You've created your first Web page!

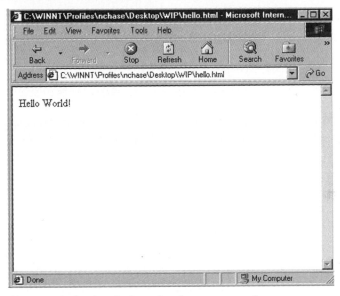

11. Leave the file open in both windows for the next exercise.

Tags

Strictly speaking, the page we just created was an HTML page, because we named it that way. It wasn't really an XHTML page, because to create an XHTML page, we need to use tags.

Tags are the foundation of a Web page. They describe how items should look and what they are. Tags tell the browser what to do with specific pieces of information, and they define the structure of a page.

Tags, as you have no doubt noticed, are enclosed between < and >. The browser sees those marks, and knows to interpret the text between them. If the browser doesn't understand a particular tag, it ignores it. In this way, old browsers can still be used with new pages without causing errors.

There is much more to tags than just formatting, however. An XHTML document is highly structured; you could, if you wanted, create a structure of data in the form of a tree, of sorts, with the pieces. This stems from its roots in XML. In fact, what we used to think of as simple tags are now much more like XML elements.

Elements

An *element* is a type of object that can contain text or even other objects. For instance, in our previous example, though we haven't talked about these specific tags yet, a page might consist of an html element, which contains a body element, which contains text and a number of other elements, and so on.

When one element is contained by another, it's said to be "nested," as mentioned earlier. One of the rules of XHTML is that elements have to be nested properly, with one section completely contained within another. For instance, we couldn't write:

\<p\>You have to listen, because this is **\<b\>**important.**\</p\>\</b\>**

(although most of today's browsers would let us get away with it), since the closing tag (\</b\>) is outside the \</p\> tag but the opening \<b\> is inside the \<p\> tags. Instead, we have to write:

\<p\>You have to listen, because this is **\<b\>**important.**\</b\>\</p\>**

In this example, the paragraph element (\<p\>\</p\>) contains a bold element (\<b\>\</b\>) that contains the text "important."

Attributes

Containing text is only one way that an element can provide information. Elements can also carry *attributes*, which are pieces of information contained within the opening tag.

In general, attributes provide more information about the tag and what we want it to do. For instance, we could create a heading on our page and tell the browser that we want to center it:

\<h1 align="center"\>Chapter 1\</h1\>

In this case, we have an h1 element. The element contains an align attribute, which has a value of center. This is known as a "name-value pair," and we enclose the value in double quotes so that the browser knows where it ends. For an image tag, we might say:

\<img src="book.jpg" alt="My Life " /\>

In this case, we have an img (image) element. We're telling the browser that the source, or src, for the image is book.jpg, and that the alternate text (alt) for this tag is My Life. (We'll talk more about the image tag and alternate text shortly.)

Some tags, such as those shown above for images, contain only attributes. Because they don't contain any text between the start and end tags, these are known as "empty elements," and we'll see more about them shortly as well.

The Basic Structure

An XHTML page has a definite structure.

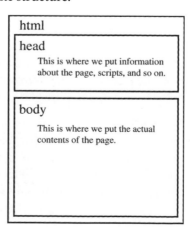

html		
head		
	This is where we put information about the page, scripts, and so on.	
body		
	This is where we put the actual contents of the page.	

Remember to use straight quotation marks (" ") not typographer's or "curly quotes" (" ") when you write your code. If you don't, the code will fail.

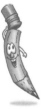

If you have been writing HTML for a while, you are probably wondering about the slash, since you were expecting it to say:

\<img src="book.jpg" alt="My Life"\>

The extra slash is one of the changes that comes with XHTML, and must be preceded with a space, or older browsers will not display properly. So it now reads correctly:

\<img src="book.jpg" alt="My Life" /\>

<html>

The html element defines the entire page. All of the content of and about the page must go within this element.

One of the requirements for any valid XHTML page is that all other tags are contained between <html> and </html>.

<head>

The head section of a page is where we put information that is not generally shown on the page but is still important to it. For instance, when we add meta information (discussed in Chapter 10), or information about the page, this is where it will go. In other situations, we may have scripts that will be run by the browser (for example, to change an image when the mouse rolls over it), and those scripts (discussed in Chapter 8) are generally placed in the head section of the page.

<title>

The title, which is included within the head of the document, doesn't actually appear on the page but typically controls the text that displays in the Title bar of the browser window.

<body>

The body is where the content of the page goes. All text, images and other items that the user sees go in this section.

We create these sections using the most basic HTML tags: html, head and body.

Add Structure to an HTML Page

Remember the text shouldn't really be bold. It's just how we know what's changed between steps.

1. In the open hello.html file in your text editor, add the <html>, <head> and <body> opening and closing tags to the existing document. The text should read:

```
<html>
  <head>
  </head>
  <body>
    Hello, World!
  </body>
</html>
```

2. Save the file.

3. If you still have hello.html open in your browser from the last exercise, click the Refresh button. Otherwise, launch IE and select File>Open to open the file, as before.

Notice that nothing has changed from before because we haven't actually added any content. All that we have done, so far, is define the structure of the document.

The appearance and content of the title bar may vary based on your browser and operating system. Your title bar may simply say "Untitled."

Title Bar

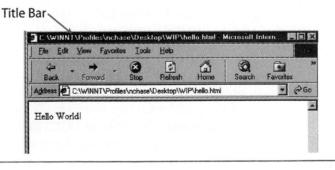

4. Now, if someone were to bookmark this page, the browser would just give "Untitled" (or "Shortcut to hello.html" in some browsers) as the document name, because we haven't given it any other title. The Title bar may display the location of the document, but that's not useful for our visitors. They need an actual title, so give them one:

```
<html>
  <head>
    <title>Hello, World, it's our first page!</title>
  </head>
  <body>
    Hello, World!
  </body>
</html>
```

5. Save the file.

6. Return to your browser, and refresh the page. Notice that we now have a title at the top of the page.

Netscape calls the Refresh button "Reload."

7. Leave the file open in both windows for the next exercise.

Validating an XHTML Page

As we mentioned earlier, there are three "flavors" of XHTML, each of which is defined in a Document Type Definition, or DTD. While our file will display correctly in the browser, it is not technically a valid XHTML page unless we can verify that it conforms to one of those DTDs.

We can check this using a special application called a "validating parser," but rather than installing one (which is well beyond the scope of this book), we can use the XHTML validation service provided by the World Wide Web Commission.

Validating an XHTML page is not strictly necessary, but can be helpful for two reasons:

- First, validation can help you to check for errors that current browsers normally forgive, so that you know that your pages won't "break" later, when browsers are not as forgiving. For example, most browsers will allow you to place text directly into the body tag (<body></body>), but it should actually be within another tag such as a paragraph tag (<p></p>).

- Second, there are times when a page just doesn't look right, and you can't figure out why. Attempting to validate the page can show you where you may have a misspelled or misplaced tag.

Let's take a look at how we would go about validating a document. First, we have to specify the DTD that we're going to follow. We do that through a special tag called the "DOCTYPE declaration." The *DOCTYPE declaration* is what links a document to the DTD to which it needs to conform. Once we've added it, we can upload the document to be checked. (We'll talk more about the different DOCTYPEs and what they mean in Chapter 12. For now, we'll look at how their presence enables us to validate files.)

Throughout this book you will find several sections that may require significant typing. To save time, we've provided some of these lengthy files on the CD. These files are organized by chapter and may be found within the RF_HTML folder within a folder called Text Files.

Validate a Document

1. Open your browser, and navigate to http://validator.w3.org/file-upload.html.

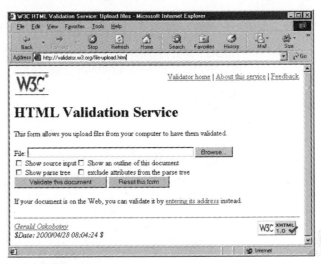

2. In the open document hello.html in your text editor, add the DOCTYPE (shown below in bold) for XHTML Strict, just above the <html> tag.

```
<!DOCTYPE HTML PUBLIC "-//W3C//DTD HTML 4.01//EN"
"http://www.w3.org/TR/html4/strict.dtd">
<html>
  <head>
    <title>Hello, World, it's our first page!</title>
  </head>
  <body>
    Hello, World!
  </body>
</html>
```

3. Save the file.

4. In your browser, navigate to the file by selecting Browse>**WIP>basics>hello.html**, and click Open.

5. Click the Validate This File button.

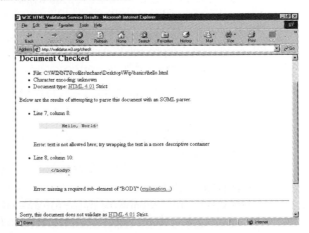

6. Notice that although our document was handled correctly by the browser, the validator didn't accept it because we had our text in the body, rather than within another tag. We'll take a look at exactly why in Chapter 12, when we discuss the different versions of XHTML in more detail.

In the meantime, change the DOCTYPE to the Transitional DTD.

```
<!DOCTYPE HTML PUBLIC "-//W3C//DTD HTML 4.01 Transitional//EN"
"http://www.w3.org/TR/html4/loose.dtd">
<html>
  <head>
    <title>Hello, World, it's our first page!</title>
  </head>
  <body>
    Hello, World!
  </body>
</html>
```

7. Save the file. Click the Back button on the browser. Navigate again to your file by selecting Browse>**WIP>basics>hello.html**, and click OK. Click Validate This File.

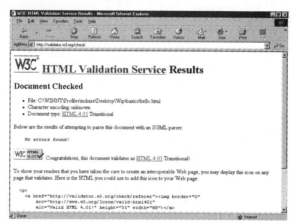

8. Notice that this time, the same document has been successfully validated.

9. Leave the file open in both windows for the next exercise.

Validation Using Transitional vs. Strict DTDs

Notice that, in the exercise, our file would not validate under the Strict DTD, but was fine under Transitional DTD. This is because there are some items that are on their way out and that won't be supported under later versions of XHTML. Items that are on the way out are said to be "deprecated." An item that is deprecated works for now but won't in the future, so should be removed from your code as soon as possible.

So why are we using Transitional DTD for this book? Because there is a fine line between being compliant and practical. Strict DTD assumes that all formatting will be done using Cascading Style Sheets (CSS), which will be discussed in Chapter 3, but not all browsers support all features of CSS. This means that if we wrote all of our pages using Strict, many browsers wouldn't get the attractive pages that we intend.

In order to have the best of both worlds, and because browsers supporting Transitional XHTML will probably be in use for some time, we will use it. We will, however, make note of situations where deprecated tags and attributes are in use.

Body Text

As we have seen above, body text is copy contained in the <body></body> tags. The actual copy is simply text like any text file. You add and subtract text in essentially the same fashion as you would in any text editor. What makes this text different is the structure in which it is placed and the formatting that we apply. Web-page body text can be formatted using white space such as line or paragraph breaks, spaces within a line, type formatting such as bold or italicized text and more. Using Cascading Style Sheets (CSS), you can also create text in different sizes and control its alignment. Some of this control is also possible using XHTML, as we can see with headings and images as discussed below.

White Space and Paragraph Breaks

White space, or the empty areas on the page that make a page easier to read, is an important element of design, and one that we often take for granted when working with word-processing or page-layout programs. With those types of programs, if we want to add several blank lines to the page, we just add them and see the results immediately. Want to break a line of text? Just add a hard return to the text.

Matters are not quite so simple in XHTML. White space in the text of our file is ignored by the browser, so if we want to see it in our final document, we must add it by using tags such as <p></p> and <br />.

For instance, if we had a block of text on the page with some white space added, the word-processed text would look like this:

> White space is an important element of design, and one that we often take for granted when working with word-processing or page-layout programs. With those types of programs, if we want to add several blank lines to the page, we just do it and see the results immediately. Want to break a line of text? Just add a hard return to the text.

> Things are not quite so simple in XHTML. White space in our file is ignored by the browser, so if we want to see it in our final document, we're going to have to add it specifically using tags.

The page in the browser, however, would not show the added space:

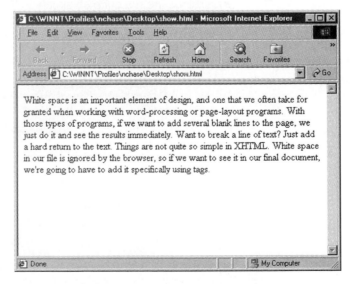

We can add a simple line break by using the <br /> tag, as in:

White space is an important element of design, and one that we often take for granted when working with word-processing or page-layout programs. With those types of programs, if we want to add several blank lines to the page, we just do it and see the results immediately. Want to break a line of text? Just add a hard return to the text:

**
**

Things are not quite so simple in XHTML. White space in our file is ignored by the browser, so if we want to see it in our final document, we're going to have to add it specifically using tags.

This would add a single line break to the page:

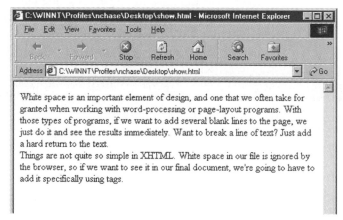

Notice that rather than an opening and closing tag, the break tag is a single tag with an extra slash, preceded by a space. This is an example of an empty tag. We'll discuss empty tags when we talk about images, later in this chapter.

Enclosing a paragraphs in <p></p> tags will create a double line break between them, as in:

<p>White space is an important element of design, and one that we often take for granted when working with word-processing or page-layout programs. With those types of programs, if we want to add several blank lines to the page, we just do it and see the results immediately. Want to break a line of text? Just add a hard return to the text.**</p>**

<p>Things are not quite so simple in XHTML. White space in our file is ignored by the browser, so if we want to see it in our final document, we're going to have to add it specifically using tags.**<p>**

which gives us:

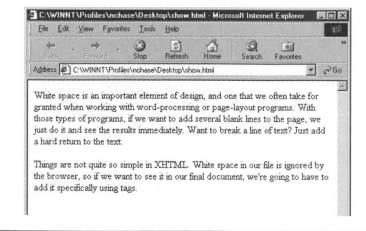

Another way to accomplish this would be to use the <pre></pre>, or preformatted tag, as in:

<pre>White space is an important element of design, and one that we often take for granted when working with word-processing or page-layout programs. With those types of programs, if we want to add several blank lines to the page, we just do it and see the results immediately. Want to break a line of text? Just add a hard return to the text.

Things are not quite so simple in XHTML. White space in our file is ignored by the browser, so if we want to see it in our final document, we're going to have to add it specifically using tags.**</pre>**

The <pre></pre> tag relieves us of the burden of adding our own white space, since the tag causes the browser to retain the formatting (preformatting) of the text, but it does add its own complications, as we can see below.

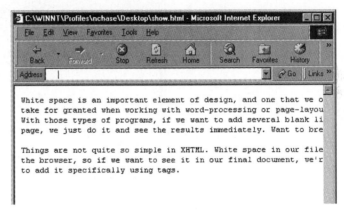

Notice that the text is now in a different font, and that the line breaks occur exactly where they are in the original text, instead of breaking at the edge of the browser window, as they did before. Note, also, that <pre></pre> sections are automatically displayed on a separate line, so they can't be placed in the middle of a line.

We also need to control horizontal white spaces, such as extra spaces within a line. The browser displays a series of spaces as a single space, so if we need to add spaces within a line, without using <pre><pre>we need to use the non-breaking space special character, " ".

Exercise Setup
We can see all of this with a simple example.

Add White Space

1. In the open file, hello.html, in your text editor, remove Hello World! and add several lines of text to the file. Type the bolded text below into the file. Be sure to press Return/Enter after each sentence.

```
<!DOCTYPE HTML PUBLIC "-//W3C//DTD HTML 4.01 Transitional//EN"
"http://www.w3.org/TR/html4/loose.dtd">
<html>
<head>
        <title>Hello, World, it's our first page!</title>
</head>
<body>
```

This is the first sentence.
This is the second sentence.
This is the third sentence.
This is the fourth sentence.
This is the fifth sentence.
</body>
</html>

2. Save the file in the text editor and refresh the page in your browser. Notice that although each sentence was on a new line, when we view it in the browser, all the lines run together.

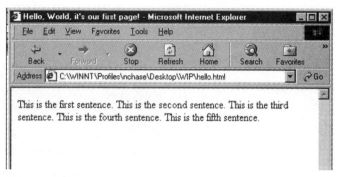

3. Enclose the first two sentences in `<p></p>` tags, as shown below:

```
<!DOCTYPE HTML PUBLIC "-//W3C//DTD HTML 4.01 Transitional//EN"
"http://www.w3.org/TR/html4/loose.dtd">
<html>
<head>
        <title>Hello, World, it's our first page!</title>
</head>
<body>
<p>This is the first sentence.</p>
<p>This is the second sentence.</p>
This is the third sentence.
This is the fourth sentence.
This is the fifth sentence.
</body>
</html>
```

4. Save the file in the text editor and refresh the page in your browser. Notice that not only do each of these sentences now appear on their own lines, but now there are also blank lines between the sentences.

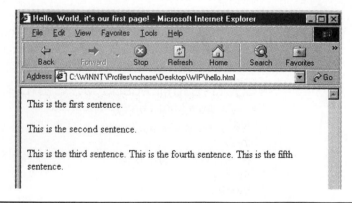

5. Of course sometimes we don't want the gaps between sentences to be too large. Instead of creating paragraphs, add a line break after the fourth sentence by typing <br />:

```
<!DOCTYPE HTML PUBLIC "-//W3C//DTD HTML 4.01 Transitional//EN"
"http://www.w3.org/TR/html4/loose.dtd">
<html>
<head>
        <title>Hello, World, it's our first page!</title>
</head>
<body>
<p>This is the first sentence.</p>
<p>This is the second sentence.</p>
This is the third sentence.
This is the fourth sentence.
<br />
This is the fifth sentence.
</body>
</html>
```

6. Save the file in the text editor and refresh the page in your browser.

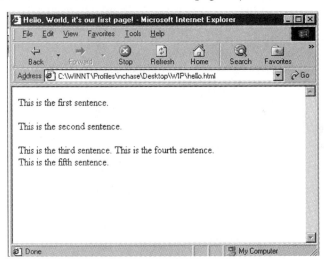

7. Add five extra <br /> tags to the file, following the fourth sentence.

```
<!DOCTYPE HTML PUBLIC "-//W3C//DTD HTML 4.01 Transitional//EN"
"http://www.w3.org/TR/html4/loose.dtd">
<html>
<head>
        <title>Hello, World, it's our first page!</title>
</head>
<body>
<p>This is the first sentence.</p>
<p>This is the second sentence.</p>
This is the third sentence.
This is the fourth sentence.
<br /><br /><br /><br /><br /><br />
This is the fifth sentence.
</body>
</html>
```

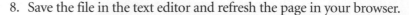

8. Save the file in the text editor and refresh the page in your browser.

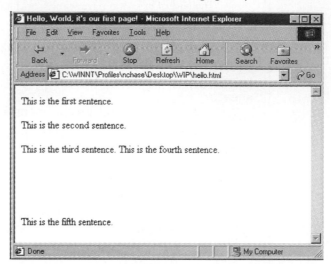

9. XHTML also ignores horizontal white space. Add a number of spaces within the third sentence.

```
<!DOCTYPE HTML PUBLIC "-//W3C//DTD HTML 4.01 Transitional//EN"
"http://www.w3.org/TR/html4/loose.dtd">
<html>
<head>
        <title>Hello, World, it's our first page!</title>
</head>
<body>
<p>This is the first sentence.</p>
<p>This is the second sentence.</p>
This is the                    third sentence.
This is the fourth sentence.
<br /><br /><br /><br /><br /><br />
This is the fifth sentence.
</body>
</html>
```

10. Save the file in the text editor and refresh the page in your browser.

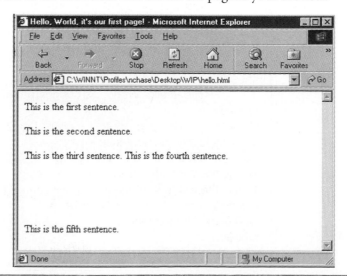

11. Notice that there is no difference in the rendered page. The browser ignored the extra white space.

12. Add white space within — tell the browser that the text is preformatted by using the <pre></pre> tag.

```
<!DOCTYPE HTML PUBLIC "-//W3C//DTD HTML 4.01 Transitional//EN"
"http://www.w3.org/TR/html4/loose.dtd">
<html>
<head>
        <title>Hello, World, it's our first page!</title>
</head>
<body>
<p>This is the first sentence.</p>
<p>This is the second sentence.</p>
<pre>This is the                third sentence.</pre>
This is the fourth sentence.
<br /><br /><br /><br /><br /><br />
This is the fifth sentence.
</body>
</html>
```

13. Save the file and refresh the browser.

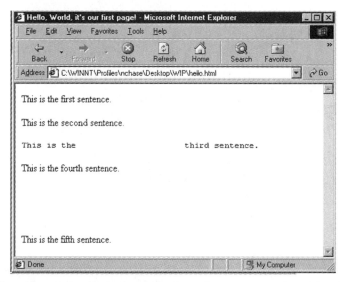

14. Notice that this text breaks incorrectly since the section enclosed by the <pre> tags must be on a separate line.

15. A more convenient way to add spaces to a line is to use non-breaking spaces. Add the bolded text to the fourth sentence.

```
<!DOCTYPE HTML PUBLIC "-//W3C//DTD HTML 4.01 Transitional//EN"
"http://www.w3.org/TR/html4/loose.dtd">
<html>
<head>
        <title>Hello, World, it's our first page!</title>
</head>
<body>
```

```
<p>This is the first sentence.</p>
<p>This is the second sentence.</p>
<pre>This is the           third sentence.</pre>
This is the fourth         
           
           
   sentence.
<br /><br /><br /><br /><br /><br />
This is the fifth sentence.
</body>
</html>
```

16. Save the file in the text editor and refresh the page in your browser.

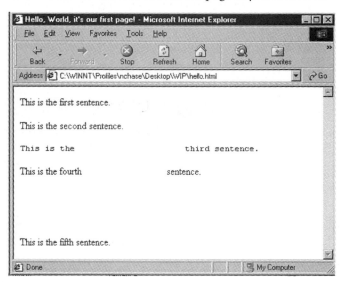

Other useful special characters are the copyright symbol (©) and the trademark symbol (™). We can also embed quotes in text using ".

17. Close the file.

Formatting Body Text

Modern XHTML allows us so much more freedom than merely using italics, bold, centered text and so on, but we still need to know how to do the basics, so let's take a look at some of the ways XHTML enables us to format text.

Bold and Italics

Bold (<b></b>) and italics (<i></i>) are among the most common of HTML tags. They are generally used to add emphasis to sections of text, such as names and places.

Exercise Setup

Let's see this in action and emphasize the names of authors in a book review by bolding them.

Make the Text Bold

1. Open **RF_HTML>Chapter 1**, and copy the contents to your **WIP>Basics** folder.

2. Open the new **WIP>Basics>article.html** file in both your text editor and your browser.

3. Make the author names in the article bold by adding the <b></b> tag in the text editor.

```
<!DOCTYPE HTML PUBLIC "-//W3C//DTD HTML 4.01 Transitional//EN"
"http://www.w3.org/TR/html4/loose.dtd">
<html>
<head><title>Recommended Books</title></head>
<body>
Dr. Know-It-All Recommendations
<p>These days, Dr. Know-It-All is reading several books by <b>Dr. C. Little</b>, including
his latest, Why Don't Chickens Have Lips? Dr. Know-It-All has also been engrossed in My
Life In Australia, by <b>Alligator Al</b> </p>
<p>Dr. Know-It-All recommends books on a weekly basis, or whenever we get around to
it.</p>
Upcoming Books
<p>At the urging of Mrs. Know-It-All, the next book Dr. Know-It-All reviews will be Weight
Loss Secrets, by <b>Sally Slinky</b>.</p>
</body>
</html>
```

4. Save the file in the text editor and refresh the page in your browser.

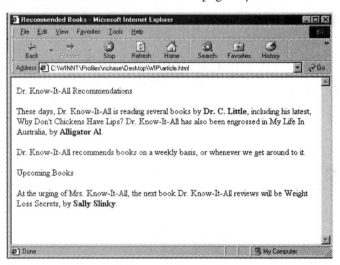

5. Leave this file open in both windows for the next exercise.

Exercise Setup

Let's emphasize the heading and subheading by italicizing them. We'll also italicize the book titles.

Add Italics

1. In the open article.html in your text editor, italicize the heading, subheading and book titles using the <i></i> tag.

```
<!DOCTYPE HTML PUBLIC "-//W3C//DTD HTML 4.01 Transitional//EN"
"http://www.w3.org/TR/html4/loose.dtd">
<html>
<head><title>Recommended Books</title></head>
<body>
<i>Dr. Know-It-All Recommendations</i>
<p>These days, Dr. Know-It-All is reading several books by <b>Dr. C. Little</b>, including
his latest, <i>Why Don't Chickens Have Lips?</i> Dr. Know-It-All has also been en-
grossed in <i>My Life In Australia</i>, by <b>Alligator Al</b>.</p>
```

```
<p>Dr. Know-It-All recommends books on a weekly basis, or whenever we get around to
it.</p>
<i>Upcoming Books</i>
<p>At the urging of Mrs. Know-It-All, the next book Dr. Know-It-All reviews will be
<i>Weight Loss Secrets</i>, by <b>Sally Slinky</b>.</p>
</body>
</html>
```

2. Save the file in the text editor and refresh the page in your browser.

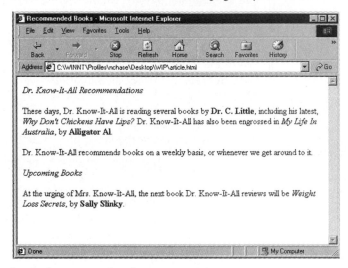

3. Leave both windows open for the next exercise.

Nesting Tags

Now, while these tags are both helpful, they would seem very limited, if that were all that we could do to text. Fortunately, they're not. To start with, applying more than one style to a section is as simple as nesting one set of tags within another. We just need to remember that tags have to be completely nested.

Exercise Setup

Let's make the upcoming reviews paragraph italic.

Nest Tags

1. In the open file, article.html, in your text editor, make the last paragraph italic, using the <i></i> tag.

```
<!DOCTYPE HTML PUBLIC "-//W3C//DTD HTML 4.01 Transitional//EN"
"http://www.w3.org/TR/html4/loose.dtd">
<html>
<head><title>Recommended Books</title></head>
<body>
<i>Dr. Know-It-All Recommendations</i>
<p>These days, Dr. Know-It-All is reading several books by <b>Dr. C. Little</b>, including
his latest, <i>Why Don't Chickens Have Lips?</i> Dr. Know-It-All has also been engrossed
in <i>My Life In Australia</i>, by <b>Alligator Al</b>.</p>
<p>Dr. Know-It-All recommends books on a weekly basis, or whenever we get around to
it.</p>
<i>Upcoming Books</i>
```

```
<p><i>At the urging of Mrs. Know-It-All, the next book Dr. Know-It-All reviews will be
<i>Weight Loss Secrets</i>, by <b>Sally Slinky</b>.</i></p>
</body>
</html>
```

2. Save the file in the text editor and refresh the page in your browser.

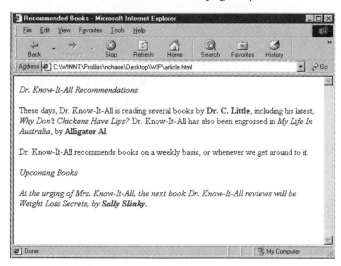

3. Notice that the text we had boldfaced in that paragraph remains bold, but now is also italicized. The book title, which was already italicized, isn't affected.

4. Leave the file open in both windows for the next exercise.

Headings

We've italicized the heading and subheading, but they still don't stand out enough from the rest of the page. What will solve this is using tags to emphasize important information, since bolding and italicizing don't seem to convey this adequately.

While we could just make the text larger or more prominent in some other fashion, we also want to indicate that this is important structural information on the page. To do that, we'll use headings, created with tags such as <h1></h1>.

Headings tell the browser that text is important, so they are normally displayed as larger and bolder than the rest of the text.

Add Headings

1. In the open article.html in your text editor, remove the italics from the heads only, and use the <h1></h1> tag to emphasize the heading and subheading.

```
<!DOCTYPE HTML PUBLIC "-//W3C//DTD HTML 4.01 Transitional//EN"
"http://www.w3.org/TR/html4/loose.dtd">
<html>
<head><title>Recommended Books</title></head>
<body>
<h1>Dr. Know-It-All Recommendations</h1>
<p>These days, Dr. Know-It-All is reading several books by <b>Dr. C. Little</b>, including
his latest, <i>Why Don't Chickens Have Lips?</i> Dr. Know-It-All has also been engrossed
in <i>My Life In Australia</i>, by <b>Alligator Al</b>.</p>
```

```
<p>Dr. Know-It-All recommends books on a weekly basis, or whenever we get around to
it.</p>
<h1>Upcoming Books</h1>
<p><i>At the urging of Mrs. Know-It-All, the next book Dr. Know-It-All reviews will be
<i>Weight Loss Secrets</i>, by <b>Sally Slinky</b>.</i></p>
</body>
</html>
```

2. Save the file in the text editor and refresh the page in your browser.

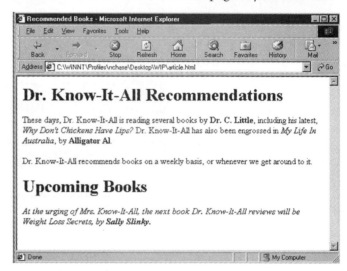

3. Leave the file open in both windows for the next exercise.

The Sizes of Headings

In the preceding exercise, we've emphasized the heading and subheading, but we haven't provided a way to distinguish them from each other. What we really need is different sizes of headings so we can tell which is more important. Fortunately, headings come in six sizes: <h1></h1> through <h6></h6>.

Now, it might seem logical that h6 would be the largest heading and h1 the smallest, if size of the heading were the only consideration. Remember, however, that different levels of headings indicate the importance of the text, not size, so the opposite is true. An h1 heading is much more important than an h3 or h6, so it's rendered as the largest.

Exercise Setup
Let's take a look at some of the smaller headings by experimenting with different sizes.

Add a Subhead

1. In the open article.html in your text editor, change the emphasis on the subheading using the <h6></h6> tag in place of the <h1><h/1> tag.

```
<!DOCTYPE HTML PUBLIC "-//W3C//DTD HTML 4.01 Transitional//EN"
"http://www.w3.org/TR/html4/loose.dtd">
<html>
<head><title>Recommended Books</title></head>
<body>
<h1>Dr. Know-It-All Recommendations</h1>
```

```
<p>These days, Dr. Know-It-All is reading several books by <b>Dr. C. Little</b>, including
his latest, <i>Why Don't Chickens Have Lips?</i> Dr. Know-It-All has also been engrossed
in <i>My Life In Australia</i>, by <b>Alligator Al</b>.</p>
<p>Dr. Know-It-All recommends books on a weekly basis, or whenever we get around to
it.</p>
<h6>Upcoming Books</h6>
<p><i>At the urging of Mrs. Know-It-All, the next book Dr. Know-It-All reviews will be
<i>Weight Loss Secrets</i>, by <b>Sally Slinky</b>.</i></p>
</body>
</html>
```

2. Save the file in the text editor and refresh the page in your browser. Leave the file open in both applications for the next exercise.

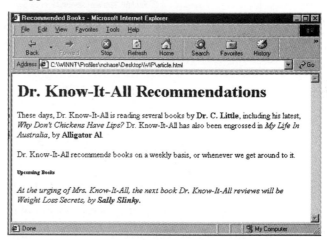

All changes to a page must be made in the text editor. The browser just displays the page and can't edit it.

Hierarchy of Headings

In the preceding graphic (at the end of the exercise), how can the Upcoming Books line be a heading if it's actually smaller than the rest of the text? Aren't headings supposed to show that something is more important than the regular body text? Well, yes and no. Remember, we're talking about a hierarchy of importance. For instance, if we were to translate this chapter so far into headings, the XHTML might look like this:

```
<h1>XHTML and HTML -- The Basics</h1>
        <h2>Origin of the Browser</h2>
                <h3>HTML Tags</h3>
                <h3>The First Graphical Browsers</h3>
                <h3>The State of Browsers Today</h3>
        <h2>HTML 4.01 and XHTML 1.0</h2>
                <h3>Then what is XHTML?</h3>
        <h2>XML + HTML = XHTML</h2>
                <h3>Content versus Presentation</h3>
                <h3>The Reformulation of HTML 4.01 into XHTML 1.0</h3>
        <h2>The Basic Web Page</h2>
                <h3>Tags</h3>
                <h3>The Basic Structure</h3>
        <h2>Validating an XHTML Page</h2>
                <h3>Validation using Transitional vs. Strict DTDs</h3>
        <h2>Body Text</h2>
                <h3>White Space and Paragraph Breaks</h3>
                <h3>Formatting Body Text</h3>
```

Many Web authors indent their content, as we've done here. Since, as we have seen, HTML normally ignores white space, it doesn't hurt anything, and it makes the code much clearer.

```
<h2>Headings</h2>
        <h3>The Sizes of Headings</h3>
        <h3>Hierarchy of Headings</h3>
```
The heading levels correspond to the level of the information. The page with that code would look like this in the browser:

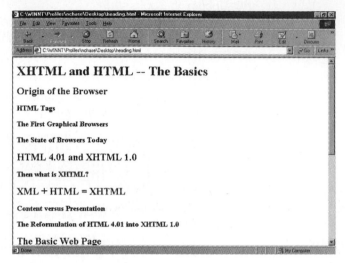

So although the more in-depth headings are comparatively small, they still serve the purpose of letting us know visually the relative importance of different pieces of information, and in a way that other programs can also understand.

Controlling Heading Alignment

Headings are convenient not only as indications of importance, but also, as we've seen, as formatting tools.

We can also use attributes to make our headings even more convenient formatting tools. One example would be the align attribute. We can use this attribute to align headings to the left or right, or to center them. We can also set the value to justify, in which case any line but the last will be stretched to take up the entire width of the page. (If the heading is only one line long, this alignment will have no effect.)

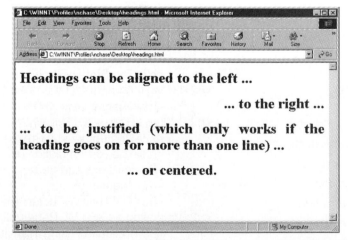

Like all attributes related strictly to the appearance of the page, the align attribute is deprecated, which means that it will not be included in the next version of XHTML. It is being replaced by CSS.

Exercise Setup

In our article, the first heading is actually the title of the article, so it makes sense to center it on the page. The best way to do that is to use the align attribute.

Center the Heading

1. In the open article.html in your text editor, make the subheading a reasonable size, such as <h2></h2>.

```
<h2>Upcoming Books</h2>
```

2. Now let's look at the article's headline. Use the align attribute to center the heading on the page.

```
<!DOCTYPE HTML PUBLIC "-//W3C//DTD HTML 4.01 Transitional//EN"
"http://www.w3.org/TR/html4/loose.dtd">
<html>
<head><title>Recommended Books</title></head>
<body>
<h1 align="center">Dr. Know-It-All Recommendations</h1>
<p>These days, Dr. Know-It-All is reading several books by <b>Dr. C. Little</b>, including
his latest, <i>Why Don't Chickens Have Lips?</i> Dr. Know-It-All has also been engrossed
in <i>My Life In Australia</i>, by <b>Alligator Al</b>.</p>
<p>Dr. Know-It-All recommends books on a weekly basis, or whenever we get around to
it.</p>
<h2>Upcoming Books</h2>
<p><i>At the urging of Mrs. Know-It-All, the next book Dr. Know-It-All reviews will be
<i>Weight Loss Secrets</i>, by <b>Sally Slinky</b>.</i></p>
</body>
</html>
```

3. Save the file in the text editor and refresh the page in your browser.

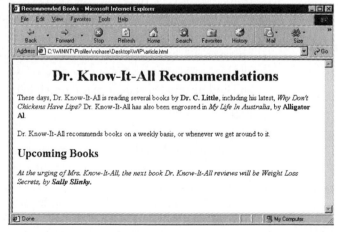

4. Experiment with different alignments, such as left and right, and with different heading sizes.

5. When you're finished experimenting, close article.html.

Images

Text formatting is important, but it would be difficult to imagine a Web site today without images. Unfortunately, using images is sometimes taken to extremes, leading to excessively large pages with long download times. Each image on a page adds to the time Web surfers must wait to see the entire page and increases the chance that they will give up and go somewhere else.

Image Formats

There are several types of images that can be added to a Web page, and each of them has their own strengths and weaknesses, including how large a file they add to your site.

GIF Images

GIF, or Graphics Interchange Format was the original Web graphics format. It uses *indexed color*, meaning that each pixel is assigned a number from 0 to 255, representing its color. Because of this, indexed color is limited to a maximum of 8-bits, or 256 colors. This format is best for images with large areas of a single color, such as line art. If an image uses less than 256 colors, it should be compressed to a smaller bit depth. GIF images also have two other advantages:

If you have created all of the images on your site with a program that is covered by a Unisys license, you can use LZW GIF images without a problem. The problem arises when sites generate their own graphics without one of these programs.

- **GIF images can be transparent.** A single color is designated as the transparent color, and any pixels that are that color simply allow the background to show through. This is useful for several reasons, not the least of which is that it allows you to create a single image that can be used on different backgrounds.

- **GIFs can be animated.** The result is much like a flip-book animation, with multiple images being changed rapidly to give the appearance of movement. These animations can repeat. Be aware that while animated GIFs can enliven a page when used properly, they can also distract from your message and are virtually guaranteed to annoy users if overdone.

JPEG

JPEG (also JPG) is the format created by the Joint Photographic Experts Group. Since one of the weaknesses of GIF images is that the format favors large blocks of a single color, photographic images in GIF format usually end up with a huge files. The JPEG format, however, is created with a compression specifically suited to photographs, so any image with gradual color changes (as opposed to the line art that is so well suited to the GIF format) will end up smaller (and looking much better) in JPEG format.

PNG

There are other types of media than these, of course, such as Macromedia Flash, Macromedia Shockwave, and streaming audio and video. We'll talk about them in Chapter 9.

PNG, or Portable Network Graphics, were created to fill a need created by a legal issue. Most GIF images are based on LZW compression, which is covered by a patent issued to Unisys Corporation. This patent means that any graphics program that reads or creates images with this form of compression must be licensed. The major software companies have obtained such licenses for their programs, such as Adobe Photoshop and CorelDraw, of course, but small developers and Web-site operators don't have that option, so an alternative format was needed. PNGs were standardized in 1996 and are similar to GIFs.

Adding Images

We talk about adding an image to a Web page, but in fact, we're not really adding it. When you insert an image into a Microsoft Word file, for instance, you can either insert the image or just link it to the file. If you insert the image, then send the Word document to someone, the recipient will be able to see the image in the document, even though he or she doesn't have the original image. On the other hand, if you just link the image to the file, all you've added is a reference (connection) to where Word can find the image on your hard drive. If you then send someone the file, he or she will only see a big red "X" where the image should be because Word can't locate it.

Adding an image to a Web page is similar to linking an image into a Word document. What we're actually adding is a reference to the location of the image, telling the browser where to find it. That location can be on your hard drive or on a server on the other side of the world. It doesn't even have to be on the same server as the Web page itself, although for our examples we'll assume that it is. (We'll look at images in other places in Chapter 2.)

The <img> Tag

Images are added through the <img> tag. The <img> tag is a little different from most of the tags that we've looked at so far, in that it's an empty tag.

When we want to boldface someone's name, like Bunny Hop in the following example, we put that name between the start and end tags. Bunny Hop is the content for that tag.

```
<b>Bunny Hop</b>
```

An <img> tag, however, works differently. If we want to add an image called logo.gif to a page, the image tag might read like this:

```
<img src="logo.gif" alt="Logo">
```

The src, or *source attribute*, specifies the file we want to appear, and the alt, or *alternate text attribute*, specifies the text that will appear if the image can't be loaded.

That's how it reads in HTML 4.0. One of the requirements of XHTML is that we have complete pairs of tags. So in XHTML, technically, that tag should read:

```
<img src="logo.gif" alt="Logo"></img>
```

Of course, since there's no actual content, the closing tag can look rather silly. In addition, if a browser understands only HTML (and not XHTML), it may not be able to display the results of this code properly.

The designers of XML (and XHTML) understood this browser problem, and defined a "shorthand" for empty elements, like the image and line break tags. So, in XHTML, this element is written as:

```
<img src="logo.gif" alt="Logo"/>
```

Unfortunately, older browsers don't understand this shorthand. In order to prevent errors in these browsers, we also need to add a space before the slash, so the tag becomes:

```
<img src="logo.gif" alt="Logo" />
```

In this way, the tag will be readable by older browsers, current browsers and programs designed to read XML.

Alternate Text

Although *bandwidth*, or the speed of a user's connection to the Internet, is getting better in general, many users, particularly outside the United States, still surf with images turned off in their browser. Other users surf using text-only browsers, for various reasons. For all of these people, it has always been a good idea to put alternate text into the image tag. This text, which is specified with the alt attribute, is what appears if for some reason the image doesn't. With the advent of XHTML this has become a requirement. This is text that will be displayed by the browser under five circumstances:

- The user has turned off images.

- The image has not yet downloaded.

- The image is not available.

- The browser is not capable of displaying images .

- The browser is part of specialized hardware used by persons with disabilities (as we'll discuss more in Chapter 11).

Adding alternate text to an image is easy, as we saw above. For instance, to add it to our book1.jpg image, we would write:

<img src="book1.jpg" align="right" width="150" height="224" **alt="My Life In Australia, by Alligator Al"** />

Exercise Setup

Now that we understand the requirements, let's add some photos to our article.

Add an Image

1. Open **WIP>basics>images.html** in both the text editor and the browser.

2. Add the images to the page, as shown in bold:

```
<!DOCTYPE HTML PUBLIC "-//W3C//DTD HTML 4.01 Transitional//EN"
"http://www.w3.org/TR/html4/loose.dtd">
<html>
<head><title>Recommended Books</title></head>
<body>
<h1 align="center">Dr. Know-It-All Recommendations</h1>
<p><img src="book1.jpg" alt="My Life In Australia" />These days, Dr. Know-It-All is
reading several books by <b>Dr. C. Little</b>, including his latest, <i>Why Don't Chickens
Have Lips?</i> Dr. Know-It-All has also been engrossed in <i>My Life In Australia</i>, by
<b>Alligator Al</b>.</p>
<p>Dr. Know-It-All recommends books on a weekly basis, or whenever we get around to
it.</p>
<h2>Upcoming Books</h2>
<p><img src="book2.jpg" alt="Weight Loss Secrets" /><i>At the urging of Mrs. Know-
It-All, the next book Dr. Know-It-All reviews will be <i>Weight Loss Secrets</i>, by
<b>Sally Slinky</b>.</i></p>
</body>
</html>
```

3. Save the file in the text editor and refresh the browser.

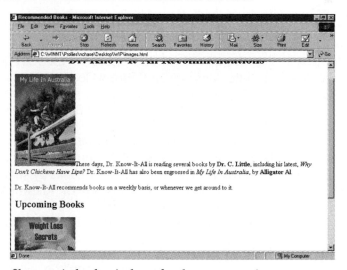

4. Leave the file open in both windows for the next exercise.

Controlling the Image

At the end of the previous exercise, the images were added, but this certainly wasn't the most attractive way to display them.

Images, like body copy and headings, can carry a number of attributes that can affect the image's appearance, for example. These attributes enable you to control alignment, the way

In order to be in compliance with the Americans with Disabilities Act, or ADA, a Web site must, among other things, use alternate text for all images.

that text does or does not wrap around the image, the size of the image, and the appearance of a small temporary image while the main image loads.

Alignment and Wrapping Text around an Image

In the graphic at the end of the last exercise, notice that the image sits on the same line as the text, but only one line of the text. This used to be the only way to display text and images on the same line. Now we can control the relationship of text and images using the align attribute for images, in similar fashion to controlling the alignment of headings.

The align attribute has five possible values: top, bottom, middle, left and right. If we don't indicate our preference, the browser will use the default value. A *default* is the value that is assumed if no other value is provided. For the align attribute on images, the default value is bottom. Bottom alignment is what we're seeing in the last image of the exercise. While we may assume that bottom means that the image will be lower than the text, in fact it means that the text will go to the bottom of the image.

If we use top, bottom or middle alignment, only a single line of text will appear next to the image, no matter how much room there is on the page. In order to cause text to wrap around the image, the image must be aligned to the left or right.

If we are using left or right alignment, there will be situations where we need to move content below an image. To do that, we can add a special attribute to the <br /> tag — clear. For instance, if we set clear to left, the next text will move down the page until there are no more images to the left.

Alignments can produce different results, including causing text to wrap around an image.

Align the Images

1. In the open file images.html in the text editor, set the alignment on the first image to middle and the second to top.

```
<!DOCTYPE HTML PUBLIC "-//W3C//DTD HTML 4.01 Transitional//EN"
"http://www.w3.org/TR/html4/loose.dtd">
<html>
<head><title>Recommended Books</title></head>
<body>
<h1 align="center">Dr. Know-It-All Recommendations</h1>
<p><img src="book1.jpg" align="middle" alt="My Life In Australia" />These days, Dr.
Know-It-All is reading several books by <b>Dr. C. Little</b>, including his latest, <i>Why
Don't Chickens Have Lips?</i> Dr. Know-It-All has also been engrossed in <i>My Life In
Australia</i>, by <b>Alligator Al</b>.</p>
<p>Dr. Know-It-All recommends books on a weekly basis, or whenever we get around to
it.</p>
<h2>Upcoming Books</h2>
<p><img src="book2.jpg" align="top" alt="Weight Loss Secrets" /><i>At the urging of
Mrs. Know-It-All, the next book Dr. Know-It-All reviews will be <i>Weight Loss Secrets</i>,
by <b>Sally Slinky</b>.</i></p>
</body>
</html>
```

The align attribute has been deprecated, but it is an example of the reason that we are using Transitional XHTML. Without this attribute, older browsers would be unable to duplicate our page layouts.

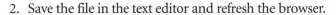

2. Save the file in the text editor and refresh the browser.

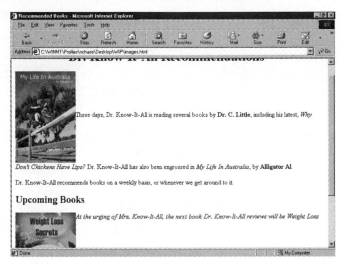

3. Notice that although we've moved the text up and there's plenty of room next to the image, only one line of text displays next to the image.

4. In order to cause the text to wrap, we need to use two (relatively) new alignments, left and right. Set the alignment on My Life In Australia to the right and on Weight Loss Secrets to the left.

```
<!DOCTYPE HTML PUBLIC "-//W3C//DTD HTML 4.01 Transitional//EN"
"http://www.w3.org/TR/html4/loose.dtd">
<html>
<head><title>Recommended Books</title></head>
<body>
<h1 align="center">Dr. Know-It-All Recommendations</h1>
<p><img src="book1.jpg" align="right" alt="My Life In Australia" />These days, Dr. Know-
It-All is reading several books by <b>Dr. C. Little</b>, including his latest, <i>Why Don't
Chickens Have Lips?</i> Dr. Know-It-All has also been engrossed in <i>My Life In Austra-
lia</i>, by <b>Alligator Al</b>.</p>
<p>Dr. Know-It-All recommends books on a weekly basis, or whenever we get around to
it.</p>
<h2>Upcoming Books</h2>
<p><img src="book2.jpg" align="left" alt="Weight Loss Secrets" /><i>At the urging of Mrs.
Know-It-All, the next book Dr. Know-It-All reviews will be <i>Weight Loss Secrets</i>, by
<b>Sally Slinky</b>.</i></p>
</body>
</html>
```

5. Save the file in the text editor and refresh the browser.

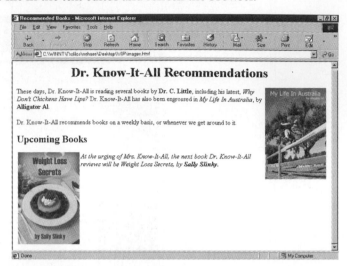

6. So once we align an image to the left or the right, all the remaining content will wrap around it, including other images. Of course, there may be times when we don't want this to happen. Fortunately, we can use the <br /> tag to tell the browser to move down to the next clear area.

Insert the break tag before the Upcoming Books heading, as shown in bold:

```
<!DOCTYPE HTML PUBLIC "-//W3C//DTD HTML 4.01 Transitional//EN"
"http://www.w3.org/TR/html4/loose.dtd">
<html>
<head><title>Recommended Books</title></head>
<body>
<h1 align="center">Dr. Know-It-All Recommendations</h1>
<p><img src="book1.jpg" align="right" alt="My Life In Australia"  />These days, Dr. Know-
It-All is reading several books by <b>Dr. C. Little</b>, including his latest, <i>Why Don't
Chickens Have Lips?</i> Dr. Know-It-All has also been engrossed in <i>My Life In Austra-
lia</i>, by <b>Alligator Al</b>.</p>
<p>Dr. Know-It-All recommends books on a weekly basis, or whenever we get around to
it.</p>
<br clear="right" />
<h2>Upcoming Books</h2>
<p><img src="book2.jpg" align="left" alt="Weight Loss Secrets"  /><i>At the urging of Mrs.
Know-It-All, the next book Dr. Know-It-All reviews will be <i>Weight Loss Secrets</i>, by
<b>Sally Slinky</b>.</i></p>
</body>
</html>
```

7. Save the file in the text editor, and refresh the browser window. Notice that by using the clear attribute, we can force the browser to move down to the next clear area.

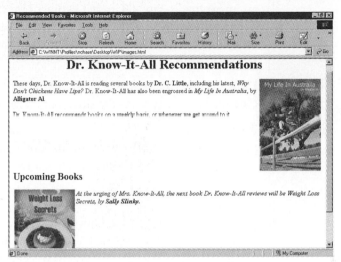

8. Leave the file open in both windows for the next exercise.

Specifying Height and Width

Alignment is only one of many attributes that can be used with images. Two of the most important such attributes are height and width. Until comparatively recently, browsers were unable to display any part of a page until they "knew" where every item would be placed on that page. Without the height and width being specified within the image tag, the browser had to download all images completely before it could begin to display any text, rather than just placing the text around placeholders (empty boxes) for the images and then downloading the images afterwards.

While this limitation is becoming the exception rather than the rule, browsers with these limitations are still in common use and must be considered when we build our pages. Besides, because there aren't really any restrictions on the height and width attributes, other than the fact that they must be numbers, there are some convenient effects that we can create using these attributes. They don't have to be just the actual size of the images.

For instance, the images we've been using so far are pretty small. We could scale them up or down using just the height and width attributes. Bear in mind, however, that reducing the amount of space the images take up on the page does not reduce the size of the file! If you display a 300K image in a 5 × 5 px area, it's still going to be 300K, and download that slowly.

If we're not worried about download and display time, we can use the height and width to force an image to fit into a particular area, even if we're not sure of the dimensions. This works because if we leave out one of the dimensions, the browser automatically scales the image based on the other.

You should only use this technique, however, for the initial planning of the site. Eventually, when it's ready to go into production, all images should be brought back down to their final size. Cleaning up image size is important because a file's size is determined by the number of pixels it has, not by how many it displays. What might appear to be a small thumbnail might actually be a huge file. What's more, because it's just the resolution that changes, sizing up can cause an image to look pixilated and distorted.

Scaling up an image using height and width can result in severely jagged-looking images.

There's one more point to keep in mind when it comes to image sizes. Most graphics programs allow you to set both the size and the resolution of an image, so you might have an image that is 2 in. × 3 in. at 144 dpi, or one that is 4 in. × 6 in. at 72 dpi. These images will appear different in a page-layout program, but not in a browser. Why? Because both of these images are 288 px wide × 432 px high, and that's all the browser looks at, unless we set the size specifically.

Determining Image Size

Of course, in order to set the size of an image, we need to know what the size is.

There are several ways to accomplish this, such as opening the image in a graphics-editing program, such as Adobe Photoshop, Adobe Illustrator or Macromedia FreeHand. In certain situations, you can also determine this information from the browser.

On Netscape for the Macintosh, for example, you place your mouse over the image and hold down the mouse button. When the menu pops up, you choose "View Image In New Window." The height and width appear in the Title bar. You can accomplish the same effect on Netscape for Windows by Right-clicking the image and choosing View Image.

On Internet Explorer for Windows, you Right-click the image and choose Properties. The height and width are listed under Dimensions. Unfortunately, this does not work on the Macintosh version of Internet Explorer.

Exercise Setup

Now that we know what the sizes are, let's add them to the page.

Add Height and Width to the Images

1. Double-check that images.html is open in both your browser and your text editor.

2. In your text editor, set the height and width of our images to 120% of their full size, or 180 px × 269 px:

```
<!DOCTYPE HTML PUBLIC "-//W3C//DTD HTML 4.01 Transitional//EN"
"http://www.w3.org/TR/html4/loose.dtd">
<html>
<head><title>Recommended Books</title></head>
<body>
<h1 align="center">Dr. Know-It-All Recommendations</h1>
<p><img src="book1.jpg" align="right" alt="My Life In Australia" width="180"
height="269" />These days, Dr. Know-It-All is reading several books by <b>Dr. C. Little</
b>, including his latest, <i>Why Don't Chickens Have Lips?</i> Dr. Know-It-All has also
been engrossed in <i>My Life In Australia</i>, by <b>Alligator Al</b>.</p>
<p>Dr. Know-It-All recommends books on a weekly basis, or whenever we get around to
it.</p>
<br clear="right" />
<h2>Upcoming Books</h2>
<p><img src="book2.jpg" align="left" alt="Weight Loss Secrets" width="180"
height="269" /><i>At the urging of Mrs. Know-It-All, the next book Dr. Know-It-All reviews
will be <i>Weight Loss Secrets</i>, by <b>Sally Slinky</b>.</i></p>
</body>
</html>
```

3. Save the file in your text editor and refresh the browser.

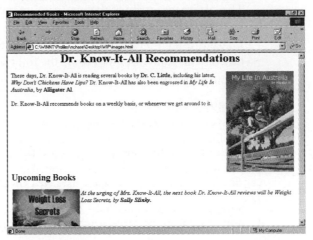

4. Set the first image to 200 px wide, and the second to be 200 px tall:

```
<!DOCTYPE HTML PUBLIC "-//W3C//DTD HTML 4.01 Transitional//EN"
"http://www.w3.org/TR/html4/loose.dtd">
<html>
<head><title>Recommended Books</title></head>
<body>
<h1 align="center">Dr. Know-It-All Recommendations</h1>
<p><img src="book1.jpg" align="right" alt="My Life In Australia" width="200" />These days,
Dr. Know-It-All is reading several books by <b>Dr. C. Little</b>, including his latest,
<i>Why Don't Chickens Have Lips?</i> Dr. Know-It-All has also been engrossed in <i>My
Life In Australia</i>, by <b>Alligator Al</b>.</p>
<p>Dr. Know-It-All recommends books on a weekly basis, or whenever we get around to
it.</p>
<br clear="right" />
<h2>Upcoming Books</h2>
<p><img src="book2.jpg" align="left" alt="Weight Loss Secrets" height="200" /><i>At the
urging of Mrs. Know-It-All, the next book Dr. Know-It-All reviews will be <i>Weight Loss
Secrets</i>, by <b>Sally Slinky</b>.</i></p>
</body>
</html>
```

5. Save the file in your text editor and refresh the browser.

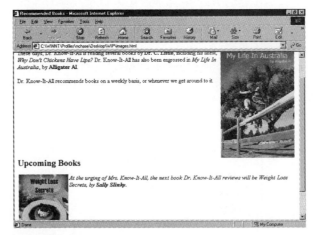

6. Close both applications.

This method (forcing an image to fit by specifying the height and width) should only be used when initially planning the site. Eventually, when it's ready to go into production, all images should be brought back down to their final size.

Lowsrc

The last image attribute that we're going to look at for now is lowsrc. Even when bandwidth was (more) scarce, this wasn't used as often as it could have been, which is a shame. A lowsrc image is usually a much smaller version of the final image. This smaller image is downloaded and displayed while the full real image is downloading more slowly, giving the visitor something to look at while awaiting the final image.

Originally, lowsrc images were just low-quality or black-and-white versions of the real images, but sometimes designers use this more creatively, such as by providing a lowsrc that is a line-art wire frame or skeletal version of the actual image. Since JPEGs load from the top down, the effect of filling in the wire frame is quite striking.

The lowsrc attribute is still in use. We can use it as follows:

```
<img src="book1.jpg" align="right" width="150" height="224" alt="Dr. C. Little at the beach, enjoying his lunch." lowsrc="book1_low.jpg" />
```

A lowsrc image only appears if the full image isn't available, usually because the full image hasn't yet loaded. Because our files are local and load rapidly, you may have difficulty seeing the lowsrc before the regular image is displayed. Once you add the page to the Web server and have to download the images over the Internet, you'll be able to see the lowsrc image.

Summary

In this chapter, you learned the history of the World Wide Web and the modern browser. Along the way, you also became familiar with some of the differences between HTML and XHTML. You discovered how to create and structure a basic XHTML file, and check to make sure that it is valid. You explored the basics of white space, certain kinds of formatting, such as bold, italic, alignment and headings, as well as using images on Web pages. You also learned about elements and attributes, and how to use them to achieve certain formatting effects on a basic Web page.

2 *Hyperlinks and URLs*

Chapter Objective:

To learn different ways to link to content on the Web. In Chapter 2, you will:

- Learn how to create a text link to another page.

- Become familiar with adding a link to an image and controlling the combined appearance.

- Observe the appropriate times to use relative and absolute URLs versus the <base /> tag.

- Discover how to distinguish between URLs using different protocols.

- Learn how to plan file organization for easier maintenance of your site.

Projects to be Completed:

- News Web (A)

- Cyber Travel (B)

- Hunter Films (C)

- North Star Adventure Gear (D)

Hyperlinks & URLs

If you have surfed the Web at all, you have almost certainly experienced *hyperlinks*, those clickable areas that take you to another page or show you more information. In the last chapter we discussed the fact that when we add an image to a page, we are actually adding a reference to the image, not the image itself. To make either of these references work, we need a way for the browser to know exactly where that image is. So far, that's been easy: the image has been in the same folder as the page itself. When it comes to linking to other pages, however, that is frequently not the case.

There is some question as to how you pronounce "URL." Some people say "U-R-L," and some say "earl." While neither is technically incorrect, for the purpose of this book, we will use "U-R-L."

A URL, or *Uniform Resource Locator*, is the Web address of a particular resource, such as an image or a Web page. If you've surfed the Web at all, URLs should not be completely unfamiliar to you. They can be simple, like:

http://www.yahoo.com

and:

http://home.netscape.com

or they can be more complicated, such as:

http://www.amazon.com/exec/obidos/search-handle-form/002-4812613-4372068

Let's start with the simplest type of URL usage: a text link to another page.

Adding Hyperlinks to Text

As we mentioned in Chapter 1, hypertext and links have been around, at least in concept, since the 1940s. On the Web, the most common form of link is one that uses text to show the user that there is more information. This is coded using the <a></a> tag.

There are two different types of <a></a>, or anchor, tags, but the most common sends the user to a different page. This page might be within the same site, or it might be somewhere else entirely. This destination, called the "target," is stored in the href, or hypertext reference attribute.

The "Uniform" in Uniform Resource Locator shouldn't be underestimated. A URL is used whenever we want to reference information, whether it's with a hyperlink to another page, an image to display, or even a sound or movie that we want the browser to play.

For instance, if we wanted to add a link to a page that would go to home.html, it would look like this:

<a href="home.html" title="Home Page Link">Click here to go to our home page!**</a>**

Anything between the start and end tag will display formatted as a link. If the browser supports it, the title attribute will also cause a tool-tip-style piece of information to appear when the user points to a link. Tool tips can be used to provide additional information about a link without disrupting the flow of content.

This creation of links is deceptively simple. The URL contained in the link can point to anything, from a page on the same server (as it does in the following exercise) to a page halfway across the world or even to another application for the browser to launch. Anything that can be expressed as a URL can be linked to the Web page in this way.

Remember to use straight quotation marks (" ") not typographer's or curly quotes (" ") when you write your code. If you don't, the code will fail.

Exercise Setup

Let's use an exercise to take a look at adding a hyperlink to our file.

Special note: In most of the exercises in this book you see the three dots "…" in the code. This is not part of the code to type. It indicates that there's more code that hasn't changed, and we don't want to take up your time showing this. In the exercises, add only the type that we have made bold.

Add a Text Link

1. Create a new folder called "urls" in the WIP folder. Navigate to **RF_HTML>Chapter 2**, and copy its files to the **WIP>urls** folder.

2. Open **recs.html** in your text editor and browser. At the top of the file, we added a reference to our question-and-answer page (faq.html), as well as a horizontal rule, or line, (using the <hr /> tag). Using the <a></a> tag, add a link to the faq.html page.

```
<!DOCTYPE HTML PUBLIC "-//W3C//DTD HTML 4.01 Transitional//EN" "http://
www.w3.org/TR/html4/loose.dtd">
<html>
<head><title>Recommended Books</title></head>
<body>
<p><img src="q.gif" align="middle" alt="?" />Got questions? Dr. Know-It-All has the
<a href="faq.html">answers</a>.</p>
<hr />
<h1 align="center">Dr. Know-It-All Recommendations</h1>
…
```

3. Save the file in the text editor and refresh the browser window.

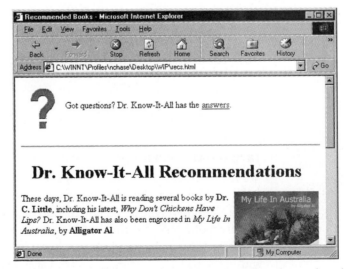

Start and end tags are sometimes referred to as "open" and "close" tags. The terminology is interchangeable.

4. Add a title attribute for "Frequently Asked Questions" to the anchor (<a>) tag.

```
…
<p><img src="q.gif" align="middle" alt="?" />Got questions? Dr. Know-It-All has the <a
href="faq.html" title="Frequently Asked Questions">answers</a>.</p>
<hr />
<h1 align="center">Dr. Know-It-All Recommendations</h1>
…
```

5. Save the file in the text editor and refresh the browser. Roll your mouse over the new link, but don't click it.

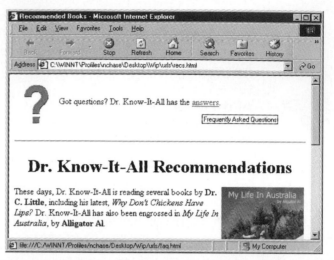

The title attribute is not supported in Netscape 4.x.

6. Click the link. We specified faq.html as the href, so we should see it in the browser.

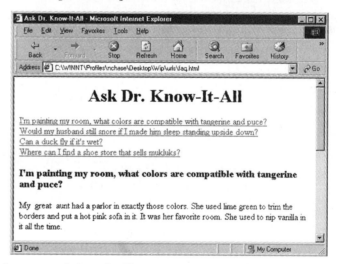

Notice that the text is underlined and blue. We can change the look of the link later using style sheets, but that's the default appearance.

7. Save the changes and close the file.

Targets within a Page

We've looked at linking to a full page. We can also link to a specific location, like a particular point within a page, by using the name attribute of a link. The name attribute enables us to create a different type of anchor. Instead of an anchor that's a link, we create an anchor that's the target of a link. Creating such targets is common on longer Web pages. Since it can be distracting to scroll up and down a long page, we provide convenient links to specific places within the page. These target links can also serve as a form of table of contents to specific points on a page, for easy reference.

To use an attribute, such as the name attribute, we include the name of the attribute and the value for that attribute within quotes. In adding the name attribute to the <a></a> tag, this works out to:

```
<a name="specific choice">some text</a>
```

where "specific choice" is the name of the target.

We also need to create the link to point to this anchor. That uses the anchor format:

<a href="name of the page**#specific choice**">link text</a>

In this instance, "name of the page" is the HTML page on which the target appears, and what follows the pound sign (#) is the name we have chosen for the target. In an instance where the link and the target refer to the same page, the target would omit the page name and begin with the pound sign and the name of the target.

We can change our example above to point directly to the answer to question three by adding the location, or *anchor*, to the page. First we create the target, using an <a></a> tag with the name attribute:

<h3>**<a name="duck">**Can a duck fly if it's wet?**</a>**</h3>

Then we create the link that points to that anchor:

<p>Got questions? Dr. Know-It-All has the <a href="faq.html**#duck**">answers</a>.</p>

We can see this in action in faq.html:

```
<!DOCTYPE HTML PUBLIC "-//W3C//DTD HTML 4.01 Transitional//EN" "http://
www.w3.org/TR/html4/loose.dtd">
<html>
<head><title>Ask Dr. Know-It-All</title></head>
<body>
<h1 align="center">Ask Dr. Know-It-All</h1>
<a href="#room">I'm painting my room. What colors are compatible with tangerine and
puce?</a><br />
<a href="#snore">Would my husband still snore if I made him sleep standing upside
down?</a><br />
<a href="#duck">Can a duck fly if it's wet?</a><br />
<a href="#mukluk">Where can I find a shoe store that sells mukluks?</a><br />
<h3><a name="room">I'm painting my room. What colors are compatible with tangerine
and puce?</a></h3>
<p>My great aunt had a parlor in exactly those colors. She used lime green to trim the
borders and put a hot pink sofa in it. It was her favorite room, she used to nip vanilla in it
all the time.</p>
<h3><a name="snore">Would my husband still snore if I made him sleep standing
upside down?</a></h3>
<p>Personally, I think you and your husband have more serious issues than snoring.
While standing upside down on his head may stop him from snoring, after a time his head
may get flat. I think you should look towards more conventional methods for help. Have
you tried putting a clothespin on his nose?</p>
<h3><a name="duck">Can a duck fly if it's wet?</a></h3>
<p>The question should not really be can he, but would he want to? There could also be
other factors involved, such as lightning and wind. The duck could suffer from migraines
and would want to avoid thunder as well. My advice to you is to find a duck, wait until it
rains and follow it.</p>
<h3><a name="mukluk">Where can I find a shoe store that sells mukluks?</a></h3>
<p>This is a very silly question for which there is only one answer: Sam's Mukluk and
Igloo Shop just south of the North Pole.</p>
</body>
</html>
```

The questions have links that point to the anchors within the same page. Since they point to a location within the same page, we don't have to specify the page, as we would otherwise do.

<h3>**<a name="room">**I'm painting my room. What colors are compatible with tangerine and puce?**</a>**</h3>

As you look at the page, notice that when we're answering the questions, they aren't underlined, even though they're enclosed by <a></a> tags. In fact, they don't give any outward sign that there is anything different about them. Only the browser needs to know where to find them, so the underlines are not necessary.

One important design concept: if we enable users to jump down the page, we should also enable them to jump back up. Don't forget to add links at the bottom of the page to return the visitor to the top of the page.

The browser will move to the location specified by the target anchor, no matter what it's called. Make certain that you put your anchors where you actually want the browser to go.

Exercise Setup
We will use this same principle to add a series of "Back to Top" links to our page. First we'll add the links, and then we'll add the anchor to the top of the page (well, just below the top).

Add an Anchor within a Page

1. Open **WIP>urls>faq.html** in your text editor and in the browser.

2. Add a Back to Top link to each of the questions:

…
<h3><a name="room">I'm painting my room. What colors are compatible with tangerine and puce?</a></h3>
<p>My great aunt had a parlor in exactly those colors. She used lime green to trim the borders and put a hot pink sofa in it. It was her favorite room. She used to nip vanilla in it all the time.</p>
<p><a href="#top">Back To Top</a></p>
<h3><a name="snore">Would my husband still snore if I made him sleep standing upside down?</a></h3>
<p>Personally, I think you and your husband have more serious issues than snoring. While standing upside down on his head may stop him from snoring, after a time his head may get flat. I think you should look towards more conventional methods for help. Have you tried putting a clothespin on his nose?</p>
<p><a href="#top">Back To Top</a></p>
<h3><a name="duck">Can a duck fly if it's wet?</a></h3>
<p>The question should not really be can he, but would he want to? There could also be other factors involved, such as lightning and wind. The duck could suffer from migraines and would want to avoid thunder as well. My advice to you is to find a duck, wait until it rains, and follow it.</p>
<p><a href="#top">Back To Top</a></p>
<h3><a name="mukluk">Where can I find a shoe store that sells mukluks?</a></h3>
<p>This is a very silly question for which there is only one answer: Sam's Mukluk and Igloo Shop just south of the North Pole.</p>
<p><a href="#top">Back To Top</a></p>
</body>
</html>

Rather than add anchor tags (<a name="anchor"></a>) exactly at the first line of the related content, sometimes designers choose to put the tags ahead of or below the beginning of this material. The reason is that the browser places the exact spot where the anchor tag is located at the very top of the window. If the tag slightly precedes the relevant text, the visitor sees the information a little lower on the screen, which is often a little easier to read. If the tag is a little lower on the page, it may move the reader to a position within the text that is a little closer to the sense of the purpose of the link. Experiment with placing your anchor points to see how it affects the jump of the browser to best effect.

Since the browser won't add blank space to the end of the page, you may need to shrink your browser window or add <p></p> tags to the end of the page to cause this question to move to the top of the page.

3. Add the target for these links to the top of the page:

```
...
<body>
<h1 align="center">Ask Dr. Know-It-All</h1>
<a name="top"></a>
<a href="#room">I'm painting my room.What colors are compatible with tangerine and puce?</a><br />
...
```

4. Save the file in the text editor and refresh the browser window.

5. Click the third question. The browser immediately jumps to the text of the third question in the page.

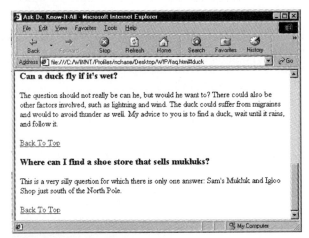

6. Click any Back to Top link.

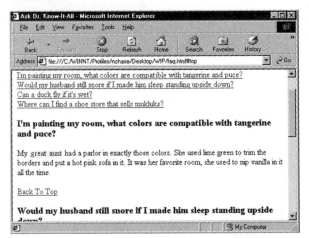

7. Notice that our heading is cut off. The browser moved us to the target we specified. When we created the Back to Top link, we specified in our code a particular target location below the heading. So although the link seems to say that it will jump to the top of the page, it actually jumps to a slightly lower place, because that's where the target anchor was placed.

8. Save and close the file.

Adding Hyperlinks to Images

When we add a hyperlink to text, we do so by enclosing the text in an <a></a> tag. By doing so, we tell the browser that whatever is between that start and end tag is clickable, and will transport the user to whatever destination was specified by the href attribute.

Adding a link to an image works in exactly the same fashion. The process is the same, except that the text that we're enclosing is actually the image tag, thus making the image clickable.

Add a Hyperlink to an Image

1. Open **WIP>urls>recs.html** in your text editor and browser.

2. Add a link to the image so that when it is clicked, the browser will jump to faq.html.

```
<!DOCTYPE HTML PUBLIC "-//W3C//DTD HTML 4.01 Transitional//EN"
"http://www.w3.org/TR/html4/loose.dtd">
<html>
<head><title>Recommended Books</title></head>
<body>
<p>
<a href="faq.html"><img src="q.gif" align="middle" alt="?" /></a>
Got questions? Dr. Know-It-All has the <a href="faq.html">answers</a>.</p>
<hr />
…
```

3. Save the file in the text editor and refresh the browser window.

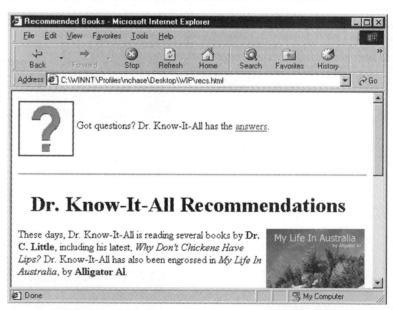

4. Notice that the graphic has now become a link. Click the image to verify that it takes you to faq.html.

5. User the browser's Back button to return to recs.html.

6. Leave the file open in both windows for the next exercise.

On the Macintosh, some browsers will remove the border by default.

Removing Borders

Adding the link to the image was easy, but if you look at the page, you'll notice that the image now has a big blue (or purple) border around it. In the early days of the Web, many Web-page authors used this border as an indication that the image would do something (move you to another page, replace a small image with a larger image, provide additional details about the image) if you clicked on it. These days, however, designers typically prefer to use the image as a supplemental link (as we're doing in this example) or to create a clickable image that doesn't need such obvious cues.

This improvement of the look of Web pages has been expedited by the increasing sophistication of the average Web user. If you put a set of navigation buttons on the page, you can expect your users to understand that they should click the buttons.

So how do we remove the border? Simple: by using the border attribute. With the border attribute, we can control the border's width in pixels. (The default border is 2 px. wide.) To remove the border on a linked image, we set the border width to 0:

`<a href="home.html"><img sre="home.gif" `**`border="0"`**` alt="Home" /></a>`

Notice that the border attribute is actually specified as part of the image tag, but that a border only appears if there is a link. In this way, we can control the presence (or absence) of borders, even if we don't yet know whether or not an image will ever be linked. This can prevent an unintended border from appearing later.

Remove the Image Border

1. In the open recs.html file in your text editor, set the border to "0 px" wide, effectively removing it.

```
<!DOCTYPE HTML PUBLIC "-//W3C//DTD HTML 4.01 Transitional//EN" "http://
www.w3.org/TR/html4/loose.dtd">
<html>
<head><title>Recommended Books</title></head>
<body>
<p><a href="faq.html"><img src="q.gif" align="middle" alt="?" border="0" /></a>Got
questions? Dr. Know-It-All has the <a href="faq.html">answers</a>.</p>
<hr />
…
```

2. Save the file in the text editor and refresh the browser window.

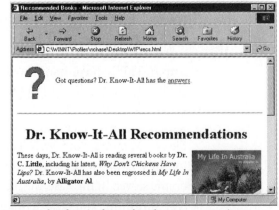

The border attribute is deprecated, but the functionality has been replaced by Cascading Style Sheets.

3. Leave the file open in both windows for the next exercise.

Avoiding Artifacts

As you know, white space doesn't appear on a Web page unless we specifically create it with our code. Despite this, when we added a link to our image in one of the exercises, we made sure there were no returns or spaces between the tags, as in:

```
<p><a href="faq.html"><img src="q.gif" align="middle" alt="?" border="0" /></a>Got questions? Dr. Know-It-All has the <a href="faq.html">answers</a>.</p>
```

This avoidance of unintentional returns or spaces is more than just a question of being neat, however. You may notice that when we add a link to text, the spaces are also underlined. The same thing can happen to spaces around an image in older browsers, leading to what looks like an artifact. *Artifacts* are occasional unwanted lines and spots, like digital dirt on a page. For instance, if we wrote:

```
<p><a href="faq.html">
      <img src="q.gif" align="middle" alt="?" border="0" />
   </a>
   Got questions? Dr. Know-It-All has the <a href="faq.html">answers</a>.
</p>
```

we might wind up with something like this small line that we have circled here:

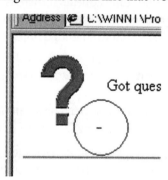

Spaces within <a></a> tags can result in unwanted digital "dirt," as blank spaces wind up as underlined links.

Relative vs. Absolute URLs

All of the URLs that we have looked at so far have been fairly simple, but there's much more going on than these links might suggest. Let's take a moment to analyze the parts of a URL. Observe this sample code:

http://www.againsttheclock.com/xhtml/contents.html

There are four parts to this URL:

- **http://.** This is the protocol. We'll discuss the different types of protocols below (in "Other Types of URLs"), but for now, just be aware that the http:// protocol tells the browser that this is a traditional Web request.

- **www.againsttheclock.com.** This is the name of the actual computer on which the file can be found. For a Web site, this is also known as the "Web server."

- **xhtml.** Coming between the server and the file, this is the folder where the file lives on the server. In this case, the file is in a folder called "xhtml."

- **contents.html.** This is the name of the file.

Such artifacts as this small line shown here can be extremely frustrating to a designer, particularly since they don't vanish when the border is set for zero with an image. As a precaution, always double-check to ensure that there are no extraneous spaces within your <a></a> tags.

A URL is constructed by combining all of these parts and separating them with a forward slash (/). When we put a URL in a link or image, the browser needs to interpret this URL. How it does depends on whether the URL is absolute or relative.

An *absolute URL* is one that has all of the information, from the protocol to the file name. Some examples of URLS are:

http://www.yahoo.com/index.html
http://www.nicholaschase.com/xmlfs/jdom.html
http://www.againsttheclock.com/

This last URL requires some explanation. We've said that an absolute URL has all of the information, from the protocol to the filename but this one doesn't seem to have a filename.

If you've surfed at all, however, you've used URLs just like this. They work because Web servers have default files specified for just this purpose, usually called "index.html" or something similar. So the URL:

http://www.againsttheclock.com

is actually the same as:

http://www.againsttheclock.com/index.html

A *relative URL* is one that omits some of the location information and expects the browser to figure it out. This expectation is reasonable because the browser assumes that any information missing from the URL is to be supplied relative to the current page. Therefore, the file will be in the same location (in this case in the same folder) as the page referring to it, unless the code tells it to look somewhere else. For instance, it's common practice, and a good idea, to put images in their own folder, typically within the main Web site folder.

We can also move up and down the structure of folders using "dot notation." For instance, if we wrote:

<img src="./logo.gif" alt="Logo" />

then the browser knows to look in the same directory as the page. So if this was WIP>urls>recs.html, the browser is going to look for WIP>urls>logo.gif.

On the other hand, if we use two dots, then we're looking for the parent of this folder. (The parent is the folder that contains the folder.)

If we had the file WIP>urls>recs.html, and we wrote:

<img src="../logo.gif" alt="Logo" />

then the browser is going to look for WIP>logo.gif.

Exercise Setup
In this exercise, you will move some files around to see how the browser looks for them. In doing so, you want to make sure that you're always looking at the latest version of a page.

Put Images in Their Own Folder

1. Create an "images" folder within the **WIP>urls** folder. Move urls>q.gif into this new folder.

2. Close all browser windows, then restart the browser.

3. Open **WIP>urls>recs.html** in the browser.

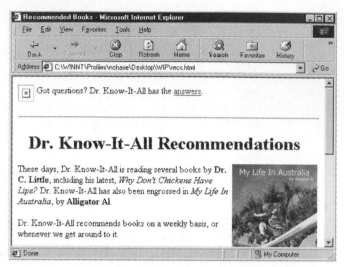

Notice that the image no longer appears on the page, even though it's still on the hard drive. This is because the browser is still looking for it in the urls folder.

4. Open **WIP>urls>recs.html** in your text editor, if it's not already open.

5. Change the image tag so that the browser will look in the images folder.

```
<!DOCTYPE HTML PUBLIC "-//W3C//DTD HTML 4.01 Transitional//EN" "http://
www.w3.org/TR/html4/loose.dtd">
<html>
<head><title>Recommended Books</title></head>
<body>
<p>
<a href="faq.html"><img src="images/q.gif" align="middle" alt="?" border="0" /></a>
Got questions? Dr. Know-It-All has the <a href="faq.html">answers</a>.</p>
<hr />
…
```

6. Save the file in the text editor and refresh the browser window.

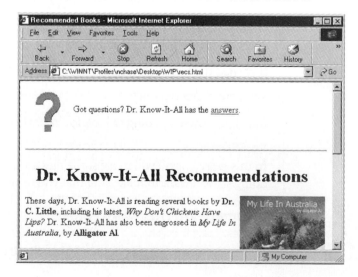

As you surf the Web, your browser caches, or saves information about pages that it's already seen to a storage spot (called a "cache"). This way, when you visit the page again, it doesn't have to take the time to redownload the information. When you want to see the page as it currently exists and not as it existed the first time you visited it, you don't want the cached version. Normally, you can accomplish this by clicking Refresh (on IE) or Reload (on Netscape). Sometimes, however, and for no discernable reason, this may not be enough. In that case, you can also try Command/Control-Refresh (on IE) or Shift-Reload (on Netscape). If all else fails, quit the browser and lauch it again.

7. Notice that the browser is able to locate the image because it has the information about the images folder. But this is still a relative URL. If we move the page, we can lose the image again. Create a folder called "articles" in the urls folder.

8. Move WIP>urls>recs.html into the **WIP>urls>articles** folder.

9. Open **WIP>urls>articles>recs.html** in the browser. (Simply refreshing the page won't work, because WIP>urls>recs.html doesn't exist as a path anymore.)

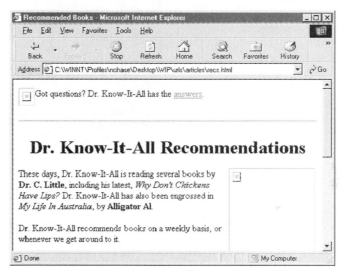

Notice that once again, we seem to have misplaced the image. Since we now are starting from the current position, we are looking for WIP>articles>images>q.gif, which doesn't exist! In this case, we want to tell the browser to start in the parent of the current folder, which would be urls, and look for the images folder there.

10. Open the newly moved **WIP>urls>articles>recs.html** in your text editor, and change the image tags to look for the parent folder:

```
<!DOCTYPE HTML PUBLIC "-//W3C//DTD HTML 4.01 Transitional//EN"
"http://www.w3.org/TR/html4/loose.dtd">
<html>
<head><title>Recommended Books</title></head>
<body>
<p><a href="faq.html"><img src="../images/q.gif" align="middle" alt="?" border="0" /></a>Got questions? Dr. Know-It-All has the <a href="faq.html">answers</a>.</p>
<hr />
<h1 align="center">Dr. Know-It-All Recommendations</h1>
<p><img src="../book1.jpg" align="right" width="150" height="224" alt="My Life In Australia" />These days, Dr. Know-It-All is reading several books by <b>Dr. C. Little</b>, including his latest, <i>Why Don't Chickens Have Lips?</i> Dr. Know-It-All has also been engrossed in <i>My Life In Australia</i>, by <b>Alligator Al</b>.</p>
<p>Dr. Know-It-All recommends books on a weekly basis, or whenever we get around to it.</p>
<br clear="right" />
<h2>Upcoming Books</h2>
<p><img src="../book2.jpg" align="left" width="150" height="224" alt="Weight Loss Secrets" /><i>At the urging of Mrs. Know-It-All, the next book Dr. Know-It-All reviews will be <i>Weight Loss Secrets</i>, by <b>Sally Slinky</b>.</i></p>
</body>
</html>
```

11. Save the file in the text editor and refresh the browser.

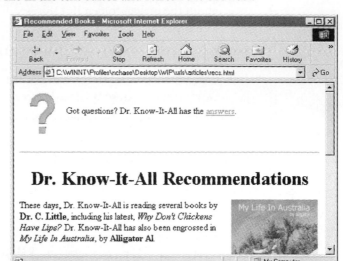

12. Notice that the .. tells the browser to move up one folder, in this case to urls, and then come back down into the image folder.

13. Leave the file open in both windows for the next exercise.

Organizing Your Files

It's important to realize how easy it is to wind up with a jumbled mess of files, if you're not careful. For instance, right now we have the q.gif file in the images folder, but the book cover images are in the urls folder. This could quickly turn into an organizational nightmare!

When we're planning the site, it's always a good idea to plan out the file structure, including folder and file locations. Assets (files), such as images and sounds, should always be in their own folders. Different content sections should have their own folders as well. The important point is to make sure that you (and anyone else working on the site) know where everything is. One way to make that easier is to have a standard location for all of our URLs to use as their consistent reference point.

Using the Document Root

Fortunately, there is a way to have a standard location that all documents can use as a reference point. It's called the "document root." Like a tree, all branches of the site grow off that root. When you move your documents to an actual Web server, you'll be able to test this, but in the meantime, let's look at how it works.

When we set up Web-server software, we have to tell it where the files will be located. For instance, if we were to set up a Web server for the files we have been using up to now, we would tell the software that our files are in the urls folder. This becomes our document root.

So if our site were called www.xhtmlclass.com, the URL for faq.html, which is still in the urls folder, would be:

http://www.xhtmlclass.com/faq.html

The URLs for recs.html and q.gif, respectively, would be:

http://www.xhtmlclass.com/articles/recs.html
http://www.xhtmlclass.com/images/q.gif

The document root is a setting that is part of the Web server software, so referring to it in this way will not work when we are accessing the files directly, as we have done in the previous exercises. It will only work once we put our pages on an actual Web server.

Since all of these files are on the same server, however, we can leave that server information out, making the three URLs:

```
/faq.html
/articles/recs.html
/images/q.gif
```

The slash "/" at the beginning (called a "leading slash") is crucial. It tells the browser to start at the document root. So we could change recs.html to read:

```
<!DOCTYPE HTML PUBLIC "-//W3C//DTD HTML 4.01 Transitional//EN"
"http://www.w3.org/TR/html4/loose.dtd">
<html>
<head><title>Recommended Books</title></head>
<body>
<p>
<a href="faq.html"><img src="/images/q.gif" align="middle" alt="?" border="0" /></a>
Got questions? Dr. Know-It-All has the <a href="/faq.html">answers</a>.</p>
<hr />
…
```

Then both the image and the links would work properly, even if we moved recs.html to a completely different location on the same server. Similarly, we could tell a browser that a link should always show the home page (or main page) of a site by using just the slash, as in:

```
<a href="/">Home</a>
```

Absolute URLs

Strictly speaking, the URLs in the last section are still relative URLs, because they are relative to a specific location. If we took all of these files and moved them to another server, such as:

http://www.anotherserver.com

they would still work. An absolute URL is different. It contains the entire location of the file, such as:

http://www.melitta.com/melittadirect/default.html
http://www.golfbusiness.com/proshop.html

With absolute URLs, the browser will always look in exactly the same place, no matter where the page is. Even if you move the page to a different server, the link or image will still work.

Using Absolute or Relative URLs vs. the <base> Tag

In most cases, you're better off using relative URLs than absolute URLs. Relative URLs allow you to move your entire site to a new location, such as a different server, and still have everything work. This flexibility is important in professional Web development, because sites are often created and tested on one server, called the "development server," then moved to the actual site, or *production server*.

Sometimes, however, using relative URLs doesn't work well. For instance, if a user were to save the page to his or her local computer, the images and links wouldn't work if the links were relative.

To correct this, however, every single link and image would have to be absolute. This would make it difficult to move the site between the development and production servers.

There is a compromise, fortunately. It's called the "<base /> tag." This tag acts as a global reference point for the page. The browser automatically adds it to the beginning of each URL. In other words, if we add a base tag to our page:

<base href="http://www.nicholaschase.com/" />

the browser will add this to every URL. So if we had a link of:

<a href="index.html">Home</a>

the browser would automatically look for:

http://www.nicholaschase.com/index.html

The <base /> tag enables us to have the advantages of both relative and absolute links. The page will still work if we download it to a local machine, but to move it from one server to another, all we need to do is change this one tag.

Exercise Setup

Let's see this in action in the following exercise.

Use the base Tag

1. In the open recs.html file in the text editor, add a <base /> tag to the page. (If you are working on a Web server, use that URL). Remove the ".." periods from the file references in the href.

```
<!DOCTYPE HTML PUBLIC "-//W3C//DTD HTML 4.01 Transitional//EN" "http://
www.w3.org/TR/html4/loose.dtd">
<html>
<head><title>Recommended Books</title></head>
<body>
<base href="http://www.xhtmlclass.com" />
<p>
<a href="faq.html"><img src="/images/q.gif" align="middle" alt="?" border="0" /></a>
Got questions? Dr. Know-It-All has the <a href="/faq.html">answers</a>.</p>
<hr />
…
```

2. Save the file in the text editor and refresh the browser.

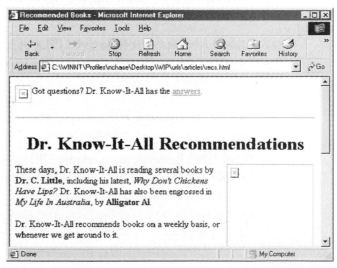

3. Close the text editor, but leave the browser open. If you were able to use an actual Web server, you may have different images than before. If not, the image will have disappeared once again. This is because the browser is now looking for:

http://www.xhtmlclass.com/images/q.gif

4. Click the image or the text link. The location bar should show:

http://www.xhtmlclass.com/faq.html

5. Close the browser.

Other Types of URLs

We have mentioned that URLs can be used to locate resources other than files over the Internet. You are no doubt familiar with http: as the beginning of a URL, but that is just one protocol, that we can use. A *protocol* is a means for communicating, a type of common vocabulary used between different computer programs. Five of the most common are http:, https:, file:, mailto: and ftp:.

The webmaster is the person who is responsible for maintaining a Web site.

- **http:**. HTTP stands for HyperText Transfer Protocol. This protocol is the method by which Web servers and browsers communicate. URLs that use this protocol start with http://, as in:

  http://www.doneger.com

- **https:**. HTTPS represents the Secure HyperText Transfer Protocol. This is just like http:, except that the messages are *encrypted*, or scrambled, so that they can't be intercepted. When you submit your credit card over the Web, you are (hopefully) using an https: page. These URLs start with https://, as in:

  https://www.melitta.com/melittadirect/default.html

- **file:**. We have been using the file: protocol throughout the chapter, though that may or may not be visible, depending on what your particular browser displays. This protocol is the method by which the browser accesses a page that is on the local hard drive. These URLs start with file:/// — note the extra slash — as in:

  file:///HardDrive/desktop/WIP/articles/recs.html

- **mailto:**. This protocol enables the user to send email to a particular person, such as the webmaster. These URLs start with mailto:, as in:

  mailto:webmaster@mysite.com

- **ftp:**. FTP stands for File Transfer Protocol. It is mainly used for downloading large files, because it is faster than HTTP. Developers and designers also use it to upload files to a Web site. These URLs start with ftp://, as in:

  ftp://ftp10.netscape.com/pub/netscape6/english/6.01/mac/macos8.5/ MacNetscape6Installer.sea.bin

Summary

In this chapter, you learned how to use text and images to create links to other pages. You also learned how to link to a specific point on a page. You discovered the distinctions between relative and absolute URLs and the <base /> tag, and when to use each of them. You explored file organization and became familiar with different types of URLs and how to refer to parent directories.

Notes:

3 Cascading Style Sheets

Chapter Objective:

Chapter Objectives

To learn to use Cascading Style Sheets to control the appearance and presentation of your content. In Chapter 3, you will:

- Discover how to apply a style to a section of text.

- Learn to determine what content will be affected, depending on how you set a particular style.

- Become familiar with the distinctions between classes, IDs and names.

- Learn how to and practice creating individual styles that work well together.

- Become familiar with how style sheets can be used.

Projects to be Completed:

- News Web (A)

- Cyber Travel (B)

- Hunter Films (C)

- North Star Adventure Gear (D)

Cascading Style Sheets

In Chapter 1, we talked briefly about separating content and presentation. Now let's explore this concept more fully.

When designers looked at the future plans for XHTML, some were alarmed to discover that certain tags, such as underline (<u>) and strikethrough (<s>), were being eliminated. How, they wondered, would they be able to control the appearance of text without these and related tags?

When HTML was first created, the intent was to make information understandable by defining the nature of each piece of text, such as a heading or a paragraph. The ability to control the appearance was an afterthought — an afterthought that has taken on such importance in the last few years that it was thought prudent to separate it from content completely. That's where XHTML and Cascading Style Sheets come in.

Tags determine the structure of the document, defining such items as the headers, individual paragraphs and tables. Style, on the other hand, is handled separately, and Cascading Style Sheets (CSS) fill that need.

For this chapter, you may find that you need to use Microsoft Internet Explorer to see the same results as the screenshots, since browsers differ in how they implement some of the CSS features that we will demonstrate.

Unfortunately, not every browser presently supports all features of CSS, as we noted when we chose Transitional XHTML over Strict for this book. Until all commonly used browsers support CSS, it is a good idea to use Transitional XHTML to make certain that the look of your content at least approximates your intent.

What Are Style Sheets?

When we design the look and feel of a site, that look includes not only the graphics but also the text and the styling or appearance of that text. This styling is crucial, and even a small change can make all the difference in the overall appearance of a site, as we can see in these images.

Cascading Style Sheets can be used to specify many of the same text properties as are handled by traditional page-layout programs, such as leading, kerning, font and size. A style sheet can also be used to specify properties for other tags, such as images and links.

Let's take a look at setting some of these styles for a specific tag.

Leading, the amount of space between lines of text, and **kerning**, the amount of space between letters in a line of text, have traditionally been difficult, if not impossible, to control on a Web page.

Adding Style to a Section of Text

Up to now, when we wanted to affect how a particular section of the page was rendered, we would use attributes such as align. Now we're going to use the style attribute, which allows us more freedom, because it enables us to designate virtually any property that controls appearance. These properties are information such as font, color and size.

For example:

```
<p>This is normal styling</p>
<p style="font-family: Verdana">This is in Verdana.</p>
```

In this case, the style attribute enables us to designate the font-family property, selecting Verdana as the font for the enclosed text. Other style properties affect the text similarly. A list of some of the most common properties used with the style attribute is available at the end of the book.

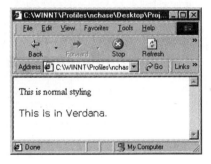

Exercise Setup
Let's see a style in action.

Add Style to a Section of Text

1. Create a new folder called "css" inside your WIP folder. Navigate to the **RF_HTML> Chapter 3** folder, and copy the entire contents of the folder — golf.html file and images folder to the new folder, WIP>css.

2. Open **WIP>css>golf.html** in the text editor and browser.

3. Change the font to Verdana on both the header and the paragraph using the style attribute and the font-family property.

```
<!DOCTYPE html PUBLIC "-//W3C//DTD XHTML 1.0 Transitional//EN"
"http://www.w3.org/TR/xhtml1/DTD/xhtml1-transitional.dtd" >
<html>
<head><title>Golfbusiness.com</title></head>
<body>
<img src="images/logo.gif" alt="Golfbusiness Logo" alt="Logo" />
<h1 style="font-family: Verdana;" >New Products</h1>
<p style="font-family: Verdana;" >Golfbusiness.com is proud to introduce three new
product lines. You can now buy your <a href="carts.html">golf carts</a> and <a
href="cartparts.html">parts</a> right here, as well as fulfilling all of your <a
href="maint.html">golf maintenance</a> needs.</p>
<p style="font-family: Verdana;" ><a href="home.html">Home</a></p>
</body>
</html>
```

4. Save the file in your text editor and refresh the browser.

5. Notice that the font has changed to Verdana.

6. Leave the file open in both the text editor and the browser for the next exercise.

The <span> Tag

One drawback of using the style attribute is having to set the style of every affected tag. Fortunately, we can take a shortcut using the <span> tag. This tag allows us to set the style for all content contained within it. In other words, if we set a style through the <span> tag, the style will affect all of the content between <span> and </span>.

```
<p>This is normal styling, while this section uses the span tag:
<span style="font-family: Verdana">This is in Verdana.</span></p>
```

A span font change works because putting a style on a tag affects everything inside that tag. The <span> tag doesn't do anything except provide a tag on which to add the style attribute.

Add Style to a Section of Text

1. In the open golf.html file in your text editor, remove the style information from the heading and paragraph tags, and replace it with the span tag. In the span tag, set the font to Verdana.

```
<!DOCTYPE html PUBLIC "-//W3C//DTD XHTML 1.0 Transitional//EN"
"http://www.w3.org/TR/xhtml1/DTD/xhtml1-transitional.dtd" >
<html>
<head><title>Golfbusiness.com</title></head>
<body>
<img src="images/logo.gif" alt="Golfbusiness Logo" />
<span style="font-family: Verdana;">

<h1>New Products</h1>
<p>Golfbusiness.com is proud to introduce three new product lines. You can now buy your
<a href="carts.html">golf carts</a> and <a href="cartparts.html">parts</a> right here, as
well as fulfilling all of your <a href="maint.html">golf maintenance</a> needs.</p>
<p><a href="home.html">Home</a></p>
</span>

</body>
</html>
```

2. Save the file in your text editor and refresh the browser. Because we are applying the same style to the same sections of text, notice that there is no change as it displays in the browser.

3. Leave the file open in both the text editor and the browser for the next exercise.

Using Internal Style Sheets

Applying styles directly to tags gives us an enormous amount of flexibility, but can be difficult to maintain. What happens if we want to change the style so that links have no underlines? If we continued to apply styles to individual tags in this way, we would have to change every link tag on every page, or at least every span tag — not very efficient!

Separating this style information into a style sheet, whether *internal* (contained in the page) or *external* (contained in a separate file), is far more convenient and much easier to maintain. A style sheet simply lists style information and information about the parts of a page to which it applies.

Style sheets allow us to associate specific style information with specific sections of our Web page. This control of specific style information is implemented using selectors.

Selectors

Selectors are the piece of the code that determines what sections of a page are affected by a specific style. A selector can consist of several different types of information:

- **Element name.** With element names, we can specify that all links have a specific hover effect or that all headings are a particular color. Element names also allow us to specify styles for combinations of elements. For example, we might want to specify a style for only the text that follows a heading and could use element names to do so.

Putting a "#" before the name tells the browser that the name is an ID.

- **Elements and attributes**. The CSS standard allows us to base styling on the existence of specific attributes as well, such as adjusting the color on only the text that has been centered with the align attribute. At the time of this writing, however, the only browser that supports this is Netscape 6. When the ability to base selectors on attributes is fully supported, it will enable us to specify our own attributes, which may have nothing to do with XHTML. This will give us a tremendous amount of control over our content simply through a well-crafted style sheet. For instance, we could add an attribute of hidden="yes" to certain sections and create a style sheet that specifies that these sections do not appear on the page.

- **Classes**. This is an easy way to create a style that could apply to more than one type of element. For instance, we might want a particular style to apply to all headers, or to all text, whether or not it is within a table. Preceding the name with a period tells the browser that it's a class. For instance:

  .crucial { color: red }

  This sets the color to red on all text that is part of the crucial class.

- **IDs.** These are similar to classes, but they are much more specific and typically are used when just a specific instance needs a particular style. Preceding the name with a # tells the browser to look for an ID, rather than a tag or a class. For example:

  #primary { color: red }

  This sets the color to red on only a tag that has specified an id attribute of primary.

- *, the universal selector. Sometimes we want a property, such as the font, to apply to everything on the page. In this case, we'd use the * selector.

In order to make use of selectors, we first create an internal style sheet on the page by using the <style></style> tag:

```
<style type="text/css">
</style>
```

We can then specify what we want to style by using a selector (such as *, which will style all text, in this case). Finally we add the style information (such as setting the text to the font Arial, in this case) in brackets.

```
<style type="text/css">
      *  { font-family: Arial }
</style>
```

There are many different ways to style text, such as changing the displayed font using the font-family property or boldfacing text using the font-weight property. We will review a list of properties and what they do a bit later in this chapter, but first we'll look at how they're used.

Exercise Setup
Let's take a look at adding styles via internal style sheets and these selectors.

Putting a period before the name indicates to the browser that what follows is a class.

Create an Internal Style Sheet

1. In the open file golf.html in your text editor, remove the span tag and add an internal style sheet. Set the font to Verdana, Arial or a sans serif font for the headline (which is indicated by the <h1></h1> tag).

```
<!DOCTYPE html PUBLIC "-//W3C//DTD XHTML 1.0 Transitional//EN"
"http://www.w3.org/TR/xhtml1/DTD/xhtml1-transitional.dtd" >
<html>
<head><title>Golfbusiness.com</title>
<style type="text/css">
   h1 { font-family: Verdana, Arial, sans-serif }
</style>
</head>
<body>
<img src="images/logo.gif" alt="Golfbusiness Logo" />
<h1>New Products</h1>
<p>Golfbusiness.com is proud to introduce three new product lines. You can now buy your
<a href="carts.html">golf carts</a> and <a href="cartparts.html">parts</a> right here, as
well as fulfilling all of your <a href="maint.html">golf maintenance</a> needs.</p>
<p><a href="home.html">Home</a></p>
</body>
</html>
```

In this case, we specified several values for the font family. This is because not every user will have every font installed. As we have written the code, the browser will first try to find Verdana. Failing that, it will try to use Arial. If it can't find Arial either, it will choose a sans-serif font that is available.

2. Save the file in your text editor and refresh the browser.

3. Use the * selector to set the font to the same fonts for all text.

```
<!DOCTYPE html PUBLIC "-//W3C//DTD XHTML 1.0 Transitional//EN"
"http://www.w3.org/TR/xhtml1/DTD/xhtml1-transitional.dtd" >
<html>
<head><title>Golfbusiness.com</title>
<style type="text/css">
   * { font-family: Verdana, Arial, sans-serif }
</style>
</head>
<body>
<img src="images/logo.gif" alt="Golfbusiness Logo" />
<h1>New Products</h1>
```

```
<p>Golfbusiness.com is proud to introduce three new product lines. You can now buy your
<a href="carts.html">golf carts</a> and <a href="cartparts.html">parts</a> right here, as
well as fulfilling all of your <a href="maint.html">golf maintenance</a> needs.</p>
<p><a href="home.html">Home</a></p>
</body>
</html>
```

4. Save the file in your text editor and refresh the browser.

5. Create a new class called "link" by adding a class attribute to each of the hyperlinks, and use it to remove the underlines by designating .link as a selector.

```
<!DOCTYPE html PUBLIC "-//W3C//DTD XHTML 1.0 Transitional//EN"
"http://www.w3.org/TR/xhtml1/DTD/xhtml1-transitional.dtd" >
<html>
<head><title>Golfbusiness.com</title>
<style type="text/css">
    * { font-family: Verdana, Arial, sans-serif }
    .link { text-decoration: none }

</style>
</head>
<body>
<img src="images/logo.gif" alt="Golfbusiness Logo" />
<h1>New Products</h1>
<p>Golfbusiness.com is proud to introduce three new product lines. You can now buy your
<a href="carts.html" class="link" >golf carts</a> and <a href="cartparts.html"
class="link" >parts</a> right here, as well as fulfilling all of your <a href="maint.html"
class="link" >golf maintenance</a> needs.</p>
<p><a href="home.html" >Home</a></p>
</body>
</html>
```

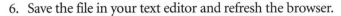

6. Save the file in your text editor and refresh the browser.

Although the links are still fairly visible in color, here they practically disappear.
Remember that if you remove such a commonly accepted visual cue as
the underline, users might not notice your links.

Notice that the Home link is still underlined, even though it's a link, because we didn't make it part of the link class.

7. Now we're going to use a more specific selector, the ID. Use it to create the homeLink ID.

```
<!DOCTYPE html PUBLIC "-//W3C//DTD XHTML 1.0 Transitional//EN"
"http://www.w3.org/TR/xhtml1/DTD/xhtml1-transitional.dtd" >
<html>
<head><title>Golfbusiness.com</title>
<style type="text/css">
  * { font-family: Verdana, Arial, sans-serif }
  .link { text-decoration: none }
  #homeLink { font-weight: bold; }

</style>
</head>
<body>
<img src="images/logo.gif" alt="Golfbusiness Logo" />
<h1>New Products</h1>
<p>Golfbusiness.com is proud to introduce three new product lines. You can now buy your
<a href="carts.html" class="link">golf carts</a> and <a href="cartparts.html"
class="link">parts</a> right here, as well as fulfilling all of your <a href="maint.html"
class="link">golf maintenance</a> needs.</p>
<p><a href="home.html" id="homeLink" >Home</a></p>
</body>
</html>
```

8. Save the file in your text editor, and refresh the browser to see that the Home link is now bold.

9. Leave the file open in both windows for the next exercise.

External Style Sheets

Using an internal style sheet is certainly more convenient than setting the specific style for each individual element, but we can go further. As we have our code set up now, to make a change we would have to edit every page. It would be much more convenient to remove the style information from all of these locations and put it, instead, in an *external style sheet*, a single separate file that can be referenced by each page. Coded this way, making a change to the site is as simple as making the change to that one file.

Creating the Style Sheet

The style sheet is just a normal text file, just as our pages have been. You create your external style sheet by creating a text file in the usual fashion and naming it with the extension ".css". (It is customary — but not essential — to use the file extension .css.)

Exercise Setup
Let's pull our current styles out into an external style sheet.

Create an External Style Sheet

1. In the open file golf.html in the text editor, create a new file in your text editor. Copy and paste the style information from golf.html into it.

```
* { font-family: Verdana, Arial, sans-serif }
.link { text-decoration: none }
#homeLink { font-weight: bold; }
```

2. Save the new file in the **WIP>css** folder as "golfstyle.css". Leave the file open for a future exercise.

Linking to the Style Sheet

Once we have created an external style sheet, we need to tell the browser to look for the style sheet to use. We do so via a new element: <link>. This is not the same as a hyperlink. Instead, it links the two files together conceptually, as in:

<link rel="stylesheet" href="golfstyle.css" type="text/css" />

As shown in the above example, we are giving the link element three different attributes. The first, rel, or relation, tells the browser what kind of link this is so it knows what to do with it. The second is the href, or hypertext reference. This, like the href on an <a></a> tag, tells the browser where to find the file. Finally, the third, type, tells the browser what language to use to do the styling. We're only dealing with CSS right now, but there are others, such as Extensible Stylesheet Language, or XSL, which we won't cover here.

Exercise Setup
Let's add the style sheet that we created to the page.

Link to an External Style Sheet

1. In the open file golf.html in your text editor, remove the internal style sheet, and replace it with a link to **WIP>Chapter3>golfstyle.css**.

```
<!DOCTYPE html PUBLIC "-//W3C//DTD XHTML 1.0 Transitional//EN"
"http://www.w3.org/TR/xhtml1/DTD/xhtml1-transitional.dtd" >
<html>
<head><title>Golfbusiness.com</title></head>
<body>
<link rel="stylesheet" href="golfstyle.css" type="text/css"  />
<img src="images/logo.gif" alt="Golfbusiness Logo" />
<h1>New Products</h1>
…
```

2. Save the file in your text editor and refresh the browser. Notice that the browser does not display any change because all we did was change the location of the styling information, not the styling information itself.

3. Leave the file open in both windows for the next exercise.

Basic Styles

There are, in fact, over 100 different properties that can be set for different XHTML elements. Some of them, such as color or font size, are obvious choices for text, but others, such as cue, azimuth or play-during, are only for audio. The most common text properties are discussed below.

You can create different style sheets for different media so that however users access your content, they will have a good experience.

For now, however, we'll look at some of the basic styles used for visual media.

Another type of link is the Shortcut icon which designates a thumbnail graphic that appears if the user bookmarks your page.

The rel attribute tells the browser what kind of link it is. The type attribute tells the browser what language to use for the styling

Certainly there were situations in which Web-page authors had no alternatives, such as changing fonts before the advent of CSS. This ability was also used, however, to replace, for example, a heading, which should be <h1>, with <font size="2">, which was not proper.

The <font> tag will be removed from version 1.1 of XHTML, but this is not cuase for panic. It is unlikely that browsers will support only XHTML 1.1, so a properly written XHTML Transitional page, such as those we have been writing here, will still be accessible to browsers. That said, content should still be tagged properly , with styling in style sheets instead of in <font> tags.

Creating Font Effects

The first style sheets weren't actually style sheets, the way that they're defined today. Instead, Web-page authors would use the <font> tag, which enabled them to specify attributes such as font family and color.

This ability to directly style text was handy for the first WYSIWYG Web-page editors. Rather than worrying about what would later become style information, a Web-page editor could act like a word processor, controlling the presentation of the material. Unfortunately, this enabled many Web-page authors to take this shortcut rather than tagging their content properly.

Today, authors should tag their content based on content, and handle presentation through text attributes in their style sheets.

Text-Related Properties

There are a number of text-related properties that can be added to a style sheet in order to control the appearance of your content. These include:

- **font-family.** Probably the most commonly used property, font-family, allows authors to set the specific font that appears in the user's browser displaying this Web page. As we saw above, we can set several alternatives, from most specific to least specific, and the browser will use the first one that's available. Always specify a generic font family among those you list, so that you can at least get close to the desired look. The generic families are serif, sans-serif, cursive, fantasy and monospace. For example:

```
* { font-family: Verdana, Arial, sans-serif }
```

- **font-size.** Font size can be set a number of ways. One way is to set font size is by specifying absolute sizes, which can be xx-small, x-small, small, medium, large, x-large and xx-large. A second way is to use relative size, whereby the text is rendered larger or smaller in proportion to the rest of the element containing the content. A third way to set size, similar to relative size, is specifying the size via percentage of the unstyled size, such as 150%. Employing relative sizes can be much more useful for style sheets that may change than setting the size with points (such as 12pt), but it is much more common to use point measurements.

In this example, we show three standard ways to set the font size:

```
h1 { font-size: xx-large }
h2 { font-size: 16pt }
b { font-size: 125% }
```

- **font-stretch**. This property permits the author to stretch or condense text. The allowable values are: ultra-condensed, extra-condensed, condensed, semi-condensed, normal, semi-expanded, expanded, extra-expanded, ultra-expanded, wider and narrower. For example:

```
h1 { font-stretch: ultra-expanded }
```

A font is a collection of information, such as the look of each glyph, or letter, how letters should line up, and so on. Part of this information that the user never sees is whether the slanted version of a font is classified as italic or oblique. In the vast majority of cases, you will jusy use italic.

*A **keyword** is a reserved word that has special meaning to the browser in a particular situation, such as when used with a style sheet property.*

- **font-style.** Font-style allows you to create an effect similar to setting text to italic. The three values are normal, which is non-slanted, italic and oblique, which is similar to italic. This property allows us to keep the style within the style sheet rather than using <i>. For example, we might create a class that is used with the <span> tag to denote sections of content. We might then use this property to set any content within this class to italic. Later, if we changed our mind and wanted to bold this content, we could just change the style sheet rather than having to change all of our <i> tags to <b> tags.

```
.destinations { font-style: italic }
```

- **font-variant.** Font-variant allows the author to choose small-caps for a section of text. Small-caps does exactly what it sounds like, setting the text to a small version of the typeface's uppercase letters, even if the original text was lowercase. Words that were already capitalized begin with a larger capital letter. This property can also be set to normal, in order to indicate that a section of text should not use small-caps.

```
* { font-variant: small-caps }

h1 { font-variant: normal }
```

In this case, all text will use small-caps except for <h1> text.

- **font-weight.** The font-weight property is like a fine-tuned bold tag. The user can set the value or weight more precisely to 100, 200, 300 and so on, up to 900. How the text appears depends on the individual browser. Four keywords are also available: normal (same as 400), bold (same as 700), bolder and lighter. This sample makes any text that is part of the crucial class bolder than the text surrounding it.

```
.crucial { font-weight: bolder }
```

- **font.** In this instance, we are discussing not the <font> tag, but the font stylesheet property. With all of these individual properties, font almost seems redundant, but it's actually a shortcut property, allowing us to set multiple properties at one time. For instance, we can apply several changes to the hyperlinks in our document at one time using the font property. We could use this one property to set the font-weight, font-style and font-family, all at one time.

```
.crucial { font: bold italic large Verdana, sans-serif }
```

- **text-decoration.** This is generally used to remove the underline from links. The allowable values are none, underline, overline (the opposite of underline), line-through and blink. For example:

```
<html>
<head>
<style>
a { text-decoration: none; }
h1 { text-decoration: line-through; }
</style>
<head>
<body>
<h1>This is a header</h1>
<a href="home.html">This is a link, even though it doesn't look like one.</a>
</body>
</html>
```

- **text-indent**. This property indents the first line of a paragraph (or other text) and can be specified in pixels (px), points (pt) or ems. As in printing, one em is the width of the m character in a particular font. The relative nature of this measurement makes it ideal for a potentially changing environment such as Web design.

  ```
  p { text-indent: 5em; }
  ```

- **text-transform**. Text-transform allows the Web-page author to designate the capitalization of a section of text. The valid values are capitalize (which makes the first letter of every word uppercase and the rest lowercase), uppercase, lowercase and none (which uses the original case of the text).

  ```
  h1 { text-transform: uppercase; }
  ```

- **text-align**. This property allows us to set the alignment of a section of text to left, right, center and justify. (Later, in Chapter 4 when we look at tables, we'll see one more use for this property.)

  ```
  h1 { text-align: center }
  ```

- **text-shadow**. When this property is supported by browsers — as is not the case as of this writing — it will allow dynamic shadows to be placed around text. Web authors will also be able to designate multiple shadows, which will overlap. Be aware that overuse of such design elements can also appear amateurish.

We can also add more than one property to a style sheet at a time, as long as the properties are separated by semicolons. For example, we could rewrite that font property above as:

```
.crucial { font-weight: bold;
font-style: italic;
font-family: Verdana, sans-serif; }
```

Exercise Setup
Let's add some of these properties to our document.

Use the font Property

1. Double-check that golf.html is open in the browser and that golfstyle.css is open in the text editor.

2. Make the hyperlinks larger, bold and small caps.

```
* { font-family: Verdana, Arial, sans-serif }
.link {
      text-decoration: none;
      font: small-caps bolder larger;
      }
#homeLink { font-weight: bold; }
```

To add more than one property to a style sheet, use semicolons to separate the properties.

3. Save the file in your text editor and refresh the browser. Notice that although we haven't touched golf.html, the page display has changed.

4. Leave the files open for the next exercise.

Colors

One of the most common uses for styles is to control the color of text. Colors can be set in a number of different ways, including named colors, RGB values and hex values.

Named Colors

One manner of setting color is using named colors, such as red, blue, green and so on. These are the easiest to use, but limited by the number of such named colors. The colors available as named colors are aqua, black, blue, fuchsia, gray, green, lime, maroon, navy, olive, purple, red, silver, teal, white and yellow. For example:

h1 { color: red }

RGB Values

One way to get around the limited number of named colors is to specify traditional RGB values.

All colors are made up of primary colors. In printing these colors are cyan, magenta, yellow and black, otherwise known as "CMYK." On works viewed on the monitor, however, we use the same color system in use by computer monitors, the Red-Green-Blue system, or RGB. Each of these values must be between 0 and 255.

For example:

h1 { color: rgb(255, 255, 255) }

RGB values as a means of specifying color are not currently supported by all browsers. You can get much the same results, however, by using the hex (short for hexadecimal) values described next. Hex values are essentially a different way of expressing the red, green and blue values.

Hex Values

Another reason for not using RGB values to set color is the issue of multiple platforms and browsers. Because of differences in the way that colors are rendered on different platforms, only 216 colors are designated as "browser safe," meaning that they exist in the system palettes of all major platforms. While these colors can be specified with RGB values, it's easier to ensure that we're using one of these browser-safe colors by using hex values.

The numbers that we're used to using in daily life are called the "decimal system" because they're based on digits that can be one of 10 values, 0-9. The *hexadecimal system*, on the other hand, is based on digits that can be 16 different values, 0-9, and then A-F. For instance, the numbers run like this:

Decimal	Hexadecimal	Decimal	Hexadecimal
0	0	1	1
2	2	3	3
4	4	5	5
6	6	7	7
8	8	9	9
10	A	11	B
12	C	13	D
14	E	15	F
16	10	17	11
18	12	28	1C
29	1D	30	1E
31	1F	160	A0
161	A1	203	BB
237	ED		

Colors are specified with hex values by translating the traditional RGB values into hex values. For instance, some sample colors and their RGB values are:

White (255, 255, 255): FFFFFF

Black (0, 0, 0): 000000

Red (255, 0, 0): FF0000

Green (0, 255, 0): 00FF00

Blue (0, 0, 255): 0000FF

Grey (170, 170, 170): AAAAAA

The important point to note here is that the only browser-safe colors are those that use double values, that is two of the same value in a row. For instance, some browser-safe colors are:

Light Blue: 3322EE

Deep Green: 22FFAA

Pink: FFAAAA

In contrast, non-browser-safe versions of these colors might be:

Light Blue: 3F29ED

Deep Green: 20FAA9

Pink: FEACA9

In most cases, these colors would be displayed in the same way as their counterparts, but they can be displayed differently depending on the browser and the color-depth of the user's computer.

By keeping this in mind, we obtain some of the flexibility of RGB values, but we can know immediately whether or not the color is browser-safe. (And, if it's not, we can find a close substitute quickly.)

Hex values use a format similar to named colors, so adding one looks like this:

h1 { color: #FF0000 }

Exercise Setup
Let's set the colors on our document.

Set the Color Using Hex Values

1. Double-check that golf.html is open in the browser, and golfstyle.css is open in the text editor.

2. Make the heading (<h1>) a browser-safe green (33FF33).

```
* { font-family: Verdana, Arial, sans-serif }
.link {
    text-decoration: none;
    font: small-caps bolder larger;
    }
h1 { color: #33FF33 }
#homeLink { font-weight: bold }
```

3. Save the text editor file and refresh the browser. Notice that the heading is now green.

4. Leave both windows open for the next exercise.

Background Images

Another way in which early Web-page authors could embellish their pages was by adding a background image. This image would tile behind the content on the page, adding textures and interest.

This capability has been expanded with CSS, allowing the author to control whether and how the image is tiled, and even whether the image scrolls with the rest of the page.

To add a background image to the page, we use the background property, as in:

body { background: url("images/watermark.gif") }

Normally, we put a background on the body of the page itself, but backgrounds can also be added to other elements. For now, we'll stick with the traditional. To tell the browser where the image is, we are using the url() command. This uses the same information as the href on a hyperlink or the src on an image.

Exercise Setup
We'll look at controlling the background shortly, but for now, let's add it to the page.

Set the Background Image

1. With golf.html open in the browser and golfstyle.css open in the text editor, add the background to the body element.

```
* { font-family: Verdana, Arial, sans-serif }
.link {
      text-decoration: none;
      font: small-caps bolder larger;
   }
 h1 { color: #33FF33 }
#homeLink { font-weight: bold }
body { background: url("images/watermark.gif") }
```

2. Save the file in your text editor and refresh the browser to see the background.

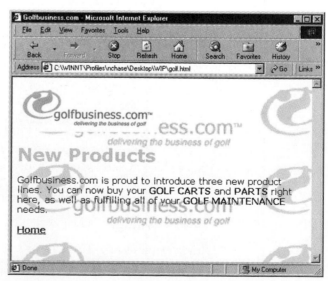

3. Leave both windows open for the next exercise.

Designing a Background Image

One thing to be careful with is the type of background images we choose. Early background images were often distracting, difficult to read over and even headache-inspiring.

In the following samples, observe that the background has a dramatic effect on the readability of the page.

Background Properties

As with fonts, there are several properties that we can set for the background of an element.

- **background-color.** Before Web-page authors could add background images, they were able to add background colors to a page. It's always a good idea to set the background color of a page, even if you're also setting an image. By doing so, if the image doesn't download for any reason, or if it's still downloading, the page should still be legible. Not all browsers display the background as white, unless it's explicitly set. For example:

  body { background-color: white}

- **background-image.** This property enables us to set the background image using a URL.

  body { background-image: url("images/watermark.gif") }

- **background-repeat**. We can control not only whether the background image tiles, but also how it tiles. Appropriate values are repeat, which causes the background image to tile normally, repeat-x and repeat-y, which cause it to tile only horizontally or only vertically, and no-repeat. For example:

```
body { background-image: url("images/watermark.gif");
background-repeat: repeat-x; }
```

- **background-position**. Using this property, we can specify where the background image should start using an offset from the upper-left corner. Repeating images will be repeated to the left and top of this point and well as below and to the right. This property takes two pixel values, the horizontal and the vertical offset. These values can be expressed using percentages, in which the size of the window is taken into account, pixel measurements, or the keywords top, center, bottom, right and left.

```
body { background-image: url("images/watermark.gif");
background-position: 20px 40px; }
```

- **background-attachment**. This is a relatively new feature, which allows us to set our background to remain in position, even if the page is scrolled. The keywords are scroll and fixed.

```
body { background-image: url("images/watermark.gif");
background-position: 20px 40px;
background-attachment: fixed; }
```

- **background**. Like the font property, this is a shorthand property, allowing the designer to specify background-color, background-image, background-repeat, background-attachment, background-position. As you can see from the last exercise, when we used the background property to specify only the background-image, not all of these values need to be specified. The browser will figure out what properties are being specified by looking at the values.

Exercise Setup
Let's add a more functional background to our page.

Add a Better Background

1. With golf.html open in the browser and golfstyle.css open in the text editor, change the background image property in golfstyle.css to base.gif. Set position to left, top; attachment to fixed; and no repeat on the page.

```
* { font-family: Verdana, Arial, sans-serif }
.link {
    text-decoration: none;
    font: small-caps bolder larger;
}
h1 { color: #33FF33 }
#homeLink { font-weight: bold }
body {

        background-image: url("images/base.gif");
        background-position: left top;
        background-attachment: fixed;
        background-repeat: no-repeat;
}
```

2. Save the file. Open **WIP>css>golf.html** in the text editor.

3. Remove the logo, and using the techniques for images that we learned in Chapter 1, add a spacer across the top and down the left side of the page.

```
<!DOCTYPE html PUBLIC "-//W3C//DTD XHTML 1.0 Transitional//EN"
"http://www.w3.org/TR/xhtml1/DTD/xhtml1-transitional.dtd" >
<html>
<head><title>Golfbusiness.com</title>
<link rel="stylesheet" href="golfstyle.css" type="text/css"  /></head>
<body>

<img src="images/spacer.gif" height="50" width="50" alt="Spacer"/>
<br clear="left" />
<img src="images/spacer.gif" height="300" width="50" align="left" alt="Spacer"/>
<h1>New Products</h1>
...
```

4. Save the file in your text editor, and refresh the browser to see the new background image. Scroll the page and notice that while the content moves, the background image stays put. (You may need to shrink your window to make the scrollbars appear.)

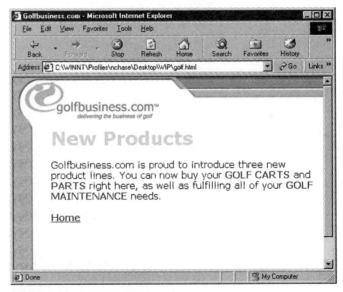

5. Leave both windows open for the next exercise.

Hover Effects and Pseudo-classes

Another effect commonly used by Web designers is a change of color or appearance of a link when the user passes his or her mouse over it. This is done with a special type of selector called a "pseudo-class."

A *pseudo-class* is a type of selector that applies to a particular type of content, whether or not we explicitly set the content to belong to that class. There are 14 pseudo-classes defined in CSS, but not all have been implemented in all browsers. The most common are related to hyperlinks.

- **:hover.** This pseudo-class affects links when the mouse rolls over them. This pseudo-class is not supported in some older CSS-enabled browsers.

- **:visited.** This pseudo-class affects links for which the content has already been visited. It's important to note that this has nothing to do with whether the user has actually clicked on this link. For instance, if the user were to come to your site through the home page, any link on your site that points back to the home page will be designated as visited.

- **:active.** This pseudo-class affects links in the process of being clicked. In other words, when the user clicks on the link, it becomes active and stays that way until the browser moves on to the next page.

Change the Rollover Color of a Hyperlink

1. Make certain that golf.html is open in the browser, and golfstyle.css is open in the text editor.

2. In golfstyle.css, add a :hover pseudo-class to the links so that when the user rolls over the links, the background color turns to yellow.

```
* { font-family: Verdana, Arial, sans-serif }
.link {
        text-decoration: none;
        font: small-caps bolder larger;
    }
h1 { color: #33FF33 }
#homeLink { font-weight: bold }
body {
            background-image: url("images/base.gif");
            background-position: left top;
            background-attachment: fixed;
            background-repeat: no-repeat;
        }
:hover { background-color: yellow }
```

3. Save the file in your text editor and refresh the browser. Roll the mouse over the links to see the color change.

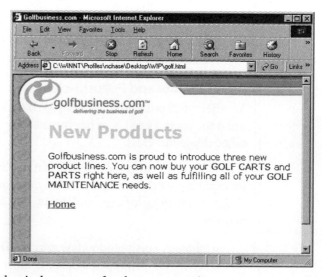

4. Leave both windows open for the next exercise.

Other Pseudo-classes

Some pseudo-classes are non-link related. For instance, :first-letter and :first-line are useful, but can require the author to specify which tags will be affected. For example:

h1:first-letter { color: #FF0000; }

Exercise Setup
Let's look at these pseudo-classes in our document.

Change the Color of Just the First Letter

1. Make certain that golf.html is open in the browser and golfstyle.css is open in the text editor.

2. Set the first letter of every paragraph to the same green as the headline.

```
* { font-family: Verdana, Arial, sans-serif }
.link {
        text-decoration: none;
        font: small-caps bolder larger;
    }
 h1 { color: #33FF33 }
#homeLink { font-weight: bold }
body {
        background-image: url("images/base.gif");
        background-position: left top;
        background-attachment: fixed;
        background-repeat: no-repeat;
    }
:hover { background-color: yellow }
p:first-letter { color: #33FF33 }
```

3. Save the file in your text editor and refresh the browser to see the color change.

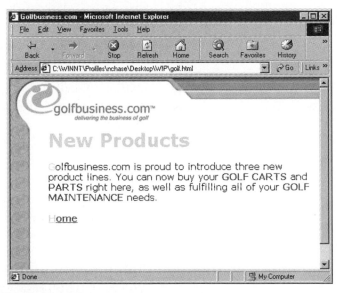

4. Close both windows.

Putting the Cascade in Cascading Style Sheets

One great advantage of style sheets is that they can be combined, allowing for easier maintenance.

They can be combined in two different ways. The first method is by applying more than one style sheet to the page. In this case, a second style sheet can override the instructions of the first. By structuring it in this fashion, a general style sheet can be created for the overall site, while a section-wide, or even page-wide style sheet can be added for specific variations. This effect, where a general style is applied and is in effect unless it is overridden, is known as "cascading."

The second way that styles can cascade is via inheritance, which we have been using throughout our exercises. We specified that our paragraph should be Verdana, and it is. When we then change the appearance of our links, the font choice remains (or is *inherited*), because it is inherited from the paragraph.

Summary

In this chapter, you learned to specify the appearance of particular sections of the page using internal or external style sheets. You also discovered the different types of selectors that are available, such as tags, classes, IDs, pseudo-classes and the universal selector, *, as well as some of the basic properties that can be set. As we move on to other areas of XHTML, we'll explore more properties that can be set.

4 *Tables and Lists*

Chapter Objective:

To learn to use tables to help format pages. In Chapter 4, you will:

- Discover how to create a table.

- Become familiar with using tables to align content.

- Learn to use attributes to span rows and columns.

- Discover how to apply styles to table content.

- Understand the advantages of and issues with nesting tables.

- Become familiar with ordered and unordered lists, and their place in presenting data effectively.

Projects to be Completed:

- News Web (A)

- Cyber Travel (B)

- Hunter Films (C)

- North Star Adventure Gear (D)

Tables and Lists

Tables were one of the first enhancements to HTML. Before tables became available, Web-page designers had virtually no way to align text vertically. Their only option was to use the <pre> tag to set their content to a monospaced font and spaces to align content. Getting exact alignment was difficult, and the results were often far from aesthetically pleasing.

Since the Web was originally used primarily by researchers, the ability to format a set of data was a definite advantage, and tables caught on quickly, despite their lack of universal support by browsers. (In particular, the AOL browser has always been slow to adopt enhancements, and Web authors will probably have to keep that in mind for some time to come.)

That was several years ago, however, and tables are now well established in Web-page coding. In fact, unless you're aiming for non-traditional audiences, such as PDAs or cell phones, you can be pretty confident that tables won't cause problems on your pages. (Non-traditional devices typically have limitations on the amount of data that can be provided at any one time, so pages usually need to be completely restructured for that audience.)

Let's take a look at how you create tables.

The Basic Table

Tables, at their most basic, are rows and columns of information. We put the information in the proper row and column, and the browser takes care of the rest.

We build a table by creating rows, designated by the <tr></tr> tag; each row has some number of data cells, designated by the <td></td> tag. The entire set of rows and cells is enclosed in the <table></table> tag.

For instance, we could create a small table:

```
…
<table border="1" width="100%">
<tr><th>First Column</th><th>Second Column</th></tr>
<tr><td>Cell 1</td><td>Cell 2</td></tr>
<tr><td>Cell 3</td><td>Cell 4</td></tr>
</table>
…
```

*A **monospaced font**, such as Courier, consists of characters that are all the same width. Unlike a non-monospaced font, such as Arial or Helvetica, in which an "m" is considerably wider than an "i", monospaced fonts can be reliably aligned using spaces.*

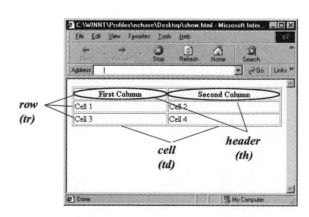

This table has three rows. Each row has two cells and two columns, and each column has a header. A header is just like a cell, except that it is formatted in bold and the text is centered. To add a column, add a <td></td> to each row. To add a row, add a <tr></tr> and its associated <td></td>s to the table. (To remove a column or row, simply remove these tags and their content.)

The table is as wide as the page, because the width is set to 100% of the page. We'll deal with heights and widths in more detail a little later, but for now, understand that the width of a table can be set as a percentage of the available area, or it can be set at a fixed pixel width.

But what about the width and height of individual cells? One of the main reasons we use tables is to align information vertically and horizontally. Tables readily achieve this alignment because they automatically adjust an entire row to the height of its tallest cell, and a column to the width of its widest cell. For instance:

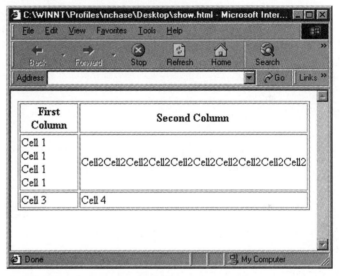

Notice that in the XHTML for this example, all text for each row is on a single line. While this may make it easier to see the individual rows, it is usually easier to read the XHTML for a page where the data is broken up, as in:

```
…
<table border="1" width="100%">
<tr>
  <th>First Column</th>
  <th>Second Column</th>
</tr>
<tr>
  <td>Cell 1</td>
  <td>Cell 2</td>
</tr>
<tr>
  <td>Cell 3</td>
  <td>Cell 4</td>
</tr>
</table>
…
```

We could use an *unordered* or bulleted list to make the information more readable. An unordered list is contained within <ul></ul> tags, with each list item contained in <li></li> tags, as in:

```
…
<ul>
<li>Item 1</li>
<li>Item 2</li>
<li>Item 3</li>
</ul>
…
```

The same process can be used to create an *ordered* or numbered list, using the <ol></ol> tag:

```
…
<ol>
<li>Item 1</li>
<li>Item 2</li>
<li>Item 3</li>
</ol>
…
```

Exercise Setup

Let's create a sample table to see how all of this works.

Create the Table

1. Create a folder called "tables" in your WIP folder.

2. Open your text editor and create a new file. Save it as "tables.html" in the **WIP>tables** folder.

3. Add the basic HTML to the empty document. Call the page "Table Demo Document".

```
<!DOCTYPE HTML PUBLIC "-//W3C//DTD HTML 4.01 Transitional//EN" "http://www.w3.org/TR/html4/loose.dtd">
<html>
<head><title>Table Demo Document</title></head>
<body>

</body>
</html>
```

4. Open the document in your browser.

5. In the text editor, add the first basic rows of our table. Add three rows with three cells each. Fill the cells across starting the first row with 1, the second row with 4 and the third row with 7.

```
<!DOCTYPE HTML PUBLIC "-//W3C//DTD HTML 4.01 Transitional//EN"
"http://www.w3.org/TR/html4/loose.dtd">
<html>
<head><title>Table Demo Document</title></head>
<body>
<table>
   <tr> <td>1</td> <td>2</td> <td>3</td> </tr>
   <tr> <td>4</td> <td>5</td> <td>6</td> </tr>
   <tr> <td>7</td> <td>8</td> <td>9</td> </tr>
</table>

</body>
</html>
```

6. Save the file in the text editor and refresh the browser.

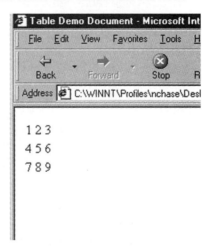

7. Notice that the browser's display of this code shows our table of information, but it doesn't make the separate cells clear. To make it a little more understandable, turn on the table's border and set the width to 75% of the page.

```
<!DOCTYPE HTML PUBLIC "-//W3C//DTD HTML 4.01 Transitional//EN"
"http://www.w3.org/TR/html4/loose.dtd">
<html>
<head><title>Table Demo Document</title></head>
<body>
<table border="1" width="75%" >
   <tr> <td>1</td> <td>2</td> <td>3</td> </tr>
   <tr> <td>4</td> <td>5</td> <td>6</td> </tr>
   <tr> <td>7</td> <td>8</td> <td>9</td> </tr>
</table>
</body>
</html>
```

8. Save the file in the text editor and refresh the browser.

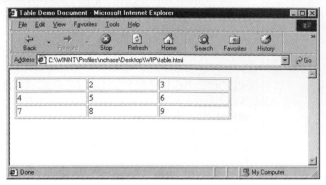

9. As we can see now, the table consists of three table rows, or <tr>s, each of which contains three table data cells, or <td>s. Now add the headers to the table, using <th>, the table header tag.

```
<!DOCTYPE HTML PUBLIC "-//W3C//DTD HTML 4.01 Transitional//EN"
"http://www.w3.org/TR/html4/loose.dtd">
<html>
<head><title>Table Demo Document</title></head>
<body>
<table border="1" width="75%">
  <tr>
    <th>First Column ...</th>
    <th>Second ... </th>
    <th>And Third</th>
  </tr>
  <tr> <td>1</td> <td>2</td> <td>3</td> </tr>
  <tr> <td>4</td> <td>5</td> <td>6</td> </tr>
  <tr> <td>7</td> <td>8</td> <td>9</td> </tr>
</table>
</body>
</html>
```

10. Save the file in the text editor and refresh the browser.

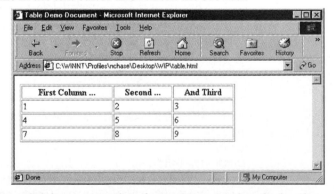

11. Although we didn't set any style information, note that the headers automatically are bold and centered within their cells. Other than that formatting, however, they are the same as table data cells. Notice also that where before all three columns were the same width, the first column is now slightly wider than the rest, allowing for the larger amount of text it contains. Remember that unless we specify otherwise, a table will adjust to its widest and longest cells.

12. Let's see the table adjust to accommodate the content of the cells. Add a To Do List of items to the first column of the second row, and format that list as an unordered list.

```html
<!DOCTYPE HTML PUBLIC "-//W3C//DTD HTML 4.01 Transitional//EN" "http://
www.w3.org/TR/html4/loose.dtd">
<html>
<head><title>Table Demo Document</title></head>
<body>
<table border="1" width="75%">
   <tr>
      <th>First Column ...</th>
      <th>Second ... </th>
      <th>And Third</th>
   </tr>
   <tr>
      <td>Things to do today:
         <ul>
            <li>Do laundry</li>
            <li>Schedule haircut</li>
            <li>Clean room</li>
            <li>Find library books</li>
            <li>Confirm vacation plans</li>
         </ul>
      </td>
      <td>2</td>
      <td>3</td>
   </tr>
   <tr> <td>4</td> <td>5</td> <td>6</td> </tr>
   <tr> <td>7</td> <td>8</td> <td>9</td> </tr>
</table>
</body>
</html>
```

13. Save the file in the text editor and refresh the browser

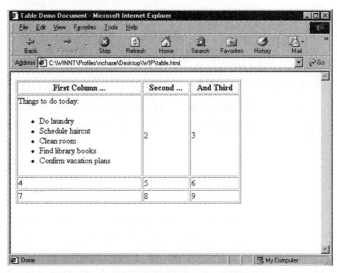

14. Notice that although cells 2 and 3 didn't need extra vertical space, they also received it because of cell 1. Leave the file open in both windows for the next exercise.

Spanning Columns and Rows

If all we could do with tables was to lay out a grid of information, tables would still be useful. We can do more, however. We can also mix and match rows and columns by merging them into each other to adjust our alignments.

For example, if we want to give a table a heading that applies to all of the columns, we can do so by adding the colspan attribute to the header tag. This attribute causes the affected cell to span one or more columns, with the value contained within the quote marks determining exactly how many columns the cell spans. The colspan attribute can even cause the cell to span the width of the entire table.

```
...
<table border="1" width="100%">
<tr>
  <th colspan="2">Title of the Table</th>
</tr>
<tr>
  <td>Cell 1<br>Cell 1<br />Cell 1<br />Cell 1</td>
  <td>Cell2Cell2Cell2Cell2Cell2Cell2Cell2Cell2</td>
</tr>
<tr>
  <td>Cell 3</td>
  <td>Cell 4</td>
</tr>
</table>
...
```

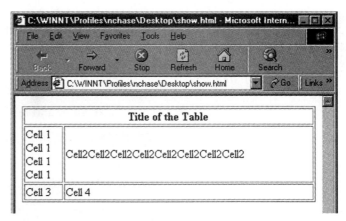

In the above example, notice that there is only one cell in the first row because that cell is set to span both columns of the table. This cell is the equivalent of two cells wide, although it looks like only one continuous cell. So if another cell were added to this first row, it wouldn't make the first cell narrower. The additional cell would expand the width of the table and take the position of a new third column.

A similar effect of expanding cells can be achieved for cells using the rowspan attribute, which extends the cell vertically along a row.

```
...
<table border="1" width="100%">
<tr>
  <th colspan="2">Title of the Table</th>
</tr>
```

```
<tr>
  <td rowspan="2">Cell 1<br>Cell 1<br />Cell 1<br />Cell 1</td>
  <td>Cell2Cell2Cell2Cell2Cell2Cell2Cell2Cell2</td>
</tr>
<tr>
  <td>Cell 4</td>
</tr>
</table>
...
```

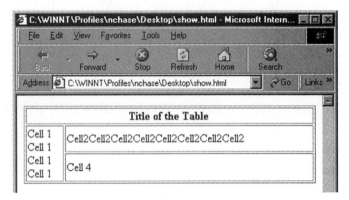

Notice that because cell 1 also occupies the first column of the second row, the second row contains only one additional cell, eliminating cell 3. The reason for this change lies in the way that browsers construct tables. Each cell is placed in the first available position, so although cell 4 appears to occupy the first position in its row, it is actually placed in the second column.

Span Multiple Rows

1. In the open file table.html in the text editor, look at the cell containing Things to Do. Notice that the list resembles a menu of options, which we would ordinarily expect to extend the length of the balance of the content.

   Use the rowspan attribute to cause this single cell to span three rows. Change the list from an unordered list to an ordered list.

```
...

  <tr>
      <td rowspan="3" >
        Things to do today:
        <ol |>
          <li>Do laundry</li>
          <li>Schedule haircut</li>
          <li>Clean room</li>
          <li>Find library books</li>
          <li>Confirm vacation plans</li>
        </ol |>
      </td>
      <td>2</td>
      <td>3</td>
  </tr>

...
```

2. Save the file in the text editor and refresh the browser.

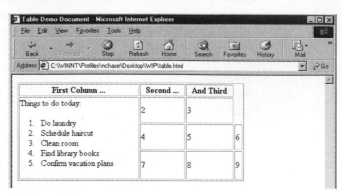

3. Look at the page in the browser. Notice how the cells have shifted.

4. Before we move on, clean up the table by removing those extraneous cells, 4 and 7, and the `<td></td>` tags around them.

Obviously, in the real world, we wouldn't remove data just because we didn't like where the browser put it. We would move it instead.

```
<!DOCTYPE HTML PUBLIC "-//W3C//DTD HTML 4.01 Transitional//EN"
"http://www.w3.org/TR/html4/loose.dtd">
<html>
<head><title>Table Demo Document</title></head>
<body>
<table border="1" width="75%">
   <tr>
      <th>First Column ...</th>
      <th>Second ... </th>
      <th>And Third</th>
   </tr>
   <tr>
      <td rowspan="3">
         Things to do today:
         <ol>
            <li>Do laundry</li>
            <li>Schedule haircut</li>
            <li>Clean room</li>
            <li>Find library books</li>
            <li>Confirm vacation plans</li>
         </ol>
      </td>
      <td>2</td>
      <td>3</td>
   </tr>
   <tr> <td>5</td> <td>6</td> </tr>
   <tr> <td>8</td> <td>9</td> </tr>
</table>
</body>
</html>
```

5. Save the file and leave it open in both windows for the next exercise.

Height and Width

Height and width in tables can apply to any of four items: cells, rows, columns and the table itself. Often the very reason that we're creating a table is to make content fit within a specific area. In such cases, it's important to have as much control over sizing as possible.

Making the Table Fill the Page

There are a number of different ways to control height and width in tables. The first such technique is using percentages, as we did in the earlier example. To do so, we tell the browser to use a particular percentage of the available area. This enables us to set the height and width of a table based on the size of the area in which it resides, and is generally more useful for text than for images. Sometimes, however, a layout requires us to set the size of the table exactly (to an absolute number), and in a situation like that, we can use pixel measurements. For example:

```
<table width="300" height="200">
…
</table>
```

Ultimately, table height and width will be controlled by CSS properties.

will produce a table that is 300 pixels wide and 200 pixels high, no matter what size the browser window may be. The table will be this size, even without units specified, because this is the only measurement that these attributes will render besides percentages, as shown below. On the other hand,

```
<table width="50%">
…
</table>
```

will produce a table that adjusts to half the width of the browser window, whatever that may be. (One exception to this rule is a situation in which the content of the table, such as an image, is larger than the specified table size. In that case, the browser will display the table as small as possible without compromising the content.)

Note that the height and width attributes are *deprecated*, which means that they are being phased out of XHTML. For many browsers, however, these attributes are still the only way to control the height and width of a table, so for now, they remain in use.

Make the Table Fill the Page

1. In the open file table.html in the text editor, set the width and height of the table to 300 pixels.

```
<!DOCTYPE HTML PUBLIC "-//W3C//DTD HTML 4.01 Transitional//EN" "http://
www.w3.org/TR/html4/loose.dtd">
<html>
<head><title>Table Demo Document</title></head>
<body>
<table border="1" width="300" height="300">
   <tr>
      <th>First Column ...</th>
      <th>Second ... </th>
      <th>And Third</th>
   </tr>
…
```

2. Save the file in the text editor and refresh the browser.

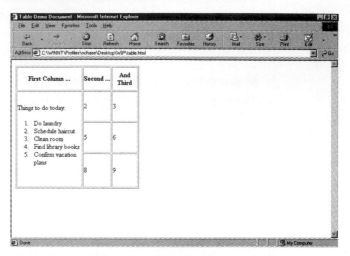

3. Resize the browser window by dragging the bottom-right corner. Notice that because we set the size of the table to an absolute number, the size of the table doesn't change.

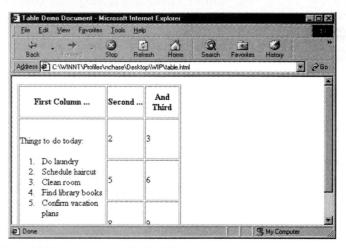

4. Change the width to 50% and the height to 100%.

```
<!DOCTYPE HTML PUBLIC "-//W3C//DTD HTML 4.01 Transitional//EN" "http://
www.w3.org/TR/html4/loose.dtd">
<html>
<head><title>Table Demo Document</title></head>
<body>
<table border="1" width="50%" height="100%">
  <tr>
    <th>First Column ...</th>
    <th>Second ... </th>
    <th>And Third</th>
  </tr>
...
```

5. Save the file in the text editor and refresh the browser.

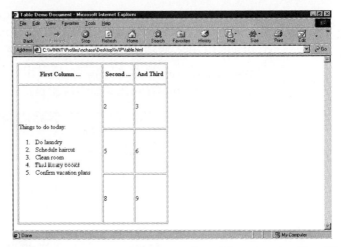

6. Again resize the window. Notice that now the table resizes itself to fill the same proportion of the window, no matter the size of the window itself.

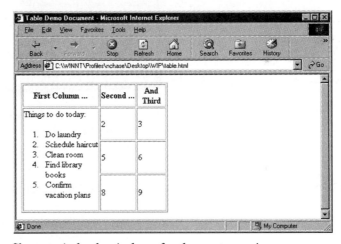

7. Leave the file open in both windows for the next exercise.

Controlling Column and Row Sizes

In addition to setting the size of the entire table, we can control the size of individual rows and columns. We do this by setting the size of the rows or the cells themselves. For example, in our sample table, we could set the height of the second row of data:

```
…
<table border="1" width="100%">
<tr>
  <th colspan="2">Title of the Table</th>
</tr>
<tr>
  <td width="100" height="150">Cell 1<br>Cell 1<br />Cell 1<br />Cell 1</td>
  <td>Cell2Cell2Cell2Cell2Cell2Cell2Cell2Cell2</td>
</tr>
<tr height="100">
  <td>Cell 3</td>
  <td>Cell 4</td>
</tr>
</table>
…
```

First, we set the width of the first cell, but because the width of the entire column follows the widest cell, it sets the width of the entire column to 100 pixels. Similarly, because we set the height of the cell to 150 pixels, the entire row grew to that height.

We can also control the height of a row directly, as we are doing here when we set the height attribute on the <tr></tr> tag to 100 pixels.

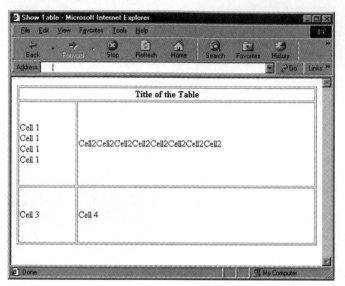

We can likewise set the size of rows and columns based on percentages. If the size of the table is larger than necessary to display the content, the browser tries to render the table so with rows and columns of roughly even size. For instance:

```
…
<table border="1" width="100%" height="100%">
<tr>
  <th colspan="2">Title of the Table</th>
</tr>
<tr>
  <td>Cell 1</td>
  <td>Cell 2</td>
</tr>
<tr>
  <td>Cell 3</td>
  <td>Cell 4</td>
</tr>
</table>
…
```

Here we've removed all height and width attributes except those on the table itself.

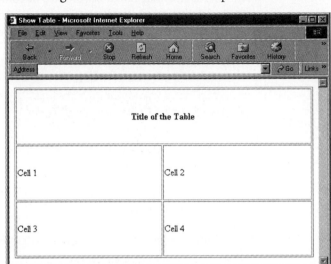

By setting heights and widths using percentages, we can control the relative size of columns and rows, while still allowing them to adjust as the table itself does:

```
…
<table border="1" width="100%" height="100%">
<tr>
  <th colspan="2">Title of the Table</th>
</tr>
<tr>
  <td width="25%">Cell 1</td>
  <td>Cell 2</td>
</tr>
<tr height="50%">
  <td>Cell 3</td>
  <td>Cell 4</td>
</tr>
</table>
…
```

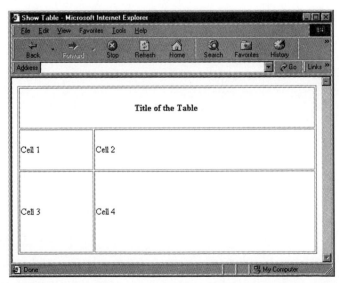

Another factor that can affect the size of columns and rows is the amount of content in a particular cell. While the browser normally tries to keep items evenly spaced in the absence of other instructions, a cell with more data necessarily will take up more room.

Exercise Setup
We can see this in the following exercise.

Set the Size of Columns and Rows

1. In the open file table.html in the text editor, let's start with the large cell. Remove the height and width from the table tag, and set the height of the second row to 200 pixels.

```
<!DOCTYPE HTML PUBLIC "-//W3C//DTD HTML 4.01 Transitional//EN"
"http://www.w3.org/TR/html4/loose.dtd">
<html>
<head><title>Table Demo Document</title></head>
<body>
<table border="1">
  <tr>
    <th>First Column ...</th>
    <th>Second ... </th>
    <th>And Third</th>
  </tr>
  <tr height="200">
    <td rowspan="3">
      Things to do today:
      <ol>
        <li>Do laundry</li>
        <li>Schedule haircut</li>
        <li>Clean room</li>
        <li>Find library books</li>
        <li>Confirm vacation plans</li>
      </ol>
    </td>
    <td>2</td>
    <td>3</td>
  </tr>
  <tr> <td>5</td> <td>6</td> </tr>
  <tr> <td>8</td> <td>9</td> </tr>
</table>
</body>
</html>
```

2. Save the file in the text editor and refresh the browser.

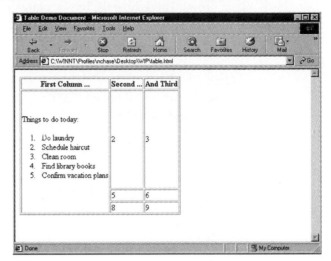

3. Notice that because we set the height on the entire row, cells 2 and 3 are 200 pixels, and the first cell is 200 pixels plus the heights of the last two rows. What we actually wanted to do was make the first cell 200 pixels high.

   Fix this by changing the location of the height setting from the row to the individual cell. Make certain that you also remember to remove it from the <tr> tag.

...

```
<tr>
    <td rowspan="3" height="200">
      Things to do today:
      <ol>
        <li>Do laundry</li>
        <li>Schedule haircut</li>
        <li>Clean room</li>
        <li>Find library books</li>
        <li>Confirm vacation plans</li>
      </ol>
    </td>
```

...

4. Save the file in the text editor and refresh the browser.

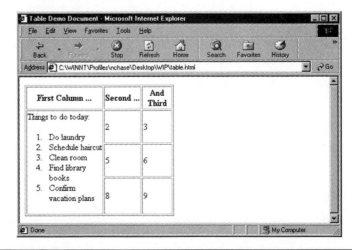

5. Notice that the second and third columns now contain more or less evenly spaced rows. This is how the browser attempts to lay out the table — by allotting equal spacing unless otherwise instructed. Such an instruction may come in the form of more content. Add some content, such as two or three sentences of text, to cell 2.

```
...
  <tr>
    <td rowspan="3" height="200">
      Things to do today:
      <ol>
        <li>Do laundry</li>
        <li>Schedule haircut</li>
        <li>Clean room</li>
        <li>Find library books</li>
        <li>Confirm vacation plans</li>
      </ol>
    </td>
    <td>
      This would be a good place for a news story.<br />
      A good Web site almost always has changing content right on the home
      page.
    </td>
    <td>3</td>
  </tr>
  <tr> <td>5</td> <td>6</td> </tr>
  <tr> <td>8</td> <td>9</td> </tr>
</table>
</body>
</html>
```

6. Save the file in the text editor and refresh the browser.

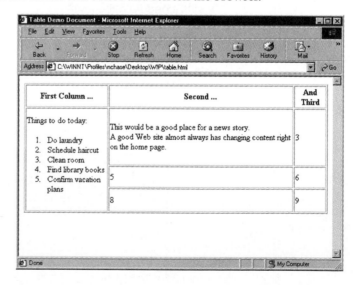

7. Notice that the browser uses as much of the window as is available, then wraps the text. It also reduces the heights on the third and fourth rows to accommodate the extra height required for the second row.

8. We can also adjust rows and columns to be a percentage of the total column size. Set the width of the news cell to 30%.

...

```
<td width="30%">
   This would be a good place for a news story.<br />
   A good Web site almost always has changing content right on the home page.
</td>
```

...

9. Save the file in the text editor and refresh the browser. Notice that although there is still room in the last column, the middle column takes up only 30% of the table.

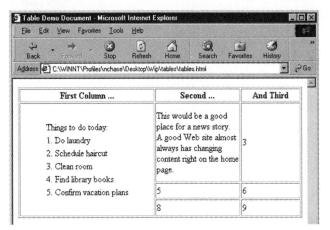

10. Leave the file open in both windows for the next exercise.

Adding a Table as Data

Another type of content that might affect the size of a table is another table included (*nested*) within a cell. We'll see a more practical example of this later, but let's look briefly at this practice. For instance, we could add a table of information within our sample table:

...
```
<table border="1">
<tr>
  <th colspan="2">Title of the Table</th>
</tr>
<tr>
  <td>Cell 1</td>
  <td>Cell 2</td>
</tr>
<tr>
  <td>Cell 3</td>
  <td>
    <table width="50%" border="1">
      <tr><td>Inner cell 1</td><td>Inner cell 2</td></tr>
      <tr><td>Inner cell 3</td><td>Inner cell 4</td></tr>
    </table>
  </td>
</tr>
</table>
```
...

In this case, we've removed all of the size information from the regular table, and added another table as the content of what was cell 4.

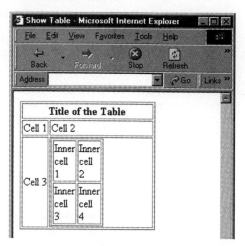

Notice that, in the absence of other instructions, the browser tries to make the table just large enough to hold all of the content. Because we set the width of the nested table to 50%, however, that cell has to be at least twice as wide as the table it contains.

Exercise Setup

To illustrate this, we'll convert the To Do List into a table. This will give us the flexibility to control the sizing and layout more completely, although the ability to automatically renumber tasks will be lost.

Add a Nested Table

1. In the open file table.html in the text editor, rework the To Do List into a table by removing the <ol> and <li> tags and adding a row for each item. In each row, add also a cell for the number, as this will no longer be added automatically.

```
...
<th>And Third</th>
</tr>
<tr>
 <td rowspan="3" height="200">
   <table>
        <tr>
           <td colspan="2">
                      Things to do today:
           </td>
           </tr>
           <tr><td>1.</td><td>Do laundry</td></tr>
           <tr><td>2.</td><td>Schedule haircut</td></tr>
           <tr><td>3.</td><td>Clean room</td></tr>
           <tr><td>4.</td><td>Find library books</td></tr>
           <tr><td>5.</td><td>Confirm vacation plans</td></tr>
   </table>
 </td>
 <td width="30%">
   This would be a good place for a news story.<br />
...
```

2. Save the file in the text editor and refresh the browser. Notice that the effect is largely the same, though we now have the opportunity for more control.

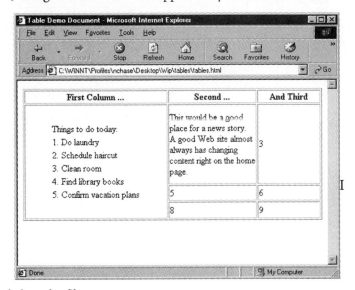

3. Save and close the file.

Using Tables to Format a Page

Now that we've covered the basics, let's take a closer look at using these techniques in formatting the pages of our Web site. This formatting includes nesting tables, setting sizes and using Cascading Style Sheets to control the appearance of the table.

Exercise Setup

In this section, we're going to create the home page for Doctor-It!, which helps people make the most of what's in their kitchen.

First let's take a look at what we're trying to achieve over the course of the next few exercises:

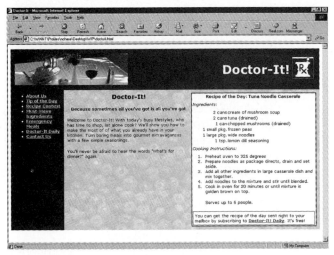

This is a fairly standard layout, with information and/or banner ads across the top, and navigational elements (in this case, a menu) down the left side.

Let's start by creating the basic layout for the page. We will start with a page that has much of the content on it already and add the table information.

Create the Basic Layout Using a Table

1. Navigate to **RF_HTML>Chapter 4**, and copy the contents of the folder to the **WIP>tables** folder.

2. Open **WIP>tables>doctorit.html** in the text editor and browser.

3. Using a table, break the page into three sections: a top bar, a menu and the content. Give the table two rows: the top row containing a single cell (for the top bar), and the bottom row containing two cells — the left cell for the navigation and the right cell for content.

```
<!DOCTYPE html PUBLIC "-//W3C//DTD XHTML 1.0 Transitional//EN"
"http://www.w3.org/TR/xhtml1/DTD/xhtml1-transitional.dtd" >
<html>
<head><title>Doctor-It</title></head>
<body>
<table>
<tr><td colspan="2">

    <img src="images/table.jpg" alt="Table Image" height="100" /><img src="images/
drlogo.jpg" alt="Logo" />

</td></tr>
<tr><td width="150">

<a href="about.html">About Us</a><br />
<a href="tip.html">Tip of the Day</a><br />
<a href="contest.html">Recipe Contest</a><br />
<a href="ingredients.html">Must-Have Ingredients</a><br />
<a href="meals.html">Emergency Meals</a><br />
<a href="daily.html">Doctor-It Daily</a><br />
<a href="mailto:webmaster@doctor-it.net">Contact Us</a>

</td><td>

<h2 align="center">Doctor-It!</h2>
<h3 align="center">Because sometimes all you've got is all you've got</h3>
<p>Welcome to Doctor-It!  With today's busy lifestyles, who has time to shop, let alone
cook?  We'll show you how to make the most of what you already have in your kitchen.
Turn boring meals into gourmet extravaganzas with a few simple seasonings.  </p>
<p>You'll never be afraid to hear the words "What's for dinner?" again.</p>
<b>Recipe of the Day: Tuna Noodle Casserole</b>
<br />
<i>Ingredients:</i>
2 cans cream of mushroom soup<br />
2 cans tuna (drained)<br />
1 can chopped mushrooms (drained)<br />
1 small pkg. frozen peas<br />
1 large pkg. wide noodles <br />
1 tsp. lemon dill seasoning<br />
<br />
  <i>Cooking Instructions:</i>
```

Although all of the pieces here are fairly standard, we will be nesting a number of tables and performing other tasks that are extremely sensitive to small errors. Be certain to copy changes exactly from the text.

```
<br />
Preheat oven to 325 degrees.<br />
Prepare noodles as package directs, drain and set aside.<br />
Add all other ingredients in large casserole dish and mix together.<br />
Add noodles to the mixture and stir until blended.<br />
Cook in oven for 20 minutes or until mixture is golden brown on top.<br />
<p>Serves up to 6 people.</p>
<p>You can get the recipe of the day sent right to your mailbox by subscribing to <a
href="daily.html">Doctor-It! Daily</a>.  It's free!</p>

</td></tr>
</table>
</body>
</html>
```

4. Save the file in the text editor and refresh the browser. Notice that the basic sections of the page are now in place.

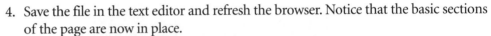

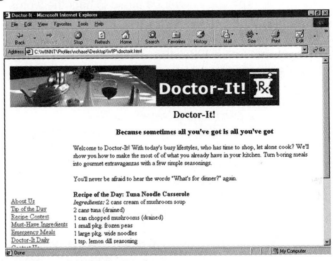

5. Leave the file open in both applications for the next exercise.

Planning Templates

If we look at the final page as planned for the exercise, we see three columns under the top bar: the menu and two columns of content. As of now, we have broken this part of the page into only two columns.

The reason is this: both the descriptive text and the menu are content that won't appear on other pages of the site. By keeping the content of these two planned cells together, for now, we can use this page (when finished) as a template. The template enables us to simply replace the content of that single cell to make a new page. If we separated the text and menu into individual columns in the main table, it would be difficult, if not impossible, to use the page as an effective template.

Templates are one of the most important concepts in the design of a Web site, for several reasons. First, they provide the common look and feel that is so important for the user experience. Second, because they provide all the user interface elements for the page, templates allow you to concentrate on content rather than on the maintenance of individual pages.

Exercise Setup

Of course, initially creating the page with one column where we eventually plan two means that we have to find a way to break up this content into two sections. We can do that using nested tables.

We can break up the content by putting our Recipe Of The Day into a table within a table. As we saw when we first looked at nested tables, we can put virtually any content into a table data cell, including another table. By coding the recipe as a table within a table, we'll have more control over the size, position and appearance of the recipe.

Add a Nested Table

1. In the open file doctorit.html in the text editor, create a table for the Recipe of the Day, and set the table width to 50%.

...

```
<p>You'll never be afraid to hear the words "What's for dinner?" again.</p>
<table width="50%">
<tr><td>
<b>Recipe of the Day: Tuna Noodle Casserole</b>
<br />
<i>Ingredients:</i>
2 cans cream of mushroom soup<br />
2 cans tuna (drained)<br />
1 can chopped mushrooms (drained)<br />
1 small pkg. frozen peas<br />
1 large pkg. wide noodles <br />
1 tsp. lemon dill seasoning<br />
<br />
  <i>Cooking Instructions:</i>
<br />
Preheat oven to 325 degrees.<br />
Prepare noodles as package directs, drain and set aside.<br />
Add all other ingredients in large casserole dish and mix together.<br />
Add noodles to the mixture and stir until blended.<br />
Cook in oven for 20 minutes or until mixture is golden brown on top.<br />
<p>Serves up to 6 people.</p>
<p>You can get the recipe of the day sent right to your mailbox by subscribing to <a
href="daily.html">Doctor-It! Daily</a>.  It's free!</p>
</td></tr>
</table>
</td></tr>
</table>
</body>
</html>
```

2. Save the file in the text editor and refresh the browser. The appearance shouldn't change yet.

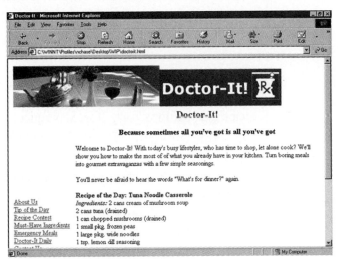

3. Leave the file open in both windows for the next exercise.

Alignment

A major part of Web-page layout is aligning content. Sometimes this involves positioning content to the right, left or center, and sometimes ensuring that content is at the top or bottom of a page section.

Most XHTML elements, such as images or tables, can be aligned using either attributes or CSS properties such as align.

Aligning the Table

Like images, entire tables can be aligned to the center, left and right, and text will then flow around them. Also like images, we need to put the code for the table ahead of the coded text we want to flow around it. For example:

```
…
<table border="1" align="right">
…
</table>
```

When a table is aligned to the left or the right, text can wrap around it.

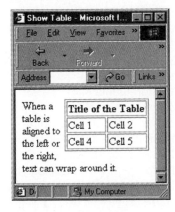

Exercise Setup

We can use this technique on the Doctor-It! home page.

So far, we don't see any change in the appearance of our recipe in our exercise. We set the width prior to aligning the two columns next to each other. So how do we align these columns?

One way to separate the content and the recipe would be to create a table in which each of them is a separate column. The problem with this approach is that it ties the content and the recipe together too closely. If we subsequently want to remove one, or simply move one to another section of the page, the entire table would have to be reworked.

We can achieve the same effect by using alignment of the recipe table. Since we want the text to flow around the table, the text must come after the table on the page. We'll move the text in the next exercise.

Align the Nested Table

1. In the open file doctorit.html in the text editor, move the "Welcome" text below the nested table, and then align the nested table to the right.

```
<!DOCTYPE html PUBLIC "-//W3C//DTD XHTML 1.0 Transitional//EN"
"http://www.w3.org/TR/xhtml1/DTD/xhtml1-transitional.dtd" >
<html>
<head><title>Doctor-It</title></head>
<body>
<table>
<tr><td colspan="2">
    <img src="images/table.jpg" height="100" alt="Table Image"/><img src="images/
drlogo.jpg" alt="Logo"/>
</td></tr>
<tr><td width="150">
<a href="about.html">About Us</a><br />
<a href="tip.html">Tip of the Day</a><br />
<a href="contest.html">Recipe Contest</a><br />
<a href="ingredients.html">Must-Have Ingredients</a><br />
<a href="meals.html">Emergency Meals</a><br />
<a href="daily.html">Doctor-It Daily</a><br />
<a href="mailto:webmaster@doctor-it.net">Contact Us</a>
</td><td>
<table width="50%" align="right">
<tr><td>
<b>Recipe of the Day: Tuna Noodle Casserole</b>
<br />
<i>Ingredients:</i>
2 cans cream of mushroom soup<br />
2 cans tuna (drained)<br />
1 can chopped mushrooms (drained)<br />
1 small pkg. frozen peas<br />
1 large pkg. wide noodles <br />
1 tsp. lemon dill seasoning<br />
<br />
  <i>Cooking Instructions:</i>
<br />
```

Preheat oven to 325 degrees.
Prepare noodles as package directs, drain and set aside.
Add all other ingredients in large casserole dish and mix together.
Add noodles to the mixture and stir until blended.
Cook in oven for 20 minutes or until mixture is golden brown on top.
<p>Serves up to 6 people.</p>
<p>You can get the recipe of the day sent right to your mailbox by subscribing to <a href="daily.html">Doctor-It! Daily</a>. It's free!</p>
</td></tr>
</table>
<h2 align="center">Doctor-It!</h2>
<h3 align="center">Because sometimes all you've got is all you've got</h3>
<p>Welcome to Doctor-It! With today's busy lifestyles, who has time to shop, let alone cook? We'll show you how to make the most of what you already have in your kitchen. Turn boring meals into gourmet extravaganzas with a few simple seasonings.</p>
<p>You'll never be afraid to hear the words "What's for dinner?" again.</p>
</td></tr>
</table>
</body>
</html>

Don't re-type this text, just copy and paste it from the top of the file.

2. Save the file in the text editor and refresh the browser. Notice that the recipe is now to the right, and the text sits to its left.

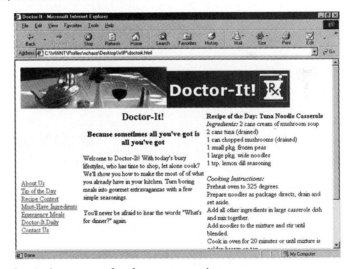

3. Leave both windows open for the next exercise.

Aligning the Data

Just as the table itself can be aligned, each individual cell can have its own alignment, both horizontally and vertically. Content can be aligned horizontally to the left (align="left"), right or center, and can be aligned vertically to the top (valign="top"), bottom or middle. With no instructions, a cell will be aligned, by default, horizontally to the left and vertically in the middle.

Consider this example:

```
...
<title>Show Table</title>
<table border="1" width="100%" height="100%">
<tr>
  <th colspan="3">Title of the Table</th>
</tr>
<tr>
  <td align="right">Cell 1</td>
  <td align="left">Cell 2</td>
  <td align="center">Cell 3</td>
</tr>
<tr>
  <td valign="top">Cell 4</td>
  <td valign="bottom">Cell 5</td>
  <td valign="middle">Cell 6</td>
</tr>
</table>
...
```

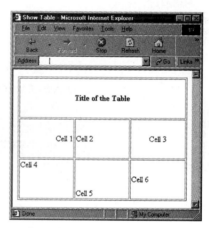

These attributes can also be combined so that data can be aligned, for example, to the bottom and right.

Notice also that cell 1 and cell 2 will come together, no matter how much content is in either one. This can come in handy when aligning different types of content, such as prices or recipe ingredients.

Exercise Setup

Well, our page is starting to take shape, but aside from the obvious styling issues, we still have some items that aren't quite in the right places yet. For instance, the menu should be at the top of the column. Also, the two images in the top bar should be spread to the far left and right. And while we're talking about alignment, wouldn't it be nice if the ingredients in the recipe lined up? In this exercise, we'll take care of all of these issues.

Align the Data

1. In the open file doctorit.html in the text editor, place the two images in the top row into a table. Make the table span the entire width of the page, and give each column 50% of that space. Align the first cell to the left and the second cell to the right.

```
<!DOCTYPE html PUBLIC "-//W3C//DTD XHTML 1.0 Transitional//EN"
"http://www.w3.org/TR/xhtml1/DTD/xhtml1-transitional.dtd" >
<html>
<head><title>Doctor-It</title></head>
<body>
<table>
<tr><td colspan="2">
  <table width="100%"><tr><td width="50%" align="left">
   <img src="images/table.jpg" alt="Table Image" />
  </td><td align="right">
   <img src="images/drlogo.jpg" alt="Logo" />
  </td></tr></table>
</td></tr>
<tr><td width="150">
...
```

2. Save the file in the text editor and refresh the browser.

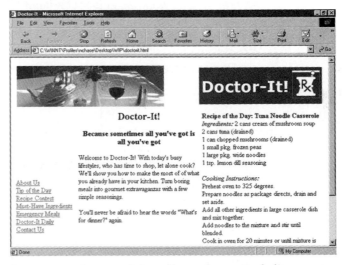

3. To move the menu to the top of the cell, use the vertical alignment, or valign, attribute to align the text to the top.

```
...
  </td><td align="right">
   <img src="images/drlogo.jpg" alt="Logo" />
  </td></tr></table>
</td></tr>
<tr><td width="150" valign="top">
<a href="about.html">About Us</a><br />
<a href="tip.html">Tip of the Day</a><br />
<a href="contest.html">Recipe Contest</a><br />
<a href="ingredients.html">Must-Have Ingredients</a><br />
<a href="meals.html">Emergency Meals</a><br />
...
```

4. Save the file in the text editor and refresh the browser. Notice that the side navigation is now at the top of the column.

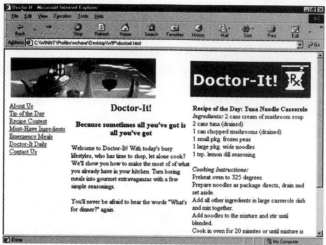

5. Align the ingredients in our recipe. Place the quantities and the items in different cells, and then align them to the right and left — the opposite of what we did with the top line. Separate the contents of this table into different rows and align them.

```
…
<a href="mailto:webmaster@doctor-it.net">Contact Us</a>
</td><td>
<table width="50%" align="right">
<tr><td colspan="2">
<b>Recipe of the Day: Tuna Noodle Casserole</b>
<br />
<i>Ingredients:</i>
</td></tr>
<tr><td align="right">2 cans</td><td align="left"> cream of mushroom soup
        <br /></td></tr>
<tr><td align="right">2 cans</td><td align="left"> tuna (drained)<br /></td></tr>
<tr><td align="right">1 can</td><td align="left"> chopped mushrooms (drained)
        <br /></td></tr>
<tr><td align="right">1 small pkg.</td><td align="left"> frozen peas<br /></td></tr>
<tr><td align="right">1 large pkg.</td><td align="left"> wide noodles <br /></td></tr>
<tr><td align="right">1 tsp.</td><td align="left"> lemon dill seasoning<br /></td></tr>
<tr><td colspan="2">
<br />
  <i>Cooking Instructions:</i>
<br />
Preheat oven to 325 degrees.<br />
Prepare noodles as package directs, drain and set aside.<br />
Add all other ingredients in large casserole dish and mix together.<br />
Add noodles to the mixture and stir until blended.<br />
Cook in oven for 20 minutes or until mixture is golden brown on top.<br />
<p>Serves up to 6 people.</p>
<p>You can get the recipe of the day sent right to your mailbox by subscribing to <a
href="daily.html">Doctor-It! Daily</a>. It's free!</p>
</td></tr>
</table>
<h2 align="center">Doctor-It!</h2>
…
```

6. Save the file in the text editor and refresh the browser. Notice that all of the quantities now line up vertically, as do all of the ingredients.

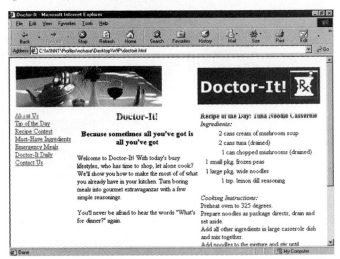

7. Leave the file open in both windows for the next exercise.

Styling a Table

We can break tables into three parts: header, footer and body. These parts can be used like their counterparts in a word-processing document, with the header and footer appearing on each page of a printout of a long table. Both the header and footer display, even if the body of the table has not yet finished loading. In order to control this loading order, we need to move footer information to the top of the table so the browser doesn't have to wait for the entire body to load in order to see the footer. We segregate the sections of our table using the <thead></thead>, <tbody></tbody> and <tfoot></tfoot> tags. Be aware, however, that at this writing, not all browsers fully support this function, so the footer might appear at the top of the table. In most cases, however, this is tolerable.

The table is constructed as follows:

```
...
<table border="1" width="100%" height="100%">
<thead>
  <tr>
    <th colspan="3">Title of the Table</th>
  </tr>
</thead>
<tfoot>
  <tr>
    <td colspan="3">The footer appears at the bottom, even though it seems like
it should be at the top.</td>
  </tr>
</tfoot>
<tbody>
  <tr>
    <td align="right">Cell 1</td>
    <td align="left">Cell 2</td>
    <td align="center">Cell 3</td>
  </tr>
```

```
    <tr>
      <td valign="top">Cell 4</td>
      <td valign="bottom">Cell 5</td>
      <td valign="middle">Cell 6</td>
    </tr>
  </tbody>
</table>
…
```

and looks like this:

Exercise Setup

Now that we've placed everything essentially where we want it, we can improve the table's appearance. We'll start by cleaning up the structure. While there's nothing technically incorrect, we can break our table into three parts: header, footer and body.

Clean Up the Table

1. In the open file doctorit.html in the text editor, separate the three sections of the recipe table, and place the footer before the body.

…

```
<a href="mailto:webmaster@doctor-it.net">Contact Us</a>
</td><td>
<table width="50%" align="right">
<thead>
  <tr><td colspan="2">
  <b>Recipe of the Day: Tuna Noodle Casserole</b>
  </td></tr>
</thead>
<tfoot>
  <tr><td colspan="2">
  <p>You can get the recipe of the day sent right to your mailbox by subscribing
to <a href="daily.html">Doctor-It! Daily</a>.  It's free!</p>
  </td></tr>
</tfoot>
<tbody>
<tr><td colspan="2">
<i>Ingredients:</i>
…
```

```
<p>Serves up to 6 people.</p>
</td></tr>
</tbody>
</table>
<h2 align="center">Doctor-It!</h2>
```
...

2. Save the file in the text editor and refresh the browser. You should see no difference in the page.

3. Leave both windows open for the next exercise.

A Column as a Single Group

We have seen that we can use an alignment attribute on a particular cell or on an entire row. We can also set an attribute for an entire column, without having to code each cell individually.

While changing the alignment on one column is relatively simple, when there are hundreds of rows, it's not as easy. The colgroup tag is placed at the top of the table. By placing an attribute on an individual col tag, we can indicate that this attribute applies to every cell in that column without having to touch each one individually. The code for each individual column and its alignment follows, using the <col align="left"> (or "right" or "center"):

```
...
<table border="1" width="100%" height="100%">
<colgroup>
  <col align="left" />
  <col />
  <col align="right" />
</colgroup>
<thead>
  <tr>
    <th colspan="3">Title of the Table</th>
...
```

This example aligns the first column to the left and the last column to the right. Note that we needed to include an empty col tag for the middle column as a placeholder, even though we were not including an alignment instruction. This placeholder was necessary so that the browser would understand to which columns to apply the alignment instructions.

Using colgroup in this way sets alignment attributes for the full columns, but we can then override the values on individual cells to compensate on the cells that we don't want to align in this way. This process enables us to control the large number of cells broadly and refine the effect on the specific cells, as needed.

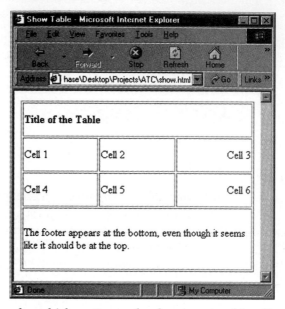

Notice also that the header, which up to now has been centered (as all <th></th> tags are), is now aligned to the left, because it, too, is considered part of the first column, even though it spans all three.

Exercise Setup
Let's see how we can apply this to our page.

Add Column Information

1. In the open file doctorit.html in the text editor, add a colgroup to the recipe table.

...

```
<table width="50%" align="right">
<colgroup>
    <col align="right" />
    <col align="left" />
</colgroup>
<thead>
   <tr><td colspan="2" align="left">
   <b>Recipe of the Day: Tuna Noodle Casserole</b>
   </td></tr>
</thead>
<tfoot>
    <tr><td colspan="2" align="left">
    <p>You can get the recipe of the day sent right to your mailbox by subscribing to <a
href="daily.html">Doctor-It! Daily</a>.  It's free!</p>
    </td></tr>
</tfoot>
<tbody>
```

```
<tr><td colspan="2" align="left">
<i>Ingredients:</i>
</td></tr>
<tr><td>2 cans</td><td> cream of mushroom soup<br /></td></tr>
<tr><td>2 cans</td><td> tuna (drained)<br /></td></tr>
<tr><td>1 can</td><td> chopped mushrooms (drained)<br /></td></tr>
<tr><td>1 small pkg.</td><td> frozen peas<br /></td></tr>
<tr><td>1 large pkg.</td><td> wide noodles <br /></td></tr>
<tr><td>1 tsp.</td><td> lemon dill seasoning<br /></td></tr>
<tr><td colspan="2" align="left">
<br />
  <i>Cooking Instructions:</i>
<br />
Preheat oven to 325 degrees.<br />
Prepare noodles as package directs, drain and set aside.<br />
...
```

Netscape does not recognize the <colgroup> attributes. To keep the alignment in the recipe, do not remove the align attribute on the individual table cells. This is another gray area. If alignment is important, put it on the cells. If it's just something that would be nice, use <colgroup>.

2. Save the file in the text editor and refresh the browser. Again, you should not see a difference in the page's appearance.

3. Leave the file open in both windows for the next exercise.

Adding Basic Style Information to Table Elements

Like other XHTML elements, tables, rows and columns can have CSS styling information attached to them. This can either be in the form of a style attribute, or in the form of a class.

In most cases, it is much better to use a class and then assign a style to that class. There are two reasons for this preference. First, and most obvious, is the ease of maintenance when using classes. If the elements on the page have the proper designations, simply changing the style information is straightforward.

The second advantage of using classes comes from the planning process. By thinking through your design in terms of classes and determining which elements belong to which class, you avoid the pitfalls of coding first and only later settling on a more efficient and consistent way of presenting material. Your site has a greater cohesion and you save time.

Exercise Setup

Now we're ready to start applying styles to our project. Our first step is to look at the page and determine which items need styles; this analysis enables us to add any required class information.

Comparing what we have now to the final page, we still need the following changes:

- Add the blue backgrounds for the top and left menus.
- Set the overall font family.
- Add the background image on the content data cell.
- Place a border around the recipe of the day.
- Add the border around the table footer in the recipe of the day.
- Change the menu links to white.
- Add bullets to the menu links.
- Number the steps in the recipe.

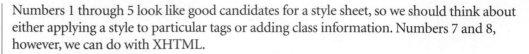

Numbers 1 through 5 look like good candidates for a style sheet, so we should think about either applying a style to particular tags or adding class information. Numbers 7 and 8, however, we can do with XHTML.

Let's add class information to the file.

Add Class Information

1. In the open file doctorit.html in the text editor, add class information to items we're going to style. Overall, there are six new classes: menu, menuLink, content, recipe, recipeHead and recipeFoot.

```
<!DOCTYPE html PUBLIC "-//W3C//DTD XHTML 1.0 Transitional//EN"
"http://www.w3.org/TR/xhtml1/DTD/xhtml1-transitional.dtd" >
<html>
<head><title>Doctor-It</title></head>
<body>
<table>
<tr><td colspan="2" class="menu">
  <table width="100%"><tr><td width="50%" align="left">
   <img src="images/table.jpg" alt="Table Image" />
  </td><td align="right">
   <img src="images/drlogo.jpg" alt="Logo" />
  </td></tr></table>
</td></tr>
<tr><td width="150" valign="top" class="menu">
<a href="about.html" class="menuLink">About Us</a><br />
<a href="tip.html" class="menuLink">Tip of the Day</a><br />
<a href="contest.html" class="menuLink">Recipe Contest</a><br />
<a href="ingredients.html" class="menuLink">Must-Have Ingredients</a><br />
<a href="meals.html" class="menuLink">Emergency Meals</a><br />
<a href="daily.html" class="menuLink">Doctor-It Daily</a><br />
<a href="mailto:webmaster@doctor-it.net" class="menuLink">Contact Us</a>
</td><td class="content">
<table width="50%" align="right" class="recipe">
<colgroup>
   <col align="right" />
   <col align="left" />
</colgroup>
<thead>
   <tr><td colspan="2">
   <b>Recipe of the Day: Tuna Noodle Casserole</b>
   </td></tr>
</thead>
<tfoot>
   <tr><td colspan="2" class="recipeFoot">
   <p>You can get the recipe of the day sent right to your mailbox by subscribing to <a
href="daily.html">Doctor-It! Daily</a>.  It's free!</p>
   </td></tr>
</tfoot>
<tbody>
...
```

2. Save the file in the text editor and refresh the browser. You should see no change.

3. Add the basic style sheet at the top of the page, and change all text to a sans-serif font such as Helvetica or Arial.

```
<!DOCTYPE html PUBLIC "-//W3C//DTD XHTML 1.0 Transitional//EN"
"http://www.w3.org/TR/xhtml1/DTD/xhtml1-transitional.dtd" >
<html>
<head>
    <title>Doctor-It</title>
     <style type="text/css">
         * { font-family: helvetica, arial, sans-serif }
     </style>
</head>
<body>
<table>
...
```

4. Save the file in the text editor and refresh the browser. All text should now be in a sans serif font.

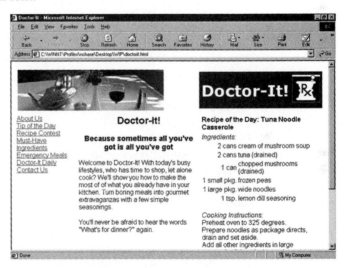

5. Leave both windows open for the next exercise.

Working with Background Images

We've explored how to add a background image to the page itself. In the same way, we can add a background to table elements. For example, to add an image to our sample table, we could write:

```
...
<table style="background-image: url('images/berries.jpg')">
...
```

The style attribute can be also used to apply a style to all of the text in the table. For example, adding:

```
style="font-style: italic"
```

to the table tag would tell the browser to render all of the text in the table as italic. Conversely, the background information shown here could be added to a CSS class, which is then applied to the table, rather than being added directly to the table, as it is here.

We can add background images to tables, rows or individual cells, but browser differences can present a definite problem when we do so. For instance, Netscape tends to rerender the background image of a table for every cell. To prevent this from happening, we can specifically assign the background on a cell to "" (called an "empty string"), which allows the overall table background to show through.

```
…
<td background="">
…
```

(Note that this code is not CSS. The bug is a leftover from preCSS days and so is the fix.)

Exercise Setup
Let's start by adding the background image to the content cell. We've created a background that goes with the theme (food), but we have tried to make it subtle enough that text can be read over it clearly.

Add the Background Image

1. In the open file doctorit.html in the text editor, add a style for the content class and add the background.

```
<!DOCTYPE html PUBLIC "-//W3C//DTD XHTML 1.0 Transitional//EN"
"http://www.w3.org/TR/xhtml1/DTD/xhtml1-transitional.dtd" >
<html>
<head>
    <title>Doctor-It</title>
    <style type="text/css">
      * { font-family: helvetica, arial, sans-serif }
        .content { background-image: url("images/berries.jpg") }
    </style>
</head>
<body>
<table>
…
```

Remember, backgrounds should be subtle enough to avoid impeding readability.

2. Save the file in the text editor and refresh the browser. Notice the berry background behind the content.

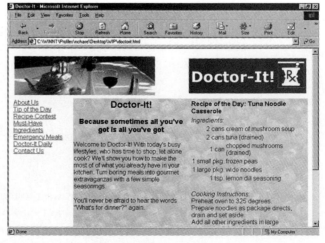

3. Leave both windows open for the next exercise.

Adding Background Colors

Backgrounds don't have to be images, however. We can add both background colors and background images directly from the style sheet:

```
…
<style>
  .myClass { background-color: #FFFFFF }
</style>
…
```

Exercise Setup

The top and left cells in our Web page are just a solid color, which we can set as a background color. Similarly, the Recipe of the Day needs a white background to block out the background behind it and make the menu more readable.

Add Background Colors

1. In the open file doctorit.html in the text editor, add the background color #000099 to the menu class, and set the background color on the recipe table to white, or #FFFFFF.

```
<!DOCTYPE html PUBLIC "-//W3C//DTD XHTML 1.0 Transitional//EN"
"http://www.w3.org/TR/xhtml1/DTD/xhtml1-transitional.dtd" >
<html>
<head>
    <title>Doctor-It</title>
    <style type="text/css">
        * { font-family: helvetica, arial, sans-serif }
        .content { background-image: url("images/berries.jpg") }
        .menu { background-color: #000099 }
        .recipe { background-color: #FFFFFF }
    </style>
</head>
<body>
<table>
…
```

2. Save the file in the text editor and refresh the browser.

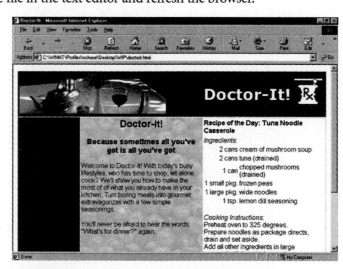

3. While that's a better look, we've apparently lost our menu links, which now blend into the background.

Change the links' color to white so that we can see them. On the sample finished page that we saw earlier, we can see that they are also bold, so let's take care of that at the same time.

```
<!DOCTYPE html PUBLIC "-//W3C//DTD XHTML 1.0 Transitional//EN"
"http://www.w3.org/TR/xhtml1/DTD/xhtml1-transitional.dtd" >
<html>
<head>
    <title>Doctor-It</title>
    <style type="text/css">
       * { font-family: helvetica, arial, sans-serif }
       .content { background-image: url("images/berries.jpg") }
       .menu { background-color: #000099 }
       .recipe { background-color: #FFFFFF }
       .menuLink {
               color: #FFFFFF;
               font-weight: bold;
               }
    </style>
</head>
<body>
<table>
...
```

4. Save the file in the text editor and refresh the browser. Notice that the links are once again visible.

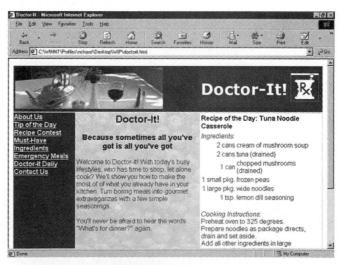

5. Leave the file open in both windows for the next exercise.

Borders

We've seen the table border on the sample that we've been discussing throughout this chapter. Borders set through CSS, however, are different. When we set the border property for a table, we're referring only to the exterior border for the entire table, not to the border on the cells, so we can easily create a line around the "box" of the table.

Borders, like backgrounds and fonts, have several different properties that can be set. These properties include the border width, style and color. We'll be dealing with them in more detail in Chapter 7, but for now, understand that border is a shorthand property. A *shorthand property* (also discussed more in Chapter 7) enables us to specify multiple properties at once, as in:

background: 2px dotted blue;

Add a Border to the Recipe

1. In the open file doctorit.html in the text editor, add a 3-px border to the table; make it the same color as the background color of the menu. Add a 1-px solid-blue border to the table footer.

```
<!DOCTYPE html PUBLIC "-//W3C//DTD XHTML 1.0 Transitional//EN"
"http://www.w3.org/TR/xhtml1/DTD/xhtml1-transitional.dtd" >
<html>
<head>
   <title>Doctor-It</title>
   <style type="text/css">
      * { font-family: helvetica, arial, sans-serif }
      .content { background-image: url("images/berries.jpg") }
      .menu { background-color: #000099 }
      .recipe { background-color: #FFFFFF;
        border: 3px solid #000099 }
        .recipeFoot { border: 1px solid #000099 }
      .menuLink {
              color: #FFFFFF;
              font-weight: bold;
              }
   </style>
</head>
<body>
<table>
...
```

2. Save the file in the text editor and refresh the browser. Notice the thick border around the recipe as a whole and the thinner one around the recipe footer.

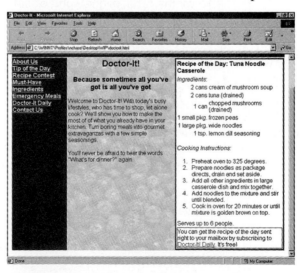

3. Leave the file open in both windows for the next exercise.

Lists

A *list* is a collection of items. Those items can be either ordered or unordered, and we can control how they're presented. An unordered list, for example, which contains items preceded by bullets, can have (instead of solid bullets) small open circles, as is normally the case, open squares or a number of other shapes. Ordered lists can use traditional Arabic numerals, Roman numerals, or even Hebrew or Russian numerals before each item.

List items, which we saw earlier were designated with the <li></li> tag, each appear on a separate line automatically, so we can also remove extraneous line breaks.

Exercise Setup

We've almost created the page we planned. We're missing bullets on the menu and the numbers on the cooking instructions but otherwise the page is looking pretty good. Both of these missing items involve the use of lists. In this case, we'll stick with the traditional Arabic numerals and remove the extra line breaks.

Add Lists

1. In the open file doctorit.html in the text editor, set the menu items as an unordered list, and make each menu option a new item. Do the same for the cooking instructions, but make that an ordered list. Remove the <br /> tags.

```
…
<tr><td width="150" valign="top" class="menu">
<ul>
<li><a href="about.html" class="menuLink">About Us</a></li>
<li><a href="tip.html" class="menuLink">Tip of the Day</a></li>
<li><a href="contest.html" class="menuLink">Recipe Contest</a></li>
<li><a href="ingredients.html" class="menuLink">Must-Have Ingredients</a></li>
<li><a href="meals.html" class="menuLink">Emergency Meals</a></li>
<li><a href="daily.html" class="menuLink">Doctor-It Daily</a></li>
<li><a href="mailto:webmaster@doctor-it.net" class="menulink">Contact Us</a></li>
</ul>
</td><td class="content">
<table width="50%" align="right" class="recipe">
<thead>
…
<br />
  <i>Cooking Instructions:</i>
<br />
<ol>
<li>Preheat oven to 325 degrees.</li>
<li>Prepare noodles as package directs, drain and set aside.</li>
<li>Add all other ingredients in large casserole dish and mix together.</li>
<li>Add noodles to the mixture and stir until blended.</li>
<li>Cook in oven for 20 minutes or until mixture is golden brown on top.</li>
</ol>
<p>Serves up to 6 people.</p>
</td></tr>
</tbody>
</table>
…
```

2. Save the file in the text editor and refresh the browser. Notice that numbers have been added to the instructions. Notice also that there are no bullets on the navigation, although it seems as if there should be.

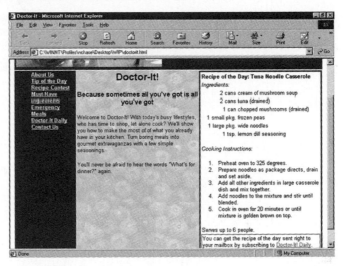

3. That takes care of the lists, but the bullets aren't showing up as white. To get that to happen, set the style on the list itself. While there, also take care of shrinking the text somewhat. Finally, because we're setting the height for all of the text, re-enlarge the headings. Set the style of the list to the color white (#FFFFFF), shrink the text to 10 pt, and enlarge the headings to 18 pt and 12 pt.

```
<!DOCTYPE html PUBLIC "-//W3C//DTD XHTML 1.0 Transitional//EN"
"http://www.w3.org/TR/xhtml1/DTD/xhtml1-transitional.dtd" >
<html>
<head>
    <title>Doctor-It</title>
    <style type="text/css">
        * {
            font-family: helvetica, arial, sans-serif;
            font-size: 10pt
            }
        h2 { font-size: 18pt }
        h3 { font-size: 12pt }
        .content { background-image: url("images/berries.jpg") }
        .menu { background-color: #000099 }
        .recipe { background-color: #FFFFFF;
                border: 3px solid #000099 }
        .recipeFoot { border: 1px solid #000099 }
        .menuLink {
                color: #FFFFFF;
                font-weight: bold;
                }
        ul { color: #FFFFFF }
    </style>
</head>
<body>
<table>
...
```

4. Save the file in the text editor and refresh the browser. Notice that the bullets are now visible, and that in general, the text is a bit smaller. Observe also that the headings have stayed the same, or nearly so.

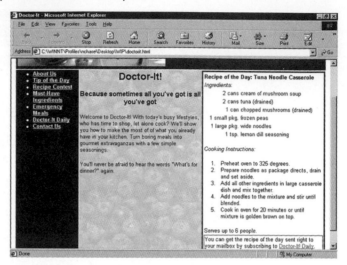

5. Leave both windows open for the next exercise.

Cellpadding and Cellspacing

Cellspacing is the gap between the cells. *Cellpadding* is the space between the content of a cell and its borders. Both are used to fine-tune the appearance and alignment of content. These attributes are both set on the table itself, and can be used independently or together. For example:

…
<table **cellpadding="15"** border="1">
…

creates a space around the content of a cell:

Cellspacing works in much the same way, but actually controls the width of the interior borders themselves, so:

...

<table **cellspacing="15"** border="1">

...

produces the page:

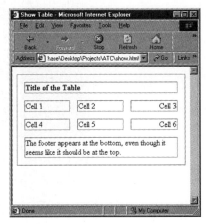

While in many cases, the positioning is the same whether we use cellpadding or cellspacing, the difference lies in whether or not we see what is behind the table.

Cellpadding and cellspacing are often used directly on a table, rather than using a style sheet, because they typically apply only to a single table.

Exercise Setup
Our page looks relatively similar to the planned design, with one exception. We still have spacing issues. The first is the line that appears between the blue-filled column on the left and the top, table-wide row containing the header graphics. Another issue is that the text sits immediately against the inside of our tables. It would be preferable to have a small amount of white space to make it seem less crowded.

Adjust Padding and Spacing

1. In the open file doctorit.html in the text editor, adjust the cellspacing and cellpadding on the main table. Because we didn't give this a class, just put the attribute right on the table. Adjust the cellpadding for the recipe table.

```
<!DOCTYPE HTML PUBLIC "-//W3C//DTD HTML 4.01 Transitional//EN" "http://
www.w3.org/TR/html4/loose.dtd">
<html>
<head>
    <title>Doctor-It</title>
    <style type="text/css">
...
    </style>
</head>
<body>
<table cellpadding="10" cellspacing="0">
```

```
<tr><td colspan="2" class="menu">
  <table width="100%"><tr><td width="50%" align="left">
  <img src="images/table.jpg" alt="Table Image" />
...
```

2. Save the file in the text editor and refresh the browser.

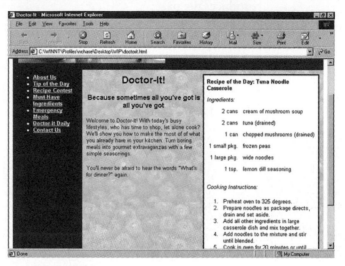

3. Check your results against the original design. Now they should look the same.

4. Close both windows.

Summary

In this chapter, you learned to use create tables and use them to format a page. You have become familiar with different ways to manipulate tables, such as spanning rows and columns, nesting tables within one another, and adding styles via a style sheet. You have worked extensively with heights, widths and alignments, and explored ordered and unordered lists.

5 Forms

Chapter Objective:

To learn to use forms to gather information from the user. In Chapter 5, you will:

- Learn how to create a form.

- Become familiar with the different types of form inputs, including a variety of button options.

- Discover how to control the appearance and initial values of elements in a form.

- Learn how data is sent back to the server and the distinction between the get and the post method.

Projects to be Completed:

- News Web (A)

- Cyber Travel (B)

- Hunter Films (C)

- North Star Adventure Gear (D)

Forms

We willingly spend time and effort working on presenting the information that we intend to send to our users, but often we don't think enough about acquiring information from users.

Obtaining information from users is important for a number of reasons. First, the Web is an interactive medium. We're meant to watch our users and interact with their actions and preferences. These interactions can be subtle, such as using knowledge about what they've already looked at to choose similar information dynamically to present to them. Interactions can also be more overt, such as surveys about their tastes and interests.

The second reason is more practical: some purposes, like e-commerce, absolutely require us to collect information. How else can we know, for example, the types of products and services that our users want to order? We could probably acquire some information with hyperlinks, but how would we safely obtain their credit card information? Likewise, searches would be difficult if we couldn't allow the users to indicate the object for their search.

The Basic Form

The purpose of a form is to acquire information from the user and send it to the server so the server can perform some variety of actions with it. (While we cannot provide a server with which to work, we have provided a script that will enable us see the form in action.)

Forms can use many different types of inputs, from text boxes to drop-down menus. Different types are appropriate for different situations, and we will explore a number of these input options in this chapter.

A form consists of a <form> tag with one or more input tags. These inputs can be different types, such as text boxes ("text") or submit buttons ("submit"). An input tag can also have a name attribute, which helps the server identify the information entered later, when that information is submitted by the browser. For example, if you were building a form that asked for a user's telephone number, you might use name="phone".

A basic form looks like this:

```
…
<form>
   Enter your information here:
   <input type="text" name="myTextField" />
</form>
…
```

This would produce a simple page:

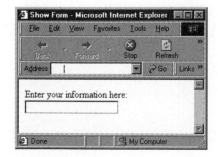

Unlike a typical Web form, there is no submit button, but because there is just one text box, this form can be submitted by pressing Return/Enter. We haven't given this form any other instructions, so submitting the form will simply return the browser to the same page, adding the form information to the URL (in the Address [Microsoft Internet Explorer] or Location [Netscape] box of the browser).

For example, if this page were called "showform.html," and we typed the text "myinfo" into the text box, when we submit the form the URL would be:

file:///<yourpathhoro>showform.html?myTextField=myinfo

If we hadn't given the input a name, it would not appear in the URL, because the browser would not have submitted it with the rest of the form. (This will become important later when we want inputs that are not submitted.)

Exercise Setup

Let's start by creating the most basic form. In this chapter we'll build an order form for Soap-To-Shawls.com, but let's start by building a login page for their administrator, Sandra.

Create the Form

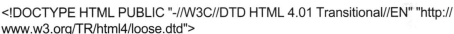

1. Create a folder called "forms" in your WIP folder. Navigate to **RF_HTML>Chapter 5**, and copy the contents of this folder to the **WIP>forms** folder.

2. Open **WIP>forms>login.html** in your text editor and in your browser. (Don't worry about the <script> tag. We'll discuss that tag in detail in Chapter 8, but for the moment just understand that the script will help us see the results of the form.) Create the basic form by adding the form tag and its input to the document.

Remember that input must be given a name if you want it to appear in the URL.

```
<!DOCTYPE HTML PUBLIC "-//W3C//DTD HTML 4.01 Transitional//EN" "http://
www.w3.org/TR/html4/loose.dtd">
<html>
<head><title>Form Test Page</title></head>
<body>
<script src="scriptvalues.js" language="JavaScript" type="text/javascript"></script>
<h2>Please Log In</h2>
<form>
   <input />
</form>
</body>
</html>
```

3. Save the file in your text editor and refresh your browser.

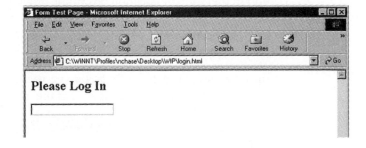

4. We've created a form and added an input box to it, but as of yet we can't do much with it. Add some text to the input box and press Return/Enter. Notice that nothing happens except that the page refreshes itself and the text that we typed vanishes.

5. Since the inputs must be named in order for the form to do anything, add a name to the text box we created.

```
<!DOCTYPE HTML PUBLIC "-//W3C//DTD HTML 4.01 Transitional//EN" "http://
www.w3.org/TR/html4/loose.dtd">
<html>
<head><title>Form Test Page</title></head>
<body>
<script src="scriptvalues.js" language="JavaScript" type="text/javascript"></script>
<h2>Please Log In</h2>
<form>
  <input name="username" />
</form>
</body>
</html>
```

6. Save the file in the text editor and refresh your browser. The page should look the same as it did before.

7. Type something, such as your name, into the input box and press Return/Enter. Notice that the form reappears with the text you typed shown at the top of the page.

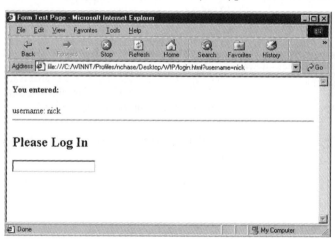

8. Leave the file open in both windows for the next exercise.

Form Data

Once the user types information into a simple form and presses Return/Enter, the information in the Address/Location box in the browser changes. In the preceding exercise, for example, in the browser window, the URL in the Address/Location box includes a question mark towards the end of the line. The question mark is what tells the server that what follows is data. The data could be one piece of information or many.

In either case, the data is sent as a name-value pair. A *name-value pair* is a combination of two elements, a *name*, which identifies the information, and a *value*, the information itself. In the example in the exercise, the name is "username" and the value is "Nick."

We can take advantage of the fact that data can be sent within URLs when building pages. For instance, we could provide a regular text link that points to a search, and includes data on what you want to find. Email marketers use this all the time by adding identifying information to the links in their messages. When users click the link, it's the same as submitting a form that identifies them to the server.

The name/value pair is the format in which all form information is sent. If our sample form were on an actual Web server, the URL might be:

http://www.againsttheclock.com/login.html**?username=Nick**

In the exercise, we can see the collected information in the URL in the Address/Location box, thanks to the script we added. (This will help us to see what we're doing. Without the script, the URL would change, but we would see no other difference in the page.)

The form created a URL and sent the browser to it. When the URL points to a script or to an application, that program can act on the data sent within the URL.

The Form Action

Of course, this page isn't much use, since it doesn't yet do anything. What we need to do is create a page that will receive our information, and then we can send the form to it. This page is called the "action" of the form, because it's the act that the browser performs with the information.

The action is written as a relative or absolute URL in the action attribute of the form element, such as in the form shown below:

```
<form action="myFormAction.asp">
  Enter your information here:
  <input type="text" name="myTextField" />
</form>
…
```

In this case, when we submit the form, the browser would try to open the URL:

file:///<yourpathhere>/myFormAction.asp?myTextField=myinfo

In almost every case, this URL represents some sort of program, such as an Active Server Page (which uses the file extension .asp) or a CGI script. This program is executed by a Web server and usually performs some action, such as processing an order or adding user information to a database, then returns an HTML page to the browser.

Creating Active Server Pages and CGI scripts are separate disciplines that are the topics of entire books. Some ISPs provide their own CGI scripts to serve these functions and require that you use their scripts — check with your ISP to see their policies and what scripts they provide, if any. Others will allow you to add your own scripts that you can create yourself or download from resources such as:

- http://www.cgiforme.com/
- http://www.cgiscripts.net/
- http://www.worldwidemart.com/scripts/

Since we don't have the luxury of using a Web server with this book, the provided script will execute and display the values you typed in the form. As before, the script will show you these values in the URL in the Address/Location box. Any URL can be used as the action of a form, and the browser will take care of the rest.

Remember, an absolute URL is one that provides the entire location, such as:

http://www.mydir/
mypage.html

A relative URL includes just part of the URL, such as:

otherdir/otherpage.html

The browser fills in the rest of the information based on the page currently being shown in the browser.

Exercise Setup

We'll see something like this when we create the login page for Soap-To-Shawls. The Soap-To-Shawls site sells handmade soap, sash belts and so on. To keep their site current, they use forms and form actions to add information to the database that contains their site content. (Database-driven sites are common, but well beyond the scope of this book.) Of course, we don't want just anyone coming in and doing that, so we'll protect the page with a script that checks for a username and password. First, let's finish creating the form itself.

Add the Form Action

1. In the open login.html file in the text editor, add an action attribute to the form, setting it for our login_action.html page.

```
<!DOCTYPE HTML PUBLIC "-//W3C//DTD HTML 4.01 Transitional//EN" "http://
www.w3.org/TR/html4/loose.dtd">
<html>
<head><title>Form Test Page</title></head>
<body>
<script src="scriptvalues.js" language="Javascript" type="text/javascript"></script>
<h2>Please Log In</h2>
<form action="login_action.html">
   <input name="username" />
</form>
</body>
</html>
```

2. Save the file in the text editor and refresh your browser. You won't see any change, but the browser will, and that's what's important right now.

3. In the browser window, type any text into the box and press Return/Enter. Notice that the browser now goes to login_action.html, which we specified as the form's action.

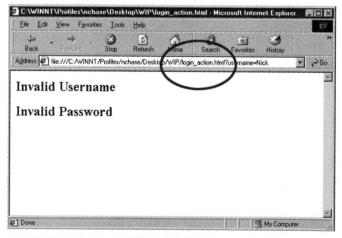

While we did receive messages telling us that our username and password were incorrect, that's not important right now. The important point is the URL — notice that it's not login.html anymore.

4. Leave the file open in both windows for the next exercise.

Form Inputs

As we've seen, we can create a form, which submits its information to a URL that we've designated as the action. We also know that only inputs that have names will be submitted. If we were only able to permit the user to type in text, this capability and the form that permits it would be useful. But we can do much more. The variety of types of form input options allows us to create powerful forms.

Text Inputs

Text inputs are the most familiar type of form input, and you've already used one, a text box, in the previous exercise.

We have some control over these text fields. Using attributes, we can control the size of the field, the number of characters the user can type into it, and the values that we want the field to contain when the page first loads.

For example, we can make our sample form load with an initial value that is explanatory text. We can also set the size of the field ("size") to 15 characters and the maximum number of characters that the user can type ("maxlength") to 30:

```
…
<form action="myFormAction.asp">
   Enter your information here:
   <input type="text" name="myTextField" value="your name here" size="15"
maxlength="30" />
</form>

…
```

This gives us a page that looks like this:

Exercise Setup
We'll use this technique in creating a login page. We'll start with a simple login page for soaptoshawls.com and then proceed to their order page.

Add the Login Box

1. Double-check that WIP>forms>login.html is open in both the text editor and the browser windows. (If the browser shows the Invalid Username page, click the back button until you get back to the login page.)

2. In the text editor, make the input a text box, add explanatory text, set the size to 20 characters (using the size attribute), change the page title to SoapToShawls.com Administration Suite, and add the top image, WIP>forms>images>soaplogo.jpg.

```
<!DOCTYPE HTML PUBLIC "-//W3C//DTD HTML 4.01 Transitional//EN" "http://
www.w3.org/TR/html4/loose.dtd">
<html>
<head><title>SoapToShawls.com Administration Suite</title></head>
<body>
<script src="scriptvalues.js" language="Javascript" type="text/javascript"></script>
<img height="133" width="246" src="images/soaplogo.jpg" alt="Logo" />
<br />
<center>
<h2>Please Log In</h2>
<form action="login_action.html">
    Please enter your username: <input type="text" size="20" name="username" />
</form>
</center>
</body>
</html>
```

3. Save the file in the text editor and refresh your browser.

4. In the browser, notice that the text box is now somewhat smaller than it was before. Type some words in the box. Notice that if you type more than 20 characters, the text scrolls to the left but lets you continue to type. Press Return/Enter to submit the form.

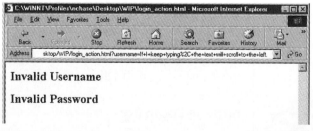

If you typed any spaces or other punctuation, you'll see that the browser converted them before submitting the data. It does this to avoid creating a URL containing spaces. Replacing these characters is known as "escaping" the text.

Notice also that the page tells us that this information is invalid. This happens because the script that is processing our data is looking for a specific username and password that we have not yet supplied.

5. Look at the URL in the Address/Location box. Observe that all of our text was submitted.

6. Press the browser's Back button until you get back to the login page. Leave the file open in both windows for the next exercise.

Limiting the Amount of Text Submitted

As you have observed, we can set the size of a text box, but that setting only affects the appearance of the box. It doesn't control the amount of text that can be submitted or the nature of that text. While this is not generally a problem for designers, programmers often need to limit the amount of text that's returned. For instance, this text may be destined for a database, where only a certain number of characters have been allotted to it. We can, fortunately, control this using another attribute — maxlength. This attribute controls the exact number of characters that can be typed into the text box.

Limit the Number of Characters

1. In the open login.html file, set the maximum length of text in the text box to 10 characters using the maxlength attribute.

```
…
<h2>Please Log In</h2>
<form action="login_action.html">
    Please enter your username: <input type="text" size="20" name="username"
maxlength="10" />
</form>
</center>
</body>
</html>
```

2. Save the file in the text editor and refresh your browser. Type in the text box in the browser. Notice that while there appears to be room in the box, the browser only allows you to type 10 characters.

3. Leave the windows open for the next exercise.

Adding an Initial Value

While Web sites started out providing information, in the last couple of years it has become common to add applications that control databases. On such a site we might want to provide a page that shows users the data they have provided and gives them a chance to edit it.

In order to provide a proofing or editing page, we need to be able to specify the initial value for a text box on the proofing page. You specify this initial value by adding the value attribute to your input tag. The copy between the quote marks following value (value=" ") displays when the page is loaded, as shown in the previous example.

Just as its name suggests, this copy is only the initial value. When the user types his or her information into the box, the new copy replaces the original (initial value) text.

Add an Initial Value

1. In the open login.html file, add explanatory text to the text box using the value attribute. Change the maximum length (in the maxlength attribute) to allow for all of the text.

```
…
<center>
<h2>Please Log In</h2>
<form action="login_action.html">
```

```
    Please enter your username: <input type="text" size="20" name="username"
maxlength="20" value="Enter Your Userid" />
</form>
</center>
</body>
</html>
```

Another reason to add an initial value for a form element might be to suggest to the user an idea of what type of information to provide.

2. Save the file and refresh the browser. Notice that the text you typed as the value appears in the box.

3. Notice that even though the text is provided as a start, you can delete it and type other text in the box.

4. Leave the windows open for the next exercise.

Passwords

Another common use for forms is to take login information (as we're doing in our exercise). One difficulty with acquiring password information is the need to hide the user's password from someone else who may be looking over his or her shoulder. On an ATM machine, this is done by not displaying the text that's typed — replacing it, instead, with placeholder characters. We can do the same thing with a password input.

A password input acts just like a text input, with one exception: the characters that the user types display as asterisks or bullets (depending on the user's browser and operating system). For example, we can change our sample form to use a password instead of a text input:

```
…
<form action="myFormAction.asp">
  Enter your information here:
  <input type="password" name="myTextField" value="your name here" size="20"
maxlength="30" />
</form>
```

The result of this is that the browser obscures the initial value, as well as anything that the user types.

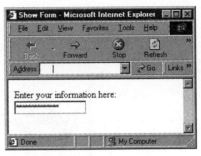

If we submit this form, however, the URL shows the flaw in this plan:

file:///<your path here>/myFormAction.asp?myTextField=mysecretinfo

As you can see, password boxes don't really encrypt the information — they just hide it from someone who may be watching the user. If the form were submitted as we just submitted our form, the password would still be visible to anyone who knew where to look. A little later on, we'll see a solution to that particular problem. For now, remember: information is not secure just because it's in a password box!

Adding a Submit Button

There is a second complication that arises with adding a password box to the login form, and it's unrelated to security. Up to now we've been submitting the form by pressing the Return/Enter key. This only worked because there was just one text box in the form. Now we will need another way to submit the form: the submit button. A submit button is just another type of input:

```
<input type="submit" />
```

The browser interprets this as a form button that, when pressed, submits the form. We'll deal with submit buttons more thoroughly later in the chapter.

Exercise Setup

Let's add both the password box and the submit button to our Soap to Shawls page.

Add a Password Box

1. In the open login.html file, add a password input box 20 characters wide and a submit button.

```
…
   Please enter your username: <input type="text" size="20" name="username"
maxlength="20" value="Enter Your Userid" />
<br />
   Please enter your password: <input type="password" size="20"
name="password" /><br />
   <input type="submit" />
</form>
</center>
</body>
</html>
```

2. Save the file in the text editor and refresh your browser. Try typing in the new box in the browser window.

3. Notice that the text in the new box is obscured by bullets or asterisks. (This may give you the impression that the information is secure, but don't be fooled.) Type a username of "sandra" and a password of "bunnies" and submit the form. Look at the URL in the Address/Location box.

4. Save changes and close the file.

Radio Buttons and Radio Groups

One typical form is the order form. Order forms can have many types of input fields, and one of the most familiar is the radio button.

Radio buttons are also known as "radio groups" because, in most cases, they're only useful when there's more than one option from which to choose. Radio buttons are perfect when we have several choices but want only one choice to be active at any given time.

For example, we can use a radio group ("radio") on our sample form:

```
…
<form action="myFormAction.asp">
  What is your choice?
  <br />
  <input type="radio" name="choice" value="Y" checked="checked">Yes
  <input type="radio" name="choice" value="N">No
  <input type="radio" name="choice" value="M">Maybe
```

```
<br />
<input type="submit" />
</form>
...
```

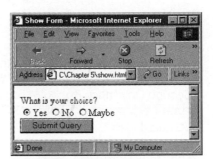

There are a couple of points to notice here. First, all three of these buttons have the same name. This is what defines a radio group. Buttons in a different group will have a different name.

Second, one button is denoted as checked. The reason for the strange notation (checked= "checked") is that in older versions of HTML, one simply included the word checked to designate which button started out selected. With the advent of XHTML, however, all attributes must have a value.

Clicking one of the other buttons selects it and deselects the previous button. This means that it's impossible to completely uncheck a radio button. You can be certain that a value will be submitted — as long as you make sure that a value is selected initially. (If not, the user may submit the form without making a choice.)

The last point to remember for radio groups is that the value submitted is the data in the value attribute and not the text next to the radio button. For example, if the user were to submit this form as is, the value passed will be "Y" and not "Yes".

Exercise Setup

Now we're ready to start creating the order form. Begin by adding two radio groups.

Add a Radio Group

1. Open **WIP>forms>order.html** in the text editor and browser.

2. In the text editor, add three radio buttons named "shipping" to the Shipping Methods and three named "card_type" to the Credit Card Type sections. Add the appropriate values.

```
...
<b>Shipping Method:</b>
<input type="radio" value="1" name="shipping" checked="checked" />
Overnight    
<input type="radio" value="2" name="shipping" />
Second Day    
<input type="radio" value="3" name="shipping" />
Standard Mail
<br /><br />
<b>Credit Card Type:  </b>
<input type="radio" value="1" name="card_type" />
American Express    
<input type="radio" value="2" name="card_type" />
Mastercard    
<input type="radio" value="3" name="card_type" />
Visa    
<br /><br />
...
```

3. Save the file and refresh the browser.

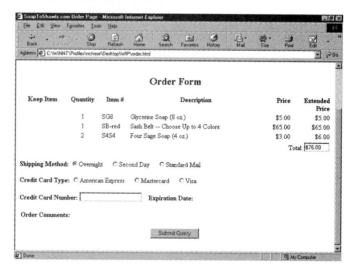

On some systems, $76.00 may appear as %2476.00 because of the way the information is encoded as part of the URL. In a production situation, the Web server would translate that back to $76.00 before passing it to the form's action.

4. Notice that we have two groups of buttons, but that only one of them has any values chosen. Submit the form just as it is and look at the values that are passed. Notice also that while the value for the selected button was passed, no value was passed for card_type because none was selected.

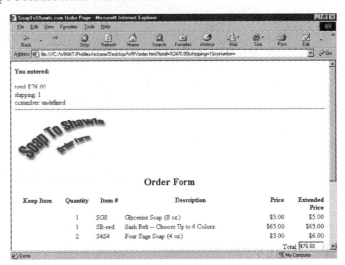

5. Leave the file open in both windows for the next exercise.

Radio Button Groupings

One important thing to remember is that radio buttons are grouped based on their name, not on where they are located on the page. Radio buttons in different areas of the page can be grouped together by giving them the same name.

Exercise Setup

We can see this process in action by making a change to our page so that one of the Shipping Method buttons belongs to the Credit Card Type group, and vice versa.

Check the Radio Groups

1. In the open order.html file, swap the names of one of the shipping and card_type buttons.

...

```
<br />
<b>Shipping Method:</b>
<input type="radio" value="1" name="shipping" checked="checked" />
Overnight   
<input type="radio" value="2" name="card_type" />
Second Day   
<input type="radio" value="3" name="shipping" />
Standard Mail
<br /><br />
<b>Credit Card Type:  </b>
<input type="radio" value="1" name="card_type" />
```

```
American Express    
<input type="radio" value="2" name="shipping" />
Mastercard    
<input type="radio" value="3" name="card_type" />
Visa    
<br /><br />
<b>Credit Card Number: </b> <input type="text" name="ccnumber" />
   
```
…

2. Save the file in the text editor and refresh your browser. Play with the two groups of buttons. Notice that one moment you may have a button selected in each of the two rows, and at the next moment you may have two buttons selected in one row and none in the other row.

3. Undo the last change in the text editor so that each button belongs to the proper group, and leave both windows open for the next exercise.

Checkboxes

Checkboxes ("checkbox") are similar to radio groups in that if they aren't clicked, their values are not submitted. They are different, however, in that they can provide several different values for the same name. This means that the user can select more than one choice without removing the check from the previous choice. Checkboxes are often used to indicate something to which the user must agree, or a group of items with which the user wants to do something.

We can change our radio buttons to checkboxes:

```
…
<form action="myFormAction.asp">
  What is your choice?
  <br />
 <input type="checkbox" name="choice" value="Y" checked="checked">Yes
 <input type="checkbox" name="choice" value="N">No
 <input type="checkbox" name="choice" value="M">Maybe
 <br />
 <input type="submit" />
</form>
…
```

Common uses for checkboxes include lists of items a user wants and categories of information in which a user is interested.

This changes our form slightly:

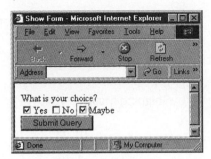

The major differences between checkboxes and radio buttons are that checkboxes can be left completely unselected, and more than one can be selected at once. For example, if the form were submitted as above, the URL would be:

file:///<your path here>/myFormAction.asp?**choice=Y&choice=M**

The script (in this case, myFormAction.asp) would then have two choice values with which to work. In the case of a real order form, the server would receive similar information and handle each item in turn, according to the program, dealing with each item appropriately.

Exercise Setup
In the case of the order form, we're going to add checkboxes that allow users to decide which items in their cart they want to keep.

Add Checkboxes

1. In the open order.html file, add checkboxes named item for each of our three products in the table at the top of the page.

```
...
<tr>
        <th>Keep Item</th><th>Quantity</th>
        <th>Item #</th><th>Description</th><th>Price</th>
        <th>Extended<br />Price</th>
</tr>
<tr>
        <td><input type="checkbox" name="item" value="SG8" checked="checked"
/></td><td>1</td><td>SG8</td>
        <td>Glycerine Soap (8 oz.)</td><td>$5.00</td><td>$5.00</td>
</tr>
<tr>
        <td><input type="checkbox" name="item" value="SB" checked="checked" /
></td><td>1</td><td>SB-red</td>
        <td valign="top" >Sash Belt — Choose Up to 4 Colors</td>
        <td>$65.00</td><td>$65.00</td>
</tr>
<tr>
        <td><input type="checkbox" name="item" value="S4S4"
checked="checked" /></td><td>2</td><td>S4S4</td>
        <td>Four Sage Soap (4 oz.)</td><td>$3.00</td><td>$6.00</td>
```

```
</tr>
<tr>
        <td colspan="3" align="left"></td><td colspan="3" align="right">Total:
        <input type="text" size="7" name="total" value="$76.00" />
</tr>
</table>
<br />
<b>Shipping Method:</b>
...
```

2. Save the file and refresh the page. Notice that the checkboxes appear at the start of each line, and that all of them are checked.

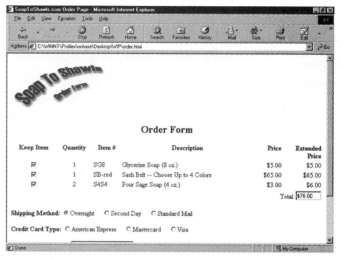

3. Uncheck one of the boxes and submit the page. Notice that the items that were checked were submitted, but the one that was unchecked was not submitted.

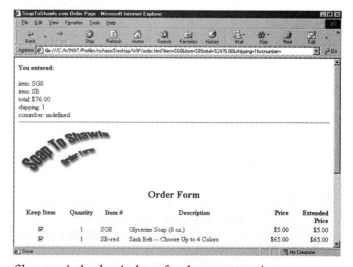

4. Leave the file open in both windows for the next exercise.

Select Boxes

Select boxes (also known as "pull-down menus," "drop-down boxes," "drag-down menus" or "drop lists") are like a cross between a radio button and a checkbox. There are two different types: one acts like a radio button and the other like a checkbox.

A select box is not simply another type of input. Instead, it is a select element that contains one or more option elements. The traditional select box shows only one value at a time and allows only one option to be selected (either through the selected attribute or through user action):

```
…
<form action="myFormAction.asp">
  What is your choice?
  <br />
  <select name="choice">
    <option value="Y" selected="selected">Yes</option>
    <option value="N">No</option>
    <option value="M">Maybe</option>
  </select>
  <br />
  <input type="submit" />
</form>
…
```

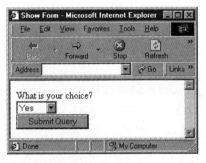

What we see here is that a select box consists of a <select></select> element with one or more <option></option> elements contained within it. The select box is the overall object, so that's where the name of the form goes. The values, on the other hand, are contained in the option elements. A select box can have any number of options, but remember, users will scroll only so far before giving up.

Also, as with checkboxes and radio buttons, the browser doesn't particularly care what the label is for a particular option — it uses the value given. Take note: in HTML, it was very common to not close the <option> tag and to omit the value. Early browsers used the label in this case, but some newer browsers use the "index" of the choice. For instance, if the second choice is selected, it might pass the value "1". (Lists are "zero-based", meaning that the first choice is number 0.) To avoid potential misunderstandings and problems, you must specify a value on each option, even if it is the same as the label.

We can also set a size on the select box:

```
…
  <select name="choice" size="3">
…
  </select>
…
```

Still, only one value can be submitted at a time, like a radio group. To make the select box act like a set of checkboxes, we can add the multiple attribute. Like checked and selected, multiple used to be written without a value, but now needs one:

…
  <select name="choice" size="3" **multiple="multiple">**

…
  </select>

…
The page looks the same in the browser, but users can choose more than one option by holding down the Shift/Control key.

Exercise Setup
On the order form, let's start with the traditional select box, where only one value can be chosen at a time.

Add a Select Box

1. In the open order.html file, add select boxes for the credit card expiration month and year.

…

```
<b>Credit Card Number: </b> <input type="text" name="ccnumber" /
>   
<b>Expiration Date: </b>
<select name="exp_month">
<option value="1">January</option>
<option value="2">February</option>
<option value="3">March</option>
<option value="4">April</option>
<option value="5">May</option>
<option value="6">June</option>
<option value="7">July</option>
<option value="8">August</option>
<option value="9">September</option>
<option value="10">October</option>
<option value="11">November</option>
<option value="12">December</option>
</select>
/
<select name="exp_year">
<option value="2001">2001</option>
<option value="2002">2002</option>
```

If you've coded HTML and worked with the <option> tag, note that there have been changes. You must close the tag and specify a value on each option or some browsers won't render this correctly.

```
<option value="2003">2003</option>
<option value="2004">2004</option>
</select>
<br /><br />
<table><tr><td valign="top"><b>Order Comments:  </b></td><td></td></tr></table>
```
...

2. Save the file and refresh the browser. Notice that the select boxes appear, and that without a value designated as selected, the first value in the list is selected.

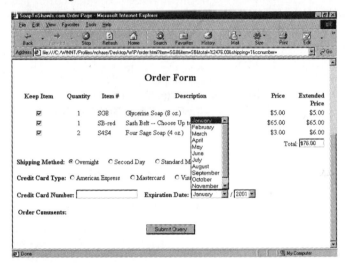

3. Leave the file open in both windows for the next exercise.

Adding Multiple-Choice Select Lists

There is also a second type of select element, which is more like a list than a menu. This list, which looks the same as the select boxes seen above, will even allow us to select multiple values.

Add a Multiple-Choice Select List

1. In the open order.html file, add the color select list to the Sash Belt item.

...

```
<tr>
        <th>Keep Item</th><th>Quantity</th>
        <th>Item #</th><th>Description</th><th>Price</th>
        <th>Extended<br />Price</th>
</tr>
<tr>
        <td><input type="checkbox" name="item" value="SG8" checked="checked" /></
td><td>1</td><td>SG8</td>
        <td>Glycerine Soap (8 oz.)</td><td>$5.00</td><td>$5.00</td>
</tr>
<tr>
        <td><input type="checkbox" name="item" value="SB" checked="checked" /></
td><td>1</td><td>SB-red</td>
        <td valign="top" >Sash Belt — Choose Up to 4 Colors
```

```
<br />
<select name="colors" size="3" multiple="multiple">
<option value="red">Red</option>
<option value="blue">Blue</option>
<option value="green">Green</option>
<option value="black">Black</option>
<option value="yellow">Yellow</option>
<option value="purple">Purple</option>
<option value="other">Other (add comments)</option>
</select>
</td><td>$65.00</td><td>$65.00</td>
</tr>
<tr>

        <td><input type="checkbox" name="item" value="S4S4" checked="checked" /></td><td>2</td><td>S4S4</td>
        <td>Four Sage Soap (4 oz.)</td><td>$3.00</td><td>$6.00</td>
</tr>
...
```

2. Save the file and refresh the browser. Notice the select list. We've created a select box, but by giving it a size attribute — even if we set the size to 1 — we're telling the browser to render it as a list, with a scroll bar, if necessary, as it is here.

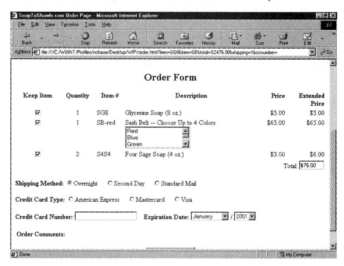

3. Scroll through the values in the list and choose a few of them.

4. Submit the form. Notice the multiple values for colors.

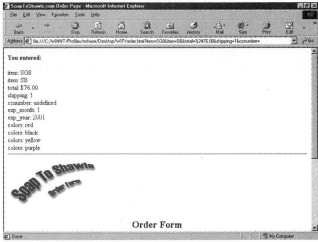

5. Leave the file open in both windows for the next exercise.

Text Area

We've explored text inputs, but there's a second type of text box with which we need to work: the text area (<textarea>). Text areas are great for free-form comments from users.

A text area can be handy because it allows users much more latitude. Instead of being limited to writing in a single tiny window, users can see all or most of what they write, depending on the size that the Web-page author has set. The textarea tag includes attributes that indicate how many columns and rows it should take up on the page, though this doesn't limit the number of characters it can hold.

For example, if we add a textarea tag to our sample form:

```
…
<form action="myFormAction.asp">
  What is your choice?
  <br />
  <textarea cols="60" rows="5">
  The initial text for a textarea goes into the textarea element.
  </textarea>
  <br />
  <input type="submit" />
</form>
…
```

we can see the results:

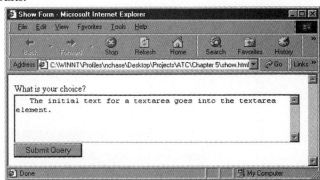

To choose more than one value on the Macintosh, Shift-click. To choose more than one on a Windows system, Control-click.

As you observe, not only did we retain the initial text, but also the spaces at the beginning of the text. Any spaces or line feeds will be preserved with this input option.

Note that there are also problems with text areas.

First, if you are receiving text that will later be displayed on a Web page (such as for a Web-based bulletin board), you will need to screen this content for malicious scripting. Such malicious scripting is JavaScript or VBScript that executes when the page is loaded, causing problems for your readers. This is typically done on the server side, which is beyond the scope of this book, but you need to keep it in mind.

The second issue is the fact that we cannot easily limit the number of characters that a user puts into this type of text box. If the application executed by the form action has a size limitation, the data must be checked against this limit before being used. (There is also a security issue involving large amounts of data being passed in order to crash the Web server. You should discuss this with the system administrator for the Web server and plan accordingly.)

Exercise Setup
Let's go ahead and add one to the Soap to Shawls order form.

Add a Text Area

1. In the open order.html file, add a text area for order comments, including some text to explain to the user how to use this text box.

...

```
<table><tr><td valign="top"><b>Order Comments:  </b></td><td>
<textarea name="comments" rows="5" cols="40">
    Enter any comments here.
</textarea>
</td></tr></table>
```

...

2. Save the file and refresh the browser. Notice the text area and its initial text.

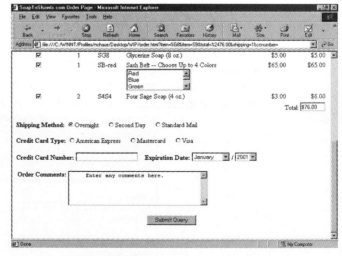

3. Leave the file open in both windows for the next exercise.

Hidden Elements

We've covered most of the visible elements on the page, but sometimes we want to include information on the form that the user doesn't need to see. It's not that we don't want the user to know the information — it's just that it's not relevant to him or her at the moment, and displaying it would only be confusing and clutter the page.

For example, we might have a session number that identifies this particular user, which we need on the script that processes the form. We might want to have information about which pages that user has already visited or the page the user visited immediately before coming to the form. Perhaps we want to include pricing information for the scripts (which we will discuss in Chapter 8) to calculate. None of this information should be shown to the user, but it must be submitted with the rest of the information on the form.

In these situations, we want to use hidden fields. A hidden field ("hidden") doesn't actually appear on the page but will be submitted. A hidden field is another type of input:

```
<input type="hidden" name="myFieldName" value="myFieldValue" />
```

Note that not only is the so-called "hidden" field submitted with the page, it is also in plain view in the URL. Just as with passwords, hidden fields are a convenience, and not a substitute for security.

One of the most common security errors made on the Web today is caused by developers who leave sensitive or important information in hidden fields. Information in such hidden fields is visible to anyone who selects "View Source" on the page. This information can even be changed, for example, to lower a price.

Exercise Setup

In this case, we'll use a hidden field to add an order number so that the server will know to what order all of this information applies.

Add a Hidden Field

1. In the open order.html file, add the order number to a hidden field on the page.

…

```
<h2 align="center">Order Form</h2>
<form action="order.html">
<input type="hidden" name="order_id" value="1234" />
<table width="100%">
<colgroup><col align="center" span="2" valign="top" /><col span="2" valign="top" /><col span="2" align="right" valign="top" /></colgroup>
```

…

2. Save the file in the text editor and refresh your browser. There should be no change in the way the page looks.

Submit the page. Notice that the hidden field was also submitted.

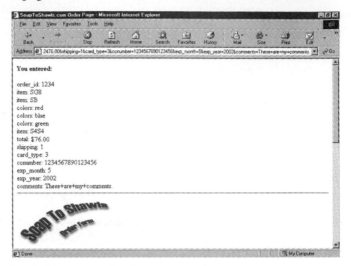

3. Leave both windows open for the next exercise.

Reset Buttons

Reset buttons ("reset") are similar to submit buttons, except that they have a different purpose. Rather than submitting the form, a reset button returns the form to its original state.

Notice that we didn't say a reset button clears the form. It doesn't, unless the form was empty originally. Instead a reset button restores the initial values that we set up with the form.

A reset button looks much like (and is coded similarly to) a submit button:

<input type="reset" value="Undo Changes To Form" />

Exercise Setup

Let's add a reset button to our order page.

Add a Reset Button

1. In the open order.html file, add a reset button and set its value to "Reset Form".

```
...
<br />
<center>
<input type="submit" />
<input type="reset" value="Reset Form" />
</center>
</form>
</body>
</html>
```

2. Save the page and refresh the browser. Notice the reset button.

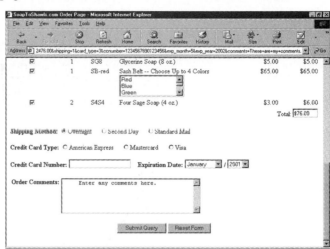

3. Experiment with changing some of the values on the page, including the total, and click the reset button. Notice that the values return to their original state.

4. Leave both windows open for the next exercise.

Button Buttons

No, "button buttons" is not a typo. There is a button input ("button"). A button input is similar to a submit button, except that when the user clicks it, it doesn't submit the form. Instead, we have to assign the button something specific to do when the user clicks it. We will deal with scripts in Chapter 8, but for now be aware that we can use the onclick event to tell the browser to execute a script when the user clicks the button:

```
<input type="button" onclick="someScript()" />
```

Exercise Setup

We're going to add a button that will update the totals based on the "keep this" checkmarks that are checked off at any given time.

Add the Update Total Button

1. In the open order.html file, add the Update Total button, along with its onclick event.

```
...
<tr>
        <td><input type="checkbox" name="item" value="S4S4" checked="checked" /></td><td>2</td><td>S4S4</td>
        <td>Four Sage Soap (4 oz.)</td><td>$3.00</td><td>$6.00</td>
</tr>
<tr>
        <td colspan="3" align="left">
        <input type="button" value="Update Total" onclick="UpdateTotal()" />
        </td><td colspan="3" align="right">Total:
        <input type="text" size="7" name="total" value="$76.00" />
</table>
...
```

2. Save the page and refresh the browser.

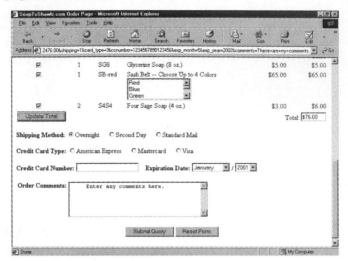

If nothing happens when you click the button, double-check that you've typed the onclick value exactly, including case. JavaScript, which we're using here, is case-sensitive.

3. At the moment, clicking the button causes the browser to run a script that we've provided, but all this script does is to display a window stating that more functionality is coming. Click the button. Close the alert box that appears.

4. Leave the file open in both windows for the next exercise.

Submit Buttons

Once the rest of the page is in place, we're ready to focus on submit buttons.

Order forms often have a pair of submit buttons — one to submit the order and one to cancel it. Of course, if we add two buttons, how will our users distinguish them from each other, if they both are labeled "Submit Query"? (And what do queries have to do with orders, anyway?)

Fortunately, we can also set the value on a submit button, just as we can with reset and other buttons. We can also name buttons. Naming them causes that value to be passed along to the server, where the program can decide what action to take based on which button was pressed.

So if we name the submit button in our sample form:

<input type="submit" name="submitButton" value="Submit Form" />

the name and value will be added to the URL and submitted.

Exercise Setup

We added a submit button when we began our exercise so that we could submit the page as we progressed through the form, but now it's time to refine it. Let's add better-suited submit buttons to the page.

Add Submit Buttons

1. In the open order.html file, add a Submit Order and a Cancel Order button to the bottom of the page, replacing the existing Submit Query (or Submit) button.

The default value of "Submit Query" is more historical than anything else. The advent of forms that do anything but initiate a search is relatively recent.

...

```
</textarea>
</td></tr></table>
<br />
<center>
<input type="submit" name="whichButton" value="Submit Order" />
<input type="submit" name="whichButton" value="Cancel Order" />
<input type="reset" value="Reset Form" />
</center>
</form>
</body>
</html>
```

2. Save the page and refresh the browser. Notice the new buttons.

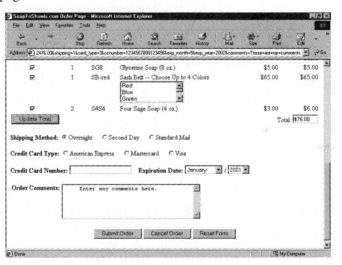

3. Press the Cancel Order button. Notice that despite what the button says, the page was submitted normally. But if we look at the values that were submitted with it, we can see that whichButton was Cancel Order, so the application in the form action can take the appropriate action.

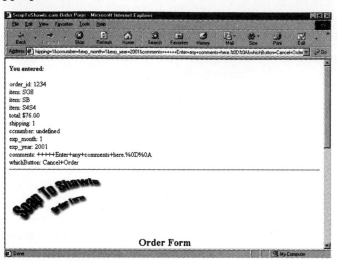

4. Leave both windows open for the next exercise.

Image Inputs

We have one more type of input to consider. Those order buttons are ugly. We can style them, but we can also replace them with an image:

```
<input type="image" name="myButton" src="images/buttonimage.gif" />
```

Images can be used like submit buttons, but they provide even more information than what was clicked. This extra information is the x and y coordinates of the exact spot where the user clicked. This allows us to include more than one button in a single image.

The form action application can take the coordinate information and use it to figure out which button the user was intending to click and act accordingly. If you knew that each button was 200 pixels wide, you would know that if x was less than 200, the user wanted to submit. If it was between 201 and 400, the user wanted to cancel the order, and so on.

Analyzing the x and y coordinates is normally handled by a server-side script, such as an Active Server Page or a Perl script.

If you have ever used server-side imagemaps, this may look familiar. In fact, these buttons use the same concepts as server-side imagemaps.

Exercise Setup
Let's replace those buttons with an image.

Replace the Buttons with an Image

1. In the open order.html file, replace the three bottom buttons with WIP>forms>images>soapbuttons.jpg as an image input.

...

```
    Enter any comments here.
</textarea>
</td></tr></table>
<br />
<center>
<input type="image" name="whichButton" src="images/soapbuttons.jpg" />
</center>
</form>
</center>
</body>
</html>
```

2. Save the page and refresh the browser.

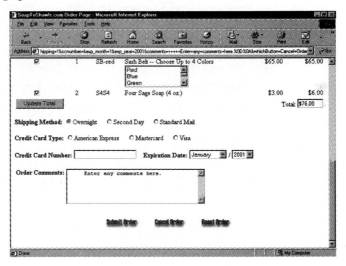

3. Notice that we replaced all three buttons with this one image. So now how would we be able to tell on what the user clicked? Click Cancel Order and watch the results.

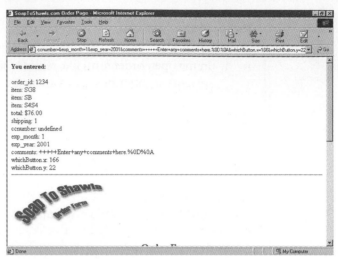

4. Notice that for whichButton, we have x and y values. These are the x and y coordinates of where the user clicked.

5. Close both windows.

Improving Security: Get vs. Post

Because we don't have a Web server, we are somewhat limited in how we can process these forms. What we've been doing is allowing the browser to add all of our information to the URL and then processing it from there. This is known as the "get" method. To use this method properly, we would need to rewrite our form element with a method attribute:

<form action="order.html" **method="get"**>

There are two problems with the get method. First, and least within our control, is the fact that most systems can only handle so much data on a form submitted via the get method. Normally this wouldn't be a problem, however, as the amount of data they can handle is fairly large, but the issue is a concern, nonetheless.

A much more significant problem is that all of our information is right there on the URL line for anyone to see. This includes the user, anyone looking at the user's screen at the time, anyone logging the URLs our user is visiting, or anyone using the user's bookmarks, if he or she happened to bookmark the page. Worse, it gives the user an opportunity to change this information. This can be devastating if you haven't followed our advice and have used a hidden variable for something essential.

Fortunately, there is an easy way to protect against these problems. A second method (again using the method attribute) for processing forms — post — is available and should be used whenever possible. A form submitted via the post method sends the information to the server in a completely different way. The data is embedded in header information the post needs to send to the server anyway.

To use the post method, simply replace "get" with "post" in the form tags method attribute. For example:

```
<form action="myFormAction.asp" method="post">
```

The only difference that you will notice when using the post method is the URL that is returned. For example, a form submitted via the get method would return:

http://www.againsttheclock.com/login.html?username=Nick

whereas the same form, submitted via the post method would return:

http://www.againsttheclock.com/login.html

because the data has been sent to the server in a different way.

There is also a drawback to the post method. If a user bookmarks a posted page, none of the form information comes with it. On the other hand, this can be a blessing. For instance, if the user bookmarks an order confirmation that had been submitted via the get method, he or she might wind up placing a duplicate order when returning to that bookmark!

Overall, however, you should use the post method wherever possible.

Summary

In this chapter, you learned how to create a form, and how to create the various types of elements that can be used on one. You also became familiar with setting initial values for these elements and with different button options. You've discovered the difference between using the get and the post methods for submitting form data, as well as the benefits of the using the post method.

Complete Project A: News Web

Notes:

6 Frames

Chapter Objective:

To learn to use frames to segregate content into individual areas of the page. In Chapter 6, you will:

- Discover the difference between a frameset and a frame, and how to create each.

- Learn to control which content appears in each area (frame) of the page.

- Become familiar with linking between frames.

- Discover how to nest framesets within each other.

- Learn how frames should and should not be used.

Projects to be Completed:

- News Web (A)

- Cyber Travel (B)

- Hunter Films (C)

- North Star Adventure Gear (D)

Frames

One truism of the Web is that users hate to scroll. Another truism is that they resent having to hunt for anything, particularly navigation. They want the navigation to be obvious, right in front of them at all times. Frames were invented to address these needs. The idea behind frames was that the page was subdivided. Certain segments, such as the navigational elements or a menu, would be fixed while other portions of the window would be scrollable or would change their content. This structure served more than one purpose.

First, the user could view a long page without ever losing sight of the navigation. Second, only the part of the page that was changing needed to be loaded by the browser, making a faster-loading page. At the height of their popularity, frames were most commonly used to add a logo and navigational elements to the top of the page and a menu down the left side.

The Frameset

When building a frame-based site, we work with two kinds of pages: the frameset and the frames. A frameset functions much like a layout document. It tells the browser how to lay out the page and what frames to include in each section. Each frame, in turn, tells the browser what content to put into its particular area. Consider the following sample framed site, looking closely at its structure.

This page was created by building a frameset that divides the window into three sections: the navigation at the top, the featured categories on the left side and the content on the right side. There are several ways to achieve this result, all of which involve dividing the page into rows and columns. Some sites take this concept further and even subdivide the rows and columns.

In the following simple example, we create a page with two columns, each of which displays a different page.

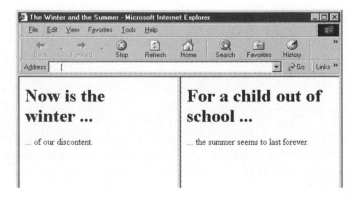

Some sites use frames to incorporate content from other sites into their own offerings. For instance, consider ask.com, which presents a found site (from a search) in the bottom frame, while displaying its own logo and navigation in the top frame.

It should be noted that ask.com makes no secret about what it's doing. Some companies, less open about the process, have attempted to hijack content in this way and have had to endure litigation as a result.

This page was created by building a frameset that split the page into two columns, and then assigning a frame with content to each of those columns. Notice the column attribute (cols=" "), which in this case divides the page evenly.

```
<html>
<head><title>The Winter and the Summer</title></head>
<frameset cols="50%, 50%">
        <frame src="winter.html" />
        <frame src="summer.html" />
</frameset>
</html>
```

The above files, winter.html and summer.html, are regular XHTML files — there is nothing special about them. The content assigned to rows or columns can be regular XHTML files of your choice. Framesets can be divided into columns or rows, each of which can be further subdivided into columns or rows. The width of columns and height of rows can be specified in percentages or in pixels. We can also use * to indicate that we want a particular row or column to take up the balance of the page.

For instance, to create a page where we have two rows, the first of which is 100 pixels high, and the second of which occupies the rest of the page, we would write:

```
<html>
<head><title>The Winter and the Summer</title></head>
<frameset rows="100, *">
        <frame src="winter.html" />
        <frame src="summer.html" />
</frameset>
</html>
```

Using an asterisk "" in a row or column tells the browser that you want this row or column to occupy the balance of the page.*

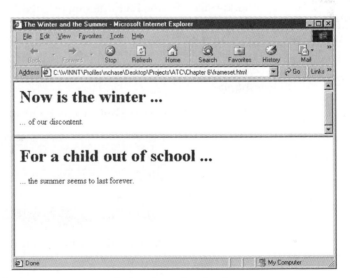

Measurements in percentages are relative sizes, that is, they represent a percentage of the page, or of the frame in which the column or row sits. Measurements in pixels, on the other hands, are fixed sizes. If you want a frame to be a specific size to match the height or width of an image, you will want to use pixels as your measurement for rows or columns. The results of this are most apparent when you resize a window. A frame specified by percentage will adjust to match the new window size, whereas a frame specified by pixels will not.

This chapter uses some non-standard HTML that browsers expect in order to achieve the desired effects. These pages will not validate, but will work in the browser.

Exercise Setup

The Free 'Til It Sells site illustrated previously is the framed Web page that we'll construct in our exercises. We've left the borders on in the above graphic so that you can see the structure clearly, but we'll turn them off when we build the page.

We'll add the logo at the top of the page, the navigational elements down the left and the content on the right, as is traditional. Let's start by constructing the frameset.

Create the Frameset

1. In the WIP folder, create a new folder and name it "frames". Navigate to **RF_HTML>Chapter 6,** and copy all of the contents in the folder to **WIP>frames**.

2. Open your text editor and create a new file. Save it in the **WIP>frames** folder as "frameset.html".

3. Create the shell of the frameset (the empty frameset). Create two rows and allot them each a portion of the window (25% and 75%). (Later we can subdivide the second row into two columns).

```
<html>
<head><title>Frameset Page</title></head>
<frameset rows="25%,75%">
</frameset>
</html>
```

4. Add frames of content — menu.html and listing.html.

```
<html>
<head><title>Frameset Page</title></head>
<frameset rows="25%,75%">
   <frame src="menu.html" />
   <frame src="listing.html" />
</frameset>
</html>
```

5. Save the page and open frameset.html in the browser.

6. Notice that you've created two rows and assigned them relative sizes. In fact, it's the sizes that determined how many rows we have, as opposed to the frames we added. Resize the window and watch the row sizes change also. That's fine in some situations, but here we need the top frame to be the same size as the menu elements, so we need to set it to a specific size.

7. Make the top row 125 pixels high, and set the second row to take up the balance of the space.

```
<html>
<head><title>Frameset Page</title></head>
<frameset rows=" 125, *">
    <frame src="menu.html" />
    <frame src="listing.html" />
</frameset>
</html>
```

8. Save the file and refresh the browser. Some browsers have difficulty refreshing frames. If you don't see a difference, you may need to open a new browser window and reopen the page.

9. You will notice that the top frame always matches the size of the menu, even if you resize the window.

10. Leave the windows open for the next exercise.

Nested Framesets

There is no way to create both rows and columns in the same frameset. Instead we replace a row with a frameset that defines the columns (or vice versa), nesting the framesets.

We can add this frameset in either of two ways: directly or through a separate frame document that contains a frameset.

To do this directly, we would add a second frameset within the code where one frame would normally be placed:

```
<html>
<head><title>The Winter and the Summer</title></head>
<frameset cols="50%, 50%">
        <frame src="winter.html" />
        <frameset rows="25%, *">
                <frame src="summer.html" />
                <frame src="spring.html" />
        </frameset>
</frameset>
</html>
```

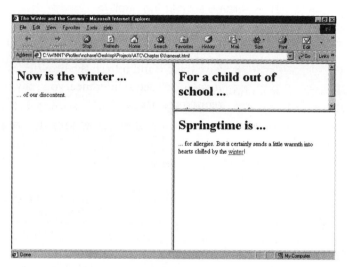

Alternatively, we could retain our original frameset but make the content of one of its frames a frameset itself. For instance, the original frameset would be:

```
<html>
<head><title>The Winter and the Summer</title></head>
<frameset cols="50%, 50%">
        <frame src="winter.html" />
        <frame src="warm.html" />
</frameset>
</html>
```

where the content of warm.html is:

```
<html>
<head><title>The Warm Months of the Year</title></head>
<frameset rows="50%, 50%">
        <frame src="summer.html" />
        <frame src="spring.html" />
</frameset>
</html>
```

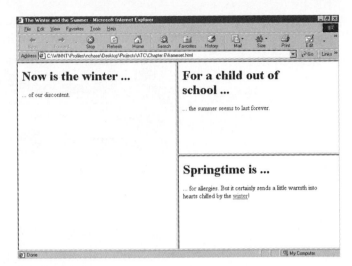

Any number of levels can be nested within each other.

Exercise Setup
In our Free 'Til It Sells site, we've created the first and second row. Now we need to split the second row into two columns.

Subdivide the Second Row

1. Double-check that frameset.html is open in both the text editor and browser.

2. In the text editor, create a new file, name it "subframe.html" and save it in **WIP>frames**.

3. Create a second frameset in subframe.html. This time, instead of specifying rows, specify columns.

```
<html>
<head><title>Subframe Page</title></head>
  <frameset cols="25%, 75%">
    <frame src="featurecat.html" />
    <frame src="listing.html" />
  </frameset>
</html>
```

4. Save subframe.html.

5. Edit frameset.html to point to subframe.html instead of listing.html.

```
<html>
<head><title>Frameset Page</title></head>
<frameset rows="125, *">
  <frame src="menu.html" />
  <frame src=" subframe.html' />
</frameset>
</html>
```

6. Save the file and refresh the browser. Notice that you have replaced the bottom frame with a document that defined its own frameset.

7. Leave the windows open for the next exercise.

Nest the Framesets

1. In the open frameset.html file in the text editor, replace the second frame with the same frameset that is in subframe.html.

```
<html>
<head><title>Frameset Page</title></head>
<frameset rows="125, *">
  <frame src="menu.html" />
  <frameset cols="25%, 75%">
    <frame src="featurecat.html" />
    <frame src="listing.html" />
  </frameset>
</frameset>
</html>
```

2. Save the file and refresh the browser. You shouldn't see any change.

3. Leave both windows open for the next exercise.

Creating Individual Frames

The frameset, of course, is only half the story. We also need to work with individual frames. We can control the appearance of these frames with the addition of attributes.

Controlling Size and Scrolling

Attributes don't affect the content of the frame, just the way that it's presented. For instance, we can control the size of a frame (with the height and width attributes), whether or not the user can change the size (using the noresize attribute), and whether or not a scroll bar will be available (using the scrolling attribute). To create a frame that is a fixed size, cannot be resized by the user and has a scroll bar, you would write the tag:

<frame src="mypage.html" **height="200" scrolling="yes" noresize="noresize"** />

The scrolling attribute has three permissible values: yes, no and auto, which adds a scroll bar only if it's needed. These values apply to both vertical and horizontal scroll bars.

The noresize attribute, like the checked attribute we discussed when we were building forms in Chapter 5, is normally written without a value. To create this as a well-formed XHTML page, we need to give it a value. This accounts for the seemingly redundant appearance.

Exercise Setup
Now we can remove the scroll bar from the top frame.

Control the Size of a Frame

1. In the open frameset.html file in the browser, position the cursor over the horizontal line separating the top frame from the rest of the page. You will see the cursor change to a two-sided vertical arrow. Hold down the mouse button and drag the frame border to resize the frame.

2. This resizing, of course, could ruin our layout. Let's prevent the user from being able to do this by adding the noresize attribute. In the text editor, add it to the first frame.

```
<html>
<head><title>Frameset Page</title></head>
<frameset rows="125, *">
  <frame src="menu.html" noresize="noresize" />
  <frameset cols="25%, 75%">
    <frame src="featurecat.html" />
    <frame src="listing.html" />
  </frameset>
</frameset>
</html>
```

Refreshing the overall page doesn't always refresh individual frames. On the Macintosh you refresh an individual frame by holding down the mouse button in the particular frame and then choosing the Refresh Page (or Refresh Frame) option. On the PC you refresh a frame by Right-clicking on it and then choosing the Refresh Frame option.

3. Save the file and refresh the browser. Now try to resize the frame again. Notice that the arrow doesn't appear.

4. This solves one problem but creates another. At this size, we see a scroll bar on the window, even though it's not really necessary. Eliminate the scroll bar through the scrolling attribute.

```
<html>
<head><title>Frameset Page</title></head>
<frameset rows="125, *">
  <frame src="menu.html" noresize="noresize" scrolling="no" />
  <frameset cols="25%, 75%">
    <frame src="featurecat.html" />
    <frame src="listing.html" />
  </frameset>
</frameset>
</html>
```

5. Save the file and refresh the browser.

Notice that the scroll bar has disappeared from the top row.

6. Leave both windows open for the next exercise.

Controlling Content Location and Borders

Two more aspects of the appearance of the frame that we can control are the location the content and whether or not the frame has a border. We control these features of the frame's appearance by using the marginheight, marginwidth and border attributes.

For instance, we could add a 5-pixel margin around the top and bottom of a frame and a 10-pixel margin on the left and right, by writing:

`<frame src="mypage.html"` **marginheight="5" marginwidth="10" border="0"** `/>`

In the above example, we've also removed the border from around the particular frame. Note that any other frames in the frameset will still have a border. Be careful if you use this process since it can sometimes result in a "half" border if one neighboring frame has a border, but the other doesn't.

Set the Margins and Border

1. In the text editor in the open frameset.html file, set the marginheight on the top frame to 4 pixels.

```
<html>
<head><title>Frameset Page</title></head>
<frameset rows="125, *">
  <frame src="menu.html" noresize="noresize" scrolling="no" marginheight="4" />
  <frameset cols="25%, 75%">
     <frame src="featurecat.html" />
     <frame src="listing.html" />
  </frameset>
</frameset>
</html>
```

It's important to keep in mind your users will be using different sized monitors, many quite different from the one on which you're working. If you were to create a frame using a percentage, then turn off scrolling and prohibit resizing, you could easily and inadvertently create a frame in which users can't see all of the content.

2. Save the file and refresh the browser. Notice that this removed the scroll bar without squeezing the graphics against the top of the frame.

3. Now let's get rid of the borders. Remove the frame borders from the top and left frames.

```
<html>
<head><title>Frameset Page</title></head>
<frameset rows="125, *" >
   <frame src="menu.html" noresize="noresize" scrolling="no" marginheight="4"
frameborder="0" />
   <frameset cols="25%, 75%">
      <frame src="featurecat.html" frameborder="0" />
      <frame src="listing.html" />
   </frameset>
</frameset>
</html>
```

4. Save the file and refresh the browser.

5. Notice that the frame border encloses just that frame. We can see where the other frames end, and we can still see half of a border on the one remaining frame from which we didn't remove borders.

The border attribute isn't actually specified for the frameset element but browsers still support it — for now.

6. Now remove the borders completely.

```html
<html>
<head><title>Frameset Page</title></head>
<frameset rows="125, *" border="0">
    <frame src="menu.html" noresize="noresize" scrolling="no" marginheight="4"
frameborder="0" />
    <frameset cols="25%, 75%">
        <frame src="featurecat.html" frameborder="0" />
        <frame src="listing.html" />
    </frameset>
</frameset>
</html>
```

7. Save the file and refresh the browser. Observe that the borders have now vanished from all frames.

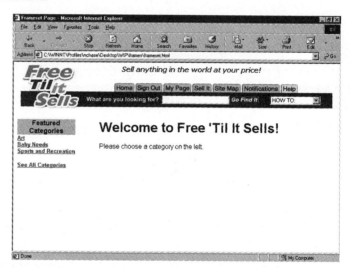

8. Leave both windows open for the next exercise.

Targets

So far we have worked on layout, but haven't yet focused on the real purpose of frames — enabling us to click a link in one frame and cause the content to display in another frame, leaving the overall layout intact.

We can create this structure by adding a target to a link. The *target attribute* tells the browser where to display the new content. There are several ways to add a target.

Named Targets

The most common way to add a target is to name the frames. Once named, we can target them directly. Names can be anything that you want, but they can't start with "_", because that's used by reserved names for special purposes, as we'll see later.

Let's see how named frames work. We can, for instance, structure our familiar seasonal frameset with named frames:

```html
<html>
<head><title>The Winter and the Summer</title></head>
<frameset cols="50%, 50%">
```

```
        <frame src="winter.html" name="winterframe" />
        <frameset rows="25%, *">
                <frame src="summer.html" name="summerframe" />
                <frame src="spring.html" name="springframe" />
        </frameset>
</frameset>
</html>
```

The most common method for adding a target is to name the frames and then add the target attribute that references the named frames.

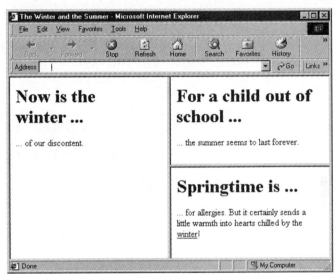

If we then add a target to the link in spring.html that references the winter frame:

...the <a href="spring.html" **target="winterframe"**>winter</a>!

we are adding the ability to change the content of the winter frame. The target attribute tells the browser where to send the content. So if we click on the new link, the browser displays the file spring.html as the content in the frame called winterframe.

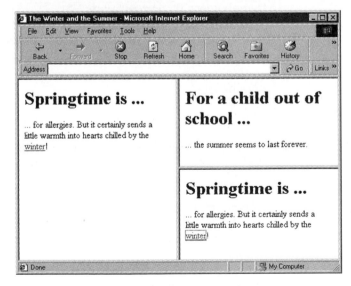

Exercise Setup
Let's apply this to our Free 'Til It Sells site. We'll begin by setting a link so that when users click a featured category, they see our listing in the main content frame.

Set a Target

1. In the browser in the open frameset.html file, click the Sports and Recreation link. Notice that the content displays in the same frame in which you clicked the link.

2. In the text editor, assign names to all frames.

```
<html>
<head><title>Frameset Page</title></head>
<frameset rows="125, *" border="0">
   <frame src="menu.html" noresize="noresize" scrolling="no" marginheight="4"
frameborder="0" name="menu" />
   <frameset cols="25%, 75%">
      <frame src="featurecat.html" frameborder="0" name="categories" />
      <frame src="listing.html" name="content" />
   </frameset>
</frameset>
</html>
```

3. Save the file. Open featurecat.html in the text editor.

4. In the text editor, add the target to the Sports and Recreation link.

```
<html>
<head>
<title>Free 'Til It Sells!</title>
<link href="images/SearchFourm.css" type="text/css" rel="stylesheet" />
<link href="images/Style1.css" type="text/css" rel="stylesheet" />
</head>
<body>
  <table cellspacing="0" cellpadding="0">
   <tbody>
   <tr>
    <td class="headerCell" align="center" width="100%">
     <b>Featured<br/>Categories</b>
```

```
        </td>
      </tr>
      <tr><td class="basefont"><b><a href = "art.html" >Art</a></b></td></tr>
      <tr><td class="basefont"><b><a href = "baby.html" >Baby Needs</a></b></td></tr>
      <tr><td class="basefont"><b><a href = "playground.html" target="content">Sports
and Recreation</a></b></td></tr>
      <tr><td> </td></tr>
      <tr><td class="basefont"><b><a href="allcat.html">See All Categories</a></b></td></
tr>
    </tbody>
  </table>
</body>
</html>
```

5. Save the file and refresh the browser.

6. Click the Sports and Recreation link. Observe that the new page comes up in the frame on the right.

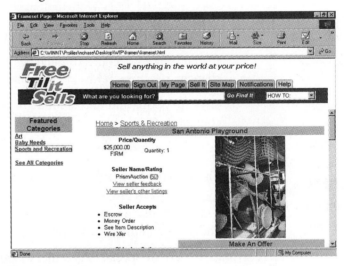

7. Close the browser window.

Using a Base Target

Using named targets is handy because it enables us to send the content to the frame we choose. But if every link on a page has the same target, such as a list of links that all send their information to the "content" frame, setting the targets on the links could be tedious! Granted, we only have four links on this page, but the idea is the same.

To avoid this problem, we can use the <base> tag that we discussed in Chapter 2. This time, instead of specifying a URL, we want to specify a target. So if we wanted to direct that all links without a target should go to the frame called "main," we would add a base tag:

```
<base target="main" />
```

Add a Base Target

1. Open **WIP>frames>featurecat.html** in the text editor and **WIP>frames>frameset.html** in the browser window.

2. Add a base tag to the list of featured categories, and remove the target from the Sports and Recreation link.

…

```
 <base target="content" />
</head>
<body>
 <table cellspacing="0" cellpadding="0">
  <tbody>
  <tr>
   <td class="headerCell" align="center" width="100%">
    <b>Featured<br/>Categories</b>
```

…

Refreshing the overall page doesn't always refresh individual frames. On the Macintosh you refresh an individual frame by holding down the mouse button in the particular frame and then choosing the Refresh Page (or Refresh Frame) option. On the PC you refresh a frame by Right-clicking on it and then choosing the Refresh Frame option.

3. Save the file and open frameset.html in the browser.

4. If your browser was already open before step 3, refresh the left frame to cause the changes to featurecat.html to take effect. You should see no change.

5. Click the Sports and Recreation Link. Notice that the new page still takes you to the content frame.

6. Leave both windows open for the next exercise.

Using Targets for Special Cases

Using a base target can save you the work of adding the target to each link individually. It can also, however, raise a new problem. What do we do if we want one or two links to replace the content in the same frame?

Fortunately, there are special targets that we can use for this and other special cases. These special targets are:

-   **_self.** This target replaces the content in the same frame.
-   **_parent.** This target sends the content to the parent document of this frame. (We'll talk more about parents in a moment.)
-   **_blank.** This target opens a new window for the content.
-   **_top.** This target replaces the main frameset.

Exercise Setup

In our example of the Free 'Til It Sells page, if we click on the See All Categories link, it also moves to the content frame, but that's not what we want. We want it to stay where it is. Not only that, but we want it to stay where it is no matter where the original page starts. Let's add a _self target to solve this problem.

Add the _Self Target

1. Double-check that featurecat.html is open in the text editor and frameset.html is open in the browser.

2. Add the _self target to the See All Categories link and remove the content target.

```
...
<tr><td class="basefont"><b><a href="playground.html">Sports and Recreation<a></
b></td></tr>
<tr><td> </td></tr>
<tr><td class="basefont"><b><a href="allcat.html" target="_self">See All Categories</
a></b></td></tr>
</tbody>
</table>
</body>
</html>
```

3. Save the file and refresh that frame.

4. Click the Sports and Recreation link to verify that the new content still goes to the content frame.

5. Click the See All Categories link. Notice that the list appears in the left frame, despite the base target indicating that it should go to the content frame.

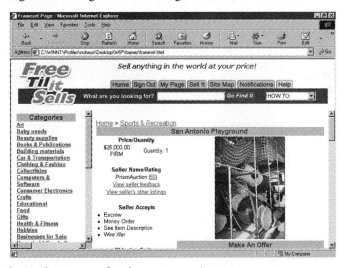

6. Leave both windows open for the next exercise.

Opening a New Window

Another option for creating targets is to open an entirely new window. This can be useful if the content to which you're linking is not directly related to what's on the present page, or if you want to display content from another site. By opening a new window, you avoid sending users away from your site. When they finish looking at the other page, your page remains open to their view.

Another reason to open a new window might be if we have an extensive list of items, such as the results of a search; a new window would prevent the user from having to continually use the Back button and reload the list page.

Exercise Setup

Let's set up our page to open a new window when a user clicks the featured category.

Open a New Window

1. Double-check that featurecat.html is open in the text editor and frameset.html is open in the browser. (If necessary, use the browser's Back button to return to the Featured Categories page.)

2. Change the <base> tag to target _blank.

...

```
 <base target="_blank" />
</head>
<body>
 <table cellspacing="0" cellpadding="0">
  <tbody>
  <tr>
   <td class="headerCell" align="center" width="100%">
    <b>Featured<br/>Categories</b>
   </td>
```

...

3. Save the file and refresh the category frame.

4. Click the Sports and Recreation link to open a new window.

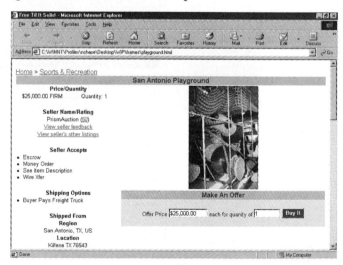

5. Close the new window.

Targeting the Top Window

What if we don't want a new window but instead want to replace the current window (as opposed to the current frame) with new content? We can do that by targeting the top window. This is normally done to "break a user out" of frames, that is, take the user from a subdivided page back to a single page with no frames.

Exercise Setup

Let's link the logo in the top menu to the home page.

Link the Logo to the Main Window

1. Open **WIP>frames>menu.html** in the text editor and **WIP>frames>frameset.html** in the browser.

2. Target the link on the logo to the _top frame.

…

```
<tbody>
<tr>
 <td valign="top" width="144" rowspan="4">
  <a href="home.html"target="_top" >
   <img height="112" src="images/FTIS_logo.gif" width="144" border="0" />
  </a>
 </td>
```
…

3. Save the file and refresh the top frame in the browser.

4. Click the logo. Observe that the page no longer has any framed sections.

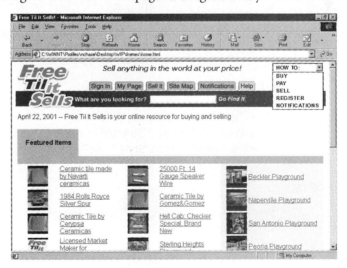

5. Close both windows, leaving the applications open.

Parents

Another common way of managing content in a frameset is to send content to the *parent*, or the frameset that calls the current frame. For instance, when we sent the playground page to its own window, it didn't look very good because the top interface disappeared.

Instead, we might decide to send this page to the bottom two frames. These two frames are part of a single frameset that can be considered the "parent" of each frame. To replace these bottom frames (and keep the top frame) with linked content, we can send the content to the parent of the link page. For instance, let's look at the frameset:

```
<html>
<head><title>Frameset Page</title></head>
<frameset rows="125, *" border="0">
   <frame src="menu.html" noresize="noresize" scrolling="no" marginheight="4"
frameborder="0" name="menu" />
   <frameset cols="25%, 75%">
      <frame src="featurecat.html" frameborder="0" name="categories" />
      <frame src="listing.html" name="content" />
   </frameset>
</frameset>
</html>
```

We're talking about a link in featurecat.html, in the categories frame, so logically the "parent" would be the frameset enclosing that frame, in bold here.

Exercise Setup
Let's test that theory by setting the base target as _parent.

Check the Parent

1. Open featurecat.html in the text editor.

2. Set the base target as "_parent".

```
<html>
<head>
<title>Free 'Til It Sells!</title>
<link href="images/SearchFourm.css" type="text/css" rel="stylesheet" />
<link href="images/Style1.css" type="text/css" rel="stylesheet" />
  <base target="_parent" />
</head>
<body>
  <table cellspacing="0" cellpadding="0">
   <tbody>
   <tr>
    <td class="headerCell" align="middle" width="100%">
     <b>Featured<br/>Categories</b>
    </td>
   </tr>
...
```

3. Save the file and refresh the frame.

4. Click the Sports and Recreation link. Notice that the entire window was replaced. Can you figure out why this occurred?

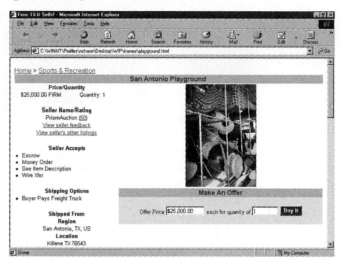

5. Close featurecat.html in the text editor.

Determining the Parent

Now, at first, this would seem to make no sense. Why would the entire window be replaced if we only specified the parent?

It's because of the definition of parent. The parent of a frame is not actually the frameset containing the frame, but the document containing that frameset. So if we want to send the listing to the bottom half of the window, we need to return to our original frameset.

Exercise Setup

Let's restructure the Free 'Til It Sells framesets.

Change the Parent

1. Open frameset.html file in the text editor, replace the second frameset with a frame containing subframe.html.

```
<html>
<head><title>Frameset Page</title></head>
<frameset rows="125, *" border="0">
   <frame src="menu.html" noresize="noresize" scrolling="no" marginheight="4"
frameborder="0" name="menu" />
   <frame src="subframe.html" name="content" />
</frameset>
</html>
```

2. Save the file and refresh the browser.

3. Click the Sports and Recreation link. Notice that the content now occupies the entire bottom portion of the page.

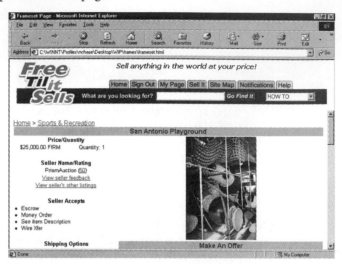

4. Close both applications.

The Future (or Nonfuture) of Frames

Now that we've discussed frames, you may be thinking that they seem to be very useful and wondering why you don't you see them used more often. For instance, even FreeTilItSells.com, which we've been using as an example, doesn't use frames on the actual site.

Why Frames Have a Bad Reputation

When frames first appeared on the scene, browsers were fairly primitive, and Web-page authoring tools even more so. There were few WYSIWYG editors, and those few were quite basic. Even Netscape, which created frames, didn't support them in the original Netscape Navigator Gold, their authoring tool!

As a result, authors learned how to work with frames in the same way that they learned to do everything else in HTML: they copied the code. At that time, the accepted method for learning HTML was to examine sites that they liked and study the code as source.

This was fine, but many Web-page authors, when coding by hand, did what they had to and no more, not coding to the standard. (This is, in fact, one of the reasons for the strictness of XHTML.)

So the majority of frames-based sites were not viewable on non-Netscape browsers — which is to say, most browsers. (At this time, the majority of Web users were still using a browser called Mosaic, or a very primitive earlier version of Netscape that didn't understand frames.)

But while it makes sense that the frames wouldn't appear, why wouldn't anything else appear? Look at the source code of frameset.html. There's no actual content in it, just instructions that a non-frames browser doesn't understand and ignores. Such browsers would see a blank window instead of the planned page.

For the last couple of years, this has become much less of an issue, as virtually all modern browsers support frames. But now that we're moving towards designing pages for other

The reason you don't often see frames is that many Web-site creators are purposely steering clear of frames, for a number of reasons.

devices like PDAs and cell phones, the issue of accessibility of framed pages is becoming important once again.

Accommodating the Frameless: noframes

Fortunately, there is a way to provide content for browsers that don't recognize frames. This is done by use of the <noframes> element. For instance, we could add some explanatory text to frameset.html.

```
<html>
<head><title>Frameset Page</title></head>
<frameset rows="125, *" border="0">
   <frame src="menu.html" noresize="noresize" scrolling="no" marginheight="4"
frameborder="0" name="menu" />
   <frame src="subframe.html" name="content" />
</frameset>
<noframes>
 <body>
   Thank you for visiting freetilitsells.com. We are currently working on a frameless
version of this site.
 </body>
</noframes>
</html>
```

Unless they're used extremely carefully, frames are one of those design elements that can mark you as an amateur.

We had previously omitted the body tag, since it would have prevented the frames from working. Now we can restore it. Any browser that understands frames also understands the <noframes> tag and knows to ignore the content within it. Any browser that doesn't understand frames won't understand <noframes> either. That means it will ignore the frameset, frame and noframes tags, displaying only (in this case) the body content.

The Elimination of Frames in XHTML 1.1

All of this will become a moot point when XHTML 1.1 becomes the standard. In their effort to more completely separate content and presentation, the authors of XHTML 1.1 have removed frames from the XHTML 1.1 recommendation (as of this writing). Frames are relegated, instead, to a separate module that may or may not be supported by the browsers.

This removal of frames from the standard is not really a loss. Many of the features of frames, such as creating multiple independent sections on a page and being able to change content in only one section, can be duplicated using other features, such as divs, which we'll discuss in Chapter 7, and scripts, which we'll discuss in Chapter 8. Still, thousands of existing Web pages use frames, and new framed sites will probably be built until supporting them becomes a problem, so it's important to understand how to work with them.

Summary

In this chapter, you learned how to create framed pages. You discovered how to create a frameset and lay it out on the page. You became familiar with manipulating the appearance of individual frames. You also learned to direct content to a specific frame, to the entire window or to a new additional window. You also became familiar with some of the issues with using frames, and the alternatives for non-frames-savvy browsers.

Notes:

Free-Form Project #1

Assignment

The owner of Scrumptious Gifts (SG), a premium fruit and vegetable dealer, plans to expand the market for their high-quality produce. Their sales are currently made from a single store location in the Castor Valley of California, or by mail and phone orders from their direct mail advertisements. They want to launch a Web site to stimulate wider consumer interest in their fresh, specialty items that can be shipped overnight anywhere in the continental United States.

You will design and construct a Web site to promote their products and encourage use of their toll-free phone number for convenient 24-hour ordering. (Keep in mind that as the site generates more sales, SG plans to add an online order system.)

Applying Your Skills

To develop the site, you will:

- Plan the design and navigation strategy of the Web site.
- Use only one primary page layout to ensure consistency across the entire site.
- Make certain that your navigation system is fully functional, with links from the home page to each individual page, and from those pages back to the home page.
- Use Cascading Style Sheets to format the text so that you can experiment with different font combinations. Edit the supplied text, as necessary, to fit your design.
- Produce a product list, with product categories and individual items hyperlinked to the appropriate page/bookmark.
- Select from the supplied images to illustrate the Scrumptious Gifts products in your layouts. You may add your own images, if necessary.

Specifications

Make certain that the home page fits in a 600 × 400 pixel space, and that it's not too large — 48k should be the maximum size.

Build your basic page and navigation strategy using tables or frames. All pages should be linked with both a graphical navigation method as well as alternative text hyperlinks. Use thumbnail images to link to larger images and more detailed information. Be sure that your navigation system within the site is easy to use and logical.

Included Files

While we have supplied images and text files for this project, you're free to add your own text and graphics. Graphic files are JPEG files. A catalog of the images has been included in PDF format (ScrumptiousCatalog.PDF). The text file that is supplied, Scrumptious Gifts.TXT, contains copy about the company and a variety of featured products. Again, supplement the copy, as you like.

Publisher's Comments

This project is typical of many real-world assignments: the client has supplied certain images that they believe have the right look and feel to represent them. Although you might prefer different images, your job is to incorporate their images with your creative vision in a site that will not only please the client, but also help expand their sales and promote their image.

Be sure to pay attention to details: image size, page download times, and easy and logical navigation. A unique and compelling Web-site design that is efficient and easy to navigate is the best solution.

Review #1

Chapters 1 through 6

In Chapters 1 through 6, you've learned most of the basic techniques that you'll need to create and produce basic professional-looking Web sites. You're familiar with basic page structure, adding hypertext links and images, Web forms, and layout using tables and frames. After completing the first half of this book, you should:

- Be familiar with the history of the World Wide Web, the foundations of HTML and XHTML, and the differences between them. You should know how to use tags, elements and attributes to create and format text and images on a page. You should also understand the difference between presentation and content.

- Be comfortable with linking both text and images to other pages or to a specific point on a page. You should know the difference between relative and absolute URLs, when each is appropriate, and how to recognize different types of URLS. You should understand file organization and directory structures, and how to access a file in a specific directory or the parent of a directory.

- Understand about internal and external Cascading Style Sheets, and how to use them to control the look and feel of your site, including via font, color and background images. You should be comfortable creating styles, and using selectors such as tags, classes, IDs, pseudo-classes and the universal selector, *, to apply them to your content. You also understand the various ways to set color values.

- Know how to use XHTML tables to lay out and align content. You understand how to create basic tables, and how to cause cells to span multiple rows or columns. You are familiar with how to structure a table, and how to nest one table within another. You know how to apply styles to tables and their content.

- Be able to create Web forms that include different types of form inputs, such as text, checkboxes, radio groups and drop-down menus, and be familiar with the different button options and how to control their appearance and initial values. You should know how to use more than one button on a form, and how to use images as buttons. You should also understand how to determine the page or script to which it is sent.

- Be comfortable creating a frameset and its frames, and understand how to determine the content contained in each frame. You are able to nest framesets within each other, and to determine the parent of a frame. You know how to create a link that will display content in a different frame, and how to control the appearance of those frames. You have practiced using frames to create a new window, and providing a page that will be usable even to those without frames-capable browsers.

7 Alignment and Placement — Divs

Chapter Objective:

To learn how to organize XHTML pages and create layers using divs. In Chapter 7, you will:

- Learn the difference between block and inline elements.

- Discover how to use spans and divs to apply style information to large and small areas of a page.

- Become familiar with creating multiple layers of information on a page.

- Learn how to control the visibility and placement of sections of a page.

Projects to be Completed:

- News Web (A)

- Cyber Travel (B)

- Hunter Films (C)

- North Star Adventure Gear (D)

Alignment and Placement — Divs

In the first half of the book, you learned the basics of Web development. You now have all of the building blocks that you need to build a Web site.

But what kind of Web site will you build? For some purposes, especially if the general public will never see a site, functionality may be all that is required. But the chances are that you want to do more — you're probably chomping at the bit to start adding all the bells and whistles that can really make a site sing.

With the basics under your belt, let's begin by learning to take more control over pages.

Block vs. Inline Elements

A Web page has a natural flow. Generally, it starts at the top and moves downward, left to right, to the bottom of the page. Along the way, we can introduce elements, such as line breaks or images, which have an impact on that flow.

For instance, as we saw in Chapter 1, if we were to present a large block of plain text, that's how it would appear — as a large, plain block of solid text.

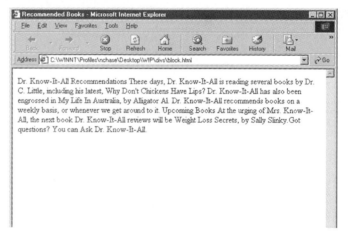

While we can add elements to it, such as links or images, it still remains a large block of solid-set text.

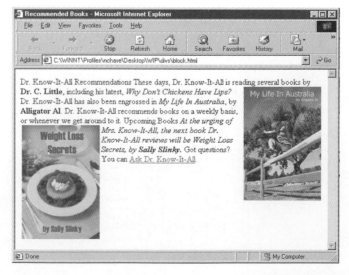

There are elements that we add, however, such as separate paragraphs or horizontal rules, to break up the visual flow.

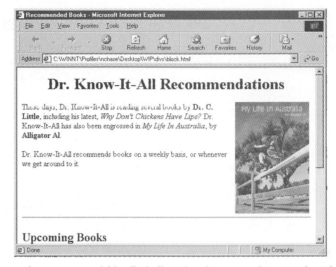

The first question, of course, would be "why"? Why do some elements break up a page and others don't? The difference lies in the types of elements. The majority of elements, such as bold, link, image and so on, are called "inline elements." They don't affect the flow of the page other than to take up a little bit of space. They don't add any extra lines or white space.

Other elements, however, such as headers, paragraphs and so on, are called "block elements." They appear on a line by themselves, no matter what else is around them. There's no need to put a line break before and after a header, for example. That's built into the nature of the header so the browser will take care of that for you.

We can see a demonstration of these elements in action if we alter the definition of a header using style sheets. Block vs. inline characteristics are handled by the display property of an element. By changing that value, we can change an element's behavior. As shown here:

```
<html>
<head><title>Block vs. Inline</title></head>
<body>
<b>Just because text is bold… </b> won't put it on a line by itself. <b style = "display:block">Unless, of course</b> it has been designated as a block element.
</body>
</html>
```

Because we designated the bold text as a block element, it appears on its own line, even though we did nothing else to cause it. So simply by adding the display value of block, we can cause an element to be separated from the preceding and following text.

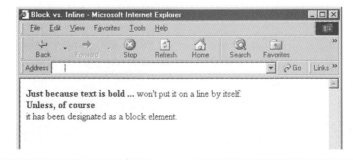

Exercise Setup

We can see this even more clearly if we look at the heading on our book recommendations page.

Change the Display Property for an Element

1. In the WIP folder, create a folder called "divs". Navigate to **RF-HTML>Chapter 7**, and copy the contents of the folder to the **WIP>divs** folder.

2. Open **WIP>divs>recs.html** in both the browser and the text editor.

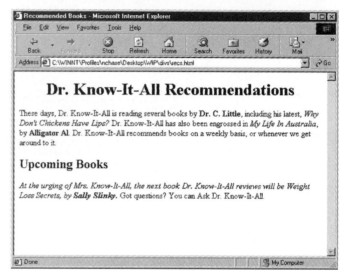

3. Add a style sheet, and alter the styles for the headers so that they are inline elements.

```html
<html>
<head><title>Recommended Books</title>
<style type=text/css">
    h1 { display: inline }
    h2 { display: inline }
</style>
</head>
<body>

<h1 align="center">Dr. Know-It-All Recommendations</h1>

These days, Dr. Know-It-All is reading several books by <b>Dr. C. Little</b>, including his
latest, <i>Why Don't Chickens Have Lips?</i> Dr. Know-It-All has also been engrossed in
<i>My Life In Australia</i>, by <b>Alligator Al</b>.
Dr. Know-It-All recommends books on a weekly basis, or whenever we get around to it.

<h2>Upcoming Books</h2>

<i>At the urging of Mrs. Know-It-All, the next book Dr. Know-It-All reviews will be
<i>Weight Loss Secrets</i>, by <b>Sally Slinky</b>.</i>

Got questions? You can Ask Dr. Know-It-All.

</body>
</html>
```

4. Save the file and refresh the browser. Notice that the headings are now within the text instead of being on their own lines.

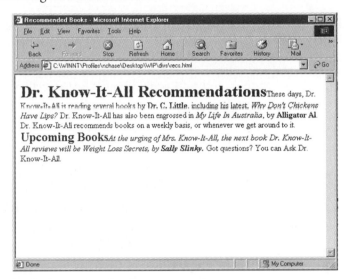

5. Leave both windows open for the next exercise.

Understanding this distinction between block and inline styles can make a difference when we want to apply styles to entire sections.

Using Span to Apply Styles

If you visit the W3C site, you will find an article entitled "<FONT> Tag Considered Harmful!". The <font> tag, on the surface, is an incredibly handy tag. For instance, we can use it to simulate a header tag, and put the header in red, by writing:

<font size="+3" color="red" face="Verdana">Dr. Know-It-All Recommendations</font>

The trouble with writing this is that this tag is now 100% presentational. There is nothing that indicates to a browser (or search engine, or text reader) that this is important content. So for example a search engine will not know to rank this text higher in importance than surrounding text.

Worse, since most of the styling that can be done to text can be implemented with the font tag, some WYSIWYG editors use it for just about everything, rather than putting in proper tags, which obliterates the idea of separating content from structure, as we discussed in Chapter 1. So one of the first tags to be removed from XHTML 1.1, when it is finalized, will be the <font> tag.

So what do we do if we really just want to apply a style to one particular section? One choice is to use the <span> tag. This is an inline element that is generally used to indicate an area that needs a particular style. For instance, the same effect that we got from the <font> tag can be achieved using span and style information:

<span style="font-family: Verdana; font-size: 16pt; color: red;">Dr. Know-It-All Recommendations</span>

Exercise Setup

We can also use the span tag, for instance, to indicate a class for our book titles, just as we added actual style information.

The size of your window will affect how this page displays because the text wraps at the edge of the window. Notice, too, that even though we changed the display property of the headers, everything else about them, such as their size and font weight, stayed the same. That's one of the great aspects of CSS: we only need to specify the properties we want to change. Everything else will remain as it was.

Add Class Information with Span

1. In the open file recs.html in the text editor, add a class for book titles (remove the header classes), and add the class to the titles.

```
<html>
<head><title>Recommended Books</title>
<style type=text/css">
    .book { color: red; }
</style>
</head>
<body>
<h1 align="center">Dr. Know-It-All Recommendations</h1>
These days, Dr. Know-It-All is reading several books by <b>Dr. C. Little</b>, including his
latest, <span class="book"><i>Why Don't Chickens Have Lips?</i></span> Dr. Know-It-
All has also been engrossed in <span class="book"><i>My Life In Australia</i></span>,
by <b>Alligator Al</b>.
Dr. Know-It-All recommends books on a weekly basis, or whenever we get around to it.
<h2>Upcoming Books</h2>
<i>At the urging of Mrs. Know-It-All, the next book Dr. Know-It-All reviews will be <span
class="book"><i>Weight Loss Secrets</i></span>, by <b>Sally Slinky</b>.</i>
Got questions? You can Ask Dr. Know-It-All.
</body>
</html>
```

While it is certainly possible to abuse the <span> tag in the same way in which the <font> tag was abused, the <span> tag is normally used in conjunction with CSS classes, as opposed to adding the style directly to the tag. This eliminates the problem by designating the content as a particular type, rather than just affecting how it looks. It just happens that this designation also sets the style.

2. Save the file and refresh the browser. Notice that the text within the spans is now red.

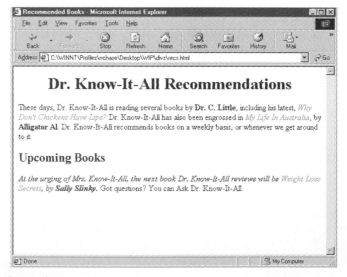

3. Close both windows.

Using Divs for Placement

When designers first began building Web pages, one point that bothered them the most was the inability to place an item in a specific location on a Web page. Sure, they could affect the flow of a page somewhat, such as by using tables with specific sizes, but for the most part, items just landed where they landed with no real control.

Divs changed all that. A *div* is a section of the page, and we can use it to place content in a particular location. As an example, let's consider a page from Doneger Online, a site for fashion manufacturers and retailers.

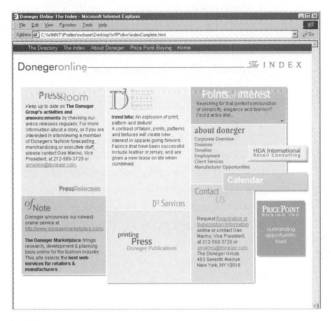

Placement on the Page

Look carefully at the page. It would be possible to build each of the text boxes as a div with a background color. This would have its advantages, such as the ability for the boxes to grow with the content, but the graphic effects, such as the overall drop shadow against a white background, make that a very complicated proposition.

Instead, we'll start out with a single background image created in Adobe Photoshop, Adobe Illustrator, Macromedia Freehand, Corel Painter or another graphics program that will let you combine graphic elements and text elements.

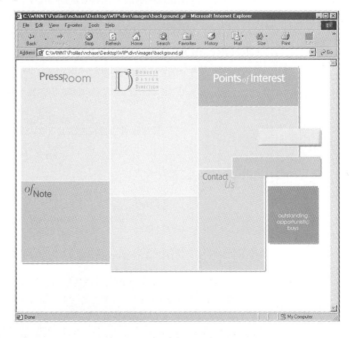

Once we have the image, we're ready to add our content. We want to cause the text to overlay the image, so just adding the graphic as an image won't work. We could add the graphic as the background of the page, but we don't really want it to be so separated from the content. Instead, we'll create a div with the image as its background and the text as its content. Doing this will require us to create several divs, some with text and images.

```
<html>
<head><title>Doneger Online The Index</title>
</head>
<body>

<div style="background:url(images/background.gif);
height=522;width=748;z-index:0;">
<div style="height:60px; width:216px; position:absolute;
top:50; left: 460;">
<p>Searching for that perfect combination of simplicity,
elegance and fashion? Find it at the Met...</p>
</div>
</div>

</body>
</html>
```

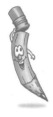

Nesting divs can have another effect. If a style, such as a font or color change, is applied to the outside div, any divs nested within it will also be affected by it.

Here we actually have two divs, one with a background image and the other with text. The second div is nested within the first in order to place the content in a particular position. Notice that the div has its own tag — <div> — that can contain a style attribute that includes positioning information. As you can see, this positioning information is given in terms of pixels. (We will discuss absolute and relative positioning later in the chapter.) In addition to the positioning information, the style attribute can include the specific URL for the image being used as a background.

Another way that divs are affected by nesting is in positioning. If we're going to set the position for the top and left edges of the div, we need a reference point. By setting the position to absolute, we're telling the browser to use the containing block, or div, as a reference point. If the containing div doesn't have any positioning information on it, however, the browser uses the page itself as a reference point.

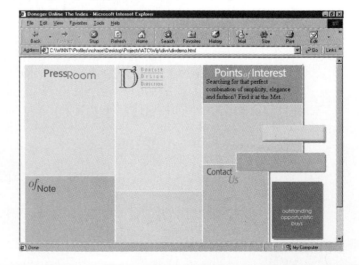

Exercise Setup

We can use this method to build our page, known on the site as "The Index." Let's start by placing the basic text.

Add and Position Basic Text

1. Open **WIP>divs>index.html** in the browser and text editor.

2. Add the base image **WIP>divs>images>background.gif** to the page.

```
...
<html><head><title>Doneger Online The Index</title>
<link rel="stylesheet" href="donegerstyle.css" type="text/css"/>
</head>
<body>
<div style="background:url(images/background.gif);">
Request <a href="/marketplace/register.asp"> Registration ... New York, NY 10018.
<p>Keep up to date on <b>The Doneger Group's activities ... </p>.
<p><b>trend bite:</b> An explosion of print, pattern and ... when combined.
<p>Searching for that perfect combination of simplicity, ... the ...</p>
<p>Doneger announces our newest online service at ... manufacturers</b>. </p>
</div>
</body>
</html>
```

It's not unusual to see style information placed directly on a div. Normally it's better to put this information into classes and assign the classes to the div, but when the purpose is mostly positioning, it's usually done this way.

3. Save the file and refresh the browser.

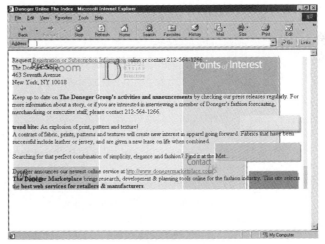

4. What a mess! The text is running off the edge of the image, nothing is in the correct box and generally the impression is confusing. Let's take care of it by first focusing on the big picture. Set the size of the overall div to be the same size as that of the background image, that is, 522 pixels high by 748 pixels wide:

```
...
<link rel="stylesheet" href="donegerstyle.css" type="text/css"/>
</head>
<body>
<div style="background:url(images/background.gif); height:522px;width:748px;">
Request <a href="/marketplace/register.asp"> Registration ...
...
```

Placement of content using divs is one area where there can be significant differences between Netscape 4.x and Internet Explorer 5.x, due to idiosyncrasies in the way that the browsers have been built. We will try to build pages that will work in both, but occasionally, something that seems trivial will cause an unexpected change in one browser or the other. When the difference is significant, we will point it out.

Style5 is the fifth style in use on the Doneger Online site. The others, in use on other parts of the site, are named style1, style2, style 3 and so on. You should also choose a consistent naming convention, whether it is hierarchical, as it is here, or descriptive, as in head1, boldtext, etc.

5. Save the file and refresh the browser.

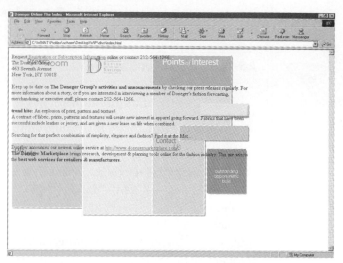

6. That's a little better, but we still have to place our text more precisely. Let's start by creating the boxes in which each of our sections will live.

Give each section of text its own div, noting that each div has a specific height and width. Set the text style information to style5 using the class attribute, since it affects the size of our boxes.

```
<link rel="stylesheet" href="donegerstyle.css" type="text/css"/>
</head>
<body>
<div style="background:url(images/background.gif); height:522px; width:748px;" class="style5">
<div style="height:155px; width:137px;">
Request <a href="/marketplace/register.asp"> Registration or Subscription Information</a> online … New York, NY 10018.
</div>
<div style="height:179px; width:200px;">
<p>Keep up to date on <b>The Doneger Group's … </p>.
</div>
<div style="height:179px; width:180px;">
<p><b>trend bite:</b> An explosion of print, …when combined.
</div>
<div style="height:60px; width:216px;">
<p>Searching for that perfect combination of … the ...</p>
</div>
<div style="height:123px; width:201px;">
<p>Doneger announces our newest online service at … manufacturers</B>. </p>
</div>
</div>
</body>
</html>
```

There are various ways to determine what the coordinates and sizes for these boxes should be. The easiest and most convenient way would be to open the background image in an image-manipulation program (like Photoshop, Illustrator, Freehand, and so on) and use the information it gives to determine the coordinates. If this is not an option, there is always the old standby of trial and error.

Note: we've reordered the text to the exact sequence in which the divs are to appear on the page. Although the positioning code places all divs where they belong on the page, some browsers have trouble if the divs aren't in the exact sequential order in which they are to appear.

7. Save the file and refresh the browser.

8. Notice that the class information that we placed on the main div carried over into the enclosed divs. In other words, the nested divs inherited the class information.

Notice also that although we set a height on the main div, it expanded to fit the amount of content that we placed in it, as you can see by the repeat of the background image at the bottom of the page. That repeat of the background image will disappear as we move our divs into position.

Some browsers, most notably Netscape 4.x, need the divs to be coded in the same order in which they will appear on the page. Rearrange the order of the divs to match the sequence in which the text will appear on the final page. In other words, the divs that appear at the top of the page should be listed before the divs that appear at the middle or bottom of the page. Also add the following positioning information.

…

```
<div style="background:url(images/background.gif); height:522px; width: 748px;"
class="style5">
<div style="height:123px; width:201px; position:absolute; top:340px; left:20px;">
<p>Doneger announces our newest online service …
<div>
<div style="height:179px; width:200px; position:absolute; top:100px; left:240px;">
<p><b>trend bite:</b> An explosion of print, …
</div>
<div style="height:60px; width:216px; position:absolute; top:55px; left: 460px;">
<p>Searching for that perfect combination of …
</div>
<div style="height:179px; width:180px; position:absolute; top:80px; left:20px;">
<p>Keep up to date on <b>The Doneger Group's …
</div>
```

```
<div style="height:155px; width:137px; position:absolute; top:340px; left:460px;">
Request <a href=" marketplace/register.asp"> Registration or Subscription Informa
tion</a> online …
</div>
</div>
</body>
</html>
```

9. Save the file and refresh the browser.

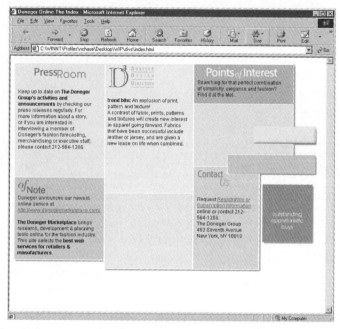

10. Leave both windows open for the next exercise.

Layers and the Z-Index

Now we need to look at a common situation: overlapping. Often, two divs will overlap, and not always in a desirable manner. Like the layers in a Photoshop or Illustrator document, however, the divs can be arranged in such a way that we control which overlaps the other, and how.

The *z-index* property determines which divs will appear in front of each other. The higher the z-index, the further to the front of the stack the div will appear. For instance, we can create three overlapping divs:

```
…
<body>
<div style="position: absolute; background-color:red; height:100px; width:100px;
top: 50px; left: 50px;"></div>
<div style="position: absolute; background-color:blue; height:100px; width:100px;
top: 100px; left: 100px;"></div>
<div style="position: absolute; background-color:green; height:100px; width:100px;
top: 50px; left: 150px;"></div>
</body>
…
```

because they're added in the order in which they appear, the first and second divs will be partially obscured.

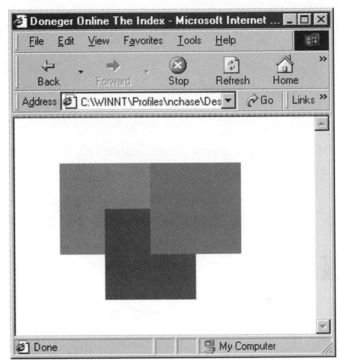

If instead, we wanted the order reversed, we could do this using the z-index, by changing the value (number) assigned to each div:

```
...
<body>

<div style="position: absolute; background-color:red; height:100px; width:100px;
top: 50px; left: 50px; z-index:2;"></div>
<div style="position: absolute; background-color:blue; height:100px; width:100px;
top: 100px; left: 100px; z-index:1;"></div>
<div style="position: absolute; background-color:green; height:100px; width:100px;
top: 50px; left: 150px; z-index:0;"></div>

</body>
...
```

The higher the number in the z-index, the closer to the "front of the page" the div will appear.

Exercise Setup

We can see in the completed page that the HDA International and Calendar boxes overlap the About Doneger box. This doesn't look like a problem, because the actual content doesn't extend into that area, but we need to be able to click these two buttons, so it could be an issue. Let's use the z-index to take care of this problem and add graphical elements.

Adjust Layers Using the Z-Index

1. In the open file index.html in the text editor, add the graphics to the page, each in their own divs.

…

```
<div style="height:155px; width:137px; position:absolute; top:340px; left:460px;">
Request <a href="/marketplace/register.asp"> Registration or Subscription Information</a> …
</div>
<div style="position:absolute; top: 239px; left: 544px;">
<img src="images/calendar.gif" alt="Calendar" />
</div>
<div style="position:absolute; top: 169px; left: 597px;">
<img src="images/hda.gif" alt="Henry Doneger Associates" />
</div>
<div style="position: absolute; top: 116px; left: 451px;">
<img src="images/about.gif" alt="About Doneger" />
</div>
<div style="position: absolute; top: 310px; left: 350px;">
<img src="images/d3.gif" alt="Doneger Design Direction" />
</div>
<div style="position: absolute; top: 400px; left: 265px;">
<img src="images/press.gif" alt="Press Releases" />
</div>
<div style="position: absolute; top: 275px; left: 100px;">
<img src="images/pressroom.gif" alt="Press Room" />
</div>
<div style="position: absolute; top: 320px; left: 623px;">
<img src="images/ppb.gif" alt="Price Point Buying" />
</div>
</div>
</body>
</html>
```

2. Notice that we've deliberately omitted the height and width from both the images and the divs in this code. We did so to make it easier for you to see the components of the code. In fact the height and width of all images should always be specified, but the divs will automatically size themselves based on the images even without these dimensions, so they don't need separate dimensions. In an actual production situation, the code would look like this:

…

```
<div style="height:155px; width:137px; position:absolute; top:340px; left:460px;">
Request <a href="/marketplace/register.asp"> Registration or Subscription Information</a> …
</div>
<div style="position:absolute; top: 239px; left: 544px;">
<img src="images/calendar.gif" alt="Calendar" width="208" height="46" />
</div>
<div style="position:absolute; top: 169px; left: 597px;">
<img src="images/hda.gif" alt="Henry Doneger Associates" width="155" height="42" />
```

```
</div>
<div style="position: absolute; top: 116px; left: 451px;">
<img src="images/about.gif" alt="About Doneger" width="254" height="122" />
</div>
<div style="position: absolute; top: 310px; left: 350px;">
<img src="images/d3.gif" alt="Doneger Design Direction" width="97" height="26"/>
</div>
<div style="position: absolute; top: 400px; left: 265px;">
<img src="images/press.gif" alt="Press Releases" width="162=" height="59" />
</div>
<div style="position: absolute; top: 275px; left: 100px;">
<img src="images/pressroom.gif" alt="Press Room" width="124" height="21" />
</div>
<div style="position: absolute; top: 320px; left: 623px;">
<img src="images/ppb.gif" alt="Price Point Buying" height="122" width="46" />
</div>
</div>
</body>
</html>
```

3. Save the file and refresh the browser. Notice that the images now appear on the page.

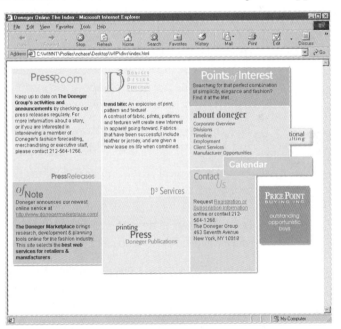

4. While all of our images are in place, the HDA International image on the right is behind the About Doneger box. Bring that image forward by adding z-index values to both divs.

...

```
<div style="position:absolute; top: 169px; left: 597px; z-index: 10;">
<img src="images/hda.gif" alt="Henry Doneger Associates" />
</div>
<div style="position: absolute; top: 116px; left: 451px; z-index: 1;">
<img src="images/about.gif" alt="About Doneger" />
</div>
```

...

5. Save the page and refresh the browser. Observe that the HDA International graphic now appears "in front of" the background.

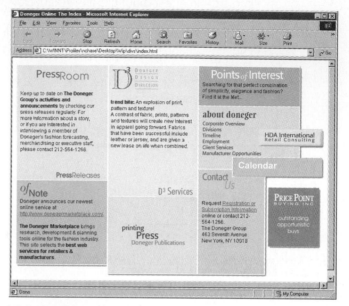

We could assign HDA International a z-index value of 2, since we are only ordering two items. It's wise, however, to plan for the unexpected. Just in case additional items later need to be placed between these two, use values with more numbers between them — the results will be the same in the short run, and you may thank yourself later if you have to make changes.

6. Leave both windows open for the next exercise.

Relative vs. Absolute Placement

In all of these examples we've considered or built, we've been using absolute positioning. With absolute positioning, specific coordinates are set for each div, and no matter what else is done on the page, those divs will be rendered at those exact places on the page.

This rigidity, however, is not always convenient. What if we would like to add other items and adjust the existing items accordingly?

As you may recall, the completed Doneger Online page includes a navigation bar across the top. If you were to add this navigation bar to the page on which you've been working in your exercises, part of your existing page would be obscured by the placement of the new bar. You would undoubtedly prefer to move all of your divs down appropriately, but what a nightmare it would be to readjust every one of those positions individually!

Fortunately, this isn't necessary. We can make positioning information relative to the normal position (that is, the position it would have appeared in if no positioning information had been added to it) of the div. For instance, consider:

```
…
<body>
<div style="position: relative; top: 100px; left: 100px; width: 300px;
border: solid 1px black;">
This text should appear 100 pixels under and to the right of where it would appear if there
were not positioning information.
</div>
</body>
…
```

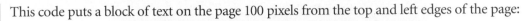

This code puts a block of text on the page 100 pixels from the top and left edges of the page:

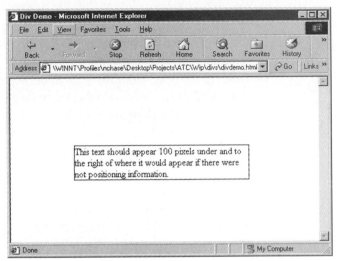

If we then add more information to the page, what will happen?

```
...
<body>
<h1>Headings take up a lot of room ...</h1>
<img src="demo.GIF" align="left" alt="blocks" />
As do images.
<div style="position: relative; top: 100px; left: 100px; width: 300px; border: solid 1px
black;">
This text should appear 100 pixels under and to the right of where it would appear if there
were not positioning information.
</div>
</body>
...
```

Although we've added information, we are able to maintain that 100-pixel margin to the top and left of our text block. That's what relative positioning does. Rather than stay at its original coordinates, the text block moves to 100 pixels right and down from where it otherwise would have appeared.

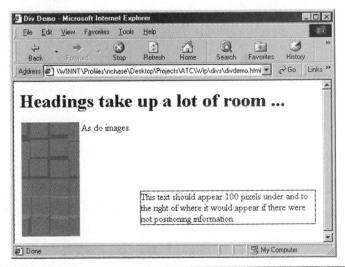

Exercise Setup

We can use this principle to shift the content of all of the divs on our Doneger Online page.

Enable Divs to Move Using Relative Placement

1. In the open index.html file in the text editor, add the background image, and then add the navigation to the top of the page. Because the text is white on a white background, we won't be able to see it, so turn on the border of the table so you can at least see the location of the table.

```
<html><head><title>Doneger Online The Index</title>
<link rel="stylesheet" href="donegerstyle.css" type="text/css"/>
</head>
<body background="images/base4.gif">
<table cellspacing="15" cellpadding="0" border="1">
<tbody>
<tr>
<td><a class="topnav" href="/directory.asp">The Directory</a></td>
<td><a class="topnav" href="/index.asp">The Index</a></td>
<td><a class="topnav" href="/index.asp#">About Doneger</a></td>
<td><a class="topnav" href="/11.0/newpricepoint.asp">Price Point Buying</a></td>
<td><a class="topnav" href="/">Home</a></td>
</tr>
</tbody>
</table>
<div style="background:url(images/background.gif); height=522;width=748;"
class="style5" >
<div style="height:123px; width:201px; position:absolute; top:340; left:20;">
...
```

2. Save the file and refresh the browser.

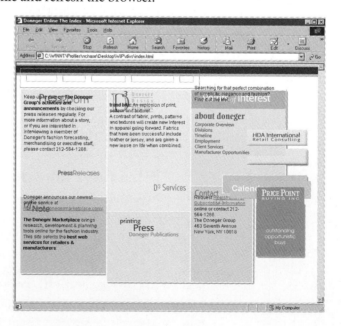

3. Notice the lower-right corner of the new table, where the div is actually in the same space as the added content. Because the main div doesn't have positioning information, the nested divs are placed relative to the page, so they didn't move.

4. What we need to do is to make a new container that will provide a stable reference point for the divs, but will also move with the page content. We'll also include the original div in this container and align it so that it's once again positioned properly. Also, our style information should be on the outermost div, so move the class designation to the new one. Make the background div part of the new div's content.

...

```
</tbody>
</table>

<div style="position: relative;" class="style5">
<div style="background:url(images/background.gif); height:522px; width: 748px;
position:absolute; top:15; left:10; z-index:0;">
</div>
<div style="height:123px; width:201px; position:absolute; top:340; left:20;">
<p>Doneger announces our newest online service at...
</div>
```

...

5. Save the file and refresh the browser.

6. Notice that you have moved the divs down the page, as desired, but the table of navigational components is not in the proper position at the top of the page. The problem lies in the rather large value for cellspacing, which was used to space out the items on the bar. To compensate for this cellspacing and cause the navigational items to appear over the dark blue (so that the white text is readable), we need to cause the table to begin above the actual top of the page.

7. Put the table in its own div and turn off the table border.

```
...
</head>
<body background="images/base4.gif">
<div style="position: absolute; top: -7px;">
<table cellspacing="15" cellpadding="0" border="0">
<tbody>
<tr>
...
</tr>
</tbody>
</table>
</div>
<div style="position: relative;" class="style5">
...
```

8. Save the file and refresh the browser.

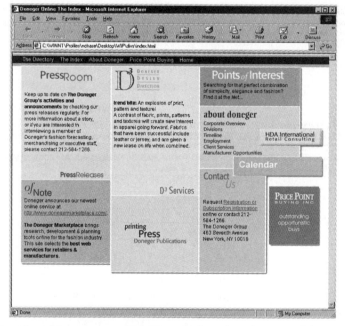

9. Notice that the table now appears correctly, but that the rest of the content (as a group) is now too high. We want to move the set of content down, but we don't want to set a particular position. We want it all to be a little bit lower than it would normally be. Set the top of the main div to be 25 pixels lower than its original position .

```
...
</tbody>
</table>
</div>
<div style="position: relative; top: 25px;" class="style5">
<div style="background:url(images/background.gif); height=522;width=748;
position:absolute; top:15; left:10; z-index:0;">
</div>
...
```

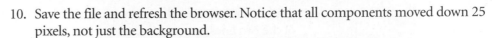

10. Save the file and refresh the browser. Notice that all components moved down 25 pixels, not just the background.

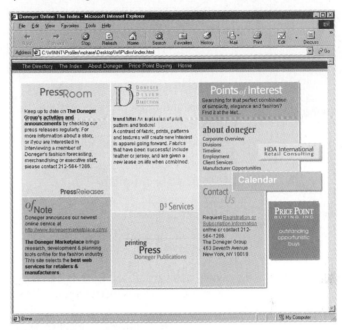

11. Leave both windows open for the next exercise.

Adding Style to Divs

We've focused primarily on how to use divs to style and position content on a page. As we've seen, this gives us enormous latitude and control over our content. Up to now, divs have been used only as a way to apply styles to the divs' content. But that's about to change. Where before the divs were simply conceptual containing blocks, we will now give them physical form using CSS properties such as borders, colors and visibility.

Borders, Border Styles and Color

You can apply borders to individual divs. There are three characteristics you can specify with borders: size, color and style. To specify size, you use absolute sizes, such as 1px, or relative sizes, such as thin, medium and thick. You can apply colors to either the border of a div or the background, but in either case, use the same values that we have used elsewhere on Web pages. You have 10 border styles from which to select for your divs. The 10 that have been defined for divs are:

- **solid**. This style specifies the traditional, familiar, single-line border.

- **none**. This style specifies that there will be no border on the div.

- **hidden**. This style is similar to none. The difference between them lies in the results of any border-conflict resolution. For instance, two objects, usually table elements, may share a common border but have different styles specified. Under normal circumstances, the browser will use the flashier style, so none will always "lose." Hidden, on the other hand, takes precedence over other styles and will always "win."

- **dotted**. This style specifies a simple line of dots. On most version 4.x and 5.x browsers, this is rendered the same as dashed.

- **dashed**. This style is similar to dotted, except that the line is made up of dashes.

See Chapter 3 for the details about specifying color on Web pages.

At the time of this writing, Netscape 6 and Internet Explorer 6 (still in beta) are the only generally available browsers that support all of these border styles. That's the bad news. The good news is that you can still use them, as long as your design isn't dependent on the borders not looking like solid lines. (This is why Doneger opted for the graphic treatment to make HDA International appear to jut out of the page.) If the browser supports it, it will look correct. If the browser doesn't support it, it will still look decent. This ability to look presentable, whether or not looking as intended, is known as "graceful degradation."

- **double.** This style results in two parallel, solid lines. The width of the combination of the two lines, however, is equal to the specified width, so the effect won't be visible unless the specified width is at least 3px.

- **groove** and **ridge.** These two styles (which are not well supported at the time of this writing) specify a border that looks like it has been carved into or juts out of the page, respectively. On version 4.x and 5.x browsers, these styles result simply in a solid line.

- **inset** and **outset.** These two, also limited to the newest browsers, make the entire box look like it's carved into or jutting out of the page. On version 4.x and 5.x browsers, this looks like a plain solid line.

Create a Border on a Div

1. In the open index.html file in the text editor, add borders of different thickness to some of the graphic divs.

…

```
<div style="position: absolute; top: 310px; left: 350px; border: 1px solid black;">
<img src="images/d3.gif" alt="Doneger Design Direction" />
</div>
<div style="position: absolute; top: 400px; left: 265px; border: 4px double black;">
<img src="images/press.gif" alt="Press Releases" />
</div>
```

…

2. Save the file and refresh the browser. The graphics are now surrounded by borders.

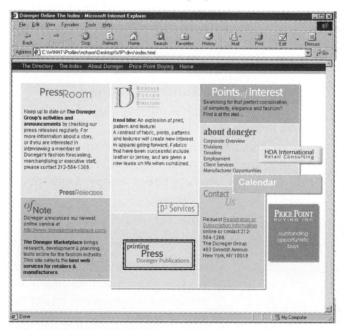

3. Leave both windows open for the next exercise.

Notice that by adding the border, we're actually offsetting the div by the width of the border, so be sure to take that into account when positioning your divs.

Using Border Shorthand Properties

The border property is known as a shorthand property because it enables us to set several properties at once. When we write:

border: 1px solid black;

it's actually the same thing as writing out more fully:

border-width: 1px; border-style: solid; border-color: black;

But actually, the shorter version is even more of a shorthand than might be obvious, because in actuality, all four sides of a border on a block can be set independently. When we specify just the border, the browser assumes that we're referring to all four sides at once. If we specify two values, the first value will be applied to the top and bottom, and the second will be applied to the left and right.

Exercise Setup

Let's change the Doneger Press div to show the border only on the bottom and right. We'll use both specific and shorthand properties.

Use Specific Border Properties

1. In the open index.html file in the text editor, remove the D3 border and the top and left borders on the Doneger Press div by specifically applying the borders to only the bottom and right side of the div.

```
...
<img src="images/about.gif" alt="About Doneger" />
</div>
<div style="position: absolute; top: 310px; left: 350px;">
<img src="images/d3.gif" alt="Doneger Design Direction" />
</div>
<div style="position: absolute; top: 400px; left: 265px; border-right: 7px double black; border-bottom-width: 7px; border-bottom-style: double; border-bottom-color: black;">
<img src="images/press.gif" alt="Press Releases" />
</div>
<div style="position: absolute; top: 275px; left: 100px;">
...
```

2. Save the file and refresh the browser. Notice that the border shows only on the bottom and right edges of the div.

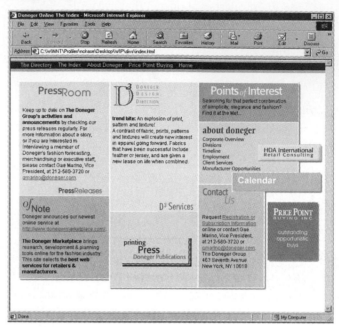

3. Leave both windows open for the next exercise.

Visibility

Sometimes we want to place content that we don't want the user to see. There can be several reasons for this, but the most common is that we want the content to remain hidden until the user does something, such as clicking a button. Then we want the content to appear.

This interaction is normally handled with scripts, which we'll discuss in the next chapter, but for the moment we can look at actually hiding and revealing content directly.

There are three values for the visibility property: visible, hidden and collapse. Visible is, of course, the default property, showing the div. Hidden and collapse both mean that the content isn't shown, but collapse is used to remove a table row or column, as well.

One point to remember is that whether or not content is visible, it still affects the layout (and download time) of the page.

If we were to add text to the previous example we used for absolute vs. relative positioning:

```
…
<body>
<div style="position: relative; top: 100px; left: 100px; width: 300px; border: solid 1px black;">
This text should appear 100 pixels under and to the right of where it would appear if there were not positioning information.
</div>

This information should appear underneath the boxed div.
</body>
…
```

we might expect that the newly added text would appear either right under the box or at the top of the page. Actually, neither happens.

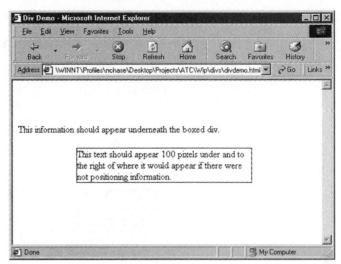

Because the original positioning of the boxed text was relative, the new text appears below where the boxed text would have been. If we then were to set the visibility of the boxed text to hidden, it would have no effect on the position of the new text:

…
```
<body>
<div style="visibility: hidden; position: relative; top: 100px; left: 100px; width: 300px;
border: solid 1px black;">
This text should appear 100 pixels under and to the right of where it would appear if there
were not positioning information.
</div>

This information should appear underneath the boxed div.
</body>
```
…

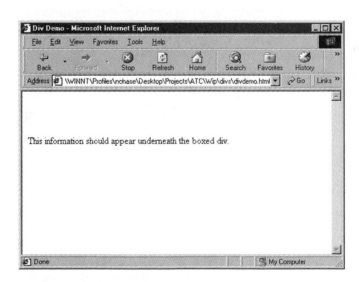

To avoid having items shift position because of other, invisible, items, we can use the display property to eliminate the boxed div's effect on the layout of the page:

```
…
<body>
<div style="display: none; top: 100px; left: 100px; width: 300px; border: solid 1px black;">
This text should appear 100 pixels under and to the right of where it would appear if there
were not positioning information.
</div>

This information should appear underneath the boxed div.
</body>
…
```

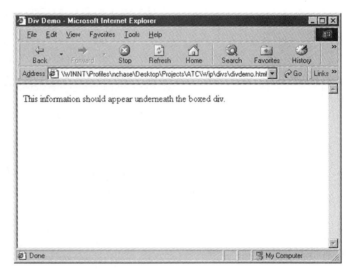

With the display property set to none, the page is laid out as though the other content didn't exist.

Exercise Setup
Let's look at this in the context of our Doneger page.

Control the Visibility

1. In the open index.html file in the text editor, add a div with more information to the top of the page.

```
…
<td><a class="topnav" href="/">Home</a></td>
</tr>
</tbody>
</table>
</div>
<div style="height:75px;width:700px;background-color: rgb(123,187,206);
"class="style5">
<div style="height:50px;width:600px;position:absolute;
top:25px;left:75px;align:center;">
```

Inspiration awaits at the \<b\>First Lady\</b\> exhibit at the Mactown Museum. Most of the 80 plus original outfits are accompanied by photographs of the First Lady wearing them, bringing both costume and First Lady to life. Redecorations of the White House are also featured. Absolutely a must-see!
\</div\>
\</div\>
\<div style="position: relative; top: 25px;" class="style5"\>
\<div style="background:url(images/background.gif); height:522px;width:748px; position:absolute; top:15px; left:10px; z-index:0;"\>
...

2. Save the file and refresh the browser.

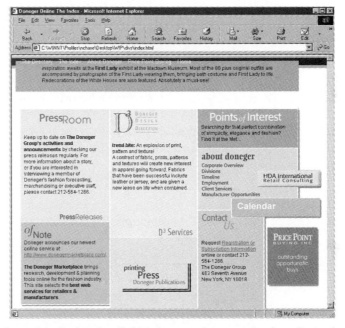

3. Notice where this div has landed in the page layout. The first div is absolutely positioned, so it has been taken out of the flow of the page. The new div, however, isn't, so it sits at the top of the page and displaces the third div downward.

4. Set the visibility to hidden.

...

\</table\>
\</div\>
\<div style="**visibility:hidden**,height:75px;width:700px; background-color: rgb(123,187,206); "class="style5"\>
\<div style="height:50px;width:600px;position:absolute; top:25px;left:75px;align:center;"\>
  ...

5. Save the file and refresh the browser.

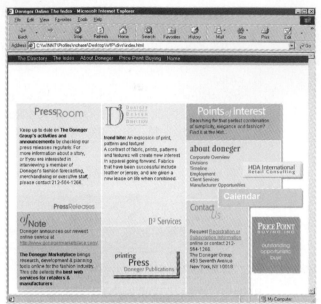

6. Notice that even though the div itself is now invisible, the bottom section is still pushed downward. Use the display property to avoid the problem.

…

```
</table>
</div>
<div style="display:none;height:75px;width:700px; background-color: rgb(123,187,206);
"class="style5">
<div style="height:50px;width:600px;position:absolute; top:25px;left:75px;align:center;">
```
…

7. Save the file and refresh the browser. Now notice that the empty space is gone, and the main div is where it should be.

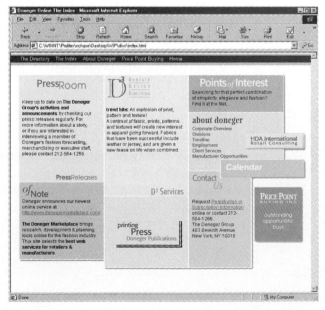

8. Close both windows.

Summary

In this chapter, you have learned to use divs to place content on a page. You've also explored how to use absolute and relative positioning to adapt content to the page, and how to make content disappear from the user's view while retaining the desired layout.

Complete Project B: Cyber Travel

Notes:

8 *Client-side Scripting*

Chapter Objective:

To learn how to use client-side scripting to create more interactive, faster and more compelling Web sites. In Chapter 8, you will:

- Learn about the different scripting language options.

- Become familiar with the concept of objects, events and functions.

- Discover how to create rollovers.

- Become familiar with validating the information on a form before it's submitted.

- Learn about the different events that can be scripted.

- Discover the advantages and disadvantages of preloading images.

Projects to be Completed:

- News Web (A)

- Cyber Travel (B)

- Hunter Films (C)

- North Star Adventure Gear (D)

Client-side Scripting

Gone are the days when Web sites were just static pages of information. Long, long gone. Today's Web site is an information resource, and there is so much information that if interactivity weren't already a buzzword, it certainly would be now. Users want an experience that's customized for them, that responds to what they do.

The first browsers were like the old mainframe dumb terminals. All they could do was retrieve and display information from a server. That meant that if there was any interactivity at all, it was managed by the server. The user clicked on a link and received that specific information from the server. Users typed in a particular search term in which they were interested and the server responded by providing that information.

Now the pendulum is swinging back in the other direction. Browsers are becoming more and more powerful, opening more options for client-side scripting.

Scripting in the Browser

Replacing applications with the browser has actually been in the works since the mid 1990s, but in these cases, the replacements were more like sophisticated Web sites than what we would think of as traditional applications.

The client in client-side is, of course, the browser. These days we can do very sophisticated things by giving the browsers instructions — if the user does this, you do that. At first this functionality was limited to displaying the date on the page or checking a form before it was submitted to ensure that it had been filled out correctly (or at least completely).

These days much more is possible. We can change images when the user rolls the mouse over them. We can create content dynamically. We can even, in some cases, replace traditional applications.

Adding Interactivity

One way that client-side scripting helps us is by enabling the user to interact with the page. For instance, we might have a section of the page that provides information on whatever topic the user happens to be viewing. As the user rolls over different objects with his or her mouse, different related information can be displayed in that designated area.

Scripting also allows us to take into consideration points like the size of the user's browser window (perhaps displaying the smaller version of an image if the window is smaller) and the color depth of the screen.

We can also use scripting to help us to overcome the differences between browsers. For instance, we might create a beautiful layout for Microsoft Internet Explorer that is rendered differently by Netscape Navigator. By using scripting, we can detect which browser is being used and display the page appropriately.

Saving Time: Eliminating a Trip to the Server

Another place that scripting can be useful to us is when users are filling out forms. This can be an unpleasant experience, and often by the time the users hit the Submit button, they're more than ready to move on to another page or another topic.

Unfortunately, without scripting, the page must be submitted and users must wait for the server to give them the next page — even if that page is just a message telling them that they couldn't possibly have been born on February 31, so to go back and correct information!

It's much more convenient to have a script that checks the form before submission and alerts users immediately if they're missing a piece of information or if something is clearly incorrect.

JavaScript vs. VBScript vs. ECMAScript

The first client-side scripting appeared in Netscape Navigator 2.0, where it was called "LiveScript." It was, however, heavily based on the then-emerging Java language, and was quickly renamed "JavaScript."

Meanwhile, back in Redmond, CA, Microsoft employees were working on their own scripting language. Based on their popular Visual Basic programming environment, VBScript was Microsoft's choice for client-side scripting. VBScript may be a bit easier to use, but it has a serious drawback: it is only available in Microsoft Internet Explorer (IE) on Windows systems. Sometimes we write pages that work better in IE, but they do still function in other browsers and on other platforms. Using VBScript for a Web page means that the scripting functionality is completely unavailable if the user isn't on a Windows system using IE.

So JavaScript remained, and still remains, the standard client-side scripting language. Still, there were differences in the way the different browsers handled it, leading to compatibility problems. Microsoft even felt that their version was so different that they had to give it a new name: Jscript.

A standard was desperately needed, and that work was taken up by the European Computer Manufacturer's Association (ECMA), which combined the various implementations into ECMAScript. So far, though, the name hasn't caught on. So for the purposes of this book, when we refer to JavaScript, Jscript or ECMAScript, we're talking about the same language.

Including a Script on the Page

Scripts can be included on the page, like any other content, but we don't want the user to see the scripts, so we include them within <script></script> tags, as in:

```
<script>
   (our script goes here)
</script>
```

By writing our code in this way, a browser that understands scripting knows not to display the content within those tags on the page, but instead to check it for instructions.

But what happens if a browser doesn't understand scripting? We said earlier that if a browser doesn't understand a tag, it will ignore that tag. For instance, if we wrote:

```
<myNewTag>Hey there!</myNewTag>
```

the browser won't show an error, it will just display:

Hey there!

without any special formatting.

This doesn't help us with scripting, however, because we don't want the browser to display the script.

This situation is precisely the opposite of the problem we had earlier with non-frames-savvy browsers. There we handled the situation by using the <noframes></noframes> tag. In that case we wanted the browser to display the information only if it didn't understand frames. In this case we don't want it to display it at all.

*Developers did have the option of **double publishing**, creating two different versions of a page. But if the functionality could be universally available by using JavaScript, why write and debug it twice? It's fairly reasonable to make minor changes to accommodate a different browser, but something else entirely to have to do the whole site over again.*

What we can do to resolve this problem is use the ability to create HTML comments. Comments are sections of text, such as information about the page itself, that the browser doesn't display. These comments are used by Web-page authors to remind themselves (or someone else looking at the page), later, of what being done, in case changes are needed. We can use this same ability to tell older browsers to ignore scripting information. So what we wind up with is:

```
<script>
<!--
    (our script goes here)
//-->
</script>
```

Written in this way, an older browser will ignore the content within the comments, and a script-aware browser will ignore the comment marks because they're within a script tag.

The Basic JavaScript: alert()

The most basic script that we can write is one that pops up a message when the page is loaded. This alert box can say anything that we want, but we don't have any control over its appearance. (The appearance of the alert box is dictated by the specific browser.) Typically, we'll use an alert box to let users know about something important, such as a change to a site's policies or a problem with a form that they're filling out. To do this, we'll use the alert() function.

HTML tags in scripts often interfere with validation even though a page works properly.

The alert() function is placed between <script></script> tags. This command takes an *argument*, information that is passed to the program. In this instance, the information is the text to be displayed in the alert box:

```
<style type="text/javascript">
        alert('Hi there!');
</style>
```

Notice that the language for the script is specified using the type attribute. Microsoft Internet Explorer also supports a language called VBScript, but it is rarely used on a page because it's not supported by other browsers. Notice also that within the script, we use single quotes to indicate text, rather than double quotes.

If we were to include this within the content of a page, it would cause the browser to render the page up to this point, then display an alert box, which includes a button the user can use to acknowledge the alert.

Add an Alert Box

1. In the WIP folder, create a new folder called "scripts". Create a new file in the text editor called "alert.html", and save it to the **WIP>scripts** folder.

2. Open **WIP>scripts>alert.html** in the browser.

3. Create the basic document. Add some minor content. We'll add the script in the next step.

```
<html>
<head><title>Script Test Document</title></head>
<body>
<p>This document will execute a script.</p>
<p>See? There it was.</p>
</body>
</html>
```

4. Save the file and refresh the browser.

5. Here we see the entire page rendered. No surprises so far — just a regular Web page. Now let's add the script, telling the browser to use JavaScript (as opposed to VBScript).

```
<html>
<head><title>Script Test Document</title></head>
<body>
<p>This document will execute a script.</p>
<script type="text/javascript">
    alert('This is an alert box.');
</script>
<p>See?  There it was.</p>
</body>
</html>
```

The language for a script used to be set via the language attribute. The language attribute is deprecated and will eventually be eliminated entirely, having been replaced by the type attribute.

6. Save the file and refresh the browser.

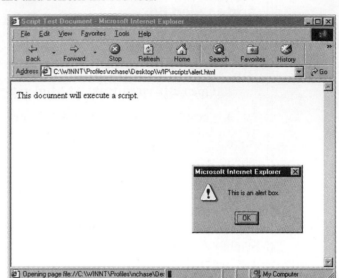

7. There are two points to notice. First, we only directed the browser to display an alert box. The browser took care of everything else — displaying not only the alert box but also the OK button and the yellow alert signal.

   The second matter to note is that unlike before, all of the content is not displayed. Instead, the browser rendered all of the content up to the script, then it executed the script and now it is waiting for a response before rendering anything else.

8. Click OK, and notice that the rest of the page is finally fully rendered when the alert box disappears.

9. Leave both windows open for the next exercise.

Events, Functions and Objects

Now that we've seen a simple script in action, let's explore how scripting works overall. In general, *scripting* is an interaction between events, functions and objects.

Events

There are times, such as when we're outputting text, that we want to execute a script in the middle of the loading of a page. In most cases, however, we want to control the timing more precisely. Usually we want a script to *fire* (execute) when a something specified happens, such as when the user clicks an item or the page finishes loading. We saw a simple example of this in Chapter 5 on forms when we clicked the Update Total button. These specified activities are called "events," and a number of them are predefined in JavaScript. (A more complete list is available later in this chapter in the section on Other Events.)

Functions

Most of the time, when we want something to happen, we're actually looking for a series of steps, not just one. When these steps are grouped together they're called a "function," like the alert() function discussed above. Fortunately for us, we can create custom functions, and then call them whenever we want.

We'll look more closely at functions shortly.

Objects

Finally, most of the time, these events and functions pertain to objects. When we say object, we don't necessarily mean in the generic sense of a physical thing. Instead, we mean a very specific kind of item, which has properties (similar to attributes, in that they describe something about the object) and *methods* (which are something that the object actually does).

For instance, the most basic object with which we'll work is the document object. Everything on the page, such as the images and form elements, is part of the document object. We'll frequently use the browser's understanding of the document object to point to these elements using a script. We'll see this more clearly when we create a rollover. Consider a brief example of using a method, document.write(), and looking at a property, document.location.

Notice the structure here. First we list the object, the document and then the property or function following a period. So document.location refers to the location property of the document object. The write() function is similar to the alert() function, in that both can take an argument.

We can also use both document.write() and document.location much as we used the alert() function, with the <script></script> tag. For instance, we could have the browser print out the current location with:

```
<script type="text/javascript">
        document.write( document.location );
</script>
```

Exercise Setup
Let's see this in action.

Look at an Object

1. Open **WIP>scripts>alert.html** in the browser and text editor if it's not already open.

2. Change the script so that instead of displaying an alert box, our text is output directly to the page using document.write().

```
<html>
<head><title>Script Test Document</title></head>
<body>
<p>This document will execute a script.</p>
<script type="text/javascript">
    document.write('This is not an alert box.')
</script>
<p>See?  There it was.</p>
</body>
</html>
```

3. Save the file and refresh the browser.

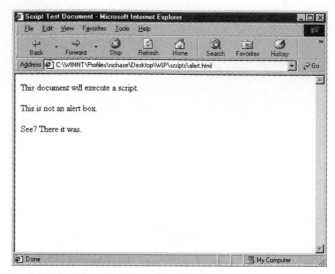

4. Leave both windows open for the next exercise.

Using the document.write() Method

So in this case, the document did its job and wrote the text in the middle of the page, but without interrupting and waiting for us, as the alert box did. We can use document.write() to write information that may only be available to scripts, such as information about the document.

Let's take a look at a common task, outputting the date, which would use another built-in function, Date().

Now, what we're outputting is plain text, which is known in programming circles as "a string" because it's a sequence of characters. Conveniently, we can build a string in the same way that we would build a string of beads, using the plus sign (+) as our connector. When a script contains more than one statement, we use a semicolon to let the browser know where one ends and the next one begins.

Output the Date

1. Open **WIP>scripts>alert.html** in the text editor and browser, if it's not already open.

2. Change the script to output today's date, using semicolons to separate the statements.

```html
<html>
<head><title>Script Test Document</title></head>
<body>
<p>This document will execute a script.</p>
< script type="text/javascript">
   document.write('<b>Today is ');
   document.write(Date());
   document.write('.</b>');
</script>
<p>See?  There it was.</p>
</body>
</html>
```

The date and time, in this case, are the date and time of the user's computer, not the server. Sometimes this is important to remember, such as when you want to display the end of an auction. The user's local time may be irrelevant; it's the server's time you want. In such situations, JavaScript won't help you.

3. Save the file and refresh the browser.

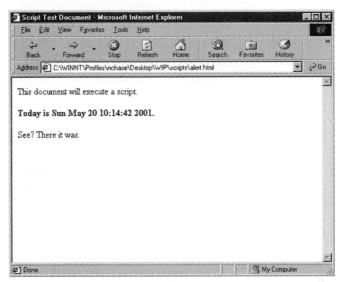

4. Notice that because we added bold tags to the script, the text is bold. If we were to view the source, we would see the script, but the browser displays the results of the output.

5. Now make this into a single string, using plus signs to connect the components.

```
<html>
<head><title>Script Test Document</title></head>
<body>
<p>This document will execute a script.</p>
< script type="text/javascript">
    document.write('<b>Today is ' + Date() + '.</b>');
</script>
<p>See?  There it was.</p>
</body>
</html>
```

Remember, an argument is information that is passed on to a function.

6. Save the file and refresh the browser. You should see no change from the previous version (except, of course, for the time, if your browser outputs it as part of the date).

7. Leave both windows open for the next exercise.

Using the document.location Property

As you can see, the mechanics of outputting information to the page are fairly straightforward. Now let's look at outputting a document property. Another common task is to output the location of the document so that when it's printed, users know where they obtained the information. We can provide this information using the document.location property.

Now, you may notice that when we wrote document.write(), we followed it with a pair of parentheses, but when we wrote document.location, we didn't. That's one way to tell the difference between a function, which might take an argument, and a property, which can't.

Exercise Setup
Let's output the location of our document.

Output a Property

1. In the open alert.html file in the text editor, add a new script to output the location of the document.

```html
<html>
<head><title>Script Test Document</title></head>
<body>
<p>This document will execute a script.</p>
<script type="text/javascript">
    document.write('<b>Today is ' + Date() + '.</b>');
</script>

<p>This page was printed from
<script type="text/javascript">
    document.write(document.location);
</script>
.</p>

<p>See?  There it was.</p>
</body>
</html>
```

2. Save the file and refresh the browser. Notice that the location is displayed on the page.

Your location will be different, of course. On a real Web site, this location would be in the form of http://www.myserver.com/ alert.html.

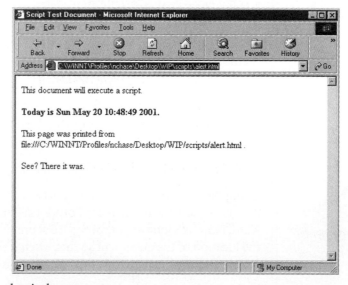

3. Close both windows.

Attaching a Script to an Event

We've covered the basic scripting concepts, so let's apply them by setting up a page where they will execute in response to particular events.

Let's consider the Doneger Online home page, which provides some typical effects through the usage of scripts.

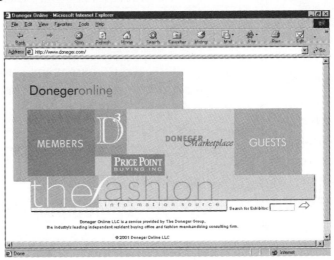

The Doneger Online home page shown here will be the focus of our exercises, as well, throughout the chapter. You will be adding the scripts to the events to make the page function as described.

This page displays a complex graphic with text positioned over the graphic, as we discussed in the previous chapter on absolute and relative positioning through divs. In this case, however, the page also uses scripts with a number of events. It provides rollovers for the squares and rectangles, verifies that users type in an Exhibitor to search for before submitting the search form, and welcomes users in a pop-up window when the page is first loaded.

onmouseover

In the graphic arts world, perhaps the most commonly used event is onmouseover. This event fires when the user rolls the mouse over any part of the affected area. Typically, the result of this event firing is that an image changes. This change stays in effect until the user's mouse leaves the area, which fires the onmouseout event.

Since this sequence of events involves a series of steps, rather than trying to put all of the steps into the event we'll create a function and execute that when the event fires. A custom function looks like this:

```
function myFunction (argument1, argument2) {
    [script goes here]
}
```

Let's look at this example step by step. First, we're telling the browser that we're creating a new function with the function keyword. Next, we're naming the function and defining any arguments we want to feed it. Not all functions have arguments, but the parentheses must be there whether or not there are any. Finally, we're using the brackets to tell the browser where the commands start and stop.

For instance, if we wanted the browser to execute myFunction() when we rolled over a link, we would write:

```
<a onmouseover="myFunction('nick', 'home')" href="home.html">Home Page</a>
```

Exercise Setup

Let's add a function to the page, setting it to be executed when the onmouseover event fires. For now, we'll just have it create an alert() box, but we'll also add comments about what it will eventually do.

You can add comments to a script by preceding them with two slashes (//). This tells the browser to ignore the rest of that line. You can also use this to make the browser ignore commands that you don't want it to execute right now.

Add a Function to the Page

1. Navigate to **RF_HTML>Chapter 8**, and copy the contents of the Chapter 8 folder into the **WIP>scripts** folder.

2. Open **WIP>scripts>homepage.html** in the browser and the text editor. Add a simple function to the page. Since we don't want the browser to display the text, add the <script></script> tags.

```
<html><head><title>Doneger Online</title>
<link href="donegerstyle.css" rel="stylesheet" type="text/css" />

<script type="text/javascript">
<!--
   function rollOver() {
     //This function will do our rollovers, when we're ready.
     alert('That tickles!');
   }
//-->
</script>

</head>
<body style="background-color:#ffffff">
  . . .
```

3. Save the file and refresh the browser. There should be no change to the appearance of the page.

4. Leave both windows open for the next exercise.

Triggering Events

In the preceding exercise, despite adding the script with a function, nothing changed. The alert box did not appear. This is because at no time did we tell it to appear. While we created a function, we haven't yet called it. Remember: we can add as many functions as we want, but they will not be executed until we call them explicitly.

One way to cause a function to execute is by calling it from an event. But which event? We know that we want the event to fire when the mouse rolls over the object, but which object? The image? The div? The link? All of these objects can have an onmouseover event specified. In our case, we'll make an arbitrary decision and use the image. To do this, we add an onmouseover attribute to the image:

```
<img onmouseover="myFunction()" src="myimage.gif" width="174" height="115"
alt="D3" />
```

Netscape 4.x doesn't support the onmouseover event on images. Instead, you would need to create a dummy link for the image, and put it on the anchor tag as shown here:

```
<a href=" "
onmouseover="rollOver()">
<img height="162"
src="images/
members_button.gif"
width="165" border="0"
alt="Members" /></a>
```

This tells the browser to do whatever we've put into that attribute when the onmouseover event fires. Also, because we're putting it directly into the event, we don't need the <script></script> tags.

One thing to remember is that the onmouseover event only fires at the moment when the user enters the area. You can roll your mouse around inside the area, and nothing will happen, but if you leave the area and reenter it, the onmouseover event will fire again.

This sort of structure, where a function is called by events, is convenient because the same function can be executed multiple times, and from multiple events.

Add a Function to an Event

1. In the open homepage.html file in the text editor, add the onmouseover attribute to the four center boxes for which we're creating rollovers.

```
...
<div style="z-index:9; left:218px; width:174px; position:absolute; top:123px; height:161px;
background-color:#c9d4e6; layer-background-color:#c9d4e6">
   <a href="http://www.doneger.com/login.asp?page=d3">
      <img onmouseover="rollOver()" height="115" src="images/d3_home1n.gif"
width="174" border="0" alt="D3" />
   </a>
</div>
...

<div style="z-index:9; left:55px; visibility:visible; width:162px; position:absolute; top:123px;
height:161px">
   <img onmouseover="rollOver()" height="162" src="images/members_button.gif"
width="165" border="0" alt="Members" />
</div>

<div style="z-index:7; left:563px; width:165px; position:absolute; top:123px;
height:115px">
   <a href="http://www.doneger.com/index_guest.asp">
      <img onmouseover="rollOver()" height="162" src="images/rightsquare_new.gif"
width="165" border="0" alt="Guests" />
   </a>
</div>
...
<div style="z-index:15; left:261px; width:140px; position:absolute; top:233px;
height:47px">
   <a href="http://www.doneger.com/11.0/newpricepoint_guest.asp">
      <img onmouseover="rollOver()" height="52" src="images/ppb_home1n.gif"
width="132" border="0" alt="Price Point Buying" />
   </a>
</div>
...
```

2. Save the file and refresh the browser. Roll over the Members box.

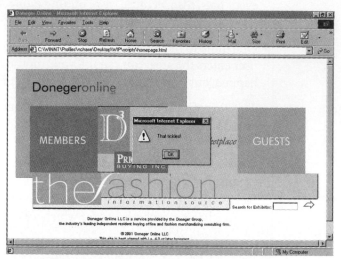

3. With your mouse still inside the Members box, press Return/Enter to acknowledge the alert box. Roll the mouse around inside the Members box, without leaving the box. Notice that even though the mouse is over this box, the event doesn't fire again. Leave the Members box and reenter it. Notice that the box pops up again.

4. Experiment by rolling over the other center boxes. Notice that even though we have just one function, we have called it from a number of different events.

5. Leave both windows open for the next exercise.

onclick

Sometimes we want to run a script when users do something such as trying to submit a form. We may want to verify whether or not they've entered a search term, such as the Search for Exhibitors box on the Doneger Online home page. To do this, we can use the onclick event in the same fashion as we used the onmouseover event.

The onclick event fires for a complete mouse click, meaning the user pressed the button and released it over the area, as opposed to holding down the button and moving to another area on the page before releasing it.

Exercise Setup
Let's add a function for verifying the form. We'll add the function to the arrow graphic in the lower-right corner.

Add a Function to the onclick Event

1. In the open homepage.html file in the text editor, add the new function. (We already have a script area, so we don't need to add a new one.)

```
...
<script type="text/javascript">
<!--
    function rollOver() {
        //This function will do our rollovers, when we're ready.
        alert('That tickles!');
```

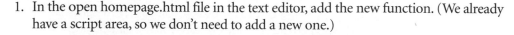

```
        }
    function checkForm() {
        alert('Did you enter a search term?');
    }
//-->
</script>
```
...

2. Add the onclick event to the arrow graphic.

...

```
<form action="homepage.html">
    <font face="arial, helvetica" size="1">Search for Exhibitor: </font>
    <input class="searchtext" size="8" name="keyword" />
    <input onclick="checkForm()" type="image" height="20" width="37"
src="images/dk_arrow.gif" border="0" alt="Submit" />
</form>
```
...

3. Save the file and refresh the browser.

4. Notice that when you click the arrow, nothing happens until you let go of the button. In this case, the new alert box should appear. Acknowledge the alert box by pressing Return/Enter.

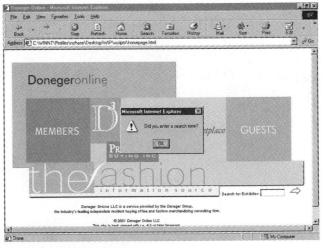

If you're using a Macintosh and hold the button down too long, you'll see a menu instead. Release the menu and click the button again more rapidly.

5. Leave both windows open for the next exercise.

Notice that the arrow graphic is a submit button for the form, not just a plain image, so when you acknowledge the alert box and complete the onclick script, the button submits the form, just as it would have done if there had been no script. (For this instance we've set the form action to be this page, so all that will happen is that the page will reload.)

onload

The easiest event to implement is the onload event, because it doesn't require the user to do anything. Instead, the onload event fires when the browser has finished gathering all of the information on the page. The entire page, including all the graphics, is displayed before the event fires. The onload event normally goes on the <body> tag, as in:

<body onload="myFunction()">

Exercise Setup

Ultimately, we're going to pop up a window welcoming the user to the site, but for now we'll just add a function with an alert box.

Execute a Function When the Page Loads

1. In the open homepage.html file in the text editor, add a new function, popup(), to the script section.

```
…
  function checkForm() {
     alert('Did you enter a search term?');
  }
  function popUp() {
     alert('Welcome to Doneger Online!');
  }
//-->
</script>
</head>
…
```

2. The page itself needs to be loaded, so add an onload attribute to the body tag.

```
…
</head>
<body style="background-color:#ffffff" onload="popUp()">

<div style="z-index:2; left:20px; width:200px; position:absolute; top:32px; height:115px;">
   <img height="266" src="images/logopanel.gif" width="418" alt="Doneger Online" />
</div>
…
```

3. Save the file and refresh the browser.

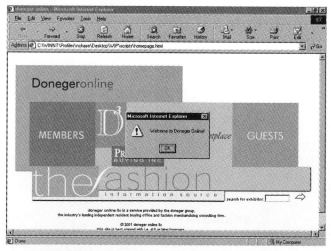

4. Acknowledge the alert box.

5. Leave both windows open for the next exercise.

It's important to realize that frequently people do not read but, instead, react to familiar shapes and symbols. That alert box might say "Congratulations, you've won $1,000,000!" but the vast majority of people will see that yellow triangle and dismiss the box, thinking "Oh, it's broken." Think about the format of the alert box, therefore, when you plan your messages. Since you cannot control the form in which the browser presents your message, decide if an alert box is the best method for that message.

Other Events

These three events — onmouseover, onclick and onload — are the most common, but they are by no means the only events that are available to us. Here is a complete list, along with the elements that they will normally affect:

- **onclick**. Just about any element that can be seen can be clicked. As we saw above, this event doesn't fire until the user releases the mouse button.

- **ondblclick**. This event is just like onclick, except that the user has to double-click. This event isn't normally used, because usually on the Web site, the user single-clicks.

- **onmouseover**. This event fires when the mouse first enters the affected area.

- **onmousemove**. Earlier, when we were testing onmouseover, we saw that once the mouse was in the area, the script didn't execute again. onmousemove fires whenever the mouse is moved within the affected area.

- **onmousedown**. If onclick isn't specific enough for you, you can have your event fire when the user actually presses the mouse, instead of when the mouse button is released.

- **onmouseup**. On the surface, this seems the same as onclick, but with onclick, the mouse has to be both pressed and released in the area. onmouseup will fire even if only the release was in the specified area.

- **onkeypress**. This is like onclick, only for keyboard presses. The user must press and release the key for this event to fire.

- **onkeydown**. Just as onclick has onmousedown, onkeypress has onkeydown, which fires when the key is pressed, regardless of when it is released.

- **onkeyup**. Of course, this fires when the key is released.

- **onfocus**. Usually seen on links and form elements, this event fires when a user clicks an element. When an element has the focus, any keystrokes the user makes will affect it. In other words, if a user clicks on a text input box, anything the user types will go into that box.

- **onchange**. This event applies to input, select and textarea boxes — it fires when their values are changed. Note that the actual event doesn't fire until the element loses focus.

- **onsubmit**. This event fires when the user tries to submit a form. We can use it to keep the submission from happening if the form hasn't been filled out properly.

- **onreset**. This event fires when the user tries to reset the form.

- **onselect**. This event is seldom used. It fires when text is selected in a text box.

- **onload**. This event has two different versions. If we put it on a body tag, then it will fire when the document is loaded. If we put it on a frameset, this event fires when all of the frames are loaded.

- **onunload**. We can fire an event when the users come to the page, and we can fire an event when they leave the page. This, obviously, fires when they leave the page.

The onunload event is often used to trap the user, opening window after window as the user tries to leave a site. Don't do this.

Creating Rollover Animations

A *rollover animation* occurs when the user's mouse rolls over an image and the image changes. This animation has been a staple of multimedia for years, but it took JavaScript to bring it to the browser. In order for us to make this animation happen, we need to cause the image to change, replacing it with a new graphic.

Let's take a look at that last sentence. We want to change the image so that a new graphic is displayed. But isn't the image the graphic?

No, the image is an object within the document. Just as our document had a location property, our image has a src (source) property. Through JavaScript, we can change that property.

Changing a Specific Image

If we want to change an image, the first thing that we do is alter the src property on the specific image. We alter it by naming the image, and then using that name to tell the browser what we want to do (with a script).

For example, if we create an image with:

```
<img src="image1.gif" name="myImage" />
```

the browser will naturally display image1.gif. If we then execute a script that includes:

```
document.myImage.src = 'image2.gif'
```

the browser will replace the original image with image2.gif.

Let's take a look at the structure for a moment. We said earlier that document.location referred to the location property of the document object. Let's take this apart, piece by piece.

Just as we had document.location, we can have myImage.src, which simply represents the src property of the myImage object. But what about:

```
document.myImage.src
```

In this case, document is still the object, so it would make sense that myImage would be the myImage property of the document. That's not strictly true, but it's close enough from the standpoint that the document object knows where to find it in the computer's memory. The difference is that instead of representing a value, as location did, myImage represents another object, which has its own property, src.

The browser interprets the src property in the same way that it interprets URLs. If we are looking for a src of "images/members_button.gif", for example, the browser will look in the same location in which it would look for <img src="images/members_button.gif" />.

In other words, the src property in a script controls the src attribute for an img tag.

Change a Specific Image

1. In the open homepage.html file in the text editor, name the Members box by adding a name attribute to the image.

Strictly speaking, the myImage object is a child of the document object, but further discussion on this topic is well beyond the scope of this book.

```
…
<div style="z-index:9; left:55px; visibility:visible; width:162px; position:absolute; top:123px; height:161px">
    <img name="members" onmouseover="rollOver()" height="162" src="images/members_button.gif" width="165" border="0" alt="Members" />
</div>
…
```

2. Just to double-check that it's working, change the rollover script to output the current source of the image when we roll over it. Also, for convenience, just as we added comments (such as "This function …") earlier, we can turn the pop-up alert box into a comment using //.

```
…
<script type="text/javascript">
<!--
    function rollOver() {
        //This function will do our rollovers, when we're ready.
        alert(members.src);
    }

    function checkForm() {
        alert('Did you enter a search term?');
    }

    function popUp() {
        // alert('Welcome to Doneger Online!');
    }
//-->
</script>
…
```

3. Save the file and refresh the browser. Roll your mouse over the Members box.

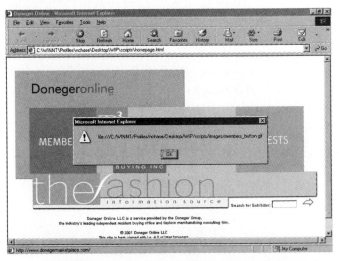

The location will be different on your machine, of course, but it shows that the members image is currently pointing to members_button.gif.

Object names are case sensitive, so be sure to type members.src and not Members.src.

4. Alter the script so that instead of displaying the src property, the script changes the property to point to the new graphic.

```
...
function rollOver() {
    //This function will do our rollovers, when we're ready.
    members.src = 'images/members_roll.gif';
}
...
```

5. Save the page and refresh the browser. Roll your mouse over the Members box.

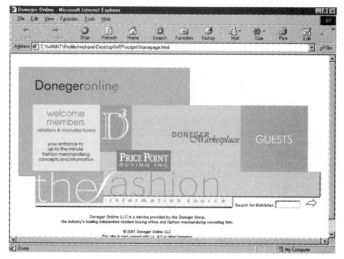

6. Refresh the page and roll over one of the other center boxes. Notice that the Members box changes whenever an onmouseover event fires.

7. Leave both windows open for the next exercise.

Turning Off a Rollover

Even when our mouse is no longer above the item that we rolled over to get the rollover effect (like the Members box in the preceding exercise), the effect remains in place. In order to cause it to change back, we need to add another function that will return the changed elements to their original state. We do this by creating a new function for the onmouseout event. We place the onmouseout event just as we placed the onmouseover event. Just as the onmouseover event fired when the user rolled over the object, the onmouseout event fires at the instant when the mouse is no longer over the object (when it leaves the object).

Turn Off a Rollover

1. In the open homepage.html file in the text editor, create the new function. Use the same concept as the rollover (but you're returning to the original image).

```
...
function rollOver() {
    //This function will do our rollovers, when we're ready.
    members.src = 'images/members_roll.gif';
```

```
    }
    function rollOut() {
        //This function will remove our rollovers.
        members.src = 'images/members_button.gif';
    }
    function checkForm() {
        alert('Did you enter a search term?');
    }
…
```

  2. Add the new function to the onmouseout event for the Members box.

…
```
<div style="z-index:9; left:55px; visibility:visible; width:162px; position:absolute; top:123px;
height:161px">
    <img name="members" onmouseout="rollOut()" onmouseover="rollOver()"
height="162" src="images/members_button.gif" width="165" border="0"
alt="Members" />
</div>
```
…

  3. Save the file and refresh the browser. Roll the mouse over the Members box and
      watch it change. Now roll the mouse out of the top or bottom of the Members box
      and watch it change back. Roll the mouse over one of the other boxes and watch it
      change. Notice, however, that when you roll out of those boxes, it doesn't change
      back because we haven't enabled the onmouseout event for those boxes. If you roll
      into and out of the Members box, however, the rollover effect vanishes.

  4. Leave both windows open for the next exercise.

Using a Disconnected Rollover

In the preceding exercise, did you notice that no matter what box we rolled over, the Members box changed? This happened because we were specifying a particular image object, no matter how the script was initiated.

This technique can be immensely helpful if we want to create a *disconnected rollover*, one in which the mouse rolls over one item and another changes. For instance, we may have a set of buttons and an area on the screen that explains what they mean. In this case, we want that area to change when we roll over the buttons, not when we roll over the information area.

In a case like this example, where we have several images with rollovers, however, this is a little inconvenient.

Using Generic Scripts

In many cases, what we want is for the script to change out whatever image we happened to be over, and to replace it with the appropriate rollover image. To do that, we'll need to create a different type of script than those we have been using so far.

Let's start by feeding the rollover script the appropriate image to swap. We'll do that by specifying an argument that the script will take and use. This argument is a *variable*, meaning that it takes whatever value we give it.

For instance, if we wrote:

```
MyText = 'Hello there!';
Document.write MyText;
```

The browser would write:

Hello there!

Basically, when we have a variable, whenever we use it, the browser substitutes the value. In this way, we can create one script that can take many different values.

Exercise Setup
Let's take a look at using variables in our scripts.

Create an Argument

1. In the open homepage.html file in the text editor, add an argument to the function.

```
...
<!--
  function rollOver(newSrc) {
    //This function will do our rollovers, when we're ready.
    members.src = newSrc;
  }

  function rollOut() {
...
```

2. Now we need to add the information that goes into the argument. For each time we call rollOver (), add the correct image.

```
...
<div style="z-index:9; left:218px; width:174px; position:absolute; top:123px; height:161px;
background-color:#c9d4e6; layer-background-color:#c9d4e6">
  <a href="http://www.doneger.com/login.asp?page=d3">
    <img onmouseover="rollOver('images/d3_roll.gif')" height="115" src="images/
d3_home1n.gif" width="174" border="0" />
  </a>
</div>
...
<div style="z-index:9; left:55px; visibility:visible; width:162px; position:absolute; top:123px;
height:161px">
  <img name="members" onmouseout="rollOut()" onmouseover="rollOver('images/
members_roll.gif')" height="162" src="images/members_button.gif" width="165" bor-
der="0" alt="Members" />
</div>
<div style="z-index:7; left:563px; width:165px; position:absolute; top:123px;
height:115px">
  <a href="http://www.doneger.com/index_guest.asp">
    <img onmouseover="rollOver('images/rightsquare_roll.gif')" height="162"
src="images/rightsquare_new.gif" width="165" border="0" alt="Guests" />
  </a>
</div>
```

```
...
<div style="z-index:15; left:261px; width:140px; position:absolute; top:233px;
height:47px">
   <a href="http://www.doneger.com/11.0/newpricepoint_guest.asp">
      <img onmouseover="rollOver('images/ppb_roll.gif')" height="52" src="images/
ppb_home1n.gif" width="132" border="0" alt="Price Point Buying" />
   </a>
</div>
...
```

3. Save the file and refresh the page. Roll over the various boxes and watch the Members box change.

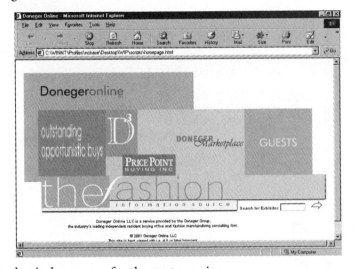

4. Leave both windows open for the next exercise.

Using the this Keyword

Now that we know how to specify different images to use for the rollover, we need to know how to tell a script which image to change. What we need is to be able to tell the browser to swap out just the image over which we're rolling.

Fortunately, JavaScript provides a way for us to do that.

Since JavaScript is oriented towards objects, we can use a special keyword, this. The this keyword always refers to whatever object fired the event or called the script. For instance, in the following example, this always refers to the image that fired the onmouseover event.

We could create a page with:

```
<img src="image1.gif" align="left" onmouseover="document.target.src=this.src" />
<img src="image2.gif" align="left" onmouseover="document.target.src=this.src" />
<img src="temp.gif" align="left" name="target" />
```

From this code, the page would look like this:

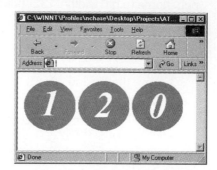

We have three images, but only one of them has a name. The other two have the onmouseover event defined so that if the user rolls over either of them, the image on the right will be replaced with whichever image was rolled over.

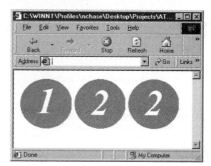

We can use the this keyword like a variable, passing it to a function just as we have passed image names and locations. For example:

```
<script type="text/javascript">
<!--
function myFunction(theImage){
    alert(theImage.src);
}
//-->
</script>

<img src="image1.gif" onclick="myFunction(this)" />
```

In this case, when the user clicks the image, myFunction() is passed a reference to the image object. This means that within the myFunction() script, theImage now represents the image object so theImage.src represents the src property of the image object.

It's interesting to note that with a rollover, the same result occurs when we first roll over the image, and when we finally leave the image: the image changes. Because of this, a single script can handle both actions.

Exercise Setup

For our page, what we need to do is pass the right image to the rollover script using the this keyword.

Use this to Make the Script Generic

1. In the open homepage.html file in the text editor, add to the script a new argument (toSwap) that represents the image object that will change.

…

```
<!--
  function rollOver(toSwap, newSrc) {
    //This function will do our rollovers, when we're ready.
    toSwap.src = newSrc;
  }

  function rollOut() {
```

…

2. Use the this keyword to feed the appropriate image to toSwap.

…

```
<div style="z-index:9; left:218px; width:174px; position:absolute; top:123px; height:161px;
background-color:#c9d4e6; layer-background-color:#c9d4e6">
  <a href="http://www.doneger.com/login.asp?page=d3">
    <img onmouseover="rollOver(this, 'images/d3_roll.gif')" height="115" src="images/
d3_home1n.gif" width="174" border="0" alt="D3"/>
  </a>
</div>
```

…

```
<div style="z-index:9; left:55px; visibility:visible; width:162px; position:absolute; top:123px;
height:161px">
  <img name="members" onmouseout="rollOut()" onmouseover="rollOver(this, 'images/
members_roll.gif')" height="162" src="images/members_button.gif" width="165" bor-
der="0" alt="Members" />
</div>
<div style="z-index:7; left:563px; width:165px; position:absolute; top:123px;
height:115px">
  <a href="http://www.doneger.com/index_guest.asp">
    <img onmouseover="rollOver(this, 'images/rightsquare_roll.gif')" height="162"
src="images/rightsquare_new.gif" width="165" border="0" alt="Guests" />
  </a>
</div>
```

…

```
<div style="z-index:15; left:261px; width:140px; position:absolute; top:233px;
height:47px">
  <a href="http://www.doneger.com/11.0/newpricepoint_guest.asp">
    <img onmouseover="rollOver(this, 'images/ppb_roll.gif')" height="52" src="images/
ppb_home1n.gif" width="132" border="0" alt="Price Point Buying" />
  </a>
</div>
```

…

3. Save the page and refresh the browser. Roll over the various boxes to see the changes.

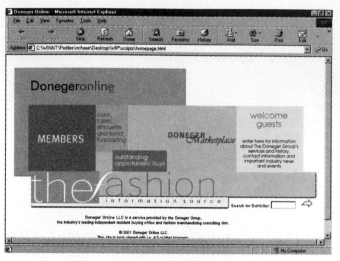

4. Now that the rollovers are created, we need to take care of canceling them. Remove rollOut() and add rollOver() to the onmouseout events.

```
…
<div style="z-index:9; left:218px; width:174px; position:absolute; top:123px; height:161px;
background-color:#c9d4e6; layer-background-color:#c9d4e6">
  <a href="http://www.doneger.com/login.asp?page=d3">
    <img onmouseout="rollOver(this, 'images/d3_home1n.gif')"
onmouseover="rollOver(this, 'images/d3_roll.gif')" height="115" src="images/
d3_home1n.gif" width="174" border="0" alt="D3" />
  </a>
</div>
…
<div style="z-index:9; left:55px; visibility:visible; width:162px; position:absolute; top:123px;
height:161px">
  <img onmouseout="rollOver(this, 'images/members_button.gif')"
onmouseover="rollOver(this, 'images/members_roll.gif')" height="162" src="images/
members_button.gif" width="165" border="0" alt="Members" />
</div>

<div style="z-index:7; left:563px; width:165px; position:absolute; top:123px;
height:115px">
  <a href="http://www.doneger.com/index_guest.asp">
    <img onmouseout="rollOver(this, 'images/rightsquare_new.gif')"
onmouseover="rollOver(this, 'images/rightsquare_roll.gif')" height="162" src="images/
rightsquare_new.gif" width="165" border="0" alt="Guests" />
  </a>
</div>
…
<div style="z-index:15; left:261px; width:140px; position:absolute; top:233px;
height:47px">
  <a href="http://www.doneger.com/11.0/newpricepoint_guest.asp">
```

```
    <img onmouseout="rollOver(this, 'images/ppb_home1n.gif')"
onmouseover="rollOver(this, 'images/ppb_roll.gif')" height="52" src="images/
ppb_home1n.gif" width="132" border="0" alt="Price Point Buying" />
    </a>
</div>
…
```

5. Save the file and refresh the page. Move your mouse around the page and watch the rollovers work.

6. Leave both windows open for the next exercise.

Preloading Images

The first time you rolled over one of those boxes in the exercise, you probably noticed that the image didn't display immediately. That's because the browser first had to load the image into memory. Now imagine what the delay would have been if you weren't dealing with images on your local drive!

Of course, once the image was loaded, the browser placed it in the browser *cache*, a temporary storage place for downloaded material. From then on, every time the browser needed that image, it retrieved the image from the cache instead of redownloading it, so the effect was nearly instantaneous.

The trick, apparently, is to get the browser to download the images before we need them. This is known as "preloading."

Preloading the Rollover Images

Before the advent of JavaScript, developers sometimes created a page with all of the site's images on it, displayed at 0 pixels by 0 pixels, so that nobody would see them. After all, we didn't want the user to see them until they're needed!

Fortunately, now that we have scripting, we can be a little more elegant about it. Instead, we can create an image object, then one by one set the src property to be each of the images we want to preload.

So what does this do? Well, since the image object exists only in the script, it won't be displayed. The browser still has to load each image, however, and each one is stored in the cache. Then, when we need an image for the rollover, the browser already has it.

So if we wanted to preload a group of images, we could do it like this:

var preloadImage = new Image();

preloadImage.src = 'images/image1.gif';

preloadImage.src = 'images/image2.gif';

preloadImage.src = 'images/image3.gif';

The first line creates the image object so that we can manipulate it. We chose to call it preloadImage, but the name is irrelevant. Each of the next three lines assigns the src property of that object, preloadImage, to a new image. This assignment causes the browser to load the graphic file.

When this script has finished executing, image1.gif, image2.gif and image3.gif will be loaded into the browser's cache.

Exercise Setup
Let's set up the preloading on our page.

Preload the Rollover Images

1. In the open homepage.html file in the text editor, create the image object within the script. Do so by declaring it, as we did in the previous example.

```
…
<script type="text/javascript">
<!--
   var preloadImage = new Image();

   function rollOver(toSwap, newSrc) {
…
```

2. Set the src property to the first image we want to preload.

```
…
<script type="text/javascript">
<!--
   var preloadImage = new Image();
   preloadImage.src = 'images/d3_home1n.gif';

   function rollOver(toSwap, newSrc) {
…
```

3. Save the file and refresh the page. You should not see any difference on the page. We've created an image and given it a graphic, but we never told the browser to display it. So it doesn't hurt anything if we then have the browser load the rest of our rollover images.

```
…
<script type="text/javascript">
<!--
   var preloadImage = new Image();
   preloadImage.src = 'images/d3_home1n.gif';
   preloadImage.src = 'images/rightsquare_new.gif';
   preloadImage.src = 'images/members_button.gif';
   preloadImage.src = 'images/ppb_home1n.gif';

   function rollOver(toSwap, newSrc) {
…
```

4. Save the file and refresh the browser. Again there should be no change, but you should see the rollovers coming up much more quickly.

5. Leave both windows open for the next exercise

The Disadvantages of Preloading

In general, preloading is a good idea. It definitely can make things run a lot more smoothly. There are a few issues to keep in mind, however.

First of all, as with the first script we created, the browser will execute this script before it does anything else. That means that if we have a large number of images to preload, the entire page will have to wait for them, which defeats the purpose. In this case, it would be better to put these instructions into the script that runs with the onload event.

Second, even when we do move it to the onload event, the browser continues to look as though it's still loading, because it is. This can have the effect of confusing users, who see "Done" in the status bar and wonder why the browser is still loading.

Third, there is the potential for downloading a large number of images that will never be seen, slowing the user's experience needlessly.

Still, managed properly, preloading images can significantly improve the user's experience.

Validating a Form

The very first Web forms were nothing more than a text box into which the user could type a search term. The forms were pretty limited, but there wasn't much that a user could do wrong.

Nowadays, a Web form is just as likely to be part of a Web-based application, and require very specific responses from the user. A form, for example, might require certain fields to be filled in, or that a field have only numbers or a date.

Nothing intrinsic in a form requires that the data be of a specific type or format. Normally, therefore, the action takes care of ensuring that the submitted information is correct. If it's not, the program provides a message for the user to go back and correct the problem, or sometimes the program repeats the form with the submitted information already in it, ready for the user to fix.

There's nothing really wrong with this process, but it's not the most efficient way of working.

It takes time for the form to be submitted to the server. If the user has made several mistakes, he or she could spend several minutes over the course of several trips, just waiting to find out what was incorrect this time.

In addition, when users submit the form, they're generally ready to move on to the next step. When they get the form back, they are often confused and frustrated.

What if, instead, we could check the form before it's submitted, giving them a message immediately asking them to correct any errors? This is the idea behind form validation.

Checking for Required Fields

The most common use for form validation is to make certain that the user has filled in one element or another. If not, the user gets a message to that effect.

In order to check for a value, we have to access properties, just as we did with document.location and image.src. In this case, however, it's a little more complex.

The document has a number of properties. Some of them are strings, such as document.location. Some of them, however, are objects, such as, in this case, a form. What's more, some of those objects have their own properties.

For example, our page has a form on it. Without the formatting, it's:

```
<form action="homepage.html">
Search for Exhibitor:
        <input class="searchtext" size="8" name="keyword" />
        <input onclick="checkForm()" type="image" height="20" width="37"
        src="images/dk_arrow.gif" border="0" />
</form>
```

Now, all of the elements in our page are part of the document object, including any and all forms. Note that we said forms, not form. We could conceivably have more than one form on the page, so all of the forms are included in:

document.forms

In this case, forms is a *array*, or a series of items. Because forms is what's known as a "zero-based array," the first form is number 0, the second one is number 1, and so on. So, since this is the first form on the page, we can refer to it by saying:

document.forms[0]

The form also has properties that happen to be objects. These are the elements of the form, such as the input box. Since it has a name, however, it's a lot easier to reference. In this case, our text box is:

document.forms[0].keyword

So now that we're down to the text box, at this moment there's only one property we're interested in — value:

document.forms[0].keyword.value

The value represents the text that currently appears in the field.

Knowing this, we can use JavaScript to look at the value of the text box. For example, if the code we typed was this:

```
…
<script type="text/javascript">
<!--
function showValue() {
    alert(document.forms[0].myText.value);
}
 //-->
</script>
<form action="mypage.html">
Enter text: <input type="text" name="myText" />
<br />
<input type="submit" onclick="showValue()" />
</form>
…
```

The resulting page would look like this:

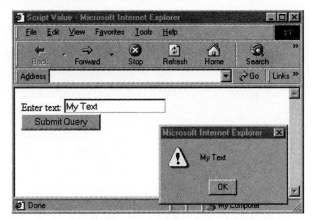

Exercise Setup

Let's use this to check the value of the search form.

Check the Value

1. In the open homepage.html file in the text editor, change the checkForm() function so that it shows the value of the text box.

```
…
function checkForm() {
  alert(document.forms[0].keyword.value);
}
…
```

2. Save the page and refresh the browser. Type something in the "Search for Exhibitor" box, and click the arrow to submit.

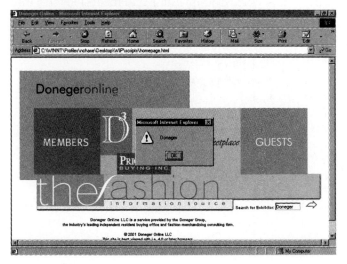

3. Acknowledge the dialog box showing what you typed in the text box. The form will be processed and return with nothing in the text box. Without typing anything in the box, click the arrow once again. Notice that the alert box shows no value.

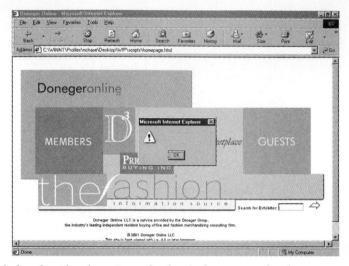

4. Acknowledge the Alert box. Leave both windows open for the next exercise.

Conditional Statements

Now we know how to access the value, but we need to figure out how to keep the form from submitting if the field is blank. To do this, we first need to look at conditional statements.

A *conditional statement*, otherwise known as an "if-then statement," is a command that we use when we want to do something only if a particular condition is true. This is the programming equivalent of "If they have chocolate ice cream, get it. Otherwise, call me with a list of what they do have."

In JavaScript, these statements look like this:

```
if (condition) {
    commands to execute
} else {
    other commands to execute
}
```

Let's take this one step at a time. We start with the keyword if, and then follow with the condition that we're looking at, in parentheses. For instance, let's say we were booking a theater with 500 seats. We might say:

```
if (ticketsSold < 500) {
    Sell more tickets
} else {
    Hang "Sold Out" sign
}
```

There is one important point that we have to note here. Earlier we used the "=" sign to assign a value, as in:

```
preloadImage.src = 'images/d3_home1n.gif';
```

In some programming languages, we can also use the = sign to show equality, but in JavaScript we need to use == instead. So if we were looking for the 500th customer, we might say:

```
If (ticketsSold == 500) {
    Congratulate buyer
} else {
    Go about your business
}
```

The brackets hold the list of commands that we want to execute in each case. We can use this format to find out if the user has typed anything at all into the keyword box.

Check for the Existence of a Value

1. In the open homepage.html file in the text editor, change the checkForm() script to output a different message depending on whether or not the user submitted any information.

```
…
    function checkForm() {
      if (document.forms[0].keyword.value == '') {
        alert('You left the form blank!');
      } else {
        alert('You entered something. Thanks!');
      }
    }
…
```

Be sure to use two single quotes (') and not one double quote ("). Sometimes we need to have a single quote in the string. To do that, we replace it with two. For instance, we could have written:

alert('You didn''t enter a search term.')

2. Save the page and refresh the browser. Click the search arrow.

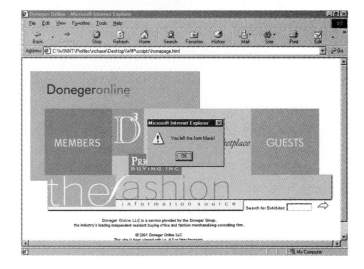

3. Acknowledge the alert box. When the form has finished submitting, type something in the search box. Click the arrow.

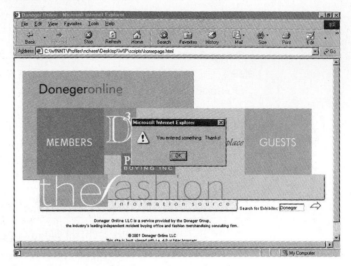

4. Leave both windows open for the next exercise.

Controlling Form Submission

Often, we want a form to submit only if the user has typed a value in the text box. With the examples we've seen so far, no matter what happens in the script, the form will submit when it's done.

By contrast, what we want to do is create a script that will make the decision as to whether or not to submit the form. To do that, we can't use a submit button. Instead, let's add an image, and then handle the submission process in a script.

To submit from a script, we just reference the submit() function of the form:

document.forms[0].**submit()**;

So, for example, a simple script that emulates the submit button could be written as:

```
function submitForm() {
    document.forms[0].submit();
}
```

Submit via the Script

1. In the open homepage.html file in the text editor, change the submit image to a regular image by changing the input to an img tag. To accommodate both Netscape and Internet Explorer, add a dummy link for the event.

…

```
<form action="homepage.html">
    <font face="arial, helvetica" size="1">Search for Exhibitor: </font>
    <input class="searchtext" size="8" name="keyword" />
    <a href="" onclick="checkForm()"><img onclick="checkForm()" height="20"
    width="37" src="images/dk_arrow.gif" border="0" alt="Submit" /></a>
</form>
```

…

2. Save the page and refresh the browser. Click the arrow.

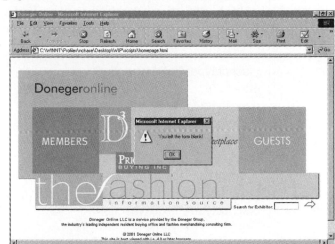

3. Acknowledge the alert box. Notice that now the form doesn't submit.

4. Change the script so that it submits the form if the user enters a search term.

...

```
function checkForm() {
  if (document.forms[0].keyword.value == '') {
    alert('You left the form blank!');
  } else {
    document.forms[0].submit();
  }
}
```

...

5. Save the page and refresh the browser. Click the arrow. Notice that the alert box displays, but the form still doesn't submit when you acknowledge it. Now type text into the box and click the arrow. Notice that the form does submit.

6. Leave both windows open for the next exercise.

Preventing the Form from Submitting

In the preceding exercise, we worked on a script that determines whether or not the form should be submitted. As long as we click the arrow, it works correctly.

But that's not the only way to submit a form. Internet Explorer will submit a form if the user presses Return/Enter, and Netscape will as well, if the form has only one text box.

This problem can happen on other pages, as well. You've created a script with an official submission process including validation, only to find that the user can circumvent your process and submit the form. Since the script in the exercise now only works if the button is clicked, the form won't be validated if the user instead presses Return/Enter.

We need a way to intercept the whole submission process. We can do that with the onsubmit event. onsubmit fires any time that the form is submitted, no matter how it is submitted. But the really helpful aspect of using an onsubmit event is that we can decide whether or not to complete the submission based on the value that we pass to onsubmit.

But how do we pass a value to onsubmit? Well, it turns out that in addition to passing a value to a function, we can also get one back out again. This is known as "returning" a value, and we can then pass, or feed, that value to onsubmit. For example:

```
…
<script type="text/javascript">
<!--
function returnValue() {
    return 'This is the value';
}
 //-->
</script>
…
<script type="text/javascript">
 <!--
   alert(returnValue());
//-->
</script>
…
```

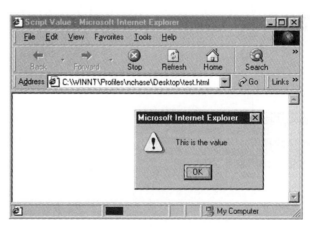

To take this a step farther, we can return a value to the onsubmit event, as in:

```
<form action="myform.html" onsubmit="return false">
```

In this case, the form won't submit, because the onsubmit event is returning false to the form.

Control the Submission with a Value

1. In the open homepage.html file in the text editor, add the onsubmit event to the form, and return to it a value of false.

```
…
<div style="z-index:20; left:550px; width:220px; position:absolute; top:350px;
height:30px">
   <form action="homepage.html" onsubmit="return false">
     <font face="arial, helvetica" size="1">Search for Exhibitor: </font>
…
```

2. Save the page and refresh the browser.

3. Click the text box and press Return/Enter. Notice that the form doesn't submit.

4. In the text editor, change the value to true.

```
...
<div style="z-index:20; left:550px; width:220px; position:absolute; top:350px;
height:30px">
    <form action="homepage.html" onsubmit="return true">
        <font face="arial, helvetica" size="1">Search for Exhibitor: </font>
...
```

5. Save the page and refresh the browser.

6. Click the text box and press Return/Enter. Notice that the form now submits.

7. Now we want to control the returned value through the script. Add the return values to checkForm(), and remove the command to submit the form.

```
...
  function checkForm() {
      if (document.forms[0].keyword.value == '') {
          alert('You left the form blank!');
              return false;
      } else {
              return true;
      }
  }
...
```

8. We need to pass the value to the onsubmit event. Turn the arrow back into a submit button. Don't forget to remove the dummy link tag. (The script no longer submits the form, so we need a submit button.)

```
...
    <form action="homepage.html" onsubmit="return checkForm()">
        <font face="arial, helvetica" size="1">Search for Exhibitor: </font>
        <input class="searchtext" size="8" name="keyword" />
        <input type="image" height="20" width="37" src="images/dk_arrow.gif" border="0"
alt="Submit" />
    </form>
</div>
...
```

9. Save the page and refresh the browser.

10. Click the arrow button. Acknowledge the alert box and notice that the form does not submit.

11. Click the text box and press Return/Enter. Acknowledge the alert box and notice that the form does not submit.

12. Type a keyword in the search box. Press Return/Enter. Notice that the form does submit.

13. Leave both windows open for the next exercise.

Confirming the User's Choices

Traditional applications often ask users to confirm their choices before they're processed (but after they're submitted), and we could certainly do that as well with the form action. Instead, however, we want to confirm the user's choices before the form is submitted.

To do this, we're going to use a function similar to the alert box, called the "confirm box." A confirm box has two buttons, generally named "OK" and "Cancel." Depending on which of these buttons the user clicks, the confirm box returns either true (if the user clicks OK) or false (if the user clicks Cancel).

Note that you don't have to add these buttons. The browser takes care of it simply because it's a confirm box. Here is an example:

confirm("Do you want to submit the form?");

Because the true and false values are automatically returned by the confirm box when the user clicks a button, we can use the confirm box to determine whether or not to submit the form. We can put whatever text we want into the confirm box, as you see above. We can also add more than one line of text. To create a line break, use the "newline" character, which is represented by \n.

Use the Confirm Box

1. Open **WIP>scripts>homepage.html** in the text editor and browser, if it's not already open.

2. Add a confirm box that pops up to echo the values that the user has entered.

…

```
function checkForm() {
  if (document.forms[0].keyword.value == '') {
     alert('You left the form blank!');
      return false;
  } else {
     return confirm ('You have entered the following search term: \n\n' +
     document.forms[0].keyword.value + '\n\nDo you want to continue?');
  }
}
```

…

3. Save the page and refresh the browser. Type a search term and click the arrow or press Return/Enter.

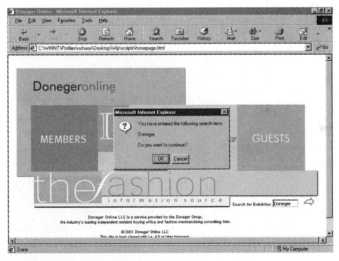

4. Click Cancel and observe that the form does not submit.

5. Press Return/Enter, click OK and observe that the form submits.

6. Leave both windows open for the next exercise.

Creating a Pop-Up Window

One more capability that you will undoubtedly use is the opening of a new window.

Opening a new window can be extremely convenient. Because it's simply an XHTML page, it can provide additional information, allow the user to make a choice without interrupting the flow of the page, feature an advertisement and so on.

To create a new window, we need the window object. We've discussed object properties — now we're going to use an object method. As we said before, a method is something that the object does, rather than information about it.

To open a new window, we can issue the command:

window.open()

Of course, it's no good all by itself like that. The open() method takes arguments that determine the page that it will display, as well as features such as the height and width and whether or not the toolbars will appear. The arguments are:

window.open(<url>, <name>, <features>, <replace>)

In our case, we'll need only <url> and <features>

This is an extremely powerful capability, and we're only going to scratch the surface. But we could use this to send information between windows, for instance, allowing the user to complete a series of steps to get to a value that could then be inserted automatically into a form on the original page.

Exercise Setup
For now, we just want to open a window to welcome the user to the Doneger Online site.

Open a New Window

1. In the open homepage.html file in the text editor, add the window.open() command to the popUp() script.

```
…
function popUp() {
    window.open('popup.html', '', 'height=130, width=230', '');
}
…
```

Those are two single quotes, not one double quote.

2. Save the page and refresh the browser.

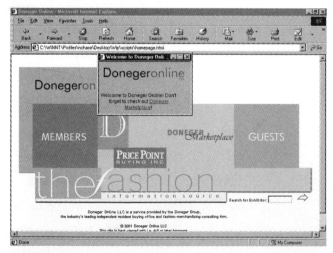

3. Close the windows.

Summary

In this chapter, you have explored all of the major and most commonly used aspects of client-side scripting. You have learned how to use events, how to validate a form and how to create rollovers by manipulating the objects that the browser provides.

Sights and Sounds

Chapter Objective:

To learn how to use sounds and other media, such as streaming audio and video, SMIL presentations, and Flash movies. In Chapter 9, you will:

- Learn how to add sounds to a Web page.

- Explore how the browser differentiates different types of content.

- Discover the differences between streaming and nonstreaming content.

- Become familiar with SMIL.

- Learn how the browser can detect the presence of a plug-in.

Projects to be Completed:

- News Web (A)

- Cyber Travel (B)

- Hunter Films (C)

- North Star Adventure Gear (D)

Sights and Sounds

New Web designers are often surprised to learn just how much can be done with a site. In fact, there are many features that aren't used as often as they could be simply because so few people know how to add them to their pages.

Sound and video are areas where that is slowly changing.

It has been possible for a few years now to add a background sound to a page. Unfortunately, however, it is extremely difficult to choose a piece of music that won't make readers hostile before they've finished reading the home page, so perhaps it's fortunate that so few designers have put this to use.

There is another reason that it has taken a while for audio and video to catch on: bandwidth. Until recently, slow connections — 28K modems or 56K, if you were lucky — were the norm for home users. Now, with cable modems and DSL becoming more common, audio and video are being taken more seriously once again.

Then there's the issue of interactivity. Java first emerged as a language for creating *applets*, small applications that ran in the browser. Programmers could create highly interactive environments, such as fancy graphical user interfaces or even games. The trouble was that while Java is not the most difficult language for a programmer to learn, it was completely impractical to ask a designer to learn it.

Bandwidth is the information-carrying capacity or amount of information that can flow through a channel. For Web users, the advent of faster and faster modems, then cable modems, DSL and more, has meant greater bandwidth and therefore greater ability to receive information rapidly.

Fortunately, we now have Macromedia Flash. A descendant of Macromedia Director (by way of Shockwave, also from Macromedia), it provides much of the same interactivity without hard-core programming. Adding a Flash movie to a page is much like adding audio or video, so we'll examine them all in this chapter.

File Extensions and MIME Types

Before we go much further, we need to have a good understanding of how the browser knows what to do with a document. After all, there is a big difference between displaying the text in a text file and rendering it as HTML, and an even greater difference between displaying an image file and playing a video.

The main cue that tells the browser what to do with a file is the file extension, the set of letters following the period (.) in the file name. If the browser sees .html, for instance, it knows that it should be looking for tags. If it sees .gif, it knows that it needs to look for the instructions to display a GIF image. If we change the name of the file, the browser will interpret the file differently.

Exercise Setup
We can see this in action by changing the extension on a file from .html to .txt.

View by File Extension

1. Create a folder in the WIP folder and name the new folder "streaming". Navigate to **RF_HTML>Chapter 9**, and copy the contents of the Chapter 9 folder into the **WIP>streaming** folder.

2. Open **WIP>streaming>detect.html** in your browser.

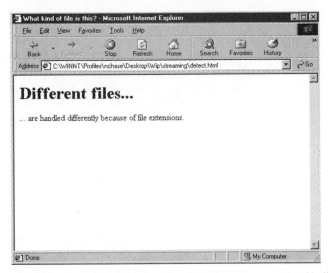

In rare cases, the browser will display the page as HTML despite the name change. If it does, it is reacting to the content of the page, which includes the html tag.

3. Here we see that the file is displayed normally. Now rename the file "detect.txt". The file is the same file, but has a different extension. Open the renamed file in the browser. The results you get will depend on the browser that you're using. Netscape will display the text in the current window, but Microsoft Internet Explorer (IE) will open a new window.

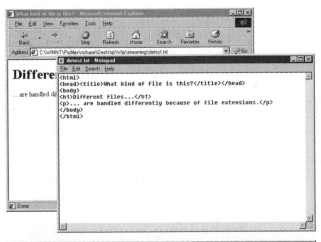

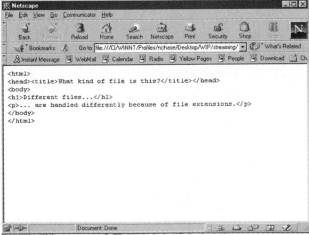

4. Leave the browser window open for the next exercise.

Before you can add sound to your Web site, you need to record it digitally. Typically, this requires special hardware, such as a cable from the headphone jack of a player to the microphone jack of your computer, and software that can be purchased or downloaded from the Web. Remember that copyrighted material should never be duplicated without permission from the copyright holders.

The first browser to add sound to a Web page was Internet Explorer's use of `<body bgsound="myfile.wav">`, but because adding a sound in this way had limited functionality, no other browsers adopted it and it never caught on.

MIME Types

To say that the browser uses the file extensions to decide what to do with the file is really only half the story, however. The file extension leads to the real information: the MIME type. The *MIME type* is a particular designation for each kind of content that a browser might encounter. For instance, an HTML page has a MIME type of text/html, where the plain text version has a MIME type of text/plain-text. Browsers were designed primarily to display HTML, but they are also designed to display other types of media. Early browsers used *helper applications*, external applications that would automatically launch when foreign types, such as a JPEG image, needed to be displayed.

Today, most of these functions are handled by plug-ins, which act like helper applications but (usually) display the content in the browser window. Let's take a look at some sample MIME types and their corresponding file extensions:

MIME Type	File Extension
html, htm	text/html
txt	text/plain-text
gif	image/gif
jpg, jpeg	image/jpeg
aiff, aif, aifc	audio/aiff
xls	application/msexcel
swf	application/x-shockwave-flash
mov, qt	video/quicktime

You may recognize some of those extensions as files that you have created in the past, such as QuickTime movies (.mov, .qt) or Flash movies (.swf). Notice that, in general, they're organized by type, such as text or video, and then by specific kind of file.

You won't usually have to deal with specific MIME types except to make certain that the Web server is handling them properly, a function normally handled by the system administrator. It helps, however, to understand how MIME types work, because system administrators don't always understand what's going on when you create a new type of content and suddenly it's not being served properly.

Embedding Sounds in a Page

Now that we understand how the browser knows what to do with multimedia, let's give it something to handle. We'll start with sound.

There are a few different types of sound that we can use on a Web page. Some of them, such as WAVs or AVI files, have to be downloaded completely before the user can listen to them. Some, such as RealAudio or QuickTime, can be streamed, so the user can hear them as they're downloading. *Streaming* is the act of sending audio or video from the server to the browser in such a way that the browser (or plug-in, or helper application) plays it as it arrives. We'll start simply, with the downloaded type, and move on to streaming in a little while.

The simplest and earliest use of sound in a Web page was as background music. Because the entire file had to be downloaded and so many Web users were on slow modem connections, it was extremely important to use the smallest files possible. MIDI files, which are actually instructions for reproducing music as opposed to the music itself, became very popular for this. As the bandwidth crunch began to ease, however, the mechanical-sounding MIDI files were replaced by the more pleasant-sounding .wav format, or its UNIX counterpart, .aiff.

Using the <embed /> Tag

The <embed /> tag is not actually standard XHTML, so pages don't include the usual DOCTYPE header seen in previous chapters, because they are "unofficial" HTML. The <embed /> tag has been replaced by the <object></object> tag, but a large number of existing browsers still require <embed /> instead, so you must understand and be able to use it to perform effectively.

Using the <embed /> tag involves designating a source for the file that the browser is to play, then adding attributes to alter the way it looks and plays. For instance, if we wanted to embed the sound file background.wav on our page and have it play continuously, we would write:

```
<embed src="background.wav" hidden="true" loop="true" autostart="true" />
```

In general, true and false determine whether or not something will happen; if it's true, it will and if it's false, it won't. When dealing with media files, however, this is not necessarily the case. Each attribute has its own idiosyncrasies and you will need to learn each on its own.

The src indicates the sound that you want to play, and the rest of the attributes determine how that sound will be played. The hidden attribute can be set to "true" or "false." The "false" setting, shown here, indicates that no controller (stop, play, rewind buttons and so on) will be visible. The loop attribute indicates that the sound will play over and over. The autostart attribute indicates that the sound will start playing automatically when the page is loaded.

The trouble with this design is that the user isn't able to control the sound, particularly to stop it. Correcting this involves compensating for some of the differences in browsers and platforms.

For instance, it would seem obvious that in order to make the sound and its controls appear, we should set the hidden attribute to false. Not so! In fact, if the hidden attribute appears in the tag at all, the controller will be hidden on IE for the Macintosh.

How do we add the controllers? On the Macintosh, we add them with the controls attribute, double-checking that we include height and width attributes. On the PC, we use the controller attribute. So… to satisfy all of these different variations, if we wanted the same sound but with controls, the tag would read:

```
<embed src="background.wav" loop="true" autostart="true" controls="true"
controller="true" height="40" width="150" />
```

Exercise Setup

Let's take a look at this in action. We've downloaded some music made available by Josh Mobely at www.flashsound.com, and we're going to add it to our Web page.

Don't irritate your users by looping sounds without a control to turn the sounds off!

Because we're focusing on audio, we won't worry about what the page looks like. (That's your job once you've chosen a project!) Instead we'll look at the use of the <embed /> tag.

Add a Background Sound to a Page

1. Create a new text file called "sounds.html", and save it in the **WIP>streaming** folder.

2. Create the basic XHTML document.

```
<html>
<head><title>Sounds!</title></head>
<body>
<h1 style="text-align:center;">Sounds!</h1>
</body>
</html>
```

3. Save the file and open it in the browser.

4. Add the sound to the page.

```html
<html>
<head><title>Sounds!</title></head>
<body>
<h1 style="text-align:center;">Sounds!</h1>
<embed src="crushing.wav" />
</body>
 </html>
```

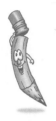

At the time of this writing, many browsers still require non-standard HTML in order to work properly.

5. Save the file and refresh the browser. The exact image that you see will vary widely depending on what browser and platform you're using, but you should hear the music. It may cycle once, then stop, or it may loop, depending on your system.

6. Leave both windows open for the next exercise.

Browser Differences

In previous exercises, we could pretty much guarantee how a page would be rendered, because we were just dealing with XHTML. In this case, however, as mentioned earlier, we are dealing with a number of different programs and implementations. Even on a single computer, there can be wide variations. This is why code standards are so important. Multimedia is one area where standards are still being worked out, and it shows in terms of browser-compatibility headaches.

For instance, the three browsers on the computer on which this chapter is being written (IE 5.5, Netscape 4.7, and Netscape 6) each produced different results for this page.

If your browser shows a plug-in icon, you don't have support for this sound. Click the icon and follow the instructions for downloading the plug-in.

Order is irrelevant when specifying attributes on a tag.

Why are the differences so great? The simple reason is that it's not the browser that's playing the sound (or not playing the sound, in one case). Another application that works with the browser plays the sound. We can't predict exactly what the user's system will do if we don't specify a behavior.

For instance, if we want to make sure that the sound will loop, we need to specify that on the <embed /> tag, as in:

```
<embed src="background.wav" loop="true" />
```

Loop the Sound

1. Open **WIP>streaming>sounds.html** in the text editor and browser, if it's not already open.

2. Add the loop attribute to the <embed /> tag.

…
```
<embed loop="true" src="crushing.wav" />
```
…

3. Save the file and refresh the browser. No matter what browser you're using, the sound should now loop.

4. Leave both windows open for the next exercise.

Giving the User Control

If you allow the sound in the preceding exercise to play long enough, you will notice that it quickly begins to drive you crazy. This is a common problem with the short clips that are used for loops. For this reason, it's extremely important to provide a way to stop sounds if they start automatically.

Sounds don't have to start automatically, of course. Instead, we can place the sound on the page and allow the user to decide when to play it. To do this, we use the autostart attribute. As we saw earlier, we can't guarantee the browser's behavior (or more specifically, the behavior of the helper or plug-in) if we don't include the attribute, so we would also want to be certain that the controller is available.

Allow the User to Start the Sound

1. In the open sounds.html file in the text editor, use the autostart attribute to ensure that the sound doesn't start automatically. Set the other attributes to make certain that the sound isn't hidden.

```
…
<embed autostart="false" height="40" width="200" controls="true"
controller="true" loop="true" src="crushing.wav" />
…
```

2. Save the file and refresh the browser. Double-check that the controller is present. Click the Play button.

3. Close the text editor.

Streaming vs. Downloading

One of the greatest advances in audio and video has been the advent of streaming. When a file is streamed, the user can start to listen almost as soon as the file begins to download. This would seem to ease the author's burden in terms of making the files smaller, but it doesn't really. After all, if you're going to stream the sound, that means that one second of sound has to be downloaded every second. The crushing.wav file in the exercise above, for instance needs approximately 100K of data every second. Even over a typical DSL connection, that would be a stretch. A modem user wouldn't have a chance. The sound would be constantly breaking up as the application waited for more data to arrive.

This becomes even more important when we move from audio to video, which has an even higher bandwidth requirement. One format that attempts to solve these problems for both audio and video is QuickTime.

QuickTime

For a long time, the de facto standard for video on the personal computer was QuickTime. Created by Apple Computer, QuickTime made it possible to watch movies over the Web.

Well, almost.

QuickTime wasn't originally a streaming platform. Instead, users had to download the (then) impossibly large files (over modems!), usually in pieces, reassemble them and only then watch the movie. Not so anymore.

The Play button may look like the play button of a VCR (a triangle pointing to the right), or it may resemble a speaker icon.

Types of QuickTime Movies

There are several types of QuickTime movies.

The first and most obvious is the traditional movie — the entire file is downloaded to the user's computer. These files can give the appearance of streaming using Fast-Start progressive downloads, Apple's way of providing streaminglike performance without the need for a server capable of actual streaming. In this case, as in streaming, the movie plays as it downloads, but it is also saved on the user's machine. These traditional movies can consist of audio and video, video only, or audio only.

The second type is a streaming QuickTime movie. This movie starts playing almost immediately and plays as it downloads, but it isn't saved on the user's computer. These movies can also be audio and video, just video, or just audio.

The third type is an interactive QuickTime movie. Special tracks and events are built into the interactive QuickTime movie. One such type of movie is the QTVR, or QuickTime VR. There are two types of QTVRs. In the first type, an object, such as a computer or a car, is represented and the user can "grab" it with his or her mouse and turn the object to see all sides. In the second type of QTVR, users can pan around an environment much as they do in interactive games. Interactive movies are typically video only, but can have audio as well. They can't be streamed.

Download or Stream?

It seems almost obvious that streaming is the best choice for displaying a movie, but it's not as simple as that. There are pros and cons to both sides.

Streaming Pros:

- A streamed movie starts playing immediately.
- A streamed movie can be randomly accessed. In other words, the user can skip ahead within the movie. If a file is being played via Fast-Start, on the other hand, it is still downloading in order from start to finish, and the user still has to wait for a section to be downloaded before it can be played.
- Streamed movies are not actually saved on the user's computer, so they can't be redistributed. You retain control over the movie.
- A streamed movie doesn't take up massive amounts of your user's available drive.

Streaming Cons:

- Streaming movies aren't cached. This means that every time the users want to watch your movie, they have to access the server. This also increases your bandwidth requirements.
- Streaming movies can't be accessed by users when they're offline.
- Streaming movies are a transient phenomenon. You won't retain user awareness.
- Users with a slow connection won't be able to view higher-bandwidth movies without downloading them first.
- Net congestion can result in a choppy appearance.
- Streaming uses a protocol called "UDP," which is sometimes blocked by firewalls.
- Special server software is needed for streaming QuickTime movies.

Firewalls are hardware or software used to prevent unauthorized access to computer systems.

When deciding whether or not to stream, consider both your resources and those of your users. Many sites choose to provide both options, so that those who can't or would prefer not to use the stream can still view the content.

Embedding a QuickTime Movie

QuickTime movies can be viewed either in the page or in a separate player. To put a movie onto the page, we can use much the same technique as we used for sound. One difference is that we need to specify the MIME type of the media that we're embedding. Another difference is the need to allow for the height of the controller when determining the height for the movie.

To embed a QuickTime movie in the page, we would use a tag like this:

```
<embed src="myMovie.mov" width="311" height="228" controller="true"
controls="true" autoplay="false" type="video/quicktime" />
```

The attributes are basically the same as they were for a sound, but the browser knows that this is a movie because it has the file extension .mov and because of the type attribute. Unlike sound, however, video files require the height and width attributes in order for the browser to allocate space for them on the page. When calculating the dimensions of the video, make certain that you allocate 25 pixels for the controller. If the height takes into account only the movie itself, the controller won't appear.

Exercise Setup
Let's take a look at this in action.

Embed a QuickTime Movie

1. Create a new file called "video.html" and save it in the **WIP>streaming** folder. Open the file in your text editor and browser.

2. Create the document, including an <embed /> tag for the cobra.mov file. To let the browser know this is a QuickTime movie, add the MIME type to the tag as well.

```
<html>
<head><title>Sights!</title></head>
<body>

<h1 style="text-align:center;">Sights!</h1>

<embed src="cobra.mov" autoplay="false" type="video/quicktime" />

</body>
</html>
```

3. Save the file and refresh the browser.

4. Depending on your browser and operating system, you may see a single image or nothing at all on the page. The video is 311 pixels wide by 228 pixels high (or 311 × 228), so add those dimensions to the file. Specify that we want to see the controller.

...
```
<embed src="cobra.mov" width="311" height="228" controller="true" controls="true"
autoplay="false" type="video/quicktime" />
```
...

5. Save the file and refresh the browser.

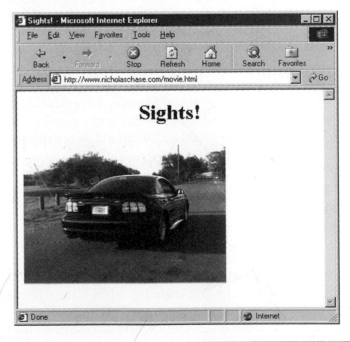

The QuickTime Plug-in actually recognizes 40 different attributes for the <embed /> tag. For more information on these attributes and what they do, see http:// www.apple.com/ quicktime/authoring/ embed2.html.

6. Notice that even though we specifically said we wanted to see the controller, it doesn't appear on the page. This is because we haven't allowed enough room for it.

Conventional wisdom says to add 16 pixels to the height to allow for the controller, but on the PC, this height is actually 25 pixels. Adjust the height of the movie.

...
```
<embed src="cobra.mov" width="311" height="253' controller="true" autoplay="false" type="video/quicktime" />
```
...

7. Save the file and refresh the browser. Notice that the controller now appears.

8. Leave both windows open for the next exercise.

Additional Attributes for <embed />

This is the simplest way to view a QuickTime movie. There are a number of other attributes that are not required but should be added to the <embed /> tag.

- **hidden**. This attribute determines whether or not the movie shows. This is probably more useful for sounds than for videos.

- **starttime**. The attribute specifies the first frame of the movie to play, in the form Hours:Minutes:Seconds:Frames, where the first frame of the movie is 00:00:00:00, so the 15th frame of the 91st second would be 00:01:31:15. For Fast-Start movies, the entire movie will still be downloaded.

- **endtime**. This attribute specifies the last frame of the movie to play, in the form Hours:Minutes:Seconds:Frames, where the first frame is 00:00:00:00. For Fast-Start movies, the entire movie is still downloaded.

- **pluginspage**. By specifying this attribute, you are telling the browser where to send the user for the plug-in, if it's not installed. For QuickTime movies, this should be http://www.apple.com/quicktime/download/.

- **scale**. If this attribute isn't specified, the movie will remain at its normal size, no matter what the height and width are on the <embed /> tag. If the height and width are smaller than the movie, the movie will be clipped, or cropped. If the dimensions specified are larger, there will be extra space around the movie. Possible values for this attribute are TOFIT, where the dimensions will be taken literally no matter what the aspect ratio of the movie; ASPECT, which will stretch to the supplied dimensions while keeping the original aspect ratio, or height/width ratio; and a number, which will scale the movie appropriately. The default value is 1, so to halve the height and width and show a smaller version, we would use .5, and so on.

TOFIT and ASPECT are values for an attribute, not the attribute itself, and are supposed to be in all capital letters.

- **volume**. This attribute is the initial volume for the movie, on a scale of 0 to 100. The default is 100, the loudest setting.

- **loop**. Just as it does for audio clips, this attribute determines whether the movie loops or not.

These properties make up just a small subset of the available attributes.

Linking to a Second Movie or to the Player

When a page loads, any media that is embedded in it, such as audio or video, is loaded as well. If you have a page that has several clips from which to choose, this can be an enormous drain on the user's system and extremely frustrating.

For this reason, it is customary instead to provide a short clip (even a single frame, for instance) that invites the user to click for the actual movie. We can also specify whether the new movie appears on the page or launches the external QuickTime player.

For instance, let's say we wanted to load a short splash-screen movie called a "poster." The poster is only a few frames long and exists solely to provide an opportunity for the user to click it to start the actual movie (as opposed to the poster). Consider, for example, the code below:

```
<embed src="poster.mov" href="newMovie.mov" target="myself" width="311" height="253" controller="true" autoplay="false" type="video/quicktime" />
```

In this case, the src movie (poster.mov) appears in the browser when the page is loaded, just as it did before. Because there is an href attribute, however, the browser knows to treat the movie as a link, as well. If the user clicks the original movie, the browser will load the movie specified by the href attribute.

What the browser does with that movie is determined by the target attribute. If the target attribute is "myself", then the browser displays the new movie in the same spot as the original movie. If the target attribute is "player", the browser will open the QuickTime player and play the movie there.

Exercise Setup
Let's take a look at loading the new movie in the player.

Open the QuickTime Player

1. In the open file video.html in the text editor, change the original movie to poster.mov. This "movie" is actually a simple animation of the phrase "Click to launch movie" moving up and down.

   …

   ```
   <embed src="poster.mov" width="311" height="253" align="middle" controller="true" autoplay="false" type="video/quicktime" />
   ```

…

2. Save the file and refresh the browser. Play the movie. Click the movie itself and verify that nothing happens.

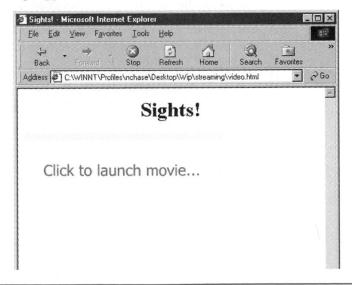

3. Add the href for the movie to open and the target to indicate where it should go.

…

```
<embed src="poster.mov" href="cobra.mov" target="quicktimeplayer" width="311"
height="253" align="middle" controller="true" autoplay="false" type="video/quicktime" />
```

…

4. Save the file and refresh the browser. Click the movie. After a few seconds, the player should appear. If the movie doesn't start playing, click the Play button.

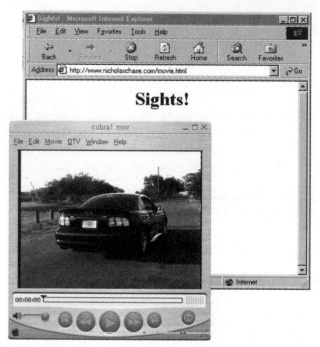

5. Leave the browser and text editor open for the next exercise, but close the QuickTime player.

Using <object> Instead of <embed>

If you look for the <embed /> tag in the HTML 4.01 standard, you won't find it. It was an offspring of the browser wars, a Netscape-specific tag for embedding media on a page.

The <embed /> tag has now been replaced in the standards by the <object></object> tag. The <object></object> tag is more general than <embed /> and enables us to do more.

One of the best features of the <object></object> tag is the codebase attribute. This is similar to the pluginspage attribute for <embed />, except that rather than directing users to a location where they can find, download and install the plug-in, codebase tells the browser where to get the plug-in without human intervention (except to confirm that this is allowed).

The codebase attribute is also a bit more convenient in situations where the browser simply can't load the object because the proper software plug-in isn't installed.

Converting an <embed> Tag to <object>

Converting the <embed /> tag to an <object></object> tag is fairly straightforward. In the simplest case, we could take code that was written as:

```
<embed src="cobra.mov" type="video/quicktime" height="311" width="253" />
```

and change it to:

```
<object data="cobra.mov" type="video/quicktime" height="311" width="253">
  </object>
```

Of course, not all users will be able to play a QuickTime movie, so we can add content within the <object></object> tag to handle that. For instance:

```
<object data="cobra.mov" type="video/quicktime" height="311" width="253">

        You do not currently have the QuickTime Plug-in installed. Please go to
        http://www.apple.com/quicktime/download/ for the latest version. Thank you!

  </object>
```

In this case, if the browser couldn't create the object, it would display the text. This is true for any plug-in, not just QuickTime.

Addressing Browser Issues

The <object></object> tag is a relatively new phenomenon, whereas the <embed /> tag has been around since Netscape 2.0. Fortunately we can employ this ability to use "fallback" content to solve the problem of browsers that don't understand <object></object>. What we do is place the <embed /> tag within the <object></object> tag, as in:

```
<object data="cobra.mov" type="video/quicktime" height="311" width="253">
<embed src="cobra.mov" type="video/quicktime" height="311" width="253" />
  </object>
```

The <embed /> tag also offers a way to provide fallback content in the event that the browser doesn't understand it. Similar to the <noframes></noframes> and <noscript></noscript> tags, we have the <noembed></noembed> tag, as in:

```
<object data="cobra.mov" type="video/quicktime" height="311" width="253">
        <embed src="cobra.mov" type="video/quicktime" height="311" width="253" />
        <noembed>
                A video of DJ Oz's Cobra taking off down the street, complete with
                musical accompaniment and screeching tires.
        </noembed>
  </object>
```

In this case, a browser that understands the <object></object> tag will use it. One that doesn't will attempt to render the content inside. If it understands <embed />, it will render that content. If not, it will render the text version. In any case, therefore, the user should get some content appropriate to his or her browser.

To test your alternative content, change the type to "bogus/bogus" or some other made-up MIME type. The browser won't know you made it up — it'll just know it doesn't understand and show you the alternative content.

The <param /> Tag and Its Issues

The <object></object> tag doesn't have nearly as many possible attributes as the <embed /> tag, and this is by design. Instead, these attributes become parameters that are fed to the <object></object> tag.

For instance, in the previous example, we might want to add the link to a second movie and have it go to the player window. To do that, we could write:

```
<object data="cobra.mov" type="video/quicktime" height="311" width="253">
        <param name="href" value="cobra.mov" />
        <param name="target" value="quicktimeplayer" />

        <embed src="poster.mov" href="cobra.mov" target="quicktimeplayer" type="video/
quicktime" height="311" width="253" />
        <noembed>
                A video of DJ Oz's Cobra taking off down the street, complete with
                musical accompaniment and screeching tires.
        </noembed>
  </object>
```

In this way, we can add as many different attributes as we want without having to tinker with the definition of <object></object>. All is not well, however, in paradise.

If you were to take the above code and move it to your browser, what you would see would depend on which browser you're using. For instance, on a Windows NT system, this page would work fine in Netscape but would not work at all in Internet Explorer 5. The culprit is the <param /> elements in this case. Other <object></object> and <param /> combinations work fine, but not this one. Other systems might have different outcomes, and for different reasons. Once again: test test test!

There will be situations where you need to fall back on something that works (such as the <embed /> tag) and note that you'll have to revisit it later, when other capabilities are more widely supported. And when you think you've got it right, test it some more.

RealMedia

Progressive Networks was the company that introduced the concept of streaming to the Web with their RealAudio product. Soon the company, which became RealNetworks, added video to their offerings, and the race was on.

The RealPlayer today is much more than just an audio or video player. We can use it to play entire presentations, which are created using *SMIL*, a tagging language similar to XHTML.

Types of Media

There are several types of media that can be viewed with the RealPlayer. They include:

- **RealAudio.** This audio is prepared for streaming by a RealServer and is typically created with a program such as RealSystem Producer.
- **RealVideo.** This video is prepared for streaming by a RealServer and is also typically created with a program such as RealSystem Producer.
- **RealText.** This text has been specially prepared for insertion into a presentation. Similar to an XHTML file, this is a text file with special tags.

For instance, we might create a file called "crawler.rt" with the following text:

```
<window type="marquee" duration="1:00" width="350" loop="true"
underline_hyperlinks="true" bgcolor="black" link="white">
        <font color="white">
                <b>These audio and video clips were provided by Dj oZ. Please visit him
                at <a href="http://www.djoz.com">http://www.djoz.com</a>. Photos
                licensed from a separate source.</b>
        </font>
</window>
```

For more information on how to build RealMedia files, see the RealNetworks Web site at http://www.realnetworks.com.

• **RealPix**. These graphic images have been prepared for insertion into a presentation. For example, you might have a file, pics.rp, which contains:

```
<imfl>
    <head title="RealPix Example" background-color="black" duration="20" bitrate="12000"
    width="300" height="300" aspect="true" timeformat="dd:hh:mm:ss.xyz" />

        <!-- Image definitions —>

        <image handle="1" name="images/boy.jpg"/>
        <image handle="2" name="images/pool.jpg"/>
        <image handle="3" name="images/hike.jpg"/>
        <image handle="4" name="images/hammock.jpg"/>

        <!-- Effects that refer back to the images —>

        <fadein start="1" duration="5" target="1"/>
        <fadein start="4" duration="5" target="2"/>
        <fadein start="7" duration="5" target="3"/>
        <fadein start="10" duration="5" target="4"/>

</imfl>
```

If these files will be streamed, you'll want to prepare your images first using a program such as the freeware JPEGTRAN, available at http://www.webdeveloper.com/advhtml/jpegtran.exe.

Other types of media, such as Flash animations (discussed later in the chapter), can also be included in these presentations.

How RealMedia Works

There are several ways for us to play RealMedia. Some of them involve the external player and some don't.

The easiest way, of course, is to embed a movie in the page. We can do this in much the same way that we did with the QuickTime movie. The trouble with this approach is that it only works for video and audio, and you can only play a single clip in that spot on the page.

We can avoid these problems by sending these clips to the player instead. Usually this is done by creating a .ram file.

The *.ram file* is a text file that lists the clips that we want to play. For instance, we can create a .ram file that plays a video and then an audio clip. To do this, we simply create a text file that lists both clips. Normally, the file would contain complete URLs, so the contents would look something like this:

http://www.againsttheclock.com/assets/movie.rm
http://www.againsttheclock.com/assets/audio.rm

In this way, we can play as many clips as we want in sequence, but we still can't play more than one simultaneously. To do that, we need one more tool: SMIL.

SMIL

Synchronized Multimedia Integration Language, or SMIL, is similar to XHTML in format; it enables us to lay out a presentation and control its flow. A comprehensive discussion of SMIL is well beyond the scope of this book, but the basics are easy to understand.

We've seen examples of SMIL already, when we discussed the different types of RealMedia. Now let's take a look at putting them together.

SMIL documents have a structure similar to XHTML documents, with the <smil></smil> element replacing the <html></html> element, as in:

```
<smil>
<head>
… layout information here
</head>
<body>
… content here
</body>
</smil>
```

SMIL is pronounced "smile."

Within the document, we can have items that run sequentially, as they did with the .ram file, and items that run in parallel, as in a presentation with background music. The difference lies in whether we use the <seq></seq>, or sequential tag, or the <par></par>, or parallel tag.

We can also control where items appear on the page by creating layouts, then assigning items to them. To do that, we create a master layout using <layout></layout> and <root-layout />, which gives information about the overall look. This combination of tags creates the window in which the presentation will appear. We then create one or more subareas using the <region /> tag. Finally, we assign different pieces of media to each region.

For example, we could create a region called "crawler":

<region id="crawler" top="260" left="0" width="400" height="60" fit="meet" />

and then assign a textstream, or crawler, to that region:

<textstream src="crawler.rt" region="crawler" />

To cause items in SMIL to run one after another, use the <seq></seq> (sequential) tags. To cause items in SMIL to run at the same time, use the <par></par> (in parallel) tags.

We can do the same thing for video, audio and other files (using the ref tag).

The end result is a file that looks something like this:

```
<smil>
<head>
  <layout>
        <root-layout background-color="black" height="300" width="400" />
        <region id="crawler" top="260" left="0" width="400" height="60" fit="meet" />
        <region id="video" top="20" left="20" width="200" height="250" fit="meet" />
        <region id="images" top="20" left="180" width="200" height="250" fit="meet" />
  </layout>
</head>
<body>
<par>
        <textstream src="crawler.rt" region="crawler" />
        <seq>
                <video src="cobra.rm" region="video" />
                <par>
                        <audio src="saturn.rm" />
                        <ref="pics.rp" region="images" />
                </par>
        </seq>
</par>
</body>
  </smil>
```

SMIL actually allows a much greater range of presentational effects, from hyperlinks within the content to animation. Even games can be created.

Streaming vs. HTTP

As with QuickTime, Web authors have to make a decision on whether or not to stream clips and entire presentations. Web authors are faced with pros and cons that are fairly similar to those of QuickTime.

To stream RealMedia you need the RealServer. You can serve RealMedia using a regular Web server, but many of the same caveats apply. Presentations served with a regular Web server can appear to be similar to streamed presentations under ideal conditions, but there are, of course, no guarantees when it comes to the quality of the stream.

If you decide to stream your content, you will need to use the Real Time Streaming Protocol, or rtsp://, rather than http://. In other words, the URL for each clip might be something like:

rtsp://www.nicholaschase.com/streaming/cobra.rm

Windows Media Player

Microsoft is also attempting to get into the streaming game. The Windows Media Player, which is also available for the Macintosh (more or less — see below) is another player that will enable you to show streaming media to your users.

Placing the Movie

Embedding a Windows Media file on a Web page works just like each of the previous formats we've seen. For instance, the <object></object> and <embed /> tags for the Windows Media version of our video files would be:

```
<object id="cobra" width="160" height="162"
   classid="clsid:22d6f312-b0f6-11d0-94ab-0080c74c7e95"
   codebase = "http://activex.microsoft.com/activex/controls/mplayer/en/
nsmp2inf.cab#version=6,0,02,902"
   standby="Loading components..."  type="application/x-oleobject">

      <param name="filename" value="cobra.wmv">
      <param name="autostart" value="false">

      <embed src="cobra.wmv" type="application/x-mplayer2"
      pluginspage = "http://www.microsoft.com/windows/mediaplayer/"
      name="embedcobra" width="160" height="162" autostart="false"
      filename="cobra.wmv" />

</object>
```

Problems on the Macintosh

Although Microsoft would, of course, like for the Windows Media Player to be the standard streaming media player (and by extension, the standard format), there have been issues in the past with non-Windows versions of the Windows Media Player, specifically on the Macintosh. These problems have reportedly been fixed, but, again, test! Your content may have that one little bit in it that causes problems.

Remember to use rtsp:// (Real Time Streaming Protocol) rather than http:// if you intend to stream your content. Of course, you must also use the RealServer.

Java applets have, for the most part, gone the way of the dinosaur. Largely replaced by DHTML and Flash movies, even their tag, <applet></applet>, has been deprecated in XHTML 1.0 and removed from XHTML 1.1. They are now run simply as <object>s, if at all.

Although we can't fit some of these URLs on a single line, be sure not to add the line breaks on your page. URLs must be typed on a single line, with no spaces.

Flash

Once upon a time, back in the Dark Ages (that is, the mid 1990s), if you wanted to create an animation on your computer, you probably did so by rolling up your sleeves and learning a $900 program called "Macromedia Director." If you wanted to do anything complex, you had to learn Director's scripting language, Lingo. And if you wanted to put your creation on the Web, well, you were pretty much out of luck, unless you wanted to create a self-running program called a "projector" for users to download and play at their leisure.

Director was never intended for the Web. It was intended for creating interactive CD-ROMs and kiosks. It did (and still does) a good job.

Macromedia, however, recognized the fact that the Web was taking over, and didn't let it escape from them. Their first step was Shockwave. Shockwave was a type of movie that Director could create and that Web authors could embed into their pages, like a QuickTime movie or a Java applet. Now artists and other Web authors who knew Director could create interactive presentations previously unheard of without learning how to program in Java.

Shockwave took off like a rocket, and Macromedia quickly capitalized on their success by creating Flash. Simply put, Flash is the parts of Director that are most useful for Web animations. Concentrating on vector graphics instead of photographic formats, Flash allows artists to create elaborate presentations, animations and games without creating huge files or spending a fortune.

Flash movies are embedded on the page just as their QuickTime and Real counterparts are. For example, to add the Flash movie chemep1.swf to our page, we would use the following:

```
<object
    classid="clsid:D27CDB6E-AE6D-11cf-96B8-444553540000"
    codebase="http://download.macromedia.com/pub/shockwave/cabs/flash/
swflash.cab#version=5,0,0,0" width="550" height="330">

        <param name="movie" value="chemep1.swf">

 <embed src="chemep1.swf" type="application/x-shockwave-flash" width="550"
height="400" pluginspage="http://www.macromedia.com/shockwave/download/
index.cgi?P1_Prod_Version=ShockwaveFlash" />

  </object>
```

This code is comparable to the code used to add other video or audio files to the page. The code uses an <embed /> tag within the <object></object> tags to cover browsers that understand one or the other. (See section on Addressing Browser Issues.)

Exercise Setup
To demonstrate, we'll create a page for The Chem Lab Chronicles.

Embed a Flash Movie

1. Create a new text file called "chemlab.html" and save it in the **WIP>streaming** folder.

2. Create the basic document.

```
<html>
<head><title>The Chem Lab Chronicles</title></head>
<body>

</body>
</html>
```

3. Add the movie information. Include both the <object></object> and <embed /> versions.

```
…
<body>

<object classid="clsid:D27CDB6E-AE6D-11cf-96B8-444553540000"
codebase="http://download.macromedia.com/pub/shockwave/cabs/flash/
swflash.cab#version=5,0,0,0" width="550" height="330">
        <param name="movie" value="chemep1.swf">

 <embed src="chemep1.swf" type="application/x-shockwave-flash" width="550"
height="400" pluginspage="http://www.macromedia.com/shockwave/download/
index.cgi?P1_Prod_Version=ShockwaveFlash" />

</object>

</body>
</html>
```

4. Save the file and open it in the browser. The movie should begin playing immediately, although you'll see it loading first.

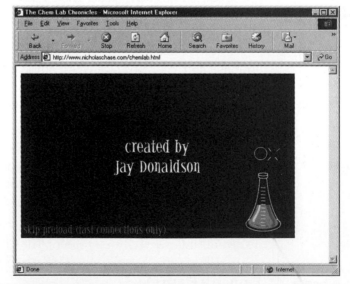

Thanks to Jay Donaldson of liquidshorts.com for the use of this movie.
The Chem Lab Chronicles *was also featured on Atom Films.*

5. Close both windows.

Because the Flash movies don't have controllers (unless they're built into the movies themselves) you will have to click the browser's Back button to stop the movie.

Designing the Overall Page

Because there is no separate player for a Flash movie, as there was for QuickTime and RealMedia, embedding a Flash movie on a page by itself leaves the page looking rather bare. Sometimes, the temptation is to build the entire page in Flash, as Jay did on his site, using Flash to accomplish rollovers and other effects rather than using XHTML and scripts.

There's one point we're forgetting, though. These movies are played by a plug-in, and that plug-in is not necessarily installed on every user's system. So there is one question that always haunts Web authors: how do we know whether or not the user can see the Flash movies?

While users of Windows Internet Explorer (post-Windows 3.1) will not have a problem because the <object></object> tag will download the plug-in, if necessary, this far from represents your entire audience. We can't be certain about what users do and do not have at their disposal, so we still have to worry about it.

Detecting the Flash Plug-in

For as long as there have been Flash movies, there have been Web authors trying to figure out whether or not the user can see them. There are several approaches, ranging from low-tech to high-tech:

- **Just ask.** This is the simplest way. In this case, users generally come to a home page that asks them whether they want to view the Flash version of the site or the non-Flash version. Depending on which link they choose, users receive the appropriate content. There is no scripting involved with this method at all.

- **Work with the user.** Sometimes users simply don't know whether or not they can view Flash movies, so asking them what they want won't necessarily do the trick. In this case, what some Web authors choose to do is to provide a small sample movie, which usually has a simple animation in it. They then provide text that says something to the effect of, "If you can see the arrows moving, you're ready for the Flash version of our site. If not, please download the Flash plug-in." Appropriate links are then provided.

- **Let the browser decide.** In this case, scripting is used to determine whether or not the plug-in is available. This, unfortunately, is complicated by the fact that Netscape and Internet Explorer both have different ways of making this information available to a script, and they are mutually exclusive.

The thinking generally goes as follows:

- If the browser says that it can handle the Flash MIME type, application/x-shockwave-flash, then use Flash. This check applies only to Netscape browsers.
- Otherwise, if they're using Windows and Internet Explorer and they're not using Windows 3.1, use Flash.
- This leaves those using Netscape without Flash, those using Windows 3.1, and those without scripting enabled. None of these people receive the Flash movie.

The script looks like this:

```
<script type="javascript">
<!--
var FlashOK = 0;
if (navigator.mimeTypes && navigator.mimeTypes["application/x-shockwave-flash"] ) {
        //Netscape with Flash
        FlashOK = true;
} else if (navigator.appName && navigator.appName.indexOf("Microsoft") != -1 &&
        navigator.userAgent.indexOf("Windows") != -1 &&
        navigator.userAgent.indexOf("Windows 3.1") == -1) {
        //Windows Internet Explorer, but not Windows 3.1
        FlashOK = true;
}

if (FlashOK) {
        // Use scripting to write the Flash tags
        document.write('<object ');
        document.write('classid="clsid:D27CDB6E-AE6D-11cf-96B8-444553540000"');
        document.write('codebase="http://download.macromedia.com/pub/shockwave/
cabs/flash/swflash.cab#version=5,0,0,0"');
        document.write('width="550" height="330">');
        document.write('<param name="movie" value="chemep1.swf">');

        document.write('<embed src="chemep1.swf" width="550" height="330"');
        document.write(' type="application/x-shockwave-flash" ');
        document.write('pluginspage="http://www.macromedia.com/shockwave/down
load/index.cgi?P1_Prod_Version=ShockwaveFlash" />');

        document.write('</object>');
} else {
        document.write('<img src="chemlab.gif" width="550" height="330">');
}
//-->
</script>
<noscript><img src="chemlab.gif" width="550" height="330"></noscript>
```

- **Use scripting to decide, but give the user final control.** This option is made much easier by Flash itself.

Options Built into Flash 5

If you're using Flash 5, you have much easier options available to you. In order to use a Flash movie on the Web, you have to publish it, and Flash gives you control over how you do so.

The Publishing Preferences enable you to choose exactly what the output will be when you publish. In all cases, your .fla file, which contains all of your authoring information, will be exported as a .swf file, the file format for which the player looks. This file can't be opened in Flash except for playing purposes, so no one will be able to use the Flash application to alter your movies.

In addition to the .swf file, you can choose a number of other formats to be exported, including GIF, JPG and PNG files, self-running projectors, QuickTime movies and RealMedia.

The publishing function will also create an HTML page with any necessary scripting, <object></object>, and <embed /> tags all ready for you to customize. You can even decide whether or not you want to force the user to use Flash or some other format, or if you want to allow the user to choose.

In this case, Flash provides a page that includes a script similar to the one above, but also allows the user to set a *cookie*, a small file on their computer indicating their preference. In this way, the next time that they come to the site, the site will already know their preference. Again, you can customize this page so that it looks like the rest of your site. You have the best of all possible worlds.

Summary

In this chapter, you've explored different types of media, such as audio and video, and how to embed them on a page. You've become familiar with the difference between streaming and non-streaming media, and when it is appropriate to use each of them. You've discovered some of the newer formats available, such as RealMedia, SMIL and Flash, as well as what is involved with their use.

Notes:

10 Meta Tags and Search Engines

Chapter Objective:

To learn how to use <meta /> tags to make your site easier for both browsers and search engines to work with. In Chapter 10, you will:

- Discover how <meta /> tags work behind the scenes.

- Learn how to add the information for which search engines are looking.

- Explore how and why to prevent search engines from visiting your site.

- Become familiar with rating information and how to add it to your site.

Projects to be Completed:

- News Web (A)

- Cyber Travel (B)

- **Hunter Films (C)**

- North Star Adventure Gear (D)

Meta Tags and Search Engines

Now that we've built the site, it's time to look under the hood and make certain that it's going to run at optimum efficiency. In this chapter, we're going to look at an underused tool in Web design — meta tags.

Meta Information

Every search engine has a different procedure for submitting links. While it might be convenient to use a service that advertises that you can "submit instantly to 15,000 search engines!" let's think about it for a moment. Do you know 15,000 search engines? Of course not. Neither do the other millions of Web surfers out there. Always submit to the major six or eight search engines manually so that you can see if there are any problems. Then use the services, if it makes you happy.

Literally, from the Greek, meta information is information that transcends information — information about information.

We use meta information to describe our pages. Sometimes, as in the case of keywords or descriptions, we're providing information for the search engines. At other times, as in the case of character sets, we're providing information to the browser. In all of these cases, we're dealing with a single empty tag, <meta />.

The <meta /> tag has just a few possible attributes — name (used to identify content by humans and other software), content (the actual information), lang (used to specify the language for a particular meta tag) and http-equiv (used to send information normally sent by the Web server) — and of these, only content is actually required.

So how do we accomplish so much with this tag? The secret is in the values that we use.

Setting General Page Information

The <meta /> tags were designed to be flexible. We can add any kind of information that we want with them, using the name and content attributes.

For instance, going back to our Dr. Know-It-All pages, we might set some very basic information, such as copyright, names and dates. This information is fairly straightforward. If we were writing a <meta /> tag about *Romeo and Juliet*, we might say:

<meta name="Author" content="William Shakespeare" />

These <meta /> tags normally belong in the <head></head> section of the document.

Exercise Setup
Lets add some basic meta information to the top of our recommendations page.

Add Basic Meta Tags

1. Create a folder called "meta" in the WIP folder. Navigate to **RF-HTML>Chapter 10**, and copy the contents of the Chapter 10 folder to the **WIP>meta** folder.

2. Open **WIP>meta>recs.html** in the browser and the text editor.

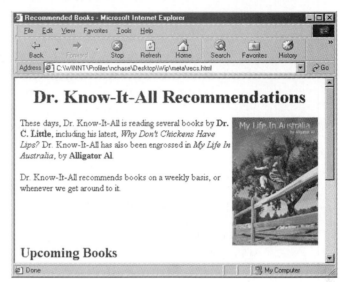

3. Add author and copyright <meta /> tags to the <head></head> section of the document.

```
<!DOCTYPE HTML PUBLIC "-//W3C//DTD HTML 4.01 Transitional//EN" "http://
www.w3.org/TR/html4/loose.dtd">
<html>
<head>
<title>Recommended Books</title>
<meta name="Author" content="John Smith" />
<meta name="Copyright" content="2001, Know-It-All Productions" />
</head>
<body>
<h1 align="center">Dr. Know-It-All Recommendations</h1>
…
```

4. Save the file and refresh the browser. Notice that nothing on the page has changed. None of the information that we added is shown to the user. Instead, it's used by other programs, such as search engines.

5. Leave both windows open for the next exercise.

Search Engines

There will come a time, possibly soon, when <meta> tags are important for alternate types of browsers, such as those for cell phones or devices for the disabled. Today, however, the most common use for these tags is to improve a site's standing and/or display on the search engines.

A search engine works by reading a page that has been submitted to it and recording, or *indexing*, its content. Most search engines will also visit the pages that are linked and index them as well. This indexed information is then used to determine which sites and pages to display for any particular search.

Each search can result in dozens, hundreds or even thousands of matches, and each engine has its own way of deciding which ones to show first. This is important, because most users will not get past the first or second page of results, so there can be a huge difference between spot number 20 and spot number 21.

First, however, let's be clear about a few points concerning search engines:

- There is nothing that we can teach you that will guarantee that your pages will jump to the top of any search engine.

- The best way to improve your search engine rankings is to provide good, relevant content. Search engines, in general, look for the frequency of search terms and their location. Search engines assume that if a term appears early on the page, it must be more relevant to the rest of the content. In general, the items that have the largest net effect on rankings are the page title, headings and alt text, so make certain that they're relevant and contain your keywords, wherever possible. The domain name is also weighted heavily on most engines.

- While not all search engines look specifically for keywords in <meta /> tags, these tags can't hurt and frequently help.

Keywords

When planning your site, it's important to know your particular keywords. A *keyword* is a word or phrase that the user is likely to type into a search engine when looking for Web pages. The best way to develop your keywords is to think about what you would type into a search engine if you were looking for information on your topic.

Next, consider variations on those terms. Singular, plural and particularly multi-word phrases are important. For example:

```
<meta name="keywords" content="xhtml, html, web, internet, instruction, instructions, web development, web developer, web developers" />
```

Some people pack their <meta> tags with keywords that are either unrelated or unnecessarily repeated, in hopes of tricking the engines into giving them better placement. For instance:

```
<meta name="keywords" content="xhtml, html, html, html, html, web, web, web, web, internet, instruction, instructions, web development, web developer, web developers" />
```

This use of unrelated or repetitious words is also known as "spamming" a search engine and can seriously backfire. Search engines are constantly refining their methods of detecting spamming and frequently ban a site using spamming from the search engine altogether.

Adding a <meta /> tag for keywords involves the same technique that we used for author and copyright information, but with different content:

```
<meta name="keywords" content="food, recreation" />
```

Exercise Setup
Let's set some keywords for our recommendation page.

Add Keywords

1. Develop a list of keywords based on the content of the page and the search terms that you would expect a user to employ. Some obvious choices are the names of the authors and books, the Dr. Know-It-All site name, and the fact that the site has book reviews. Other choices might include the subject matter of the books. Also choose variations on these words, including plurals. Your list will looks something like:

Dr. Know-It-All
Dr. C. Little
Little
Why Don't Chickens Have Lips
Alligator Al
Alligator
Al
My Life in Australia
Sally Slinky
Sally
Slinky
Weight Loss Secrets
Chickens
Farming
Lips
Australia
childhood memories
memoirs
weight loss
diet
diets
dieting
book reviews
book
books

2. In the open recs.html file in the text editor, add the keyword <meta /> tag to the recs.html file.

```
…
<head>
<title>Recommended Books</title>
<meta name="Author" content="John Smith" />
        <meta name="Copyright" content = "2001, Know-It-All Productions" />
        <meta name="keywords" content="Dr. Know-It-All, Dr. C. Little, Little, Why
Don't Chickens Have Lips, Alligator Al, Alligator, Al, My Life in Australia, Sally Slinky,
Sally, Slinky, Weight Loss Secrets, Chickens, Farming, Lips, Australia, childhood
memories, memoirs, weight loss, diet, diets, dieting, book reviews, book, books" />
</head>
<body>
…
```

3. Save and refresh the browser. There should be no change in the displayed page.

4. Leave both windows open for the next exercise.

Description

The description <meta /> tag is sometimes used in the search, but it is more often used to help control the display if a site is part of the results.

Normally, a search engine will display the first sentence or so of a page. For instance, depending on the search engine, our site might look something like this:

Recommended Books: Dr. Know-It-All Recommendations. These days, Dr. Know-it-All is reading …

While that certainly is accurate, we would probably prefer something more like:

Recommended Books: Dr. Know-It-All reviews new books on a weekly basis. This week: Why Don't Chickens Have Lips by Dr. C. Little and Alligator Al's My Life In Australia.

We would do this by adding a description <meta /> tag:

<meta name="description" content="Dr. Know-It-All reviews new books on a weekly basis. This week: Why Don't Chickens Have Lips by Dr. C. Little and Alligator Al's My Life In Australia." />

Description is used as the value of name, and its content is the text that describes the page. This text also appears next to the page title on many search engines when a page is listed.

In the above example, Recommended Books is the page title. We can add the description by adding a description <meta /> tag, just as we added one for keywords.

Add the Description

1. In the open file recs.html in the text editor, add the description to the document.

```
…
<head>
<title>Recommended Books</title>
<meta name="Author" content="John Smith" />
        <meta name="Copyright" content = "2001, Know-It-All Productions" />
        <meta name="keywords" content="Dr. Know-It-All, Dr. C. Little, Little, Why Don't
Chickens Have Lips, Alligator Al, Alligator, Al, My Life in Australia, Sally Slinky, Sally, Slinky,
Weight Loss Secrets, Chickens, Farming, Lips, Australia, childhood memories, memoirs,
weight loss, diet, diets, dieting, book reviews, book, books" />
        <meta name="description" content="Dr. Know-It-All reviews new books on
a weekly basis. This week:  Why Don't Chickens Have Lips by Dr. C. Little and
Alligator Al's My Life In Australia." />
</head>
<body>
…
```

2. Save the file and refresh the browser to ensure that nothing has changed.

3. Leave both windows open for the next exercise.

Always check your file when you make a change. By doing so, if something does suddenly break, you'll know where to look for the problem. If you wait until you've made several changes, deciding which one is the problem will be a lot harder.

Searches in Different Languages

The globalization of the Web means that not everyone who's reading your pages necessarily speaks English, or even uses what we might consider to be the typical alphabet.

Some search engines, such as AltaVista, enable users to search for content in particular languages. To maximize our reach, if we offer content in different languages, we can include keywords and descriptions for those languages as well. We do this by utilizing the lang attribute for <meta /> tags. For instance, to designate that our description is for speakers of American English, we can change our tag to read:

<meta name="description" **lang="en-us"** content=" Dr. Know-It-All reviews new books on a weekly basis. This week: Why Don't Chickens Have Lips by Dr. C. Little and Alligator Al's My Life In Australia." />

The browser sends this code, en-us, in the background to any site that requests it. In order to avoid leaving out those whose browsers are set for the British (England) version of English, we would want to include a copy for them, as well using en as the value for lang:

<meta name="description" **lang="en"** content=" Dr. Know-It-All reviews new books on a weekly basis. This week: Why Don't Chickens Have Lips by Dr. C. Little and Alligator Al's My Life In Australia." />

More information on language codes can be found at http:// www.w3.org/International/ O-HTML-tags.html.

Exercise Setup
Let's also add a German version of the description to our page.

Add Support for Different Languages

1. Open **WIP>meta>recs.html** in the text editor and browser if it's not already open.

2. Add the language attribute, lang="en-us", as well as additional versions of our description such as British English, signified by the language code en, and German, as signified by de.

…

    <meta name="keywords" **lang="en-us"** content="Dr. Know-It-All, Dr. C. Little, Little, Why Don't Chickens Have Lips, Alligator Al, Alligator, Al, My Life in Australia, Sally Slinky, Sally, Slinky, Weight Loss Secrets, Chickens, Farming, Lips, Australia, childhood memories, memoirs, weight loss, diet, diets, dieting, book reviews, book, books" />
    <meta name="description" **lang="en-us"** content=" Dr. Know-It-All reviews new books on a weekly basis. This week: Why Don't Chickens Have Lips by Dr. C. Little and Alligator Al's My Life In Australia." />
    <meta name="description" lang="en" content="Dr. Know-It-All reviews new books on a weekly basis. This week: Why Don't Chickens Have Lips by Dr. C. Little and Alligator Al's My Life In Australia." />
    <meta name="description" lang="de" content="Dr. Know-It-All wiederholt neue Bücher auf einer wöchentlichen Grundlage. Diese Woche: Warum Hühner Don't Lippen durch Dr. C. Little und Alligator Al's Meine Lebensdauer in Australien Haben." />
</head>
<body>
…

3. Save the file and refresh the browser to verify that nothing has changed.

4. Leave both windows open for the next exercise.

The name of a <meta /> tag is not case sensitive generally. The http-equiv attribute, however, tells the browser to emulate information that the server normally sends. It's quite important, therefore, that we match the case that it's expecting and capitalize the value of the http-equiv.

Multilanguage Web Sites

In addition to providing descriptions in different languages, it is often a good idea to provide actual content in different languages. How much you provide is going to depend on your intended audience. Some sites opt for providing all of their content in many different languages; some opt for just a few main pages. Your choice will depend on the composition of your customers.

Alternate Character Sets

While we see how to address searches in different languages, there's still the problem of the character sets (alphabets, characters and more) in which our content may need to be presented. Imagine the complications if we'd tried to translate our description into Japanese!

The best way to solve this problem is to specify the character set right in our document. It's convenient to do that when we specify the type of document this file is. For instance, the following code specifies our alphabet (character set):

`<meta http-equiv="Content-Type" content="text/html; `**`charset=ISO-8859-1"`**` />`

http-equiv is similar to name, but has a slightly different purpose. We will talk more about it in the section on Refreshing the Page. ISO-8859-1 is also known as Latin-1, the typical character set used in the United States.

Exercise Setup

Let's add the character set to our document.

Add Character Encoding Information

1. In the open recs.html file in the text editor, add the character encoding charset=ISO-8859-1 to the document using the http-equiv meta tag.

```
…
<meta name="description" lang="de" content="Dr. Know-It-All wiederholt neue Bücher auf einer wöchentlichen Grundlage. Diese Woche: Warum Hühner Don't Lippen durch Dr. C. Little und Alligator Al's Meine Lebensdauer in Australien Haben." />
<meta http-equiv="Content-Type" content="text/html; charset=ISO-8859-1" />
</head>
<body>
…
```

2. Save the file and refresh the browser to verify that nothing has changed.

3. Leave both windows open for the next exercise.

Spiders, Crawlers and Robots

As we mentioned previously, search engines obtain their lists of pages by reading each page on a Web site, then following each link and reading that page, and repeating the process throughout your entire site. This process is called "spidering" or "crawling" a site. There's no human interaction, for the most part. Some search engines crawl your entire site. Others just crawl two or three levels deep from the page you submit to them.

This multipage crawl comes as a surprise to many people. You may want an engine to crawl deeper into your site. That can usually be accomplished by submitting deeper pages as a starting point, as well. The problem occurs when you have content that you don't want indexed. You may not even submit it to a search engine, but what happens when someone with a link to your content does? The search engine doesn't know the difference — it's just following the links.

Fortunately, we can prevent a search engine from indexing our site in a number of ways.

In the early days, these crawling programs were called "robots," and to stop them, a webmaster would add a file called "robots.txt" to the root directory of the Web site. This file specifies the spiders that are affected by each directive, then defines what they can and cannot crawl. For instance, if we wanted to allow all spiders to crawl our main directory and our books directory but not our membership or internal directories, the robots file would look like this:

```
User-agent: *
Disallow: /membership/
Disallow: /internal/
```

Use a trailing slash after the disallowed items indicates that you're telling the robot to ignore the directory. If you do not use the slash after that item, you are directing it to skip any file that starts with that name, as well.

The trailing slash tells the robot that we're referring only to the directory. If we were to say instead:

```
Disallow: /membership
```

then crawlers also would skip a file called "membership.html."

This is a little awkward, though, because often Web authors don't have access to the robots.txt file, and because the file doesn't use the same formats that we're accustomed to using. Using <meta /> tags, we can control what a crawler can do on each page. We can even separately control whether or not it can crawl the page looking for other links and whether or not it can index the content on the page. For instance, if we had a page with public information but links to sensitive content, we might want to allow it to be indexed but not crawled. We would create a <meta /> tag like this:

```
<meta name="robots" content="index, nofollow" />
```

On the other hand, if we didn't want the content indexed, but we didn't want to ruin chances for the pages to which we link, we could create this <meta /> tag:

```
<meta name="robots" content="noindex" />
```

This tells the crawler that we don't want this particular page indexed, but that it's welcome to follow any referenced links and index them.

Of course, under normal circumstances, we want our pages to be both indexed and crawled.

To summarize:

- **index**. This value tells the crawler to index this page
- **noindex**. This value tells the crawler not to index this page
- **nofollow**. This value tells the crawler not to follow any links referenced on this page.

Exercise Setup

Let's add the <meta /> tag to the page.

Define Crawler Preferences

1. In the open recs.html file in the text editor, add the robots <meta> tag to our page.

```
…
<head>
        <title>Recommended Books</title>
        <meta name="robots" content="all" />
        <meta name="Author" content="John Smith" />
        <meta name="Copyright" content = "2001, Know-It-All Productions" />
…
```

2. Save the page and refresh the browser to double-check that nothing has changed.

3. Leave both windows open for the next exercise.

Refreshing/Redirecting the Page

All current major Web browsers support this feature, but not necessarily those for cell phones, PDAs, etc. Older browsers (released prior to 1997) might also lack support for this feature.

The Web is what is known as a "stateless medium." Once we request a page from the server and it delivers this page, we are no longer connected to the server. If the page changes, we wouldn't know about the change unless we refreshed the page.

In most cases, this disconnect from the server isn't a problem. But what about situations where things are changing, like a weather page watching a storm, or a stock market information page with pricing information? In a situation like these, we want to be able to force the page to refresh without user interaction so the most current information is always present.

Refreshing the Page

We can force this update with the refresh <meta /> tag. All that we do is specify the interval and the address of the page, and if it supports this tag, the browser will do the rest.

To make these specifications, we use headers to tell the browser that we're approximating a function that's normally performed by the server. We're not talking about headers like the <h1></h1> tags that we learned about in Chapter 1. Rather, we're talking about information that's sent to the browser before the page content. Some sample headers are:

```
Status: 200
Content-type: text/html
```

These sample headers indicate that the page was delivered successfully, and that the MIME type is text/html.

As Web-page authors, we normally don't have the opportunity to affect those headers, since they're handled by the server. Instead, we use the <meta /> tag to provide equivalents. So rather than using the name attribute, we use the http-equiv attribute, which tells the browser to treat the information as though it were contained in a header. For instance, to refresh our recs.html page every 30 seconds, we would write:

```
<meta http-equiv="Refresh" content="30; URL=recs.html" />
```

The meta tag performs the same function of this header normally sent by the Web server:

```
Refresh: 30; URL=recs.html
```

This tells the browser that it should refresh the page in 30 seconds, at which time it should load recs.html. Usually the interval is set for anywhere from 30 seconds to 10 minutes (that is, 600 seconds).

Exercise Setup

For our page, let's set the interval to 10 seconds and see how it works.

Refresh the Page

1. In the open recs.html file in the text editor, add the refresh <meta> tag to the page.

```
...
<head>
<title>Recommended Books</title>
<meta http-equiv="Refresh" content="10; URL=recs.html" />
<meta name="robots" content="all" />
...
```

2. Save the page. At this moment, the browser still is using the code of our old page, without the new <meta /> tag in it. Until we refresh the browser to give it this version of the page, nothing is going to happen. Refresh the browser.

3. Wait 10 seconds and notice that the page refreshes itself.

4. Make a change to the page, such as adding a brief promo to the top of the page. (The actual content doesn't matter. We just want to see if the page changes.)

```
...
</head>
<body>
<h2 align="center">Next Week: Shed Those Pounds!</h2>
<hr />
<h1 align="center">Dr. Know-It-All Recommendations</h1>
...
```

Choose your interval carefully. The browser is going to refresh the page whether or not all of the graphics have loaded. If you set the interval too short, your users may never see all of the content.

5. Save the file. Look at the browser, but do not refresh it. Notice that within 10 seconds, the browser refreshes the page, showing you the new content.

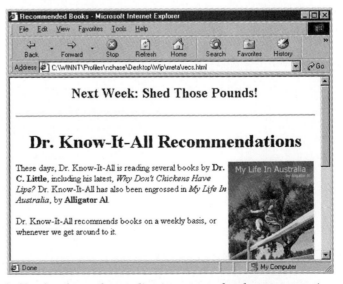

6. Close both files, but leave the applications open for the next exercise.

Redirecting the Page

One of the major problems with search engines and other directories is called "link rot." Link rot occurs when many of the references on the Web page are outdated and the URLs no longer exist, so the user is frustrated by broken links.

Sometimes the problem isn't so much that the content doesn't exist but that it's been moved. Some large corporations, for example, are notorious for moving content on their sites without giving any hint as to where it might have gone.

There is a certain virtue to maintaining an old page for a significant period of time. Other sites may link to your page, your offline advertising may promote your URL, or, if you're fortunate, magazine writers may have published it. All of these references can last much, much longer than you ever anticipated.

Sometimes you really do want an "instant" redirect. If so, it's better to do so through the Web server. This will eliminate problems with older browsers and search engines, but requires the assistance of your system administrator.

Sometimes, however, maintaining an old page simply isn't practical. So what do you do? You provide a way to send the user from the old page to the new one.

When the browser uses the <meta /> tag for refreshing the page, it's just reading the location from the content attribute. There's nothing that says that the URL needs to be the same as the current page. This means that we can use this method to send the browser to a totally different location, such as a new URL, i.e. a new page.

The temptation, of course, is to set the interval to 0 seconds, so that it appears seamless to the user. There are two problems with doing so.

The first problem is that if you're making a change to the URL, such as for a new domain name, you want people to know about the change so that they can update their bookmarks. By encouraging them to make this update, you ensure that you won't lose your users if you can't maintain the old page forever.

A more important problem is the fact that search engines and those with older browsers won't ever see the new page, because the <meta /> tag doesn't affect them.

The solution is a somewhat hybrid approach. We can create a page that does the redirect, but that also both notifies users that they need to change their bookmarks and provides a link for those who aren't automatically redirected.

In this case, we add both the redirect:

```
<meta http-equiv="Refresh" content="30; URL=recs.html" />
```

and more text that includes a text link that users can click if the redirect doesn't work. We wind up with an explanatory page that also contains a link for users and search engines.

Exercise Setup

Let's assume that our recommendations used to be in a different location and create a page directing users to the new page.

Redirect the User

1. Open **WIP>meta>oldrecs.html** in your text editor.

2. We want to create a page that redirects the browser to another page after 30 seconds, but also provides a link to the new page. To do this, add the Refresh meta tag.

```
<!DOCTYPE HTML PUBLIC "-//W3C//DTD HTML 4.01 Transitional//EN"
"http://www.w3.org/TR/html4/loose.dtd">
<html>
<head>
<title>We've Moved!</title>
<meta http-equiv="Refresh" content="30; URL=recs.html" />
</head>
<body>
<h1 align="center">We've Moved!</h1>
Dr. Know-It-All's book recommendations are no longer at this URL.
Please update your bookmarks. If you are not taken to the new
page in 30 seconds, please <a href="recs.html">click here</a>.
Thanks for your patronage!

</body>
</html>
```

3. Save the file and open it in the browser.

4. Wait 30 seconds and then verify that the browser automatically takes you to recs.html.

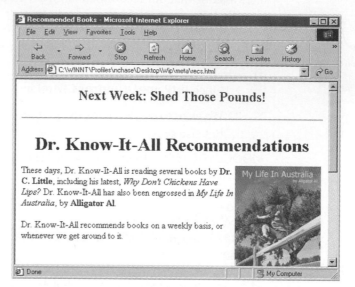

5. Leave both windows open for the next exercise.

Caching and Proxies

A *proxy server* acts as a gateway, making many users seem like one to the Internet. Instead of making the request directly to the Internet, the browser makes the request to the proxy, which then goes out and retrieves the page and feeds it back to the browser.

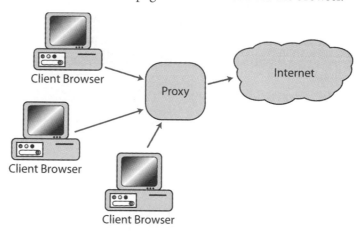

This process, in and of itself, is not a problem. The problem arises when we are dealing with a caching proxy. You may be familiar with your browser's cache. This is where the browser stores information that it has already seen, so that if you request the information again, the browser won't have to download the same material all over again. A caching proxy acts the same way, but for multiple users.

For instance, if Joe in Akron requests the Dr. Know-It-All recommendations page, the proxy gets a copy of it and serves it to him, then saves a copy for anyone else. Then, if Jeff in Dallas requests the same page, the proxy saves time by sending him the copy it has already stored. This makes it seem to Jeff as though the request was processed quite quickly, but he may not realize that the page has changed since it was last saved by the proxy. This probably isn't a major issue, in most cases, but it is always a good idea to take control over this process.

Expiring Content

The best way to take control is to set a date for when our content will expire. This will help us not only with caching proxies, but also with those users whose browsers are set to never check for new content. By setting an expiration date, we force new content in both of those situations.

The expires <meta /> tag is similar to the refresh version, in that we're mimicking headers, so again we'll use http-equiv instead of name.

Times are set using GMT, or Greenwich Mean Time. GMT is 5 hours ahead of Eastern Standard Time, so the tag:

```
<meta http-equiv="Expires" content="Wed, 4 July 2002 12:00:00 GMT" />
```

means that this page expires at 7AM EST on July 4, 2002.

Exercise Setup

Let's set the expiration date for our recommendations page.

Set the Expiration Date

1. In the open recs.html file in the text editor, remove the Refresh <meta /> tag and replace it with an Expires tag.

```
…
<head>
<title>Recommended Books</title>
<meta http-equiv="Expires" content="Wed, 4 July 2002 12:00:00 GMT" />
<meta name="robots" content="all" />
…
```

2. Save the file and refresh the browser to ensure that nothing has changed.

3. Close both applications

Preventing Caching Completely

If we have extremely time-sensitive or frequently changing information, we may want to prevent caching altogether. This covers all bases.

This global prevention of caching should be used sparingly, however. Caching was invented for a reason. If your content isn't changing, your users will be forced to download unnecessarily, and this can lead to their impression that your site is extremely slow.

The best way to prevent caching is to set the expiration time for your content to some time in the past. By doing so, your content will never be cached.

Rating Systems

Unfortunately, there is plenty of content out there that you wouldn't want your children to stumble upon. Fortunately, there are also many programs available that filter out sites with specific characteristics, such as violence and nudity. These filtering programs have different methods for determining whether or not a site is appropriate for children, but one way that they use is a PICS (Platform for Internet Content Selection) rating.

There are several different ratings vocabularies. In order to obtain a rating, you generally have to go to one of these services, answer some questions about your content, and then take the <meta /> tag they build and insert it into your pages. Every system is different, and you'll need to follow their instructions.

As an example, www.nicholaschase.com was rated with the Internet Content Rating Association, which received the following <meta /> tag to insert onto the site:

```
<meta http-equiv="pics-label" content="(pics-1.1 "http://www.icra.org/ratingsv02.html" l gen
true for "http://www.nicholaschase.com" r (cz 1 lz 1 nz 1 oz 1 vz 1) "http://www.rsac.org/
ratingsv01.html" l gen true for "http://www.nicholaschase.com" r (n 0 s 0 v 0 l 0))"  />
```

PICS is the subject of some controversy at the moment, stemming from the unintended use of PICS ratings for governmental censorship of content, as some governments choose to mandate that certain types of pages are unlawful. For more information on ratings systems, visit http://www.w3.org/PICS/overview.html.

Summary

In this chapter, you learned ways to add information about a Web page to that Web page. You became familiar with the role of search engines, how they work and how to provide keywords and descriptions for them. You also discovered how to control what content search engines are allowed to see on a site, and whether or not and for how long your content is cached, as well as how to refresh or redirect the page automatically. Finally, you explored the basics of content-rating systems.

Complete Project C: Hunter Films

11 *Usability and Accessibility*

Chapter Objective:

To learn how to make your site more accessible to those with disabilities and more usable for those without them. To discover how, in the process, to make the site more accessible to other users and potential customers, as well. In Chapter 11, you will:

- Become familiar with the various kind of disabilities for which you should plan.

- Learn about the features built into XHTML specifically to assist with accessibility.

- Discover how to design a site for maximum accessibility and usability.

Projects to be Completed:

- News Web (A)

- Cyber Travel (B)

- Hunter Films (C)

- North Star Adventure Gear (D)

Usability and Accessibility

When you or your designers think about what you're going to do with your site, it is virtually inevitable that a good portion of the discussion (at least at first) is going to center around how it's going to look, how cool it's going to be and how exciting users are going to find it. Unfortunately, for many novice designers, the conversation stops there.

Particularly, in the early days of the Web, this resulted in sites that were beautiful to look at — for about 15 seconds — which was how long it took users to realize they couldn't figure out how to do what they came to do. Most such sites were mainly branding vehicles, so if the site generated "buzz," it was considered a success. Those days are gone now. Your Web site is a crucial part of your business. If it's not usable, it's worthless.

Usability Constituents

On the Web, there's usability and there's usability. Some companies are satisfied if it's possible to perform the desired action on their site, even if the process isn't intuitive. Unfortunately, the majority of sites don't clear even that bar for a significant number of users, and the sites' owners don't even realize it.

Disabled Web Users

If you ask most designers how a blind person would interact with their site, after no more than a few moments of thought they would probably tell you that blind people have "screen readers or something." They might even tell you proudly that all of their images have alternate text, so that these readers no longer read those nifty navigation sections as "image image image image image," as was common before alternate text was a required attribute.

Many of these same designers create pages with such small text that those with poor eyesight using a normal browser can't read them, or use color combinations that make their content invisible to someone who is colorblind.

Even some of the most experienced designers, however, who would regard those issues as elementary and wouldn't even consider designing a site with those problems, don't think of providing a text transcript of audio files for Web users who are hearing-impaired. The thrust today in Web accessibility is in realizing that a Web site must be accessible in different ways, by different people, using different devices.

International Web Users

International Web users have a different set of problems. In Chapter 10 we talked about <meta /> tags that designate the character set in which the page should be displayed, in order to accommodate other languages. In this chapter, we will look at ways to provide alternate versions not only of the <meta /> tags, but also of the page's content.

Another issue is one of access to the Internet itself. In the United States, broadband Internet access, such as cable modem or DSL, is becoming common. Even in a worst-case scenario, local phone calls are generally included with monthly phone service. In many other countries and even in some rural areas of the U.S., however, it is not unusual for an Internet connection to be via an extremely slow modem (some countries make a 28.8K modem look like broadband!) or over a phone connection that is charged by the minute (or both). To make better or worse, these connections are frequently unreliable or simply unavailable. These users need to be able to get in, find what they want, and get out quickly, or you're going to lose them.

Screen readers *are speech synthesis software that reads the words on the screen in a computer-generated voice.*

*Usability guru Jakob Neilsen points out that a site's business is the number of users times the **conversion rate** or percentage of users who actually buy something. To double your business, you can double one number or the other. With conversion rates near 1%, it must be cheaper to fix usability problems and improve the conversion rate than to spend millions on advertising to encourage people to come to a site that they can't use.*

Filling the site with promotional information about the company without providing user-desired information is also known as "brochureware," as it's really just the contents of the brochure, shoveled onto the Web. Less tactful users often refer to this as "shovelware."

The Bottom Line: Getting More Business

International users aren't the only ones who want to get in quickly, do what they came to do, and get out. Americans are more impatient than ever. It used to be that 60 seconds was an acceptable download time for a page. Now that time is estimated at 8 seconds. At the very least, in that time it had better be apparent to users that they will be able to figure out how to accomplish their goals.

If you have problems with your local grocery store, you might try to resolve the issues with them, since it's more convenient than taking your business to the store in the next town. If there are three grocery stores within walking distance, however, you're likely to give up and try one of the alternatives.

How much worse is this situation on the Web, where millions of alternatives are a mouse click away, and there isn't even the personal contact with your favorite cashier to tempt you to keep trying?

Fortunately, many of the changes that we make to a site to make it more accessible by those with disabilities have the pleasant side effect of also making the site more usable by those without them. The bottom line is this: do absolutely anything you can to make your users' experience as pleasant and satisfying as possible. In most cases, the quality of that experience is all that distinguishes you from the competition.

The First Step: The Information Architecture

"Content is King," as the saying goes. Once you've decided to build a Web site and even before you decide on the look, you need to decide what you're providing on the site.

In most cases, what you're providing will be a combination of content and functionality. You offer information to the user, and you acquire information (such as data about what they want to see in a search, or (you hope) their credit card number for a transaction) from the user. The ideal way to organize all of the material depends on whose eyes you look through.

What You Want vs. What the User Wants

Aspiring writers are always told, "write what you know," and this usually works for them. That kind of approach in Web development, however, can cause problems.

The most obvious example of trouble caused by following this approach is the company that loads its Web site with promotional information about the company. There's lots of history and a prominent letter from the president right on the home page, but little product information and no pricing. Most users will take a minute or two to realize what's there and what's not, and then they're off to your competitors.

Instead, you need to look at your Web site through your customer's eyes. As a company, you want to bring in business through your Web site, whether it's directly through e-commerce or indirectly through branding. As a user, you want to obtain the information you need quickly and then act on it.

To make your site work for all, your must first determine your primary, secondary and additional audiences, as well as what each wants to accomplish on your site. Next, you determine what you want from them when they come. You then prioritize all of those objectives.

Finally you assemble all of the content and build the functionality that you're going to need in order to accomplish those objectives.

Creating Metrics

At the end of the day, how will you know whether or not you were successful? When your boss asks you to justify the money that was spent on the site, how will you do it?

Your objectives will help you do so. Determine, in advance, a *metric*, or measurement, that you will be able to use to determine whether or not the site is working. If your objective is to get users in order to increase brand awareness, you might measure the number of people who sign up for your email newsletter. If your objective is to increase sales for your distributors, you might measure the number of times that users click on a link for distributor address and phone number information.

What you decide to measure isn't necessarily important and doesn't even have to be on the Web site itself. If your objective is to save money on customer service calls by diverting some of the inquiries to your Web site, you might measure the number of calls that come in to your call center.

The important point is that you have a objective, quantifiable measurement, with a definition of "success" before you start.

Organizing Content: Wide vs. Deep

Once you have determined all of your content, you have to decide how to organize it. If you don't have a large amount of content, this is usually fairly easy to decide. If you do have a lot of content, you have to answer a fundamental organizational question. Do I need many main categories with a few subpoints each (known as a "wide site"), or just a few main categories with many subcategories and subsubcategories (known as a "deep site")?

The conventional wisdom is that a user should be able to get anywhere within three clicks of the home page. With the use of DHTML for items like dynamic menus (much like the submenus in the computer's operating system), this is much easier than it used to be, because a user can move down through several layers of subcategories with a single click.

Once you've decided on your categories, map them out, determining where all of your content belongs. This is often referred to as the "content tree."

The Second Step: Layout and Metaphor

Now that you've prepared your content, you are ready to start laying out your pages. Again, there are a few points to consider.

One temptation that is becoming less common is to use an extended metaphor throughout your site. To do so, you choose an item that can represent your company or service, such as a sailing ship for a boat company or a kennel for a dog club.

From there, all of your design, text and icons follow this lead. In the boat example, to write to the webmaster you might "talk to the captain," the site map might look like a navigational chart, and menu icons might be sea- or sailing-related objects.

The trouble with using extended metaphors is that you sometimes have to strain to make the connection between the image and what it represents. You might be able to make a case for why a sexton would be a good icon for the help section, but the user isn't there to hear it and will likely be confused. In addition, an extended metaphor, like background music, can become tiresome after a while. That's not to say that metaphors can't be used, but they must be well thought out, and you have to be prepared to sacrifice perfect adhesion to them in exchange for user clarity.

Don't forget to check your site organization plan to ensure that users won't have to click more than three times off the home page to arrive at any particularly important content.

Since your goal is to make your site usable and accessible, you must decide whether or not an extended metaphor makes using your site more pleasant and convenient, or confusing and unclear.

Consistency

One of the most important aspects of good Web design is consistency. Your Web site must give users a sense of "place." While not all of your pages can or should look exactly the same, there must be a common look and feel to tie them together. Once you've established that commonality, don't change it. A sudden difference in the appearance of a page can lead users to believe that they have left your site. The resulting confusion may well cause them to make it a self-fulfilling prophecy.

Likewise, while it is common for navigation to be different on subpages than it is on the home page, all subpages should have the navigational elements in the same position on the page, even if the navigational content itself is slightly different. This consistency will help your users to feel comfortable with the site.

Common Elements

There are certain elements every Web site should have.

First and foremost, every single page on your site (with one exception, noted below) must have a link (usually the logo) back to the home page. Just because a user is on one of your subpages doesn't mean that he or she has ever been to your home page, or even knows which company this site is about or anything about that company. Users might have arrived on your page through a link from another site, or they might have pulled up the particular page from a search engine. A link back to the homepage gives you a chance to introduce yourself (or your company).

The only exception to this rule is the home page itself. This page should not have a link to the home page, as users are confused by a link that doesn't appear to do anything. It should be obvious, however, that this is the home page.

A second feature that should appear on every page is a way for users to contact you, either through a form that they fill out or through a simple link to the webmaster's email address. If a user is frustrated enough to want to contact you, they are not going to want to take the time to figure out how to contact you. They'll simply leave. Besides, users often have helpful points or compliments to share. Why discourage them?

The third feature that should appear on most sites is a site search function. Power users often don't want to take the time to find what they want on a site. They just want to type a keyword and have the results returned to them. Of course, providing a site search engine is not a simple undertaking. On smaller sites the site search engine can usually be replaced by a site map, which lists all pages of the site, or at the very least, the pages for which users are likely to look.

The fourth and final feature is less about usability and more about credibility. Always include information about your company on the site so people know you're not a fly-by-night operation. Especially important is to give an offline address and phone number.

Even large sites should heed this advice. Too many large sites are now adding email addresses which have a standard response that they won't respond to you individually, and then don't provide any offline contact information. The usual answer about why they do this is that "they're not set up to respond." Think about that! It's true and the message is clear.

To keep consistency while avoiding links that don't appear to work because they point to the current page, many Web authors keep all of the links on the page, but deactivate, or "gray out" the link to the current page.

Your webmaster's email should always be webmaster@mysite.com, even if that email address is merely an alias that points to that individual's real email address. Many users will simply write to this address, no matter how many alternatives you provide on the site, and especially if you don't provide any address at all.

Screen Size

It's unfortunate, but while most designers are blessed with large monitors, most users are cursed with small ones. If you design your site for a 1024 × 768 screen, users with 800 × 600 screens will find it difficult, and users with 640 × 480 screens will find it impossible to use.

The best course of action is to design a site that doesn't depend on a particular size. This approach means that users with smaller monitors won't have to scroll horizontally, and users with larger monitors will receive the full impact.

If you must choose a size, however, what you choose should depend on your audience. If you are building a corporate intranet where you know everyone has at least 800 × 600 resolution, then it's acceptable to create a site that is 760 pixels wide. The extra 40 pixels are taken up by browser elements such as the scroll bar. On the other hand, if you are building for a general audience, it's still better to plan for a 600-pixel-wide design.

Multiple Columns

Some companies compromise, creating a design that is built with columns, where the main content is 600 pixels wide, and a third column, to the right, is visible on larger screens. This is better than ignoring the size of the typical user's monitor, but it is still not ideal. Users hate to scroll horizontally even more than they hate to scroll vertically.

A more common use of columns is to run the main and subnavigation down the left side, with the content in a column on the right. This is, in fact, so common as to be practically universal, but can cause its own problems with accessibility.

The problems occur because, as we mentioned when talking about search engines, reading the table literally puts the navigation at the top of the page. The result is that users with screen readers have to listen to all of the navigation, when what they really want to hear is your content. Fortunately, there are ways to avoid that problem, such as by providing a link that skips directly to the content.

Using Structure Rather than Presentation

The first step that we can take in making our pages more accessible is to make sure that we're using tags for structure, and not for presentation.

This sword cuts two ways. For instance, we would want to use headers such as <h1></h1> and <h2></h2> to indicate headlines rather than using a style sheet to make the content large and bold. On the other hand, however, if content is not a headline or other important content, it would be inappropriate to use header tags. That would be a situation for using a style sheet instead.

There are a number of structural tags that are appropriate for providing information that the browser can also use in determining its appearance, most of which are not used nearly as often as they should be.

Quoted Material

One type of content that can benefit from some underutilized tags is quoted material. The <q></q> tag can indicate inline quotes, and the <blockquote></blockquote> tag can indicate larger quoted sections that need to be set off from the rest of the text.

Exercise Setup
We'll add these tags to our recommendations.

Check that your site design allows for fixed elements in the browser, like the scroll bar and the browser menus and toolbars, when determining the size of your layout.

Add Quotes

1. Create a folder called "access" in the WIP folder. Navigate to **RF_HTML>Chapter 11**, and copy the contents of the Chapter 11 folder into the **WIP>access** folder.

2. Open **WIP>access>recs.html** in the text editor and browser.

3. Add a quoted section to the text.

```
…
<p><img src="images/book1.jpg" align="right" width="150" height="224" alt="My Life In Australia" />These days, Dr. Know-It-All is reading several books by <b>Dr. C. Little</b>, including his latest, <i>Why Don't Chickens Have Lips?</i> It's a subject close to Dr. Little's heart.</p>
<blockquote>
<p>Everyone is always jabbering on about chickens, but who has really taken the time to study them? We talk about things being rarer than hens' teeth, but who has taken the time to worry about lips? Nobody.</p>
<p>(from <i>Why Don't Chickens Have Lips?</i>)</p>
</blockquote>
<p>Dr. Know-It-All has also been engrossed in <i>My Life In Australia</i>, by <b>Alligator Al</b>.</p>
…
```

4. Save the file and open it in the browser.

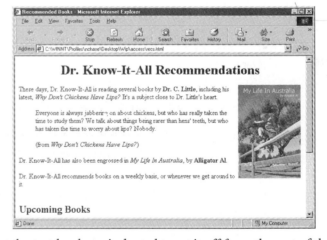

5. Notice that the text has been indented to set it off from the rest of the page, so some authors use this tag specifically for formatting, which is not, of course, its intended function. Let's also take a moment to set the content off even more with a background color.

```
…
<html>
<head><title>Recommended Books</title>
<style type="text/css">
        blockquote { background-color:#CCCFF }
</style>
</head>
<body>
```

6. Save the file and refresh the browser.

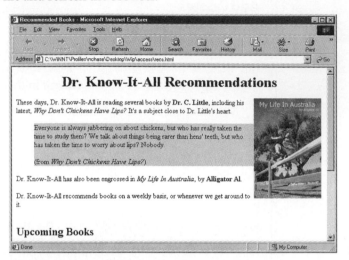

7. The style sheet will ensure that all <blockquote></blockquote> sections are set off from the page with a background color (if the browser supports it). Add a second, shorter quote by Alligator Al, using the <q></q> tag.

...
```
</blockquote>
<p>Dr. Know-It-All has also been engrossed in <i>My Life In Australia</i>, by <b>Alligator
Al</b>. The tone of the book varies between the exhilaration of discovery and the
stark terror of realizing that <q>"perhaps that wasn't such a good idea after all. It's a
wonder I made it through in one piece,"</q> he says.</p>
<p>Dr. Know-It-All recommends books on a weekly basis, or whenever we get around to
it.</p>
...
```

8. Save the file and refresh the browser.

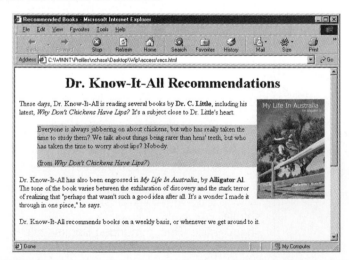

9. Notice that the text is added, but the quoted text doesn't look any different than the nonquoted text.

10. Leave both windows open for the next exercise.

Why Use the <q></q> Tags?

If there is no difference in the appearance of the text when we add the <q></q> tags around the quote, why do we bother?

We bother for two reasons. First of all, just because there is no difference now doesn't mean that there won't ever be a difference. Even now, browsers are beginning to add support for these tags. For instance, Netscape 6 inserts a double-quote before and after a quoted section. This underscores the necessity of checking your site in multiple browsers.

Al. The tone of the book varies between the f discovery and the stark terror of realizing that ""perhaps that wasn't such a er all. It's a wonder I made it through in one piece,"" he says.

The second and more important reason is that just because the text doesn't look any different to us doesn't mean that the tags are not useful. By using style sheets, we can make the quotes sound different from the rest of the text, so someone using an audio browser can tell that it's a quote. There's an entire range of uses for alternative browsers.

Alternate Browsers and Additional Media

Most of us are so accustomed to looking at our pages in Netscape or Internet Explorer that we forget that there are many more ways to peel a banana.

In addition to WebTV, browsers are also appearing in PDAs, cell phones and eventually in other devices where we might only imagine them today.

The most common example of an alternate browser is the text browser Lynx. Lynx can be found on most UNIX and Linux machines and can be downloaded on the Web. The difference between what we expect and what we see in this browser can be astonishing. Even Yahoo, widely regarded as one of the Web's most useful sites, can be disorienting when viewed in text for the first time.

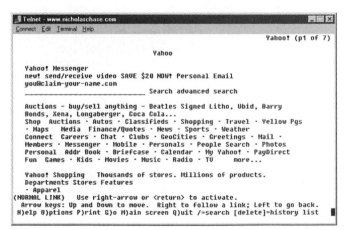

Text browsers such as Lynx, combined with a screen reader, used to be the primary way that visually impaired users accessed the Web, but today there are audio browsers specifically for that purpose.

Audio

Audio browsers are not just for visually impaired users. Browsers are being put into situations where users shouldn't be looking at the computer screen, such as: Volkswagen has announced a version of one of its cars that includes an Internet connection. In cases like this, the user had better be able to connect to the Internet without looking at the screen!

There are already voice-activated consoles in some higher-end cars. It stands to reason that a driver should be able to hear the Web page and surf it without taking his or her eyes off the road. This means that we should pay attention not only to how our pages look, but how they sound. When we create a style sheet for our page, we can specify particular properties for screen readers or other aural media.

We can do this in two ways. One is to add the properties to the page using the @media keyword, which can be included with style sheet information to indicate styles that apply only to a single type of media. This tells the screen reader whether or not to pay attention to the properties. We can, for instance, make our two quotes sound different from the text. We can also add other properties to tweak the performance of the page.

(Style sheet properties are listed in Appendix C on CSS Properties.)

```
…
<head><title>Recommended Books</title>
<style type="text/css">
blockquote { background-color: CCCCFF }
@media aural {
        body {
                azimuth: center;
                pitch: medium;
                play-during: url(backgroundmusic.wav);
                richness: 50;
                speak: normal;
                speak-header: once;
                speak-numeral: continuous;
                speak-punctuation: none;
                voice-family: paul, male;
        }
        blockquote {
                azimuth: center-left;
                speech-rate: fast;
                voice-family: vader, male;
        }
        q {
                azimuth: center-right;
                volume: soft;
                voice-family: kit, male;
        }
        h1 {
                cue: url(ping.wav);
                elevation: higher;
                stress: 80;
                volume: loud;
        }
        h2 {
                pause-before: 3;
                stress: 60;
        }
}
</style>
</head>
<body>
<h1 align="center">Dr. Know-It-All Recommendations</h1>
…
```

You can see that there is a lot of variety that we can put into the way a page is presented, even by a computerized voice. The code in the previous example shows a relatively long list of properties, of course, so it might be better to separate it out into a separate file. We can do that by specifying the media when we link in the style sheet, as in:

```
…
<html>
<head><title>Recommended Books</title>
<link rel="stylesheet" type="text/css" media="aural" href="recs_audio.css" />
<style type="text/css">
        blockquote { background-color: #CCCCFF }
</style>
</head>
<body>
…
```

Paged Media

Voice is not the only alternative presentation for your content. If you've ever tried to print out a Web page, you know that what you see is not always what you get. Nor should it be. Designed properly, a page can look completely different when it is converted to a printed, or *paged* format.

For instance, we might decide that the printed version shouldn't have ads, so we could put all the ads into a class that is hidden in the paged style sheet. We might replace a Flash movie with a still shot, since the movie obviously won't be accessible on a printed page. We could even specify that page breaks should occur before or after certain elements.

Special properties for paged media include marks, page-break-before, page-break-after, page-break-inside, widows and orphans, which specifies the number of lines that must be left at the top and bottom of pages, respectively, and size which enables us to force the page to use, say, the landscape layout, instead of the portrait layout.

Media Groupings

Different types of media are grouped together, making it easier to apply appropriate styles to the entire set. For instance, print is only one type of media that falls into the paged grouping. Others, such as projection, for uses such as presentations, and emboss, which applies to Braille printers, also fall into this grouping.

Media types are grouped in several ways. If a type is not considered paged, it's continuous. The media type tty, which is not based on pixels, is considered to be in the grid group, rather than in the bitmap group. Sometimes a type can be in more than one group. For instance, the media group tv is visual, of course, but since users may have limited pointing abilities (with no mouse), it is also in the aural group. Media types are classified as follows:

Media	Paging	Sensory	Interactivity	Layout
screen	continuous	visual	interactive, static	bitmap
aural	continuous	aural	interactive, static	
print	paged	visual	static	bitmap
tv	continuous, paged	visual, aural	interactive, static	bitmap
handheld	continuous, paged	visual	interactive, static	bitmap, grid
projection	paged	visual	static	bitmap
tty	continuous	visual	interactive, static	grid
braille	continuous	tactile	interactive, static	grid
emboss	paged	tactile	interactive, static	grid

For more information on special Cascading Style Sheet properties for sound and other media, point your browser to http://www.w3.org/CSS2.

Other Structural Tags

Some structural tags look new to those who have been writing HTML for a while, but have actually been around since the beginning of HTML. The <strong></strong> and <em></em> tags are perfect examples of helpful tags that have fallen out of common usage. The first pages usually employed these tags rather than bold or italic, as they're usually rendered. Other underutilized tags (which could, arguably, be considered presentational) are <big></big> and <small></small>.

These tags can be combined or nested:

Several of the tags that have been neglected over the last few years are **<strong>**strong**</strong>**, **<em>**emphasis**</em>**, **<big>**big**</big>**, and **<small>**small**</small>**. **<big>**These can also be **<strong>**nested**</strong>** so that they take on an even **<big>**greater**</big>** effect.**</big>**

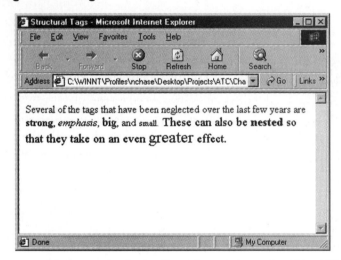

Early browsers even enabled users to change how these tags rendered text. You could, for instance, decide that in addition to being bold, strong text would be displayed in red.

This ability can greatly improve accessibility, and today users can perform the same function in some browsers, such as Microsoft Internet Explorer, using internal style sheets. To use this ability, choose Internet Option>Accessibility to designate your own style sheet to be used for all pages.

Exercise Setup
We can see some of these tags in action in our recommendations page.

Add Inflections

1. In the open recs.html file in the text editor, use the <strong></strong> and <em></em> tags to add inflection to the quotes when spoken, and emphasis when displayed.

```
...
<blockquote>
<p>Everyone is always jabbering on about chickens, but who has really taken the time to
study them? We talk about things being rarer than hens' teeth, but who has taken the time
to worry about lips? <strong>Nobody.</strong></p>
<p>(from <i>Why Don't Chickens Have Lips?</i>)</p>
```

```
</blockquote>
<p>Dr. Know-It-All has also been engrossed in <i>My Life In Australia</i>, by <b>Alligator
Al</b>. The tone of the book varies between the exhilaration of discovery and the stark
terror of realizing that <q>"perhaps that <em>wasn't</em> such a good idea after all. It's a
<em>wonder</em> I made it through in one piece,"</q> he says.</p>
```
…

2. Save the page and refresh the browser. Notice the difference in formatting. Although
   we could have accomplished the same thing by making those sections bold and italic,
   we have the added advantage that aural browsers can make the distinction and read
   the quotes appropriately.

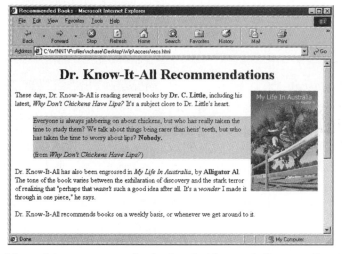

3. Use the <big></big> tag to emphasize book titles, and the <small></small> tag to
   format the attribution after the <blockquote></blockquote>. Nest these tags to
   create a cumulative effect.

…
```
<p><img src="images/book1.jpg" align="right" width="150" height="224" alt="My Life In
Australia" />These days, Dr. Know-It-All is reading several books by <b>Dr. C. Little</b>,
including his latest, <big><i>Why <big>Don't</big> Chickens Have Lips?</i></big> It's a
subject close to Dr. Little's heart.</p>
<blockquote>
<p>Everyone is always jabbering on about chickens, but who has really taken the time to
study them? We talk about things being rarer than hens' teeth, but who has taken the time
to worry about lips? <strong>Nobody.</strong></p>
<p><small>(<small>from</small> <i>Why Don't Chickens Have Lips?</i>)</small></p>
</blockquote>
<p>Dr. Know-It-All has also been engrossed in <big><i>My Life In Australia</i></big>, by
<b>Alligator Al</b>. The tone of the book varies between the exhilaration of discovery and
the stark terror of realizing that <q>"perhaps that <em>wasn't</em> such a good idea
after all. It's a <em>wonder</em> I made it through in one piece,"</q> he says.</p>
<p>Dr. Know-It-All recommends books on a weekly basis, or whenever we get around to
it.</p>
<br clear="right" />
<h2>Upcoming Books</h2>
<p><img src="images/book2.jpg" align="left" width="150" height="224" alt="Weight Loss
Secrets" /><i>At the urging of Mrs. Know-It-All, the next book Dr. Know-It-All reviews will
be <big><i>Weight Loss Secrets</i></big>, by <b>Sally Slinky</b>.</i></p>
```
…

Note that most users will not think to roll over text looking for a tool tip unless the text is part of a link, so if not, it would be a good idea to somehow highlight the acronym, such as by adding a color to the style sheet for the <acronym></acronym> tag.

The <abbr></abbr> tag is normally used in the same fashion for table headers.

4. Save the file and refresh the browser.

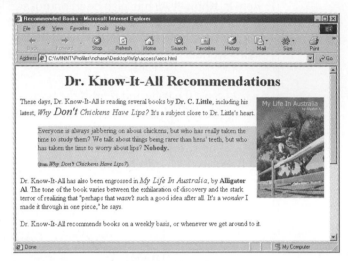

5. Leave both windows open for the next exercise.

Adding Tool Tips with the <acronym></acronym> Tag

If the browser supports it, we can provide additional information for the user through the title attribute. For instance, if we label an abbreviation or acronym using the acronym tag and give it a title attribute, that title attribute becomes the content of a "tool tip" that the user can use to get more information. For instance:

The work for this book goes in the <acronym title="Work In Progress">WIP</acronym> folder.

If a user rolls the mouse over the WIP and the browser supports this tag, he or she will see a small box that says Work in Progress, explaining what the acronym means.

Exercise Setup

We can add this to our page to clear up any question about what FAQ stands for.

Add Information to an Acronym

1. In the open recs.html file in the text editor, add the <acronym></acronym> tag and title attribute to the FAQ text.

…
```
<p><img src="images/book2.jpg" align="left" width="150" height="224" alt="Weight Loss
Secrets" /><i>At the urging of Mrs. Know-It-All, the next book Dr. Know-It-All reviews will
be <big><i>Weight Loss Secrets</i></big>, by <b>Sally Slinky</b>.</i></p>

<p>Got questions? You can Ask Dr. Know-It-All. Check out our <acronym
title="Frequently Asked Questions">FAQ</acronym>!</p>
</body>
</html>
```

2. Save the file and refresh the browser.

3. Using the mouse, point to the FAQ text. If your browser supports it, a tool tip will appear with the text Frequently Asked Questions. If your browser doesn't support this, nothing will happen.

Check out our FAQ!

Frequently Asked Questions

4. Leave both windows open for the next exercise.

Using Insert and Delete Tags to Indicate Changes

One pair of tags is much more useful for editors than it is for the eventual readers of a page. That pair is the <ins></ins>, or insert, and <del></del>, or delete tags. These two tags can be used to show what has changed between versions of pages, for instance.

Note that these tags don't actually change the content, just the appearance of it. "Inserted" text shows up as underlined in most browsers, and "deleted" text appears with a strike through it. For example:

…
This is <ins>regular</ins> text that does <del>not</del> appear.
…

would create a page that looks like:

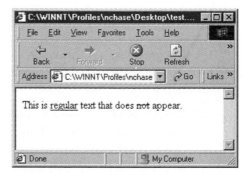

While this may, at first, seem cumbersome and not very useful, consider the fact that with style sheets, we can control how both the inserted and deleted material looks. We could, for instance, maintain all changes to a page, but suppress the rendering of the deleted material so that only the current content shows. What's more, we could do that for just the printed version, or just the screen version, and so on. In this way, the same content can serve different purposes, depending on the style sheet. For example, you might use this to show clients proposed changes to their Web pages.

Exercise Setup

If we wanted to change next week's feature article, we could show that in our page.

Insert and Delete Text

1. In the open recs.html file in the text editor, make changes to the upcoming feature section, marking the insertions and deletions.

…
```
<h2>Upcoming Books</h2>
<p><img src="images/book2.jpg" align="left" width="150" height="224" alt="Weight Loss
Secrets" /><i><del>At the urging of Mrs. Know-It-All</del><ins>At the suggestion of Dr.
Know-It-All's physician</ins>, the next book Dr. Know-It-All reviews will be
<big><i>Weight Loss Secrets</i></big>, by <b>Sally Slinky</b>.</i></p>
<p>Got questions? You can Ask Dr. Know-It-All. Check out our <acronym title="Frequently
Asked Questions">FAQ</acronym>!</p>
```
…

2. Save the file and refresh the browser. Notice the change in formatting.

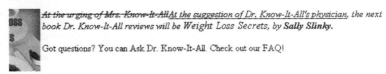

3. Save changes and close the file.

Making Tables Accessible

The first point to realize about making your tables accessible is that they will, in some situations, vanish completely. That doesn't mean that the content is gone. It means that the structure of the table has been *linearized*, or read literally from top to bottom with no cell distinctions.

While frustrating, this is not necessarily a disaster, if your pages are constructed properly. For example, when we created the Doctor-It! home page, it may have seemed to you that the layout was overly complicated, resulting in a page that couldn't possibly be accessible. While it is true that there are situations where we will want to provide an alternative to that page, the existing Doctor-It! home page actually linearizes quite well. If we were to look at the page in Lynx, a text-only browser, the content is slightly reordered, but quite readable.

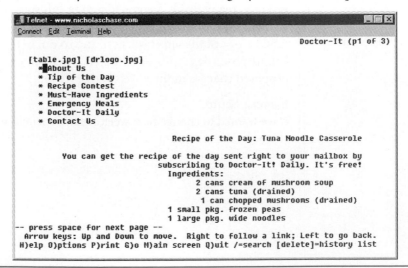

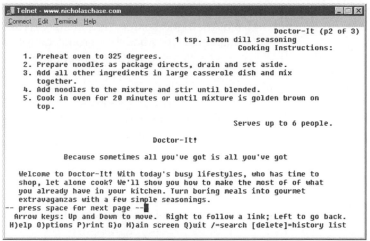

If the order of your content is crucial and linearizing is going to change it, be sure to provide a text alternative for browsers that do not read tables.

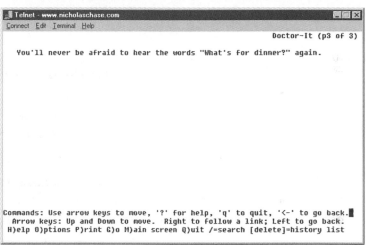

Notice that the recipe, which on the standard browser page appears third, displays second in the linearized version. In our case it doesn't much matter, but if it does for your content — for example, if the recipe's instructions had been reordered — you will want to provide a text alternative for the table. There is much more that we can do to make tables more usable. The first step would be to make certain that you include information about the table, such as a caption or summary.

A caption can be useful not only from an informational perspective, but also from a formatting perspective, as it is normally centered on the table, no matter how the table is aligned. For instance, we could create this table, including text within the <caption></caption> tag, and when we align the table to the right, the caption will remain centered on the table.

```
<!DOCTYPE HTML PUBLIC "-//W3C//DTD HTML 4.01 Transitional//EN"
"http://www.w3.org/TR/html4/loose.dtd">
<html>
<head><title>Accessible Tables</title></head>
<style type="text/css">
        .mediatype { text-align: center;
                            font-weight: bold; }
        caption { font-weight: bold;
                  font-size: 18pt; }
</style>
```

```
<body>
<table align="right" border="1" summary="This table shows the relationships between
different media types and their groupings with respect to paging, interactivity, and so on.">
        <caption>Media Groups</caption>
        <tr>
                <th></th>
                <th>Paging</th>
                <th>Sensory</th>
                <th>Interactivity</th>
                <th>Layout</th>
        </tr>
        <tr>

                <td class="mediatype">screen</td>
                <td>continuous</td>
                <td>visual</td>
                <td>interactive, static</td>
                <td>bitmap</td>
        </tr>
        <tr>

                <td class="mediatype">aural</td>
                <td>continuous</td>
                <td>aural</td>
                <td>interactive, static</td>
                <td></td>
        </tr>
        <tr>

                <td class="mediatype">print</td>
                <td>paged</td>
                <td>visual</td>
                <td>static</td>
                <td>bitmap</td>
        </tr>
        <tr>

                <td class="mediatype">tv</td>
                <td>continuous, paged</td>
                <td>visual, aural</td>
                <td>interactive, static</td>
                <td>bitmap</td>
        </tr>
        <tr>

                <td class="mediatype">handheld</td>
                <td>continuous, paged</td>
                <td>visual</td><td>interactive, static</td>
                <td>bitmap, grid</td>
        </tr>
        <tr>

                <td class="mediatype">projection</td>
                <td>paged</td>
                <td>visual</td>
                <td>static</td>
                <td>bitmap</td>
        </tr>
        <tr>
```

One simple way to help users with tableless browsers to see your content is to always put a <br /> at the end of each row. When you do, your content may be misaligned vertically, but at least it won't merge into a single, undifferentiated, block type mess.

```
                      <td class="mediatype">tty</td>
                      <td>continuous</td>
                      <td>visual</td>
                      <td>interactive, static</td>
                      <td>grid</td>
            </tr>
            <tr>
                      <td class="mediatype">braille</td>
                      <td>continuous</td>
                      <td>tactile</td>
                      <td>interactive, static</td>
                      <td>grid</td>
            </tr>
            <tr>
                      <td class="mediatype">emboss</td>
                      <td>paged</td>
                      <td>tactile</td>
                      <td>interactive, static</td>
                      <td>grid</td>
            </tr>
</table>
</body>
```

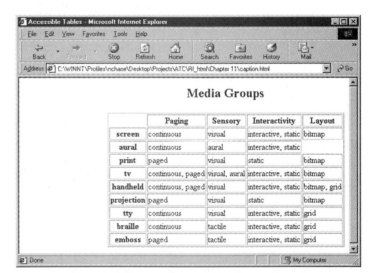

There are three important points to notice here. The first is that we have added a summary to the table. While it won't be seen by most users, it will be available for those who need it. The second point is that even though the table is aligned to the right, the caption is centered over it. Using the <caption></caption> tag is an easy and convenient way to achieve this while adding to usability by explaining the table with a title or caption.

The third point to notice is that even though the left-hand column has the same styling as the <th></th> cells, we did not cheat and simply make them <th></th> cells to achieve the effect. The reason we did not is that the table header cells serve a specific structural purpose, different from the cells in the left column, which are lead cells for each row.

Never use structural tags to achieve formatting goals, especially if you're using the tables just for formatting. It is going to be difficult enough for assistive browsers to understand the structure of the content.

Headers

To make your content easier for these browsers to handle, we can explicitly associate cells with specific table headings using the headers attribute. The headers attribute, as shown below, logically associates each cell with a particular column, which is identified by the id attribute.

…

```
<caption>Media Groups</caption>
<tr>
        <th></th>
        <th id="paging">Paging</th>
        <th id="sensory">Sensory</th>
        <th id="interactivity">Interactivity</th>
        <th id="layout">Layout</th>
</tr>
<tr>
        <td class="mediatype">screen</td>
        <td headers="paging">continuous</td>
        <td headers="sensory">visual</td>
        <td headers="interactivity">interactive, static</td>
        <td headers="layout">bitmap</td>
</tr>
<tr>
        <td class="mediatype">aural</td>
        <td headers="paging">continuous</td>
        <td headers="sensory">aural</td>
        <td headers="interactivity">interactive, static</td>
        <td headers="layout"></td>
</tr>
<tr>
        <td class="mediatype">print</td>
```

…

With these additions, the standard suggests that a speech synthesizer might read the table as:

> "Caption: Media Groups. Summary: This table shows the relationships between different media types and their groupings with respect to paging, interactivity, and so on.
>
> Screen. Paging: continuous. Sensory: visual. Interactivity: interactive, static. Layout: bitmap.
>
> Aural. Paging: continuous …"

So while tables can give us a false sense of security about accessibility, in the long run they can help us make our information more usable. In general, use style sheets for layout and positioning, and tables for structure.

Alternate Text for Sights, Sounds and Maps

With the coming of HTML 4.01 (and subsequently XHTML 1.0), alternate text on images is mandatory, but there is much more to managing images than that. Just planning for screen readers is not enough. You must remember that your content will be used in many different ways.

In addition to alternate text, you can add longer descriptions that may be accessible to users who might not be able to see the image. Similarly, you will want to provide alternate text for users who cannot hear your audio.

You can also create powerful maps that allow users to click an image to receive their desired content, but you must also provide a text alternative for those who can't use the map.

It is thought that laying out content with tables is "going the way of the dodo," but with many older browsers still in use, this device for page layout will be with us for some time to come.

Alternate Text and Long Descriptions

Alternate text, or "alt text," as it is generally known, is the text that we put into the alt attribute of an <img /> tag. It is a short name or description, used to replace the image if, for any reason, the image can't be found or loaded.

Sometimes, this alternate text is not enough for a complete description in an environment where the user has no visual cues. In this case, we can add a second attribute, longdesc, which allows us to specify a file that contains a longer description. For instance, on our recommendations page, we might add a longdesc to the cover of *My Life In Australia*, like so:

```
…
<p><img src="images/book1.jpg" align="right" width="150" height="224" alt="My Life In
Australia" longdesc="alcover.html" />These days, Dr. Know-It-All…
```

where the file alcover.html contains more information, such as:

```
<!DOCTYPE HTML PUBLIC "-//W3C//DTD HTML 4.01 Transitional//EN"
"http://www.w3.org/TR/html4/loose.dtd">
<html>
<head><title>My Life In Australia: Cover Art</title></head>
<body>
<h1>My Life In Australia cover art</h1>
This graphic depicts Alligator Al leaping over a fence on his family's farm Down Under. It is
a wooden fence, with…
</body>
</html>
```

There is no actual length limit for alt text, but it is customary to provide just enough information to identify the image.

The idea of the long description is to provide all of the information necessary for someone who is not seeing the image, table, frame, etc., to understand what it contains. Most users with traditional browsers will never see this long description.

Maps as Navigation

We've talked about images as links to other pages, as form submission buttons and even as triggers for scripts, but there is one more variation that we haven't touched upon, and that is the image map, or imagemap.

With an imagemap, the browser knows what portion of the image the user has clicked and responds appropriately, performing different actions or moving to different URLs, depending on which region the user selects. Early browsers couldn't distinguish these regions, so they sent the coordinates to the server, which processed them and returned the appropriate content. One of our goals in making our site usable and accessible, however, is to avoid such device-dependent input. We can't assume that the user will even be using a mouse, so we can't assume that there will be coordinates to send to the server.

So it's just as well that this approach, also known as "server-side imagemaps," has been almost completely replaced by client-side imagemaps, in which the browser contains both the coordinate and destination information so it can all be handled appropriately. Client-side imagemaps have other usability advantages, too. They enable us to add information that users, disabled or not, can use to decide whether or not a link is appropriate before following.

You make a client-side imagemap by creating a <map></map> element that includes individual areas, using the <area /> tag to define their shape and coordinates. An area can also be designated as a default, in case the user clicks outside of the defined areas. The image is linked to the map definition using the usemap attribute in the <img /> tag, where the value of usemap matches the id attribute of the map definition.

For instance, we might have an image with a circular button in the middle of it, and we want only the button to be a link. We would then write:

```
<map id="buttonmap" name="buttonmap">
        <area shape="circle" coords="100,100,50" href="home.html"
title="Home Page"  alt="Home Button" />
</map>
<img src="button.gif" height="300" width="300" alt="Button" usemap="#buttonmap" />
…
```

In this example, we've created an image and assigned it the usemap attribute, which links the image to the map that we created above by the name. The map itself can have one or more areas, each of which has a shape and coordinates. In this case, the shape is a circle, and the active area will be a circle with a radius of 50 pixels, centered at a point 100 pixels from the top and 100 pixels from the left edge of the image. If the user clicks anywhere else on the image, nothing will happen.

The circle is just one of the shapes that we can use when creating imagemaps. The complete list includes:

Client-side imagemaps are also much faster than server-side imagemaps, since the browser doesn't have to make an extra trip to the server to find out what to do.

- **default**. This is the link that is followed if the user clicks on an undefined area of the imagemap. For example:

```
<area shape="default" title="Click to Proceed" alt="Default Choice" href="main.html" />
```

- **rect**. This rectangular area is defined by two points, the upper-left and the lower-right corners. For instance, we created a block with corners at (545,95) and (708,253) as part of the exercise:

```
<area shape="rect" coords="545,95,708,253" title="Guests" alt="Guests Block"
href="index.html" />
```

- **poly**. This polygonal shape can be defined by any number of points. The last pair of coordinates should match the first pair in order to close the shape. For example:

```
<area shape="poly" coords="10,100, 120,20, 250,20, 360,100, 340,100, 340,300, 30,300,
30,100, 10,100" title="Home" alt="House" href="home.html" />
```

- **circle**. This circular shape is defined by a center point and a radius. For instance, a circle with a center at the (50,100) coordinate with a 25-pixel radius would be:

```
<area shape="circle" coords="50,100,25" title="Play Ball!" alt="Baseball"
href="baseball.html" />
```

Notice in the example above that the area tag includes a shape attribute that has a value of one of the shapes listed above. The coordinates are the pixel positions of the points defining the shape. The title attribute provides tool tip information (in this case, "Play Ball!") when the user rolls over this area of the map. The alt and href attributes provide their usual alternate text and URL functions.

Areas can be specified in any order, but in the event that two areas overlap, the standard says that the first defined area should take precedence.

Exercise Setup

Let's take a look at this by converting the Doneger Online home page from individual <div>s to a single imagemap.

Add a Client-side Imagemap

1. Open **WIP>access>homepage.html** in the text editor and browser.

2. Add an imagemap to the page, and link the Navigation Buttons (images>topmap.gif) image to it. For the moment, don't add any areas to it.

```
...
<body style="background-color:"#ffffff">

<div style="z-index:2; left:20px; position:absolute; top:32px;">
  <map name="buttonmap"id="buttonmap">
  </map>
  <img src="images/topmap.gif" usemap="#buttonmap" height="264" width="712"
alt="Navigation Buttons" border="0" />
</div>

<div style="z-index:5; left:62px; width:671px; position:absolute; top:284px; height:90px">
  <img height="92" src="images/thefashion_new.gif" width="700" />
...
```

3. Save the file and refresh the browser. Notice that nothing has yet changed. Although we added the imagemap, there are no active areas to link.

A client-side imagemap is obviously not the ideal way to handle the Doneger Online home page, since we lose the rollovers and other effects we have worked to achieve. It's not impossible to use them with this approach, but it's not practical.

4. Now add one area. In this case, we're using a rectangular-shaped area. The coordinates of the upper-left corner are (545,95) and the coordinates of the lower-right corner are (708,253).

```
...
<div style="z-index:2; left:20px; position:absolute; top:32px;">
  <map name="buttonmap"id="buttonmap">
      <area shape="rect" coords="545,95,708,253" title="Guests" alt="Guests
Block" href="index.html" />
  </map>
  <img src="images/topmap.gif" usemap="#buttonmap" height="264" width="712"
alt="Navigation Buttons" border="0" />
</div>
...
```

5. Save the file and refresh the browser. Notice that if you point to any of the boxes but Guests, they show no link, but that if you point to Guests, it shows a link to index.html. If your browser supports it, it will also show a tool tip that says "Guests."

6. Add the rest of the areas.

There are a number of products that can be downloaded to give you imagemap coordinates and information. You can also open the image in a graphics program such as Adobe Photoshop and use the Information palette to acquire the relevant coordinates.

```
…
<div style="z-index:2; left:20px; position:absolute; top:32px;">
  <map name="buttonmap"id="buttonmap">>
      <area shape="rect" coords="37,95,200,253" title="Members" alt="Member Login Block" href="login.html" />
      <area shape="rect" coords="201,95,279,209" title="D3" alt="D3 Block" href="d3.html" />
      <area shape="rect" coords="243,205, 373,253" title="Price Point Buying, Inc." alt="PPB Block" href="PPB.html" />
      <area shape="rect" coords="374,95,544,253" title="Doneger Marketplace" alt="Doneger Marketplace Block" href="http://www.donegermarketplace.com" />
      <area shape="rect" coords="545,95,708,253" title="Guests" alt="Guests Block" href="index.html" />
  </map>
  <img src="images/topmap.gif" usemap="#buttonmap" height="264" width="712" alt="Navigation Buttons" border="0" />
</div>
…
```

7. Save the file and refresh the browser. Notice that each box has its own URL. (You can see this by looking at the status bar in the browser.)

8. Notice that when you point to the overlapping area between D3 and Price Point Buying, the D3 URL shows, even though the graphic by its color implies that Price Point Buying should be active. To correct this, switch the two areas.

```
…
<div style="z-index:2; left:20px; position:absolute; top:32px;">
  <map name="buttonmap"id="buttonmap">
      <area shape="rect" coords="37,95,200,253" title="Members" alt="Member Login Block" href="login.html" />
      <area shape="rect" coords="243,205, 373,253" title="Price Point Buying, Inc." alt="PPB Block" href="PPB.html" />
      <area shape="rect" coords="201,95,279,209" title="D3" alt="D3 Block" href="d3.html" />
      <area shape="rect" coords="374,95,544,253" title="Doneger Marketplace" alt="Doneger Marketplace Block" href="http://www.donegermarketplace.com" />
      <area shape="rect" coords="545,95,708,253" title="Guests" alt="Guests Block" href="index.html" />
  </map>
  <img src="images/topmap.gif" usemap="#buttonmap" height="264" width="712" alt="Navigation Buttons" border="0" />
</div>
…
```

9. Save the file and refresh the browser. Verify that the change took effect.

10. Leave both windows open for the next exercise.

Maps as Structure

Even Web page authors who haven't thought much about accessibility often know that they need to provide text alternative links to imagemaps. What many of them don't realize, however, is that this can be done in conjunction with the map itself.

Text links, or <a></a> tags, can be included as part of the <map></map> element, and in some cases this is actually preferable. In this case, the area definitions are duplicated on the <a></a> tags, which in turn appear on the page as regular links, as in:

```
<map Id="myMap">
        <area shape="rect" coords="0,0,100,100" title="Area 1" alt="Area 1 Block"
href="page1.html" />
        <area shape="rect" coords="100,0,200,100" title="Area 2" alt="Area 2 Block"
href="page2.html" />

        <a shape="rect" coords="0,0,100,100" href="page1.html" >Page 1</a> |
        <a shape="rect" coords="100,0,200,100" href="page2.html" >Page 2</a>
</map>
```

Notice the "|" character between the links. Always include a printable character between links to prevent them from running together.

Exercise Setup

Let's add the text alternative links to our Doneger Online page.

Add Text Alternative Links

1. In the open homepage.html file in the text editor, add text alternatives to the <map></map> element.

```
…
        <area shape="rect" coords="374,95,544,253" title="Doneger Marketplace"
alt="Doneger Marketplace Block" href="http://www.donegermarketplace.com" />
        <area shape="rect" coords="545,95,708,253" title="Guests" alt="Guests Block"
href="index.html" />

        <a shape="rect" coords="37,95,200,253" href="login.html" >Member</a>
        <a shape="rect" coords="243,205, 373,253" href="PPB.html" >PPB</a>
        <a shape="rect" coords="201,95,279,209" href="d3.html" >D3</a>
        <a shape="rect" coords="374,95,544,253"
href="http://www.donegermarketplace.com" >Marketplace</a>
        <a shape="rect" coords="545,95,708,253" href="index.html" >Guest</a>
  </map>
  <img src="images/topmap.gif" usemap="#buttonmap" height="264" width="712"
alt="Navigation Buttons" border="0" />
</div>
…
```

2. Save the file and refresh the browser.

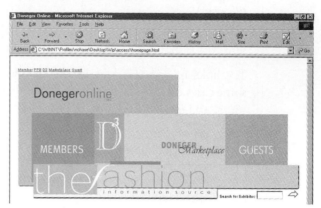

3. This code put the text links on the page, but we now have a couple of resulting issues. First, we've pushed the graphic down under the rest of the page. Second, a screen reader would read all of our links as one because there are only spaces between them. Solve both problems by putting the "|" character between them and adding positioning information.

```
…
<div style="z-index:2; left:20px; position:absolute; top:32px;">
  <div style="position:absolute; left:475px; top:5px;">
    <map name="buttonmap" class="finePrint" title="Doneger Online Navigation" "id="buttonmap">
      <area shape="rect" coords="37,95,200,253" title="Members" alt="Member Login Block" href="login.html" />
…
      <a shape="rect" coords="37,95,200,253" href="login.html" >Member</a> |
      <a shape="rect" coords="243,205, 373,253" href="PPB.html" >PPB</a> |
      <a shape="rect" coords="201,95,279,209" href="d3.html" >D3</a> |
      <a shape="rect" coords="374,95,544,253" href="http://www.donegermarketplace.com" >Marketplace</a> |
      <a shape="rect" coords="545,95,708,253" href="index.html" >Guest</a>
  </map>
  </div>
  <img src="images/topmap.gif" usemap="#buttonmap" height="264" width="712" alt="Navigation Buttons" border="0" />
</div>
…
```

4. Save the file and refresh the browser.

5. Close the file.

Always put printable characters, such as the vertical line, or pipe, surrounded by spaces, between a series of links.

Make sure your browser window is wide enough to accomodate the line of links.

Graceful Degradation

You're probably wondering why we put coordinates on the <a></a> tags. The reason is that the XHTML 1.0 Recommendation supports imagemaps that use <a></a> tags instead of <area />s, even though today's browser's don't.

What we have done in the previous example is create graceful degradation. If the browser supported the advanced functionality of imagemaps using <a></a> tags, it would know not to display the text links, because the links are available on the image. If not, it simply displays the text alternative, because that's how it handles <a></a> tags.

Another method that is not yet supported by current browsers would allow us to display the text alternative only if it were needed. As we know, the content inside an <object></object> tag will be rendered only if the object is not. If the browser supported the use of objects for imagemaps, we could write:

```
<div style="z-index:2; left:20px; position:absolute; top:32px;">
<object data="images/topmap.gif" usemap="#buttonmap" height="264"
width="712"  alt="Navigation Buttons" type="image/gif">
    <map name="buttonmap" class="finePrint" title="Doneger Online Navigation">
        <a shape="rect" coords="37,95,200,253" href="login.html" >Member</a> |
        <a shape="rect" coords="243,205, 373,253" href="PPB.html" >PPB</a> |
        <a shape="rect" coords="201,95,279,209 href="d3.html" >D3</a> |
        <a shape="rect" coords="374,95,544,253" href="http://
www.donegermarketplace.com" >Marketplace</a> |
        <a shape="rect" coords="545,95,708,253" href="index.html" >Guest</a>
    </map>
</object>
</div>
```

Alternate Text for Audio

We can also use this method for providing alternate text for audio. For instance, assuming that a deaf person would be surfing with a browser that knows audio is not acceptable, we might write:

```
<object data="/sounds/narative.wav" type="audio/wav" title="Narrative Audio">
        Narrative: Once upon a time, there was a beautiful witch who lived in a forest that
was ruled by a mean, ugly princess…
</object>
```

Because the browser knows that audio is not acceptable, the text narrative would be displayed instead. The only trouble with this approach is that the deaf are not the only people who might not get the audio.

Many users surf without audio, either because they don't have a sound card in their computer, or because their connection is so slow that by the time the audio is downloaded (assuming that the audio isn't being streamed), they've already moved on to another page.

Because of these common sound-access problems, important audio should always be accompanied by a text link that the user can follow for a text representation.

Hyperlinks, Forms and Scripting

Have you ever tried to surf the Web without using your mouse? It's not impossible. In fact, it can be extremely easy. But how, you may wonder, can you surf if you can't click anything? It's simple. We're used to clicking, but that is far from the only way to "follow a link" (which is actually the correct term for it).

Web pages and forms can both be built in such a way as to make it convenient for alternate input devices, such as keyboards. These seldom-used methods for ordering links, form fields and other functions don't take much time and can increase usability tremendously.

Tabbing Order

In fact, we could surf most Web sites with just two keys: Tab and Return/Enter. The Tab key is used to move from link to link, and the Return/Enter key is used to activate the current link, whatever it may be. For instance, if we were to pull up our Doctor-It! page, we could follow the position of the current link by watching the page.

This is neither an accident nor something helpful that browser developers threw in to make life easier for people with pencil-eraser mice. In fact, the HTML standard was written to allow for users with other input devices that do not use a mouse. Rather than forcing users to tab through every link in the navigation section (which is usually the first thing on the page), accessibility guidelines suggest giving them a way to skip the navigation, such as a Skip to Content link.

Most browsers also go a step further in terms of convenience, allowing developers to use the tabindex attribute to reorder links, so that more important links appear first, even if they're not the first links on the page. This ability to reorder links is useful, but where reordering is most often used is for form elements, where users have been used to tabbing to get from field to field since long before the Web came along.

For instance, we can reorder the tabbing for our order form. Note the tab order by the numbers on the following graphic:

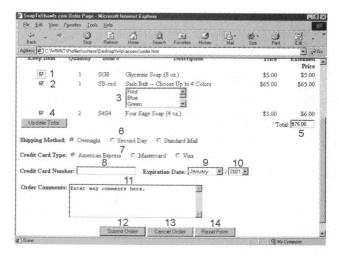

To be more user friendly, we want the tab order to be as follows, leaving out the the total, because the user shouldn't be editing it directly:

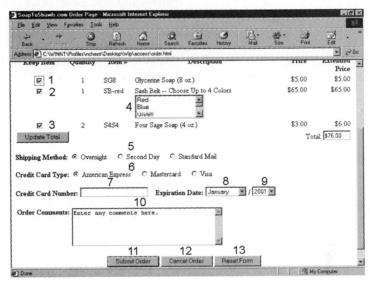

We can change the order by adjusting the tabindex values on various elements within our form. For instance, to designate that the SG8 checkbox should be the first item active on the page, we would write:

```
<input tabindex="1" type="checkbox" name="item" value="SG8" checked="checked" />
```

When the user tabs through the page, the browser will hit each form element in the order of its tabindex value.

Reorder Form Elements

1. Open **WIP>access>order.html** in the text editor and browser.

2. Tab through the form elements to verify their original order. Notice that between the second and third checkboxes, we are diverted to the color selection list.

3. Add tabindex values to our form elements in the order in which we want them to appear.

```
...
<tr>
        <td><input tabindex="1" type="checkbox" name="item" value="SG8"
checked="checked" /></td><td>1</td><td>SG8</td>
        <td>Glycerine Soap (8 oz.)</td><td>$5.00</td><td>$5.00</td>
</tr>
<tr>
        <td><input tabindex="2" type="checkbox" name="item" value="SB"
checked="checked" /></td><td>1</td><td>SB-red</td>
        <td valign="top" >Sash Belt — Choose Up to 4 Colors<br />
        <select tabindex="5" name="colors" size="3" multiple="multiple">
        ...
        </select>
</td>
        <td>$65.00</td><td>$65.00</td>
</tr>
<tr>
```

```
                    <td><input tabindex="3" type="checkbox" name="item" value="S4S4"
checked="checked" /></td><td>2</td><td>S4S4</td>
                    <td>Four Sage Soap (4 oz.)</td><td>$3.00</td><td>$6.00</td>
</tr>
<tr>
                    <td colspan="3" align="left">
                            <input tabindex="4" type="button" value="Update Total"
onclick="UpdateTotal()" />
                    </td>
…
<b>Shipping Method:</b>
<input  tabindex="6" type="radio" value="1" name="shipping" checked="checked" />
Overnight    

…
<b>Credit Card Type:  </b>
<input  tabindex="7" type="radio" value="1" name="card_type" checked="checked" />
American Express    
…
<b>Credit Card Number: </b> <input tabindex="8" type="text" name="ccnumber" /
>   
<b>Expiration Date: </b>
<select tabindex="9" name="exp_month">
…
</select>
/
<select tabindex="10" name="exp_year">
…
</select>
<br /><br />
<table><tr><td valign="top"><b>Order Comments:  </b></td><td><textarea
tabindex="11" name="comments" rows="5" cols="40">
Enter any comments here.
</textarea>
…
```

4. Save the file and refresh the browser. Click the first checkbox to put the focus on it. Press the Tab key several times and see that the focus bypasses the Total text field.

5. Keep pressing the Tab key, and notice that once all of the form elements with a tabindex are passed, the focus goes back to the Total and then to the form buttons.

6. Leave both windows open for the next exercise.

Removing Elements from the Flow

Since we don't want the user to change the value of the Total field, there's no reason to even have it in the flow. We can take it out of the tabbing order in a couple of different ways.

The first way would be to give it a tabindex that is a negative number. Set in this way, it will never be selected. The second way is to disable the field completely. To do that, we will add the disabled attribute, as in:

```
<input disabled="disabled" type="text" size="7" name="total" value="$76.00" />
```

Like checked, this attribute is a carryover from before XHTML, when attributes didn't always need a value, so it looks a little odd.

Disable the Total

1. In the open order.html file in the text editor, add the disabled attribute to the total.

```
…
<td colspan="3" align="right">Total:
        <input disabled="disabled" type="text" size="7" name="total" value="$76.00" />
</td>
…
```

2. Save the file and refresh the browser. Notice that the field is grayed out. Press Tab and notice that this field is now skipped.

3. Leave both windows open for the next exercise.

Organizing Form Elements

Earlier we looked at uses of structural tags such as <strong></strong> and <em></em> for improved access and usability for general text. Similarly there are ways to structure a form to make it more understandable to assistive devices and other browsers.

One way to make a form more understandable is to explicitly associate labels with their elements. For example, under normal circumstances, there is no relationship between the word "Overnight" on the order form and the radio button adjacent to it that signifies the user's preference. This can sometimes be frustrating to users, who are used to offline applications, in which they can click on a label and the choice is made.

We can duplicate that functionality here with the <label></label> element. The idea is to create a label, then associate it with a particular form element, using the for attribute (on the <label></label>) and the id attribute (on the <input />).

For instance, we could write:

```
…
The light was:
<input type="radio" value="red" name="light" id="redbutton" />
<label for="redbutton">Red</label>
<input type="radio" value="green" name="light" id="greenbutton" />
<label for="greenbutton">Green</label>
…
```

This code would associate the buttons with their labels, so we could click the labels instead of the buttons, and the buttons would still be activated. For instance, you could click on the word "Green."

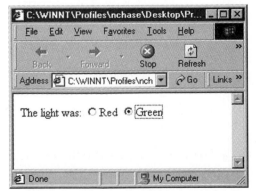

If necessary, we can also set a field to be readonly. In that case, the user won't be able to change it, but it will still be in the tabbing order.

Exercise Setup

Let's create labels for our radio buttons.

Add Labels to the Form

1. In the open order.html file in the text editor, add labels to each radio button. Each button needs an individual id.

```
…
<b>Shipping Method:</b>
<input id="over" tabindex="6" type="radio" value="1" name="shipping" checked="checked" />
<label for="over">Overnight</label>    
<input id="second" type="radio" value="2" name="shipping" />
<label for="second">Second Day</label>    
<input id="standard" type="radio" value="3" name="shipping" />
<label for="standard">Standard Mail</label>
<br /><br />
<b>Credit Card Type:  </b>
<input id="amex" tabindex="7" type="radio" value="1" name="card_type" checked="checked" />
<label for="amex">American Express</label>    
<input id="mc" type="radio" value="2" name="card_type" />
<label for="mc">Mastercard</label>    
<input id="visa" type="radio" value="3" name="card_type" />
<label for="visa">Visa</label>    
<br /><br />
…
```

Some older browsers (even as recently as Netscape 4.x) don't support this functionality, but the document is unaffected for those users, so it's still a good idea to use it.

2. Save the file and refresh the browser. If your browser supports it, you can now change the radio buttons by clicking the labels rather than the buttons themselves.

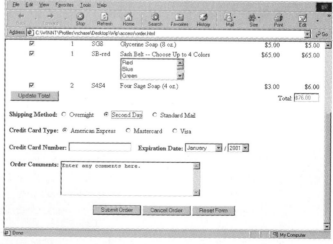

3. Close both applications.

Scripting Concerns

Another point to consider with forms is that we can't depend on the user having any particular type of input device, such as a mouse or even a keyboard. When scripting the form (or the page), we should, wherever possible, use application-level events as opposed to device-dependent events. For instance, if you want something to happen when a user gets to a particular field, use onFocus instead of onClick.

Another consideration is that not all users can access client-side scripting, such as JavaScript. This means that we need to avoid client-generated content as much as possible. If you have dynamic content, produce it on the server.

If you have functions that rely on scripting, wherever possible you should provide an alternative for those who cannot access scripting. For instance, without scripting our Update Total button won't work. To avoid frustrating users, we could include an explanation, using the <noscript></noscript> tag to provide alternate content that will only appear if it's needed, as seen below:

```
…
<td colspan="3" align="left">
   <input  tabindex="4" type="button" value="Update Total" onclick="UpdateTotal()" />
   <noscript><br />To update your total, submit the order. You will have one more
chance to confirm.</noscript>
</td>
…
```

The ideal solution in this case would be to use scripting to generate the Update Total button in the first place, and provide an alternative button that submits the form in the <noscript></noscript> section. By writing the code in this way, only the appropriate content will appear.

Frames

One of the greatest challenges to accessibility (though certainly not the very greatest) is the use of frames.

The reason for this is that, by their very nature, frames break the essential idea of the Web, which is to link directly to specific content. For instance, it is difficult, if not impossible, to bookmark a frameset with particular pages in it.

Increasing accessibility when using frames essentially consists of four tactics, which deal with providing information and not confusing the user.

As far as providing information, there is nothing new. Always provide title and longdesc attributes for your frames, so that the user knows whether or not to attempt to access them. Also, be sure to provide a <noframes></noframes> section on the page, as we discussed earlier, to provide information for users who do not have frames available. Typically, this should link to a nonframed version of the site.

To avoid confusing the user, accessibility guidelines suggest staying away from opening new windows, such as by using target=_blank, as they can be disorienting. Perhaps the best way to avoid accessibility problems with frames is to simply avoid using them entirely.

Linking Related Content

Although most of us, when surfing, tend to view a single Web page at a time, most Web-page authors like to think of their site as a logical grouping of content. We can encourage our users to see this larger grouping with additional information that ties a page to other pages. In many cases this information is nonsequential, in that the user can choose content in any order, but sometimes it's not. We might also want to provide the browser with information on where to find alternate versions of a page, such as one designed for text-only viewing.

Sequential Pages

If we had an article that spanned three pages, we could provide information about them in the <head></head> section of each page. The first page of our mylife1.html might read:

```
…
<head><title>Book Review: My Life In Australia</title>
<link rel="start" href="mylife1.html" />
<link rel="next" href="mylife2.html" />
<link rel="end" href="mylife3.html" />
</head>
<body>
…
```

whereas page 2 might read:

```
…
<head><title>Book Review: My Life In Australia</title>
<link rel="start" href="mylife1.html" />
<link rel="prev" href="mylife1.html" />
<link rel="next" href="mylife3.html" />
<link rel="end" href="mylife3.html" />
</head>
<body>
…
```

and page 3,

```
…
<head><title>Book Review: My Life In Australia</title>
<link rel="start" href="mylife1.html" />
<link rel="prev" href="mylife2.html" />
<link rel="end" href="mylife3.html" />
</head>
<body>
…
```

This is one of those situations where you do something knowing that you will need it later. Today's browsers do not use this linking and grouping information, but sooner, rather than later, there will be applications that do.

Alternative Content

We can also use this method for providing links to alternative content. For instance, if we wanted to provide a text-only version of the article, we might add:

```
<link title="My Life In Australia: Text Only Version" rel="alternate" href="mylifeText.html"
media="aural, braille, tty, handheld" />
```

Or to provide a version in German, we might add:

```
<link title="Meine Lebensdauer in Australien: Deutsche Version" rel="alternate"
href="mylifeGerman.html" lang="de" />
```

Why Bother?

It is natural for humans to stick with their own experiences, and in general, Web developers have come to take for granted some of the tools that are in common use. Even now, it is not uncommon for an experienced Web author, when reminded that tables should always have a line break at the end of each row to accommodate browsers that don't support it, to remark, "sure, but what is that, .3% of the marketplace?"(Clients often feel the same way, wondering why you're "wasting" time on accessibility issues.)

That kind of thinking can quickly turn a site into a dinosaur, unable to keep up. Web content is appearing on more and more devices, such as cell phones and PDAs. At this moment there are plans to provide Web content in public restroom stalls. You cannot and should not assume that all of these devices will have all features available. When providing your content, you must seek to make it accessible in as many ways as possible. But there is perhaps a more compelling reason: legal requirements.

The Web Accessibility Initiative (WAI)

All United States government Web sites are already required to be accessible under the Americans with Disabilities Act. Web sites have been ruled in court to be a public accommodation and must be accessible to those with disabilities.

In some countries, including not only the U.S. and Canada but also Australia, Web access is considered a civil right. Many European countries, and specifically the European Union, have or are considering policies ensuring Web access for those with disabilities.

The Web Accessibility Initiative is proposing the standards for accessibility. The WAI covers accessibility for Web sites, for those creating browsers (otherwise known as "user-agents") and for authoring tools.

There are various tools that will help you evaluate your site, such as *Bobby*, a Web site that allows you to enter a URL for evaluation. Bobby will rate your accessibility and tell you how to improve it. Bobby is available at:

http://www.cast.com/bobby

For those using Dreamweaver, there is also a new extension called the "508 Accessibility Suite Extension," named for U.S. accessibility legislation.

The basic guidelines can be summarized in the WAI Checklist.

The Checklist

The WAI Checklist has three levels. Priority 1 is absolute, must-do items. If any of these are missing, some users will be unable to access some or all of your content.

1. Provide alternate text, such as alt, title and longdesc information for all non-text elements.

2. Ensure that pages are understandable in a noncolor environment.

3. Identify changes in language. This enables readers to adjust for pronunciation. For instance:

Just press the button, and <span lang="fr">voilà</span>, it's complete.

4. Organize the page so that it can be read without style sheets. Dynamic positioning is good, but should not be essential to the page.

Look over the three Web Accessibility Initiative checklists (priority 1, 2 and 3) at http://www.w3.org/WAI. The WAI also lists resources for assistive devices and software.

5. Avoid flickering. Seizures can be caused by flickering in the range of 4 to 59 beats per second. (Peak sensitivity is at 20 beats per second.) Also avoid strobe effects for this reason.

6. Use the clearest, simplest language possible.

7. Provide text equivalents for imagemap regions.

8. Use client-side imagemaps rather than server-side imagemaps.

9. Identify column and row headers on all tables.

10. If a table has more than two logical levels, associate cells with the appropriate headers.

11. Provide titles for all frames.

12. Ensure that pages are usable even without any scripting, applets and other external objects.

13. Provide an auditory track for visual multimedia. Be sure that both tracks are synchronized, if appropriate.

14. Provide a visual presentation of auditory multimedia. Be sure that both tracks are synchronized, if appropriate.

15. When all else fails, provide an alternative version of content that is accessible, but be sure that this version is updated as frequently as the original.

Priority 2 and 3 checklists center around items that make your site difficult, but not impossible, to use. All three checklists can be found on the Web Accessibility Initiative site, at http://www.w3.org/WAI.

Summary

You have learned that accessibility and usability go hand in hand, and usability is an absolute necessity for success on the Web. In this chapter, you explored ways to make a site more usable, from the overall structure to the page layout. You also became familiar with specific approaches that should be used on all sites, such as text alternatives for visual and audio elements and, perhaps most importantly, using structure to define a page as much as possible. You learned many of the disabilities for which you will need to plan and became familiar with the WAI checklists to help you plan how to ensure that your site is accessible to and usable by all.

12 Where Do We Go from Here?

Chapter Objective:

To become familiar with the nuances of XHTML and where it is going. In Chapter 12, you will:

- Learn how to convert existing HTML content to XHTML.

- Discover the differences between versions of XHTML.

- Become familiar with the direction in which XHTML is going.

Projects to be Completed:

- News Web (A)

- Cyber Travel (B)

- Hunter Films (C)

- **North Star Adventure Gear (D)**

Where Do We Go from Here?

Over the last 11 chapters, we've touched on all aspects of XHTML as it exists and, more specifically, as it is supported by browsers today.

It's important to remember, however, that XHTML is just the beginning of a new era in Web authoring. The reformulation of HTML 4.01 into XHTML 1.0 is the first step in preparing for innovations that become necessary as the Web becomes available in more and more places.

Let's take a look first at how to move from our existing HTML pages to XHTML, and then at the directions in which XHTML is moving in the near future.

Converting Existing HTML to XHTML

Perform simple cleanup of old pages with HTML Tidy, from http://www.w3.org/People/Raggett/tidy/.

We started this book with the assertion that a properly written HTML page was virtually indistinguishable from a properly written XHTML page. While we're not backing away from that statement, there are millions of HTML pages that were written before XHTML came into the picture, and before the importance of writing pages properly was really known.

It was these documents that almost forced the creation of XHTML just to bring some sanity to the process of rendering pages.

What can be done to salvage these pages? For simple conversions, you can use a tool such as HTML Tidy, which is available at http://www.w3.org/People/Raggett/tidy/. This useful program, written by the W3C's Dave Raggett, will clean up many of the problems that we'll discuss below, but in some situations, we will need to do some or all of the conversion manually.

Missing Closing Tags

The most common problem in pre-XHTML pages is probably a lack of closing tags. The most prominent of these is the <p></p> tag. For years, browsers have allowed authors to use a single <p> as a sort of double line break, completely ignoring the original intention of the tag.

All tags must have closing tags, except empty tags, which should be written with a space and a slash as in <br />.

This is not entirely the fault of Web authors, however. The original standards classified many closing tags, such as </td>, as "optional."

All tags, with the exception of empty tags such as <img /> and <br />, must have a closing tag.

Empty Tags

If a tag is defined as empty, however, it shouldn't have a closing tag. In HTML, these tags were expressed simply as <img> or <br> or <hr>. In XHTML, this would cause the document to be "non-well-formed." In other words, the missing closing tag would be a problem.

The natural temptation would be to use
</br>, but some browsers will have a problem with this, so the best course of action is to use the abbreviated versions, such as <br />. Please note that space before the slash. Without it, many browsers will have difficulty interpreting the tag.

Uppercase vs. Lowercase

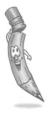

All tags should be written in lowercase.

All tags in XHTML are lowercased, but in previous versions, HTML was specifically case-insensitive. Unfortunately, the general convention then was to uppercase tags to distinguish them from the rest of the content.

To convert older pages, make sure that all tags and attribute names are in lowercase.

Attributes

Using quotation marks (double quotes) around attribute values was also optional in HTML, particularly if the value was a number. For instance, it was perfectly acceptable to place an image on the page by writing:

<img src="/images/myimage.gif" **height=300 width=200** align=right>

This would be illegal in XHTML, with the correct version reading:

<img src="/images/myimage.gif" **height="300" width="200"** align="right" />

For some elements, such as checkboxes, it was also normal in HTML to use "attribute minimization." This means that authors would write:

<input type="checkbox" **checked** name="first" value="firstval" />

which is incorrect, rather than:

<input type="checkbox" **checked="checked"** name="first" value="firstval" />

which is correct.

Nested Tags

When talking about nested tags, there are two points to consider.

The first, which we talked about in Chapter 1, is the fact that tags can't overlap. In other words, rather than writing:

<h3>Upcoming Books</h3>

we need to write:

<h3>Upcoming Books</h3>

The second is less obvious — tags that can't be contained within each other. The list is fairly short and includes mostly items that should be obvious, such as the following:

Tag	Can't Contain...
a	another a
form	another form
label	another label
button	input, select, textarea, label, button, form, fieldset, iframe or isindex
pre	img, object, big, small, sub or sup

Name vs. Id

When we use the # notation, we are typically referring to a particular spot, such as an anchor on a page, as in:

http://www.myserver.com/faq.html**#mukluk**

A particular spot, as indicated here, is known as a "document fragment," and was previously designated with the name attribute of an <a></a> tag, as in:

<a **name="mukluk"**></a>

Converting this code to XHTML means converting it to the id attribute, but this is one area where browsers will definitely notice the difference — many older browsers won't recognize the id attribute. To prevent problems, add an id attribute beside the name attribute, as in:

`<a name="snore" id="snore"></a>`

This problem and solution affect the following tags: <a></a>, <applet></applet>, <form></form>, <frame></frame>, <iframe></iframe>, <img /> and <map></map>.

DOCTYPE

The designers of HTML knew that the language would evolve fairly quickly, and that browsers would inevitably run into tags that they didn't recognize. To ensure that this discrepancy wouldn't break anything when it happened, browsers are designed to ignore a tag that they don't recognize.

This means that in HTML, we could have all sorts of unofficial tags, which was one by-product of the browser wars.

In XHTML, we use an established *grammar*, or set of tags. The way that we tell the browser which set of tags we're using is through the DOCTYPE declaration. For example, the DOCTYPE declaration that we've used on all of our files throughout this book is:

```
<!DOCTYPE html PUBLIC "-//W3C//DTD HTML 4.01 Transitional//EN"
"http://www.w3.org/TR/html4/loose.dtd">
```

This declaration tells the browser the grammar that we're using is XHTML Transitional, and has five basic components:

- **<!DOCTYPE**. This component indicates the beginning of the declaration.
- **html**. This component indicates the name of what's called the "root element," or the main element of the document.
- **PUBLIC**. This component indicates that we want to use the public identifier, which comes next, as opposed to the system identifier, which comes last.
- **"-//W3C//DTD HTML 4.01 Transitional//EN"**. This component is the public identifier, which may or may not be recognizable to the processor (in this case, the browser). The general public identifiers for XHTML are standard, but authors can create their own. If they do, the result could be a situation where the public identifier is unknown and the processor needs to use the system identifier.
- **"http://www.w3.org/TR/html4/loose.dtd"**. This component is the system identifier. This is a URL for the Document Type Definition, or DTD, which defines the possible elements and attributes, and what can be nested within what. This is the document against which the page is *validated*, or checked.

Namespace

By their very nature, XHTML documents are also XML documents, which means that we can take advantage of features that we can use to take a Web page to the next level, such as integrating text-based graphics or a mathematical formula.

The way that we use these features is via XML namespaces. Basically, a <h1></h1> element in one namespace and an <h1></h1> element in a different namespace can exist in the same document and have two different meanings. For example, the traditional browser might interpret <h1></h1> as expected, whereas an <h1></h1> in a different namespace might tell a plug-in to do something completely different with the content.

Namespaces are beyond the scope of this book (and in most cases you won't need to even worry about them), but it's a good idea to define the default namespace for your documents, in case they are later incorporated into another document. All XHTML pages, regardless of whether they're transitional, strict and so on, have the same namespace. To indicate this in our files, we add a notation to the <html></html> element using the xmlns attribute. The namespace value for all XHTML pages is http://www.w3.org/1999/xhtml. It's also a good idea to indicate the language of the document, using the xml:lang attribute. This makes the element:

<html xmlns="http://www.w3.org/1999/xhtml" xml:lang="en" >

…

</html>

The Three Flavors of XHTML 1.0

Part of the purpose of DOCTYPE declarations is to allow different applications to use different grammars. At this time, XHTML comes in three different variations.

XHTML 1.0 Transitional

Transitional XHTML is the most common document type found when we're talking about *legacy HTML documents* (those pages that will need to be converted to XHTML but are working with current browsers). Transitional documents can contain presentation-oriented tags and attributes, such as and width. Most of these tags and attributes have been deprecated, which means that they will be removed from the next version, so they should be avoided wherever possible.

As we noted above, the DOCTYPE declaration for a XHTML Transitional document is:

```
<!DOCTYPE HTML PUBLIC "-//W3C//DTD HTML 4.01 Transitional//EN"
"http://www.w3.org/TR/html4/loose.dtd">
```

XHTML 1.0 Strict

XHTML Strict is a version of XHTML that does not include any of the tags or attributes that are deprecated — there are no presentational elements in it. All presentation is to be done through CSS style sheets. The disadvantage of using XHTML Strict is that it may be difficult to get your pages to look exactly right in browsers that have limited support for CSS. The advantage is that your documents will be ready for the next version, XHTML 1.1.

The DOCTYPE declaration for an XHTML Strict document is:

```
<!DOCTYPE HTML PUBLIC "-//W3C//DTD HTML 4.01//EN"
"http://www.w3.org/TR/html4/strict.dtd">
```

XHTML 1.0 Frameset

XHTML Frameset is identical to XHTML Transitional, except for slight differences that allow the Web author to replace <body></body> with <frameset></frameset>. Frames are also deprecated, and will be removed from the main specification in XHTML 1.1.

The DOCTYPE declaration for XHTML Frameset is:

```
<!DOCTYPE HTML PUBLIC "-//W3C//DTD HTML 4.01 Frameset//EN"
        "http://www.w3.org/TR/html4/frameset.dtd">
```

By using XHTML Strict, your pages will be ready for XHTML 1.1, because the tags are identical.

Modularization of XHTML

This doesn't mean, however, that frames can't be used at all. The W3C has put together a recommendation for the Modularization of XHTML, which will enable authors to add modules to standard XHTML in order to extend the language.

The most basic module is a tag, with all of its associated attributes. These tags are then grouped into larger modules. A tag can belong to any number of different modules, including, for example, to both forms modules.

The Forms Modules

The modularization project defined two different forms-related modules, the Basic Forms module and the Forms module.

The Basic Forms module includes:

- form
- input
- select
- option
- textarea
- label

The Forms module includes:

- form
- input
- select
- option
- textarea
- button
- label
- fieldset
- optgroup
- legend

The Legacy Module

The purpose of XHTML modularization is to provide an easy way to specify a particular group of tags that may be supported by a particular piece of software, such as a browser in a cell phone. In the future, authors will be able to find out whether a particular module is supported, and therefore provide the appropriate content.

For example, browsers may eventually remove support for the Legacy module. The Legacy module consists of the following elements:

- basefont
- center

- dir
- font
- isindex
- menu
- s
- strike
- u

The Legacy module also defines additional attributes that can be used with other elements when the module is included in a document. These include:

- body: alink, background, bgcolor, link, text and vlink
- br: clear
- caption: align
- div: align
- dl: compact, type
- hr: align, noshade, size and width
- img: align, border, hspace and vspace
- input: align
- legend: align
- li: type, value
- ol: compact, start and type
- p: align
- vpre: width
- script: language
- table: align, bgcolor
- tr: bgcolor
- th: bgcolor, height, nowrap and width
- td: bgcolor, height, nowrap and width
- ul: compact, type

XHTML 1.0 Basic

The first application of modularization to make its way to Recommendation status is XHTML Basic. The purpose of XHTML Basic is to define a set of modules that is small enough to be supported on a low-power, low-complexity device, but still adequate for authoring. If a page contains only tags included in XHTML Basic, you can be fairly certain that it will be readable under virtually any circumstances.

XHTML Basic includes the following modules:

- **Structure module**: body, head, html and title
- **Text module**: abbr, acronym, address, blockquote, br, cite, code, dfn, div, em, h1, h2, h3, h4, h5, h6, kbd, p, pre, q, samp, span, strong and var

You will be able to use XHTML modularization to identify and then develop the most appropriate content for particular devices in the future.

Proposed "standards" must go through a review process with the W3C. They begin as a Working Draft, then become a Last Call Working Draft, Candidate Recommendation, Proposed Recommendation and finally a Recommendation.

- **Hypertext module:** a
- **List module:** ol, ul, li, dl, dt and dd
- **Basic Forms module:** form, input, label, select, option, and textarea
- **Basic Tables module:** caption, table, td, th and tr
- **Image module:** img
- **Object module:** object and param
- **Metainformation module:** meta
- **Link module:** link
- **Base module:** base

The DOCTYPE declaration for XHTML Basic documents is:

```
<!DOCTYPE html PUBLIC "-//W3C//DTD XHTML Basic 1.0//EN"
"http://www.w3.org/TR/xhtml-basic/xhtml-basic10.dtd" >
```

XHTML 1.1

XHTML 1.1 is basically the next step beyond the Modularization of XHTML. Using the process of modularization, which allows for the inclusion or exclusion of particular defined modules, XHTML 1.1 removes the deprecated elements, and provides a purely structural look at a page. XHTML 1.1 is virtually identical to XHTML 1.0 Strict.

XHTML 1.1 has its own DOCTYPE definition:

```
<!DOCTYPE html PUBLIC "-//W3C//DTD XHTML 1.1//EN"
"http://www.w3.org/TR/xhtml11/DTD/xhtml11.dtd">
```

XHTML 1.1 also defines new functionality called "Ruby Annotation."

Ruby Annotation

The idea behind Ruby Annotation is that in some languages, such as those in east Asian countries, it's not unusual to have an annotation that appears as smaller text above certain expressions to add meaning or pronunciation assistance, as shown here in the specification.

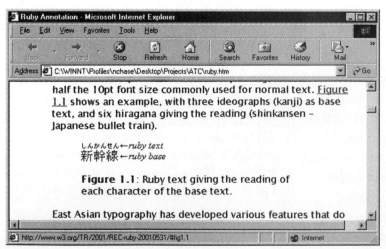

From Ruby Annotation: W3C Recommendation 31 May 2001. Edited by Marcin Sawicki, Michel Suingard, Masayasu Ishikawa, Martin Durst and Tex Texin. Latest version: http://www.w3.org/TR/ruby/

The name "ruby" comes from the name for the 5.5-point typeface generally used to produce it in traditional printed documents.

In western languages, this annotation can be used to further clarify the meaning of text within a page in such a way that if Ruby Annotation isn't supported, the text that would have appeared as an annotation will appear, instead, in parentheses. At the time of this writing, there are no browsers fully supporting ruby. We can create a page, however, that is ready when they do, but degrades gracefully enough to remain helpful in current browsers. For instance, we could create a ruby annotation for abbreviations on a page, such as FAQ, for Frequently Asked Questions. The browser won't show the annotation because ruby is not yet supported, but the annotation won't look odd, either.

Ruby Annotation consists of a section of <ruby></ruby>, which contains the ruby base and the ruby text that appears above it. In "simple ruby," there is just one section of ruby text (indicated by <rt></rt> tags), and just one ruby base (indicated by <rb></rb> tags). For instance:

```
<ruby>
<rb>FAQ</rb>
<rt>Frequently Asked Questions</rt>
<ruby>
```

would create something along the lines of:

Frequently Asked Questions

F A Q

The reason that the base is written first is so that if the browser doesn't know anything about ruby, this text will be displayed first. Of course, the way we have it written, the browser would show:

FAQ Frequently Asked Questions

which might be a little confusing. Instead, we would want something along the lines of:

FAQ (Frequently Asked Questions)

We can do this by using another tag, <rp></rp>, for ruby parentheses. These tags enable you to put in parentheses that do not reproduce in ruby-savvy browsers but do reproduce in non-ruby browsers. We might add such parentheses by writing:

```
<ruby>
<rb>FAQ</rb>
<rt><rp>(</rp>Frequently Asked Questions<rp>)</rp></rt>
<ruby>
```

In this way, a browser that understands ruby would know not to render the parentheses, but a non-ruby browser would ignore the new tags and just present the text.

Summary of XHTML Elements

Now that we've explored most of the elements defined in XHTML and its variations, here is a summary of each of them and the variations to which they belong.

Element	Strict	Transitional	Frameset	Basic	XHTML 1.1	Empty
a	X	X	X	X	X	
abbr	X	X	X	X	X	
acronym	X	X	X	X	X	
address	X	X	X	X	X	
applet		X	X			
area	X	X	X		X	X
b	X	X	X		X	
base	X	X	X	X	X	X
basefont		X	X			X
bdo	X	X	X		X	
big	X	X	X		X	
blockquote	X	X	X	X	X	
body	X	X	X	X	X	
br	X	X	X	X	X	X
button	X	X	X		X	
caption	X	X	X	X	X	
center		X	X			
cite	X	X	X	X	X	
code	X	X	X	X	X	
col	X	X	X		X	X
colgroup	X	X	X		X	
dd	X	X	X	X	X	
del	X	X	X		X	
dfn	X	X	X	X	X	
dir		X	X			
div	X	X	X		X	
dl	X	X	X	X	X	
dt	X	X	X	X	X	
em	X	X	X	X	X	
fieldset	X	X	X		X	
font		X	X			
form	X	X	X	X	X	
frame			X			X
frameset			X			
h1	X	X	X	X	X	
h2	X	X	X	X	X	
h3	X	X	X	X	X	
h4	X	X	X	X	X	
h5	X	X	X	X	X	
h6	X	X	X	X	X	

Element	Strict	Transitional	Frameset	Basic	XHTML 1.1	Empty
head	X	X	X	X	X	
hr	X	X	X		X	X
html	X	X	X	X	X	
i	X	X	X		X	
iframe	X	X	X		X	
img	X	X	X	X	X	X
input	X	X	X	X	X	X
ins	X	X	X		X	
isindex		X	X			X
kbd	X	X	X	X	X	
label	X	X	X		X	
legend	X	X	X		X	
li	X	X	X	X	X	
link	X	X	X	X	X	X
map	X	X	X		X	
menu		X	X			
meta	X	X	X	X	X	X
noframes			X			
noscript	X	X	X		X	
object	X	X	X	X	X	
ol	X	X	X	X	X	
optgroup	X	X	X		X	
option	X	X	X	X	X	
p	X	X	X	X	X	
param	X	X	X	X	X	X
pre	X	X	X	X	X	
q	X	X	X	X	X	
rb					X	
rbc					X	
rp					X	
rt					X	
rtc					X	
ruby					X	
s		X	X			
samp	X	X	X	X	X	
script	X	X	X		X	
select	X	X	X	X	X	
small	X	X	X		X	
span	X	X	X		X	
strike		X	X			
strong	X	X	X	X	X	
style	X	X	X		X	
sub	X	X	X		X	

Element	Strict	Transitional	Frameset	Basic	XHTML 1.1	Empty
sup	X	X	X		X	
table	X	X	X	X	X	
tbody	X	X	X		X	
td	X	X	X	X	X	
textarea	X	X	X	X	X	
tfoot	X	X	X		X	
th	X	X	X	X	X	
thead	X	X	X		X	
title	X	X	X	X	X	
tr	X	X	X	X	X	
tt	X	X	X		X	
u		X	X			
ul	X	X	X	X	X	
var	X	X	X	X	X	

Future Specifications

Technology keeps marching on, and of course the "X" in XHTML stands for extensibility. Several new initiatives are in the works, some of which are similar to the HTML we now know and love, and some of which will fundamentally change the way that we build Web sites.

XHTML Events

As we saw when we examined scripting in XHTML, we can specify actions to take place when a particular event, such as a rollover or button click, happens. This is, however, fairly rudimentary.

The XHTML Events module, which is, at the time of this writing, a Working Draft, defines a set of elements and attributes that will allow for much more comprehensive event handling.

For instance, suppose we create a script that should execute if someone rolls over an image. With today's XHTML, that script will always fire, unless we specifically turn it off on that image. With XHTML events, we can get closer to the functionality of, say, Macromedia Director. For instance, we might have rollover events on each of our images, but we could deactivate an entire section of the page by interrupting the event chain.

XHTML Events also gives us more freedom by associating an element, such as an image, with an event handler. So rather than specifying an onmouseover, an onmouseout and an onclick script, we would instead create an event handler. That handler would sort out what has actually happened and take the appropriate action.

Because XHTML Events is a module, it is either supported or not supported; there's no guesswork involved.

XForms

XForms is being billed as "the next generation in Web forms," and that's probably accurate. Where current XHTML forms are based on elements that have very specific functionality, XForms take the separation of structure and presentation one step further.

With XForms, there are three pieces to the puzzle: the form itself, the rendering of the form and the data collected by the form.

The form itself controls the processing of the data, which can be limited in very specific ways. For instance, if we were writing a car-rental reservation screen, we could require that a drop-off destination be entered, but only for one-way reservations. Where we now have to create that set of conditions with fairly complex scripting, it would be inherent in the form.

Separating the presentation also enables us to adapt to the environment where the form is being processed. For instance, if we specify that we're looking for a date, an XForms-aware browser might automatically render three pulldowns, or drop-down menus, one each for the month, the day and the year, and the years would already be limited by maximums and minimums that we've established for the data.

As of this writing, XForms is still a Working Draft, but it is likely that this will be most helpful to authors of programs such as Dreamweaver, who will integrate the functionality into their authoring environment. Hand-coding XForms is considerably more complex than hand-coding traditional XHTML.

XLink

The XML Linking Language specification, or XLink, became a W3C Recommendation in June of 2001. Although not yet supported by current browsers, XLink may start appearing in the next versions.

We're already familiar with hyperlinks, where we create an <a></a> tag that jumps to another location when we click on it. This is similar to the most basic XLink link, in which we activate the link on request, and replace the current content in the window.

XLink allows us to expand on this functionality. For instance, we might specify that a link be followed when the page is loaded, and that the new content be embedded in the current page instead of replacing the page. In this way, we could include external content in our page without touching either page. If the external content changed, our page would be updated automatically.

XLink also allows for more complex links. For instance, imagine that we were creating a Web page that talks about the new season's television shows. With a complex link, the user could click a show's title and be given a choice of linking to a summary, a schedule or a bio for each cast member. What's more, as authors we could decide whether that information replaces the page or is added to it.

SVG

With the growth of Macromedia Flash, many designers are becoming familiar with vector graphics. Scalable Vector Graphics, or SVG, which at the time of this writing is a Candidate Recommendation, defines tags and attributes that enable a designer to create not only artwork, but also animations right in the page.

The advantage of this is that, just as today we can create a page with dynamic content, a designer can, with the help of an engineer, create dynamic graphics and animations.

When to Switch

As new capabilities become available, they will ultimately include the ability to determine what is supported and what is not, so you can choose accordingly. But what about those pages that you already have? When do you worry about upgrading them to XHTML, or more specifically, to XHTML Strict?

The answer to this question is going to depend on several factors, such as what you're presenting, to whom you're presenting it, and how.

The biggest question that needs to be answered is "how bad are they now?" If your pages are "mostly" in compliance, you probably don't need to worry too much about it, as long as you clean up any problems when you update the content. (You are updating your content, aren't you?) If there are serious problems, however, such as missing end tags for table elements, you'll want to take up the effort as soon as possible. New browsers, such as Netscape 6, are beginning to interpret the recommendations much more strictly, removing much of the legacy capabilities upon which lax authors have relied.

This brings up a second question: how are users accessing your content? If your users are mostly using traditional browsers, you'll be able to get away with leaving your legacy content alone much more successfully than if your content is likely to be accessed by users on mobile phones and PDAs. Even in the best of circumstances, these devices need special versions of your content, which will be difficult to provide if legacy issues exist.

Finally, do your users expect the "latest and greatest" from you? If so, you'll want to start migrating as soon as possible. Browser support for advanced features is currently fractured, and while deviations from the standard are sometimes necessary, what seems like a small issue can destroy the capabilities of your page.

In the final analysis, it comes to this: put yourself in your user's shoes periodically. Every few months, and certainly when a new browser is released, look at your audience and determine how they're accessing your site, or will be likely to in the next few months, then try it. If your home page suddenly disappears in the latest browser, it's time to upgrade.

Summary

In this chapter, you explored the differences between the main versions of XHTML — Strict, Transitional and Frameset — and how to convert existing HTML documents to XHTML. You also learned about the modularization of XHTML, and the new capabilities that it will create. Finally, you became familiar with the new specifications that are on the way, such as XForms, XLink and Scalable Vector Graphics.

Complete Project D: North Star Adventure Gear

Free-Form Project #2

Assignment

Perfect Partner Dating Service (PP) is expanding into online services to broaden their reach and expand their client base. PP feels that one of their strengths is their excellent reputation for providing "that personal touch," so they want their site design to reflect that — a pleasant experience that simulates the relaxed and friendly atmosphere of one of their offices.

You have been hired to design the new PP Web site that will enable their potential clients to obtain the information that they want as well as to "meet" potential partners who are already enrolled with their service. Your design should reflect PP's values, with an easy-to-use navigation system, and a relaxed and friendly tone and look. You are creating a functional "proof of concept" that the client will review in order to approve the page designs.

Applying Your Skills

To develop this site, you will:

- Plan the structure of the site by sketching a flowchart or tree of pages.

- Design the overall layout of the pages. While the home page doesn't have to match the subpages, the look must be similar enough to avoid jarring the user.

- Design a layout template that can be modified to create new pages. Include style sheet information in a separate file.

- Create a home page using the supplied temporary text to give an idea of the type of information needed.

- Create a navigation scheme that enables a user to get to any page from any other page.

- Design the "Find a Partner" pages based on the look of the home page, including a combination of different form elements based on the questions listed in the included files.

- The actual search logic will be created by engineers later, but create a sample results page using the supplied photos to give them an idea of what it

should look like. Use this sample results file as the action for your "Find a Partner" form.

Specifications

The site should be designed for systems set for a resolution of 800×600, but must be usable at 640×480 pixels.

Pages must be usable even when images are turned off in the browser, and each page must include keyword and description information for search engines.

The "Find a Partner" results page should show, for each member listed, the photo, name, age, gender, location, occupation, income range, indoor and outdoor interests, religion, language, preferred date and other preferences. You can decide how to lay out this information, but assume at least five members are returned as possible matches.

Publisher's Comments

As Web sites become more complex, more of their functions are created by engineers, who write the scripts to pull information from databases and other applications. It is still up to you, however, to provide the design, and in many cases, the overall vision for the site. You see that in this project in two ways.

First, the copy — the client has provided little information other than their goals. While it may not be your official job to write copy, in designing the overall Web experience, you define the types of copy that the client must provide. Often, the client has reams of promotional material that they think is right for the Web, but usually isn't. You use different copy for the Web than for a brochure. As a designer, it is often your job to determine what that copy should be.

Second, the design — while you could provide it using sketches and even full images, that still leaves the engineers to create the XHTML that realizes your vision. Creating the actual pages allows you to control the presentation much more tightly, and to find out whether your ideas are possible and workable before they go to the next level. By providing pages with "for placement only" (FPO) information, you provide the essential framework into which programmers can plug functionality.

Review #2

Chapters 7 through 12

In Chapters 7 through 12, you've learned advanced techniques — absolute placement, scripting, streaming media and more — for developing your Web site. You also learned methods for improving accessibility, both for users and for search engines and other applications. After completing the second half of this book, you should:

- Be familiar with block and inline elements. You should know how to use divs to apply style to your content, to place content in an absolute position on the page or to allow content to adjust to the rest of the page. You should also understand how to create layers of information that sit on top of each other, and how to control the visibility of those layers, as well as their appearance.

- Know how to add scripting to a Web page using JavaScript. You should be familiar with objects, events and functions, and know how to use them to create effects such as image rollovers, form validation and pop-up windows. You should be able create alert boxes and confirm boxes, and know how to use scripts to create dynamic content on the page.

- Be able to add sounds and video to a page and give the user control over them. You should be familiar with sounds, QuickTime movies, RealMedia, Windows Media and Macromedia Flash movies, and know how to compensate for differences between browsers. You should understand the differences between streaming and non-streaming content, and when each is appropriate.

- Understand search engines and how they work, and understand <meta /> tags and how they can assist search engines in indexing and describing your content. You should know how to use <meta /> tags to refresh or redirect your pages automatically, or to control whether and for how long your pages are cached by the browser.

- Be able to improve a Web site's accessibility and usability. You should be familiar with the various kinds of disabilities for which you must plan, and know the features (such as style sheets for different types of media) that you can use to improve accessibility. You know how to increase the usability of your site, understanding both how to do so (layout and structure) and why doing so is important. You know how to make forms more usable, how to create client-side imagemaps, how to structure tables to prevent accessibility problems, and how to handle accessibility concerns for frames and scripts. You are familiar with the Web Accessibility Initiative guidelines.

- You understand the current state of XHTML and its variations, the direction in which it is moving, and which elements belong to which variations. You have discovered how and when to convert current pages to meet new specifications. You also explored upcoming specifications.

Project A: News Web

You are a member of the Web development team at a full-service ISP and Web-Design agency. Your agency has just won the account for a local newspaper that is trying to "move into the 21st century" by providing their content online as well as in print. In addition to their traditional printed newspaper, they want to be an online news agency by the name of "News Web."

Your team is creating the News Web site, and you are producing the front page. Other team members have set out the parameters of the project. Your job is to create a Web page within those parameters.

You have been given the *comp* (a hand-drawn rough sketch) and the images for the News Web site. You need to determine the best way to structure the layout. This project depends on your abilities to create simple XHTML elements, format with CSS and produce complex tables, all tailored to the plan in the comp.

Planning for News Web

The creative group prepared a number of comps to review with the client and, after revisions, this is the approach that the client approved. This hand-drawn comp shows the look of the page from which you can plan the structure to create that look and layout.

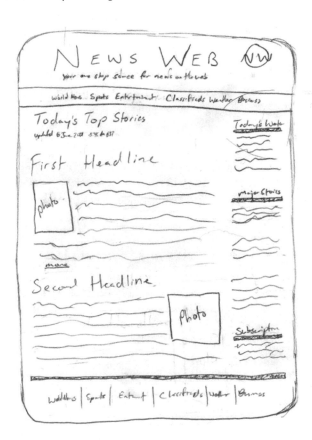

You've already made the usual photocopies of the comp, written notes on them, such as file names for images, and drawn the structure of the table that you will use for layout.

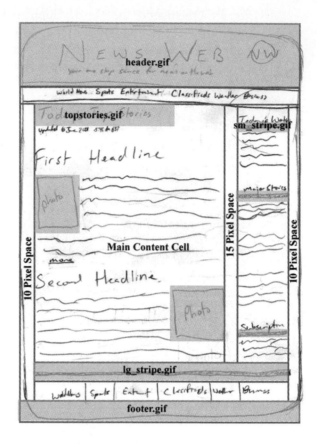

The comp annotated in preparation for creating the page

The lines represent the cell borders for the table. By looking at this comp, you can determine the number of rows and columns that you need. (This table will require five columns and six rows.) You will also need to create a nested table for the sidebar area. Now that you have planned out the layout table, you can start to build the structure of the News Web front page.

Create the Page Structure

1. Navigate to **RF_HTML>A_Project_HTML**, and copy the entire A_Project_HTML folder to your WIP folder.

2. Inside this folder are all of the images that will be needed to create the News Web main page. Take note that the images are in a subfolder named "images". You will need to remember this location when you later insert images into the front-page file.

3. Open your text editor and save a new file as "newsweb.html" to **WIP>A_Project_HTML**.

4. Type in the basic required XHTML page elements, and entitle the page "News Web".

```
<!DOCTYPE html PUBLIC "-//W3C//DTD XHTML 1.0 Transitional//EN"
"http://www.w3.org/TR/xhtml1/DTD/xhtml1-transitional.dtd">
<html>
<head>
<title>News Web</title>
</head>
<body>
</body>
</html>
```

5. Create the following table within the body element. It is a five-column, six-row table to match the comp. Some of the cells span multiple rows or columns. Set the appropriate rowspan and colspan attributes.

```
…
<body>
<table cellspacing="0" cellpadding="0" width="590" border="1">
<tr>
        <td colspan="5"></td>
</tr>
<tr>
        <td colspan="5"> </td>
</tr>
<tr>
        <td width="10" rowspan="3"></td>
        <td width="430"></td>
        <td width="15"></td>
        <td width="125"></td>
        <td width="10" rowspan="3"></td>
</tr>
<tr>
        <td colspan="3"></td>
</tr>
<tr>
        <td colspan="3"></td>
</tr>
<tr>
        <td colspan="5"></td>
</tr>
</table>
</body>
…
```

6. Save the document.

Note the indention of the <td> elements. While not required, this indentation will make the code easier to read. This is especially true as more content is added into the document.

Document the Table

1. Insert the comment tags:

```
…
<body>
<table cellspacing="0" cellpadding"0" width="590" border="1">
<tr>
        <td colspan="5"><!-- header --></td>
</tr>
<tr>
        <td colspan="5"><!--navigation bar --> </td>
</tr>
<tr>
        <td width="10" rowspan="3"><!--Left 10 pixel spacer --></td>
        <td width="430"><!--Main Content --></td>
        <td width="15"><!--Middle 15 pixel spacer --></td>
        <td width="125"><!--Side Bar --></td>
        <td width="10" rowspan="3"><!--Right 10 pixel spacer --></td>
</tr>
<tr>
        <td colspan="3"><!-- Long Stripe--></td>
</tr>
<tr>
        <td colspan="3"> <!--Bottom Text Links --></td>
</tr>
<tr>
        <td colspan="5"><!--Footer --></td>
</tr>
</table>
</body>
…
```

Due to the way in which tables are rendered, it is very important to make certain that your code looks exactly like the example. Placing elements in the wrong cell or adding elements that are not in the examples may give you strange results.

2. Save the document.

Exercise Setup
Browsers do not display cells that contain no contents. We will use temporary text to keep the cells that will have content while we are working. To keep open the cells that will have no content but are used for spacing, we will use non-breaking spaces.

Keep the Cells Open

1. Insert the following temporary text into the appropriate cells:

```
…
<body>
<table cellspacing="0" cellpadding"0" width="590" border="1">
<tr>
        <td colspan="5"><!-- header -->header.gif</td>
</tr>
<tr>
        <td colspan="5"><!--navigation bar -->Navigation Bar</td>
</tr>
<tr>
```

```
        <td width="10" rowspan="3"><!--Left 10 pixel spacer --></td>
        <td width="430"><!--Main Content -->Main Content</td>
        <td width="15"><!--Middle 15 pixel spacer --></td>
        <td width="125"><!--Side Bar -->Side Bar</td>
        <td width="10" rowspan="3"><!--Right 10 pixel spacer --></td>
</tr>
<tr>

        <td colspan="3"><!-- Long Stripe-->lg_stripe.gif</td>
</tr>
<tr>

        <td colspan="3"><!--Bottom Text Links -->Bottom Text Links</td>
</tr>
<tr>

        <td colspan="5"><!--Footer -->footer.gif</td>
</tr>
</table>
</body>
…
```

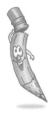

Adding comment tags will make our code easier to read. It will not only be easier for us to read, but also for others who may need to update or maintain the code in the future.

2. Add non-breaking spaces in the spacer cells.

```
…
<tr>

        <td width="10" rowspan="3" > <!--Left 10 pixel spacer --></td>
        <td width="430">Main Content<!--Main Content --></td>
        <td width="15">  <!--Middle 15 pixel spacer --></td>
        <td width="125">Side Bar<!--Side Bar --></td>
        <td width="10" rowspan="3"> <!--Right 10 pixel spacer --></td>
</tr>
…
```

3. Now that you have content in the cells, let's see how the table looks. Save the document.

4. Open **WIP>A_Project_HTML>newsweb.html** in your browser and compare it to the following screenshot.

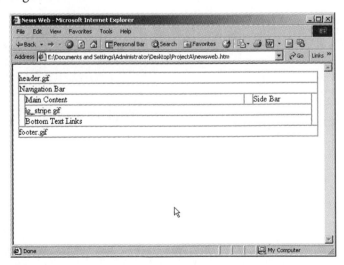

5. Keep both windows open so that you can continue to watch your progress.

Insert the Header and Footer

1. Insert the header.gif image in the topmost cell. (Remember, all images are in the images folder in your A_Project_HTML folder.) Notice that since we now have content in this cell, we no longer need the temporary text.

```
…
<body>
<table cellspacing="0" cellpadding"0" width="590" border="1">
<tr>
        <td colspan="5"><!-- header --><img src="images/header.gif" height="68"
        width="590" alt="News Web - Your one stop source for news on the
        web." /></td>
</tr>
…
```

2. Add the lg_stripe.gif image to the cell that contains the comment Long Stripe. Be sure to remove the temporary text.

```
…
<tr>
        <td colspan="3"><!-- Long Stripe--><img src="images/lg_stripe.gif" height="3"
        width="570"   alt="Long Blue Stripe" /></td>
</tr>
…
```

3. Add the footer.gif image to the bottom cell. It should have a comment that says Footer. Be sure to remove the temporary text.

```
…
<tr>
        <td colspan="5"><!--Footer -->
        <img src="images/footer.gif" height="25" width="590" alt="Footer Image" />
        </td>
</tr>
</table>
…
```

4. Save the file and refresh the browser.

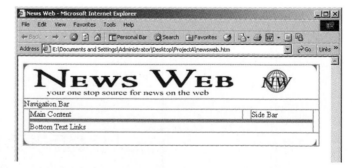

Exercise Setup

Now that there is some content in the table, let's add the background image for the document. This is also a good opportunity to do some formatting of the table.

Format the Document

1. Set the background image for the document to back.gif.

…
```
</head>
<body background="images/back.gif">
<table cellspacing="0" cellpadding"0" width="590" border="1">
```
…

2. Set the table border size to 0 (zero).

…
```
</head>
<body background="images/back.gif">
<table cellspacing="0" cellpadding"0" width="590" border="0">
```
…

3. Set the background color of the table to white.

…
```
</head>
<body background="images/back.gif">
<table cellspacing="0" cellpadding"0" width="590" border="0" bgcolor="white">
```
…

4. Center the table on the document.

…
```
</head>
<body background="images/back.gif">
<table cellspacing="0" cellpadding"0" width="590" border="1" bgcolor="white"
align="center">
```
…

5. Set the height of the Long Stripe cell to 15 pixels.

…
```
<tr>
        <td colspan="3" height="15"><!-- Long Stripe--><img src="images/lg_stripe.gif"
        height="3" width="570" alt="Long Blue Stripe" /></td>
</tr>
```
…

6. Save the file and refresh the browser.

Exercise Setup

Now we will add the site's navigation. Since we will only be creating this single page, we will use # as the hypertext reference for links.

Add the Navigation Bar

1. Create the following links in the Navigation Bar cell. Be sure to remove the temporary text.

```
...
<tr>
        <td colspan="5"><!-- Navigation Bar -->
        <a href="#">World News</a> |
        <a href="#">Sports</a> |
        <a href="#">Entertainment</a> |
        <a href="#">Classifieds</a> |
        <a href="#">Weather</a> |
        <a href="#">Business</a>
        </td>
</tr>
...
```

Using # as the hypertext reference for links is a useful technique for creating "dummy links." It enables you to give a value to the required href attribute, and it only reloads the page if you click on any of the links.

2. Save the file and refresh the browser.

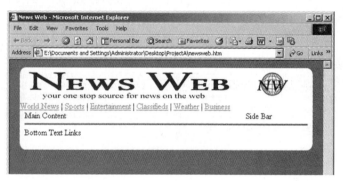

It is important to put a space both before and after the pipe symbol (|). Otherwise the links will appear immediately next to the pipe symbols. If the above links were on the same line, the first two would look like:

```
<a href="#">World
News</a> | <a
href="#">Sports</a>
```

3. Now let's make the Navigation Bar a little more interesting visually. We will begin by adding some CSS style information.

Insert the following code between the head tags:

```
...
<head>
<title>News Web</title>
<style type="text/css">
*           {font-family: "Times New Roman", Times, serif}

#navbar {background: url("images/nav.gif");
         text-align: center;
}

a {color: #0066cc;
   font-weight: bold;
   text-decoration: none;
}
```

```
a:hover {color: #ffff99;
  background-color: #0066cc;
  font-weight: bold;
  text-decoration: none;
}
</style>
</head>
```
…

4. Apply the navbar style to the Navigation Bar cell.

…
```
<tr>
        <td colspan="5" id="navbar"><!-- Navigation Bar -->
        <a href="#">World News</a> |
        <a href="#">Sports</a> |
        <a href="#">Entertainment</a> |
        <a href="#">Classifieds</a> |
        <a href="#">Weather</a> |
        <a href="#">Business</a>
        </td>
</tr>
```
…

5. Set the height of the Navigation Bar cell to 35.

…
```
<tr>
        <td colspan="5" id="navbar" height="35"><!-- Navigation Bar -->
        <a href="#">World News</a> |
        <a href="#">Sports</a> |
        <a href="#">Entertainment</a> |
        <a href="#">Classifieds</a> |
        <a href="#">Weather</a> |
        <a href="#">Business</a>
        </td>
</tr>
```
…

6. Save the file and refresh the browser.

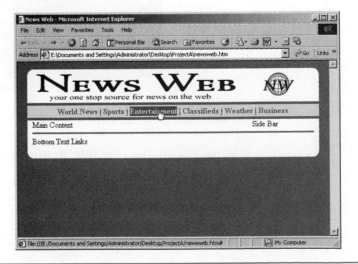

Add the Bottom Links

1. Copy the links from the Navigation Bar cell, and paste them into the Bottom Text Links cell. Be sure to remove the temporary text.

```
…
<tr>
        <td colspan="3"><!-- Bottom Text Links -->
        <a href="#">World News</a> |
        <a href="#">Sports</a> |
        <a href="#">Entertainment</a> |
        <a href="#">Classifieds</a> |
        <a href="#">Weather</a> |
        <a href="#">Business</a>
        </td>
</tr>
…
```

2. Center the contents of the Bottom Text Links cell.

```
…
<tr>
        <td colspan="3" align="center"><!-- Bottom Text Links -->
        <a href="#">World News</a> |
        <a href="#">Sports</a> |
…
```

Remember that if your page does not look like the screenshots you should check the code very carefully. Your syntax has to be correct in order for the page to work properly.

3. Save the file and refresh the browser.

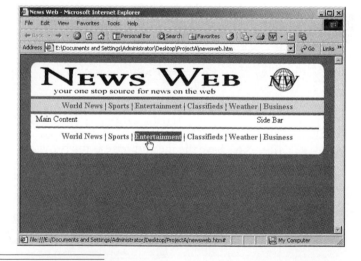

Add the Main Content Text

1. Navigate to and open **WIP>A_Project_HTML>stories.txt**.

2. Select and copy the contents of the file into your clipboard.

3. Close the stories.txt file.

4. Paste the contents into the Main Content cell. Be sure to remove the temporary text.

```
        <td width="430"><!-- Main Content -->
        Teachers Awarded A Raise
        Congress passed a bill today that will change the state of
        education in the U.S. The <i>Alder's Education Reform Bill</i>,
        sponsored by Florida Democrat David Alders, gives teachers a
        raise as part of a major overhaul of the entire education system.
        The raise is expected to be between 33% and 47%, depending
        upon years of service. The entire package will cost the federal
        government billions over the next 10 years. In a press conference,
        Congressman Alders said: "It's the least we can do for tomorrow's
        future." more...

        Kingfish Return Early
        From all reports this week it seems we are getting a little early
        push of kingfish in the area. Some nice ones were caught close
        to the beach at Redington as well as off St. Pete. Beach near the
        artificial reef. They all were nice sized fish over 20 pounds and
        were caught among schools of large Spanish mackerel. Of course
        Spanish mackerel is just about their favorite food when they are
        around. The Spanish have been large as well, from 4 to 7 pounds
        being the average size caught by the live bait fishermen. The only
        problem right now is that you will have to move around enough
        to find water that is free of red tide and that can be difficult as
        windy as it has been. more...     </td>
        <td width="15"> <!-- Middle 15 pixel Spacer --></td>
```

…

5. Set the headlines to level 2 headings.

…

```
        <td width="430"><!-- Main Content -->
        <h2>Teachers Awarded A Raise</h2>
Congress passed a bill today that will change the state of
```

…

```
        <h2>Kingfish Return Early</h2>
        From all reports this week it seems we are getting a little early
```

…

6. Mark up the paragraphs with the <p> element.

…

```
        <td width="430"><!-- Main Content -->
        <h2> Teachers Awarded A Raise</h2>

        <p> Congress passed a bill today that will change the state of
        education in the U.S. The <i>Alder's Education Reform Bill</i>,
        sponsored by Florida Democrat David Alders, gives teachers a
        raise as part of a major overhaul of the entire education system.
        The raise is expected to be between 33% and 47%, depending
        upon years of service. The entire package will cost the federal
        government billions over the next 10 years. In a press conference,
        Congressman Alders said: "It's the least we can do for tomorrow's
        future."  more...</p>
```

```
<h2> Kingfish Return Early </h2>
<p> From all reports this week it seems we are getting a little early
push of kingfish in the area. Some nice ones were caught close
to the beach at Redington as well as off St. Pete. Beach near the
artificial reef. They all were nice sized fish over 20 pounds and
were caught among schools of large Spanish mackerel. Of course
Spanish mackerel is just about their favorite food when they are
around. The Spanish have been large as well, from 4 to 7 pounds
being the average size caught by the live bait fishermen. The only
problem right now is that you will have to move around enough
to find water that is free of red tide and that can be difficult as
windy as it has been. more... </p>
</td>
```

...

7. Create links out of the "more…" text.

...

```
<h2> Teachers Awarded A Raise </h2>
<p> Congress passed a bill today that will change the state of
```

...

```
future." <a href="#">more...</a>
```

```
<h2> Kingfish Return Early </h2>
<p> From all reports this week it seems we are getting a little early
```

...

```
windy as it has been. <a href="#">more...</a>
```

...

8. Save the file and refresh the browser.

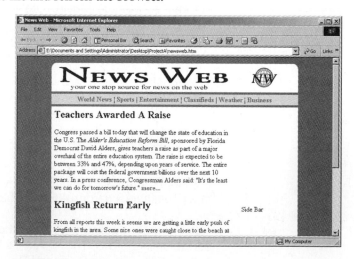

Add the Main Content Images

1. Insert the topstory.gif image into the top of the Main Content cell.

...

       \<td width="430">\<!-- Main Content -->
       \<img src="images/topstory.gif" height="40" width="283" alt="Today's Top
Stories" />
       \<h2>Teachers Awarded A Raise\</h2>

...

2. Add the teachers.jpg image to the first paragraph and set it to align to the left.

...

       \<h2>Teachers Awarded A Raise\</h2>
       \<p>\<img src="images/teachers.jpg" width="165" height="125"
alt="Teacher" align="left" />
       Congress passed a bill today that will change the state of

...

3. Add the boat.jpg image and set it to align to the right.

...

       \<h2> Kingfish Return Early \</h2>
       \<p>\<img src="images/boat.jpg" width="125" height="187" alt="Fishing
Boat" align="right" />
       From all reports this week it seems we are getting a little early...

...

4. Save the file and refresh the browser.

Exercise Setup

In order to format the sidebar we need to use a nested table. The table will have one column and 11 rows.

Create a Nested Table

1. Insert the <table> element into the Side Bar cell of the main table. Be sure to remove the temporary text.

...

```
<td width="125"><!-- Side Bar -->
<table>
</table>
</td>
```

...

2. Set the border and the cellspacing of the table to 0 (zero) and the width to 100%.

...

```
<td width="125"><!-- Side Bar -->
<table border="0" cellspacing="0" width="100%">
</table>
</td>
```

...

3. Create the following cells and add the appropriate comments in the sidebar table. Notice that some of the cells do not have comments, but have non-breaking spaces instead. These cells are for spacing only, and no content will go in them.

...

```
<td width="125"><!-- Side Bar -->
<table border="0" cellspacing="0" width="100%">
<tr>
        <td> </td>
</tr>
<tr>
        <td> </td>
</tr>
<tr>
        <td><!-- Weather Title --></td>
</tr>
<tr>
        <td><!-- Weather Info --></td>
</tr>
<tr>
        <td> </td>
</tr>
<tr>
        <td><!-- Stories Title --></td>
</tr>
<tr>
        <td><!-- Story 1 --></td>
</tr>
<tr>
        <td><!-- Story 2 --></td>
</tr>
<tr>
        <td> </td>
```

```
            </tr>
            <tr>
                    <td><!-- Subscribe Title --></td>
            </tr>
            <tr>
                    <td><!-- Subscribe Info --></td>
            </tr>
            </table>
            </td>
...
```

4. Save the file. Since there are no changes displayed in the browser at this point, we will refresh the browser at the end of the next section.

Fill in the Weather Information

1. In the Weather Title cell, type the text "Today's Weather", and mark it up as a level 3 heading.

...

```
        <tr>
                <td><!-- Weather Title -->
                <h3>Today's Weather</h3>
                </td>
        </tr>
```

...

2. Insert the sm_stripe.gif image immediately below the title. Do not put in a break element.

...

```
        <tr>
                <td><!-- Weather Title -->
                <h3>Today's Weather</h3>
                <img src="images/sm_stripe.gif" height="3" width="123" alt="Small
blue stripe" />
                </td>
        </tr>
```

...

3. Insert the following content into the Weather Info cell.

...

```
        <tr>
                <td><!-- Weather Info -->
                <b>In Gainesville, FL<br />
                Currently:</b> Clear, 86&deg;<br />
                <b>Precip. Today:</b> n/a <br />
                <b>Heat Index:</b> 91&deg; <br />
                <b>Today's Outlook:</b><br />
                Thunderstorms, 86&deg; <br />
                <b>Tomorrow's Outlook:</b> <br />
                Thunderstorms <br />
                High 90&deg;, Low 69&deg;
                <a href="#">Change Location</a>
                </td>
        </tr>
```

...

4. Save the file and refresh the browser.

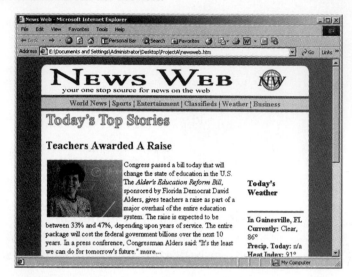

Exercise Setup

There are three problems at this point. First, the sidebar table is not positioned at the top of the page. Second, the text in the sidebar is a little too large. Finally, the headings are also little large and would be better with less space on the bottom.

Format the Sidebar

1. Set the vertical alignment value of the Sidebar cell of the main table to top.

...

```
<td width="125" valign="top"><!-- Sidebar -->
<table border="0" cellspacing="0" width="100%">
<tr>
        <td> </td>
```

...

2. Add the following CSS information to the style sheet in the head of the document:

...
```
a:hover {color: #ffff99;
background-color: #0066cc;
font-weight: bold;
text-decoration: none;
}

h3 {margin-bottom: 0px;
   font-size: 1em;
}

.sidebar-text {font-size: .8em}
</style>
</head>
```
...

3. Apply the sidebar-text style to the Sidebar table.

...

```
<td width="125" valign="top"><!-- Side Bar -->
<table border="0" class="sidebar-text" cellspacing="0" width="100%">
<tr>
        <td> </td>
```

...

4. Save the file and refresh the browser.

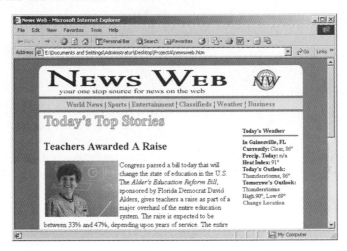

Fill in the Breaking Stories

1. In the Stories Title cell, type the text "Breaking Stories", and mark it up as a level 3 heading.

...

```
<tr>
        <td><!-- Stories Title -->
        <h3>Breaking Stories</h3>
        </td>
</tr>
```

...

2. Insert the sm_stripe.gif image immediately below the heading. Do not put in a break element.

...

```
<tr>
        <td><!-- Stories Title -->
        <h3>Breaking Stories</h3>
        <img src="images/sm_stripe.gif" height="3" width="123" alt="Small
blue stripe" />
        </td>
</tr>
```

...

3. Add the following content into the Story 1 cell:

...

```
    <tr>
            <td><!-- Story 1 -->
            <a href="#">Cloning Advancement</a><br />
            A major advancement in the cloning field occurred today, as an
            ant was cloned.
            </td>
    </tr>
```

...

4. Insert the following content into the Story 2 cell:

...

```
    <tr>
            <td><!-- Story 2 -->
            <a href="#">Poor Sports</a><br />
            Today, in a Virginia baseball game, the Mavericks stormed the field
            and a riot broke out.
            </td>
    </tr>
```

...

5. Save the file and refresh the browser.

Fill in the Subscription Options

1. In the Subscribe Title, cell type "Subscription Options", and mark it up as a level 3 heading.

...

```
    <tr>
            <td><!-- Subscribe Title -->
            <h3>Subscription Options</h3>
            </td>
    </tr>
```

...

2. Insert the sm_stripe.gif image immediately below the image. Do not put in a break element.

...

```
    <tr>
            <td><!-- Subscribe Title -->
            <h3>Subscription Options</h3>
            <img src="images/sm_stripe.gif" height="3" width="123" alt="Small
blue stripe" />
            </td>
    </tr>
...
```

3. Add the following content to the Subscribe Info cell:

...

```
    <tr>
            <td><!-- Subscribe Info -->
            Get News Web delivered to your front door. Well, at least to
            your email client.<br />
            <a href="#">Subscribe</a>
            </td>
    </tr>
...
```

4. Save the file and refresh the browser.

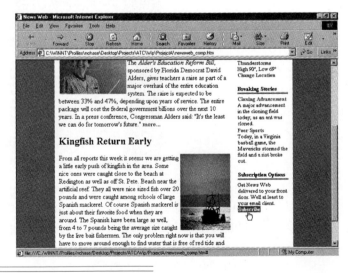

Add the Last Updated Information

1. In the Main Content cell of the main table, insert a break after the topstory.gif image.

...

```
    <td width="430"><!-- Main Content -->
    <img src="images/topstory.gif" height="40" width="283" alt="Today's Top
Stories" /><br />
    <h2>Teachers Awarded A Raise</h2>
...
```

2. Type the following text:

...

```
<td width="430"><!-- Main Content -->
<img src="images/topstory.gif" height="40" width="283" alt="Today's Top Stories" /><br />
Last Updated Sunday 24 June 2001 5:30 PM EST
<h2>Teachers Awarded A Raise</h2>
```

...

3. Save the file and refresh the browser.

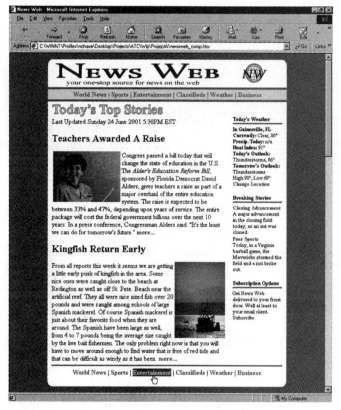

Congratulations you have just helped the local newspaper achieve their goal of providing online news content. They can now meet their marketing goals! You created their Web page using tables for layout and CSS for formatting.

Project B: Cyber Travel

A local travel agency, Cyber Travel, has retained you to help them with their Web site. They have the basic site in place, but now they want to make their site more interactive. They hope that by adding a questionnaire-style form, they can encourage potential customers to submit their travel questions, plans and desires as well as contact information, thus creating additional business online and building a better marketing database.

You will create the form to help Cyber Travel meet their needs. The proper planning is complete and how the structure should be built has been decided. Now it's time to work on the form.

Creating this form will call on your abilities to produce all of the XHTML form elements. You will begin by building your form using only paragraphs and breaks. Then you will use tables to make the form more attractive.

Build the Basic Form

1. Navigate to **RF_HTML>B_Project_HTML**, and copy the B_Project_HTML folder to your WIP folder.

2. Open your text editor. Create a new file and save it as "ctform.html" to **WIP>B_Project_HTML**.

3. Write the basic required XHTML page elements, and entitle the page "Cyber Travel Arrangements".

```
<!DOCTYPE html PUBLIC "-//W3C//DTD XHTML 1.0 Transitional//EN"
"http://www.w3.org/TR/xhtml1/DTD/xhtml1-transitional.dtd">
<html>
<head>
<title>Cyber Travel Arrangements</title>
</head>
<body>
</body>
</html>
```

4. Set the page's background color to white.

```
..
<title>Cyber Travel Arrangements</title>
</head>
<body bgcolor="#ffffff">
...
```

5. Insert the basic <form> element within the body element.

```
...
</head>
<body>
<form name="flights" action="post">
</form>
</body>
...
```

6. Insert the travel options using the following paragraph, text and select box:

```
…
<form name="flights" action="post">
<p>
Choose your destination:
        <select name="destination">
        <option></option>
        <option>Chicago</option>
        <option>New York City</option>
        <option>Orlando</option>
        <option>San Francisco</option>
        </select>
</p>
</form>
…
```

7. Add the submit and reset buttons.

```
…
        </select>
</p>
<p>
        <input type="submit" value="Submit" />
        <input type="reset" value="Reset" />
</p>
</form>
</body>
…
```

8. Save the file.

9. Open **WIP>B_Project_HTML>ctform.htm**l in your browser.

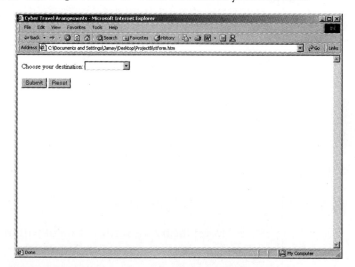

10. Keep both windows open so that we can watch our progress.

Exercise Setup

The rest of the form is broken into four subforms. These will be formatted as blocks, eventually, each with its own individual background color. For now, though, we'll just use paragraphs and comments to denote each of these subforms. This is purely for organization of our data.

Create Subforms

1. Give the form structure by inserting the following paragraph elements and comments before the submit element:

```
…
        </select>
</p>

<p><!-- Accommodations Subform -->
</p>

<p><!-- Travel Habits Subform -->
</p>

<p><!-- Contact Info Subform -->
</p>

<p><!-- Newsletter Subform -->
</p>

<p>
        <input type="submit" name="submit" value="Submit" />
…
```

2. Add the key statements or questions to each of the subforms.

```
…
        </select>
</p>

<p><!-- Accommodations Subform -->
Travel Accommodations Selector
</p>

<p><!-- Travel Habits Subform -->
Tell us about your travel habits
</p>

<p><!-- Contact Info Subform -->
How can we contact you?
</p>

<p><!-- Newsletter Subform -->
Which of our travel newsletters would you like to receive?
</p>

<p>
        <input type="submit" name="submit" value="Submit" />
…
```

3. Save the file and refresh the browser.

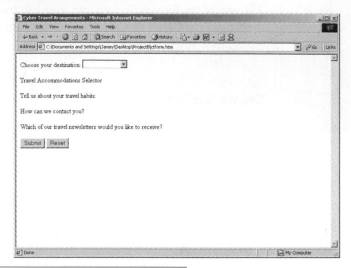

Adding Form Elements to the Subforms

1. Label the six select boxes by adding the breaks and text elements to the accommodations subform.

```
…
<p><!-- Accommodations Subform -->
Travel Accommodations Selector<br />
Class:

<br />
Snacks:

<br />
Seating:

<br />
Reading:

<br />
Food:

<br />
Movies:

</p>
<p><!-- Travel Habits Subform -->
…
```

2. Insert the appropriate select element and options for each of the labels. Make certain that the breaks follow the ending of the select elements.

```
…
<p><!-- Accommodations Subform -->
Travel Accommodations Selector<br />
```

```html
Class:
<select name="class">
        <option></option>
        <option>First Class</option>
        <option>Coach</option>
</select>
<br />
Snacks:
<select name="snacks">
        <option></option>
        <option>Yes</option>
        <option>No</option>
</select>
<br />
Seating:
<select name="seating">
        <option></option>
        <option>Window</option>
        <option>Aisle</option>
</select>
<br />
Reading:
<select name="reading">
        <option></option>
        <option>Yes</option>
        <option>No</option>
</select>
<br />
Food:
<select name="food">
        <option></option>
        <option>Yes</option>
        <option>No</option>
</select>
<br />
Movies:
<select name="movies">
        <option></option>
        <option>Yes</option>
        <option>No</option>
</select>
</p>
<p><!-- Travel Habits Subform -->
…
```

3. Save the file and refresh the browser.

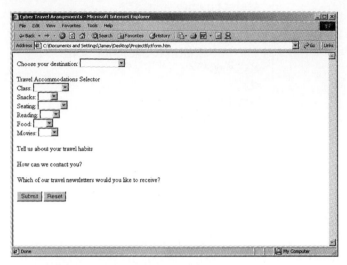

4. Add the travel-habits options to the travel habits subform, using the following text elements, breaks and radio buttons:

```
…
<p><!-- Travel Habits Subform -->
Tell us about your travel habits<br />
<input type="radio" name="TravelHabits" value="Infrequently" />
I travel infrequently<br />
<input type="radio" name="TravelHabits" value="Often" />
I am a travel maniac<br />
<input type="radio" name="TravelHabits" value="Necessity" />
I travel only when necessary<br />
<input type="radio" name="TravelHabits" value="Business" />
I only travel for business<br />
</p>
<p><!-- Contact Info Subform -->
…
```

5. Save the file and refresh the browser.

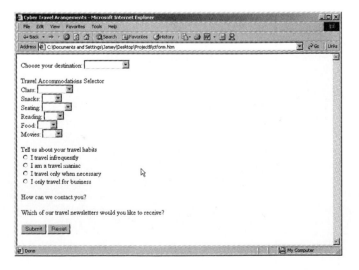

6. Label the six text boxes by adding the following breaks and text elements to the contact information subform:

```
...
<p><!-- Contact Info Subform -->
How can we contact you?<br />
Name:

<br />
Address:

<br />
City:

<br />
Zip:

<br />
Phone:

<br />
Email:
</p>
<p><!-- Newsletter Subform -->
...
```

7. Add a text box element for each label. Make certain that you put breaks after the ending of each text box element.

```
...
<p><!-- Contact Info Subform -->
How can we contact you?<br />
Name:
<input type="text" name="Name" size="40" />
<br />
Address:
<input type="text" name="Address" />
<br />
City:
<input type="text" name="City" />
<br />
Zip:
<input type="text" name="Zip" />
<br />
Phone:
<input type="text" name="Phone" />
<br />
Email:
<input type="text" name="Email" size="40" />
</p>
<p><!-- Newsletter Subform -->
...
```

8. Save the file and refresh the browser.

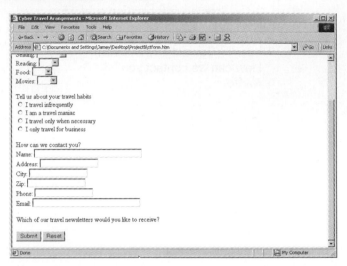

9. Add the travel-newsletter options to the newsletter subform, using the following text elements, breaks and checkboxes:

```
…
<p><!-- Newsletter Subform -->
Which of our travel newsletters would you like to receive?<br />
<input type="checkbox" name="Leisure" value="Subscribe" />
Leisure Time
<input type="checkbox" name="Pets" value="Subscribe" />
Traveling With Pets
<br />
<input type="checkbox" name="USA" value="Subscribe" />
USA Parks
<input type="checkbox" name="Seniors" value="Subscribe" />
Senior Trips
</p>
…
```

10. Save the file and refresh the browser.

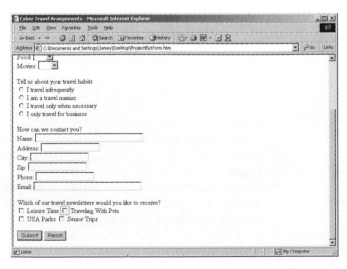

Exercise Setup
Now that we have a functional form, we can start to add some visual appeal. Let's begin by adding some images.

Add the Images

1. Insert the triangle.gif image next to the label for the first select box. Use the align attribute value, middle, to cause the text to align to the absolute middle of the triangle.

```
…
</head>
<body>
<form name="flights" action="post">
<p>
<img src="images/triangle.gif" alt="Triangle" align="middle" />
Choose your destination:
        <select name="destination">
…
```

2. Insert the triangle.gif image after each of the comments for the subforms. (This will cause the image to appear immediately in front of the label for each subform.)

```
…
<p><!-- Accommodations Subform -->
<img src="images/triangle.gif" alt="Triangle" align="middle" />
Travel Accommodations Selector<br />

…

<p><!-- Travel Habits Subform -->
<img src="images/triangle.gif" alt="Triangle" align="middle" />
Tell us about your travel habits<br />

…

<p><!-- Contact Info Subform -->
<img src="images/triangle.gif" alt="Triangle" align="middle" />
How can we contact you?<br />

…

<p><!-- Newsletter Subform -->
<img src="images/triangle.gif" alt="Triangle" align="middle" />
Which of our travel newsletters would you like to receive?<br />
…
```

Remember, all images are in the images folder in your WIP>B_Project_HTML folder.

3. Save the file and refresh the browser.

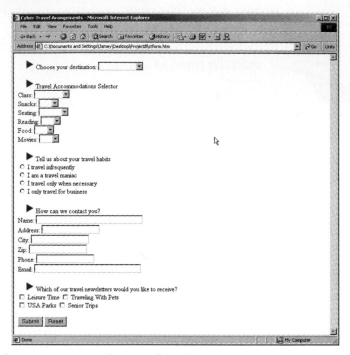

4. Add the logo.jpg image at the top of the document, within the form element.

```
…
<body>
<form name="flights" action="post">
<img src="images/logo.jpg" alt="Cyber Travel" />
<p>
<img src="images/triangle.gif" alt="Triangle" align="middle" />
Choose your destination:
…
```

5. Save the file and refresh the browser.

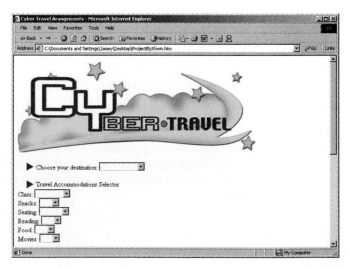

Exercise Setup

We will now use a table to format the entire form and to add a 10% margin on each side of the form.

Format the Document with a Table

1. Add a table to format the entire form. Set it as 80% width, centered, 5 pixels of padding and no border. Insert the opening and closing table tags with the following attributes within the form element:

…

```
</head>
<body>
<form name="flights" action="post">
<table width="80%" cellpadding="5" border="0" align="center">
<img src="images/logo.jpg" alt="Cyber Travel" />

…

<p>
        <input type="submit" name="submit" value="Submit" />
        <input type="reset" name="reset" value="Reset" />
</p>
</table>
</form>
</body>
</html>
```

2. Within the table tags, create a single row and single cell to contain the data.

…

```
<title>Cyber Travel Arrangements</title>
</head>
<body>
<form name="flights" action="post">
<table width="80%" cellpadding="5" border="0" align="center">
<tr>
<td>
<img src="images/logo.jpg" alt="Cyber Travel" />
<p>

…

<p>
        <input type="submit" name="submit" value="Submit" />
        <input type="reset" name="reset" value="Reset" />
</p>
</td>
</tr>
</table>
</form>
</body>
</html>
```

3. Save the file and refresh the browser.

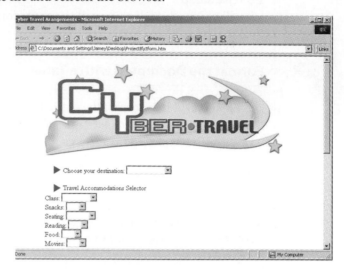

Exercise Setup

Now that we have content, we need to clean up our subforms. We will use tables to give a clean alignment and add some color. Each table will be centered, with a width of 75% of its parent element, 5 pixels of padding and a background color of #99ccff.

We will now create the table for the accommodations subform. This particular table will have three rows and four columns.

Format the Accommodations Subform

1. Create the table to format the accommodations subform. Add the following table element and attributes inside of the paragraph tags of this subform. The table should begin after the image and the "Travel Accommodations Selector" text.

…

```
<p><!-- Accommodations Subform -->
<img src="images/triangle.gif" alt="Triangle" align="middle" />
Travel Accommodations Selector<br />
<table border="1" cellpadding="5" width="75%" align="center" bgcolor="99ccff">
Class:
<select name="class">
```

…

```
<select name="movies">
        <option></option>
        <option>Yes</option>
        <option>No</option>
</select>
</table>
</p>
```

…

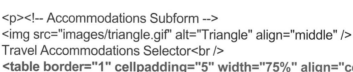

Notice that the border is set to 1. This setting enables us to see that we are getting the results that we want when we look at the table in the browser. Later we will set the border to 0.

2. Currently there is a problem with the nesting of elements. We have a table nested within a paragraph.

   To fix this, move the end of the paragraph element so that it is in front of the beginning table tag.

```
…
<p><!-- Accommodations Subform -->
<img src="images/triangle.gif" alt="Triangle" align="middle" />
Travel Accommodations Selector<br />
</p>
<table border="1" cellpadding="5" width="75%" align="center" bgcolor="#99ccff">
Class:
…

</select>
</table>
<p><!-- Travel Habits Subform -->
…
```

3. Now we need to add table rows. Create a total of three rows by placing table row tags around select elements in pairs. Make certain that you add the following comments as well:

```
…
<p><!-- Accommodations Subform -->
<img src="images/triangle.gif" alt="Triangle" align="middle" />
Travel Accommodations Selector<br />
</p>
<table border="1" cellpadding="5" width="75%" align="center" bgcolor="#99ccff">
<tr> <!--Accom. Row 1 -->
Class:
<select name="class">
        <option></option>
        <option>First Class</option>
        <option>Coach</option>
</select>
<br />
Snacks:
<select name="snacks">
        <option></option>
        <option>Yes</option>
        <option>No</option>
</select>
<br />
</tr>
<tr> <!--Accom. Row 2 -->
Seating:
<select name="seating">
        <option></option>
        <option>Window</option>
        <option>Aisle</option>
</select>
<br />
```

```
Reading:
<select name="reading">
        <option></option>
        <option>Yes</option>
        <option>No</option>
</select>
<br />
</tr>
<tr> <!--Accom. Row 3-->
Food:
<select name="food">
        <option></option>
        <option>Yes</option>
        <option>No</option>
</select>
<br />
Movies:
<select name="movies">
        <option></option>
        <option>Yes</option>
        <option>No</option>
</select>
</tr>
</table>
<p><!-- Travel Habits Subform -->
…
```

4. Save the file and refresh the browser. Notice that the background color has not been applied. This is because there are no data cells in the table yet.

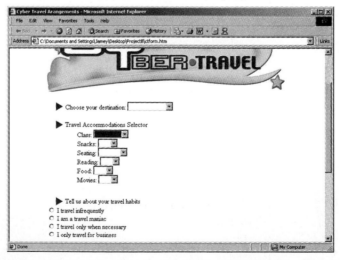

5. Add table data elements to each select element and its label in the first row.

```
…
<table border="1" cellpadding="5" width="75%" align="center" bgcolor="99ccff">
<tr><!--Accom. Row 1 -->
<td>Class:</td>
<td>
<select name="class">
```

```
        <option></option>
        <option>First Class</option>
        <option>Coach</option>
</select>
<br />
</td>
<td>Snacks:</td>
<td>
<select name="snacks">
        <option></option>
        <option>Yes</option>
        <option>No</option>
</select>
<br />
</td>
</tr>
<tr><!--Accom. Row 2 -->
…
```

6. Add table data elements to each select element and its label in the second row.

```
…
<tr><!--Accom. Row 2 -->
<td>Seating:</td>
<td>
<select name="seating">
        <option></option>
        <option>Window</option>
        <option>Aisle</option>
</select>
<br />
</td>
<td>Reading:</td>
<td>
<select name="reading">
        <option></option>
        <option>Yes</option>
        <option>No</option>
</select>
<br />
</td>
</tr>
<tr><!--Accom. Row 3 -->
…
```

7. Add table data elements to each select element and its label in the third row.

```
…
<tr><!--Accom. Row 3 -->
<td>Food:</td>
<td>
<select name="food">
        <option></option>
        <option>Yes</option>
        <option>No</option>
```

```
</select>
<br />
</td>
<td>Movies:</td>
<td>
<select name="movies">
        <option></option>
        <option>Yes</option>
        <option>No</option>
</select>
</td>
</tr>
</table>
...
```

8. Save the file and refresh the browser.

9. Now that we have the table looking the way that we planned, set the table border to 0 (zero).

```
...
<table border="0" cellpadding="5" width="75%" align="center" bgcolor="#99ccff">
<tr><!--Accom. Row 1 -->
<td>Class:</td>
<td>
<select name="class">
...
```

10. Save the file and refresh the browser.

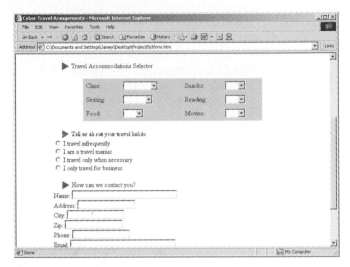

Exercise Setup

The table for this subform will be a single cell of different dimensions, but with the same formatting.

Format the Travel Habits Subform

1. Create the table to format the travel habits subform. Add the following table element and attributes inside the paragraph tags of this subform:

```
…
<p><!-- Travel Habits Subform -->
<img src="images/triangle.gif" alt="Triangle" align="middle" />
Tell us about your travel habits<br />
<table border="0" cellpadding="5" width="75%" align="center" bgcolor="#99ccff">
<input type="radio" name="TravelHabits" value="Infrequently" />
I travel infrequently<br />
<input type="radio" name="TravelHabits" value="Often" />
I am a travel maniac<br />
<input type="radio" name="TravelHabits" value="Necessity" />
I travel only when necessary<br />
<input type="radio" name="TravelHabits" value="Business" />
I only travel for business<br />
</table>
</p>
<p><!-- Contact Info Subform -->
…
```

2. Move the ending of the paragraph element so that it is in front of the ending table element.

```
…
<p><!-- Travel Habits Subform -->
<img src="images/triangle.gif" alt="Triangle" align="middle" />
Tell us about your travel habits<br />
</p>
```

```
<table border="0" cellpadding="5" width="75%" align="center" bgcolor="#99ccff">
<input type="radio" name="TravelHabits" value="Infrequently" />
I travel infrequently<br />
<input type="radio" name="TravelHabits" value="Often" />
I am a travel maniac<br />
<input type="radio" name="TravelHabits" value="Necessity" />
I travel only when necessary<br />
<input type="radio" name="TravelHabits" value="Business" />
I only travel for business<br />
</table>
<p><!-- Contact Info Subform -->
…
```

3. Since this table only needs a single cell, add one set of opening and closing row and data tags.

```
…
<p><!-- Travel Habits Subform -->
<img src="images/triangle.gif" alt="Triangle" align="middle" />
Tell us about your travel habits<br />
</p>
<table border="0" cellpadding="5" width="75%" align="center" bgcolor="#99ccff">
<tr>
        <td>
        <input type="radio" name="TravelHabits" value="Infrequently" />
        I travel infrequently<br />
        <input type="radio" name="TravelHabits" value="Often" />
        I am a travel maniac<br />
        <input type="radio" name="TravelHabits" value="Necessity" />
        I travel only when necessary<br />
        <input type="radio" name="TravelHabits" value="Business" />
        I only travel for business<br />
        </td>
</tr>
</table>
<p><!-- Contact Info Subform -->
…
```

4. Save the file and refresh the browser.

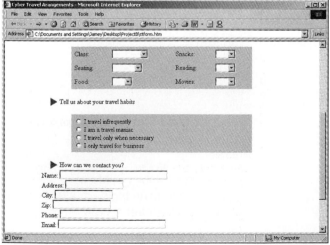

Exercise Setup

For this sub-form we will create a row for each element, and one column for the labels and one for the text boxes. This table will use the same formatting as the other subform tables.

Format the Contact Info Subform

1. Create the table to format the contact info subform. Add the following table element and attributes inside of the paragraph tags of the this subform:

```
…
<p><!-- Contact Info Subform -->
<img src="images/triangle.gif" alt="Triangle" align="middle" />
How can we contact you?<br />
<table border="0" cellpadding="5" width="75%" align="center" bgcolor="#99ccff">
Name:
<input type="text" name="Name" size="40" />
<br />
Address:
<input type="text" name="Address" />
<br />
City:
<input type="text" name="City" />
<br />
Zip:
<input type="text" name="Zip" />
<br />
Phone:
<input type="text" name="Phone" />
<br />
Email:
<input type="text" name="Email" size="40" />
</table>
</p>
<p><!-- Newsletter Subform -->
…
```

2. Move the ending of the paragraph element so that it precedes the beginning of the table.

```
…
<p><!-- Contact Info Subform -->
<img src="images/triangle.gif" alt="Triangle" align="middle" />
How can we contact you?<br />
</p>
<table border="0" cellpadding="5" width="75%" align="center" bgcolor="#99ccff">
Name:
<input type="text" name="Name" size="40" />
<br />
Address:
<input type="text" name="Address" />
<br />
City:
<input type="text" name="City" />
<br />
```

```
Zip:
<input type="text" name="Zip" />
<br />
Phone:
<input type="text" name="Phone" />
<br />
Email:
<input type="text" name="Email" size="40" />
</table>
<p><!-- Newsletter Subform -->
...
```

3. Add a row for each pair of labels and text boxes.

```
...
<table border="0" cellpadding="5" width="75%" align="center" bgcolor="#99ccff">
<tr>
        Name:
        <input type="text" name="Name" size="40" /><br />
</tr>
<tr>
        Address:
        <input type="text" name="Address" /><br />
</tr>
<tr>
        City:
        <input type="text" name="City" /><br />
</tr>
<tr>
        Zip:
        <input type="text" name="Zip" /><br />
</tr>
<tr>
        Phone:
        <input type="text" name="Phone" /><br />
</tr>
<tr>
        Email:
        <input type="text" name="Email" size="40" />
</tr>
</table>
...
```

4. Add opening and closing table data tags for each label and each text box.

```
...
<table border="0" cellpadding="5" width="75%" align="center" bgcolor="#99ccff">
<tr>
        <td>Name:</td>
        <td><input type="text" name="Name" size="40" /><br /></td>
</tr>
<tr>
        <td>Address:</td>
        <td><input type="text" name="Address" /><br /></td>
```

```
        </tr>
        <tr>
                <td>City:</td>
                <td><input type="text" name="City" /><br /></td>
        </tr>
        <tr>

                <td>Zip:</td>
                <td><input type="text" name="Zip" /><br /></td>
        </tr>
        <tr>

                <td>Phone:</td>
                <td><input type="text" name="Phone" /><br /></td>
        </tr>
        <tr>

                <td>Email:</td>
                <td><input type="text" name="Email" size="40" /></td>
        </tr>
</table>
…
```

5. Save the file and refresh the browser.

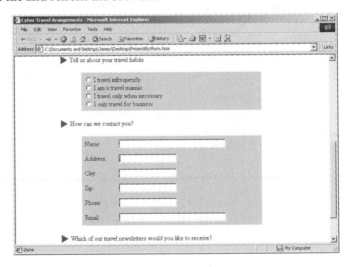

Exercise Setup

The final subform table will require a two-row, two-column table with the same formatting as the other subform tables.

Format the Newsletter Subform

1. Create the table to format the newsletter subform. Add the following table element and attributes inside the paragraph tags of the newsletter subform:

```
…
<p><!-- Newsletter Subform -->
<img src="images/triangle.gif" alt="Triangle" align="middle" />
Which of our travel newsletters would you like to receive?<br />
<table border="0" cellpadding="5" width="75%" align="center" bgcolor="#99ccff">
<input type="checkbox" name="Leisure" value="Subscribe" />
Leisure Time
```

```
<input type="checkbox" name="Pets" value="Subscribe" />
Traveling With Pets
<br />
<input type="checkbox" name="USA" value="Subscribe" />
USA Parks
<input type="checkbox" name="Seniors" value="Subscribe" />
Senior Trips
</p>
</table>
<p>
        <input type="submit" name="submit" value="Submit" />
…
```

2. Move the end of the paragraph element so that it precedes the table beginning element.

```
…
<p><!-- Newsletter Subform -->
<img src="images/triangle.gif" alt="Triangle" align="middle" />
Which of our travel newsletters would you like to receive?<br />
</p>
<table border="0" cellpadding="5" width="75%" align="center" bgcolor="#99ccff">
<input type="checkbox" name="Leisure" value="Subscribe" />
Leisure Time
<input type="checkbox" name="Pets" value="Subscribe" />
Traveling With Pets
<br />
<input type="checkbox" name="USA" value="Subscribe" />
USA Parks
<input type="checkbox" name="Seniors" value="Subscribe" />
Senior Trips
</table>
<p>
        <input type="submit" name="submit" value="Submit" />
…
```

3. Insert two table rows, one for the first pair of checkboxes and another for the second pair of checkboxes. These checkboxes and their labels will be rendered next to each other.

```
…
<table border="0" cellpadding="5" width="75%" align="center" bgcolor="#99ccff">
<tr>
        <input type="checkbox" name="Leisure" value="Subscribe" />
        Leisure Time
        <input type="checkbox" name="Pets" value="Subscribe" />
        Traveling With Pets<br />
</tr>
<tr>
        <input type="checkbox" name="USA" value="Subscribe" />
        USA Parks
        <input type="checkbox" name="Seniors" value="Subscribe" />
        Senior Trips
</tr>
</table>
…
```

4. Insert opening and closing table data tags for each pair of checkboxes and labels.

```
...
<table border="0" cellpadding="5" width="75%" align="center" bgcolor="#99ccff">
<tr>
        <td>
        <input type="checkbox" name="Leisure" value="Subscribe" />
        Leisure Time
        </td>
        <td>
        <input type="checkbox" name="Pets" value="Subscribe" />
        Traveling With Pets<br />
        </td>
</tr>
<tr>
        <td>
        <input type="checkbox" name="USA" value="Subscribe" />
        USA Parks
        </td>
        <td>
        <input type="checkbox" name="Seniors" value="Subscribe" />
        Senior Trips
        </td>
</tr>
</table>
...
```

5. Save the file and refresh the browser.

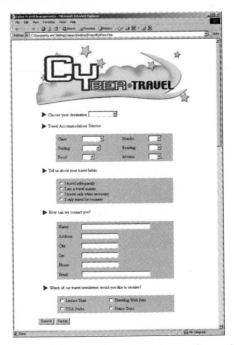

Congratulations! You have created the new customer-input form that will help Cyber Travel make their Web site more interactive and, potentially, expand their their marketing database and their business. Through the power of XHTML, you have helped them meet both their customers' needs and their marketing objectives.

Notes:

Project C: Hunter Films

Hunter Films is your own company through which you sell movies that you craft. You plan to use your Web site, hunterfilm.com, as a marketing venture to promote your abilities. It will serve both as a portfolio of your films and filmmaking abilities, and as a sales site for your products.

You have decided that your Web site should use some of the bells and whistles available to Web designers, especially given the product and services you are marketing. You plan to use JavaScript to help make your multimedia site more visually appealing.

You've determined the site design and are ready to build the page based on that layout. You are now working on the main page for this movie site. You plan to place thumbnails for three of your movies on the home page, and then use JavaScript to open individual Web pages for each of them.

Create the First Movie Page

1. Navigate to **RF_HTML>C_Project_HTML** and copy the C_Project_HTML folder to your WIP folder.

2. Open your text editor. Create and save a new file as "nessie.html" to **WIP>C_Project_HTML**.

3. Write the basic required XHTML page elements, and entitle the page "Nessie's Lost World Trailer".

```
<html>
<head>
<title>Nessie's Lost World Trailer</title>
</head>
<body>
</body>
</html>
```

To make current browsers display correctly, this project uses non-standard HTML.

4. Set the page's background color to white.

```
…
<title>Nessie's Lost World Trailer</title>
</head>
<body bgcolor="#ffffff">
…
```

5. Add a center-aligned div that will contain the contents of the page.

```
…
<body bgcolor="#ffffff">
<div align="center">
</div>
</body>
…
```

6. Add the text "Nessie's Lost World Trailer" and mark it up as a level 1 heading.

```
...
<div align="center">
<h1>Nessie's Lost World Trailer</h1>
</div>
</body>
...
```

7. Save the file.

8. Open **WIP>C_Project_HTML>nessie.html** in your browser.

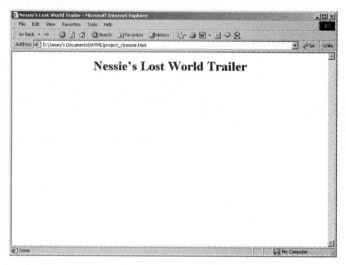

9. Keep both windows open so that you can watch your progress.

Add the Movie to the Page

1. Add the movie to the page using the embed tag, setting the height, width and type as follows:

```
...
<body bgcolor="#ffffff">
<div align="center">
<h1>Nessie's Lost World Trailer</h1>
<embed src="movies/nessie.mov" width="320" height="255"
type="video/quicktime" />
</div>
</body>
...
```

2. Save the file and refresh the browser.

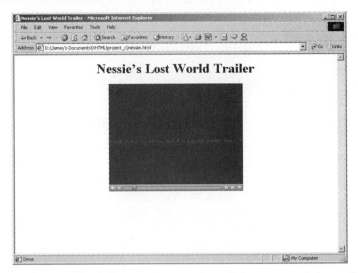

3. As you may have noticed, the movie started up right away, and depending on your browser and operating system, it may have no controls. Add the appropriate attributes so that the controls are available and autoplay is turned off.

```
...
<body bgcolor="#ffffff">
<div align="center">
<h1>Nessie's Lost World Trailer</h1>
<embed src="movies/nessie.mov" width="320" height="255" type="video/quicktime"
controls="true" controller="true" autoplay="false" />
</div>
</body>
...
```

4. Save the file and refresh the browser.

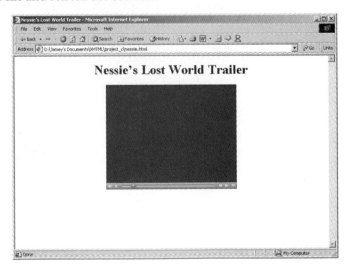

Exercise Setup

Now that we have the movie working properly, we need to offer the end-user a way to easily close the pop-up window in which this page will display. By adding a link with simple JavaScript, we can give the user that control.

Add a Close-Window Link

1. Add a break element after the embed element.

```
…
<div align="center">
<h1>Nessie's Lost World Trailer</h1>
<embed src="movies/nessie.mov" width="320" height="255" type="video/quicktime"
controls="true" controller="true" autoplay="false"  /><br />
</div>
</body>
…
```

2. Add the close-window link by inserting a link element with the following JavaScript as the value for the href attribute:

```
…
<div align="center">
<h1>Nessie's Lost World Trailer</h1>
<embed src="movies/nessie.mov" width="320" height="255" type="video/quicktime"
controls="true" controller="true" autoplay="false"  /><br />
<a href="javascript:self.close();">Close Window</a>
</div>
</body>
</html>
…
```

3. Save the file and refresh the browser.

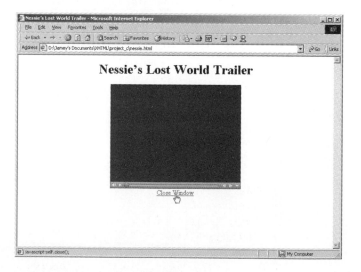

4. Click the link.

If you have only this one window open, you may see a message box asking if you want to close the window. If you get this message box, click Yes. This message box will not appear if you click the link from a pop-up window that is not the only open window.

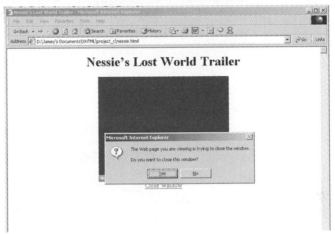

Exercise Setup

Since the code for the other two movie pages will be exactly the same except for the path and title information, we will use the Nessie's-Lost-World-Trailer page as a template for the other two.

Create the Second Movie Page

1. In the text editor, save the open file nessie.html as "logo.html" to
   WIP>C_Project_HTML.

2. Edit the file's title information so that it now reads "USA Logo Competition".

```
<html>
<head>
<title>USA Logo Competition</title>
</head>
<body bgcolor="#ffffff">
…
```

3. Change the contents within the level 1 heading tag so that it reads the same as the new title information.

```
…
<title>USA Logo Competition</title>
</head>
<body bgcolor="#ffffff">
<div align="center">
<h1>USA Logo Competition</h1>
<embed src="movies/nessie.mov" width="320" height="255" type="video/quicktime"
controls="true" controller="true" autoplay="false"  /><br />
<a href="javascript:self.close();">Close Window</a>
</div>
…
```

4. Change the file name in the src attribute of the embed element to "logo.mov".

```
…
<body bgcolor="#ffffff">
<div align="center">
<h1>USA Logo Competition</h1>
<embed src="movies/logo.mov" width="320" height="255" type="video/quicktime"
controls="true" controller="true" autoplay="false" /><br />
<a href="javascript:self.close();">Close Window</a>
</div>
</body>
…
```

5. Save the file.

6. Open **WIP>C_Project_HTML>logo.html** in the browser.

Exercise Setup

Again we will use the page that is loaded in our text editor as a springboard to create another page.

Create the Third Movie Page

1. In the text editor, save the open file logo.html as "egypt.html" to **WIP>C_Project_HTML**.

2. Edit the file's title information so that it now reads "MediEgypt Trailer".

```
<html>
<head>
<title>MediEgypt Trailer</title>
</head>
<body bgcolor="#ffffff">
…
```

3. Change the contents within the level 1 heading tag so that it reads the same as the title information.

```
…
<title>MediEgypt Trailer</title>
</head>
<body bgcolor="#ffffff">
<div align="center">
<h1>MediEgypt Trailer</h1>
<embed src="movies/logo.mov" width="320" height="255" type="video/quicktime"
controls="true" controller="true" autoplay="false"  /><br />
<a href="javascript:self.close();">Close Window</a>
</div>
…
```

4. Change the file name in the src attribute of the embed element to "egypt.mov".

```
…
<body bgcolor="#ffffff">
<div align="center">
<h1>MediEgypt Trailer</h1>
<embed src="movies/egypt.mov" width="320" height="255" type="video/quicktime"
controls="true" controller="true" autoplay="false"  /><br />
<a href="javascript:self.close();">Close Window</a>
</div>
</body>
…
```

5. Save the file.

6. Open **WIP>C_Project_HTML>egypt.html** in the browser.

7. Close the egypt.html file in your text editor.

Exercise Setup

Now that we have our three pages that we will open in pop-up windows, we need to create the main page.

Start the Main Page

1. Create a new file in your text editor and save it as "movies.html" to **WIP>C_Project_HTML**.

2. Write the basic required XHTML page elements, and entitle the page "Hunter Films".

```
<html>
<head>
<title>Hunter Films</title>
</head>
<body>
</body>
</html>
```

3. Set the page's background color to white.

```
…
<title>Hunter Films </title>
</head>
<body bgcolor="#ffffff">
…
```

Remember, all images, as in previous projects, can be found in the images subfolder (WIP>C_Project_HTML>images).

4. Add a center-aligned div that will house the contents of the page.

```
…
<body bgcolor="#ffffff">
<div align="center">
</div>
</body>
…
```

5. Insert the header.jpg image.

```
…
<body bgcolor="#ffffff">
<div align="center">
<img src="images/header.jpg" alt="Welcome to Hunter Films" />
</div>
</body>
…
```

6. Save the file.

7. Open **WIP>C_Project_HTML>movies.html** in your browser.

Add a Table for Layout

1. Add a table to control the page layout. Make certain that you put the correct number of cells in each of the four rows.

```
…
<div align="center">
<img src="images/header.jpg" alt="Welcome to Hunter Films" />
<table width="665" cellpadding="0" cellspacing="0" border="0">
<tr><!-- Row 1 -->
        <td></td>
        <td></td>
        <td></td>
        <td></td>
</tr>

<tr><!-- Row 2 -->
        <td></td>
</tr>

<tr><!-- Row 3 -->
        <td></td>
        <td></td>
        <td></td>
</tr>

<tr><!-- Row 4 -->
        <td></td>
        <td></td>
        <td></td>
</tr>
</table>
</div>
…
```

2. Add the rowspan, colspan and width attributes to the table cells.

```
<div align="center">
<img src="images/header.jpg" alt="Welcome to Hunter Films" />
<table width="665" cellpadding="0" cellspacing="0" border="0">
<tr><!-- Row 1 -->
        <td width="175" rowspan="2"></td>
        <td width="50" rowspan="2"></td>
        <td width="220"></td>
        <td width="220"></td>
</tr>

<tr><!-- Row 2 -->
        <td width="442" colspan="2"></td>
</tr>

<tr><!-- Row 3 -->
        <td width="175"></td>
        <td width="50"></td>
        <td  width="440" colspan="2"></td>
</tr>

<tr><!-- Row 4 -->
        <td width="175"></td>
        <td width="50"></td>
        <td  width="440" colspan="2"></td>
</tr>
</table>
</div>
```

3. Add the height attributes to the table rows.

```
…
<table width="665" cellpadding="0" cellspacing="0" border="0">
<tr height="105"><!-- Row 1 -->
        <td width="175" rowspan="2"></td>
        <td width="50" rowspan="2"></td>
        <td width="220"></td>
        <td width="220"></td>
</tr>

<tr height="115"><!-- Row 2 -->
        <td width="442" colspan="2"></td>
</tr>

<tr height="220"><!-- Row 3 -->
        <td width="175"></td>
        <td width="50"></td>
        <td width="440" colspan="2"></td>
</tr>

<tr height="220"><!-- Row 4 -->
        <td width="175"></td>
        <td width="50"></td>
```

```
                <td width="440" colspan="2"></td>
        </tr>
</table>
...
```

4. Save the file and refresh your browser. As you might expect, there will be no apparent change to the page.

Add the Contents to Row One

1. Add the thumbnail of the Nessie movie — nessie.jpg —to the first cell of row one.

```
...
<table width="665" cellpadding="0" cellspacing="0" border="0">
<tr height="105"><!-- Row 1 -->
        <td width="175" rowspan="2">
        <img src="images/nessie.jpg" alt="screenshot of Movie: Nessie's Lost
        World" />
        </td>
        <td width="50" rowspan="2"></td>
        <td width="220"></td>
        <td width="220"></td>
</tr>
...
```

2. Add the orange arrow image -- arrow.jpg -- to the second cell of row one.

```
...
<table width="665" cellpadding="0" cellspacing="0" border="0">
<tr height="105"><!-- Row 1 -->
        <td width="175" rowspan="2">
        <img src="images/nessie.jpg" alt="Screenshot of Movie: Nessie's Lost World" />
        </td>
        <td width="50" rowspan="2">
        <img src="images/arrow.jpg" alt="Orange arrow" />
        </td>
        <td width="220"></td>
        <td width="220"></td>
</tr>
...
```

3. Save the file and refresh your browser.

4. Add the Hot Movie and sun images — hot.jpg and sun.jpg — to the third cell of row one.

```
…
<table width="665" cellpadding="0" cellspacing="0" border="0">
<tr height="105"><!-- Row 1 -->
        <td width="175" rowspan="2">
        <img src="images/nessie.jpg" alt="Screenshot of Movie: Nessie's Lost World" />
        </td>
        <td width="50" rowspan="2">
        <img src="images/arrow.jpg" alt="Orange arrow" />
        </td>
        <td width="220">
        <img src="images/hot.jpg" alt="Hot Movie" />
        <img src="images/sun.jpg" alt="Picture of the sun" />
        </td>
        <td width="220"></td>
</tr>
…
```

5. Add the navigational-choice images -- new.jpg, archives.jpg, submit.jpg and contact.jpg -- to the fourth cell of row one.

```
…
<table width="665" cellpadding="0" cellspacing="0" border="0">
<tr height="105"><!-- Row 1 -->
        <td width="175" rowspan="2">
        <img src="images/nessie.jpg" alt="Screenshot of Movie: Nessie's Lost World" />
        </td>
        <td width="50" rowspan="2">
        <img src="images/arrow.jpg" alt="Orange arrow" />
        </td>
        <td width="220">
        <img src="images/hot.jpg" alt="Hot Movie" />
        <img src="images/sun.jpg" alt="Picture of the sun" />
        </td>
        <td width="220">
        <img src="images/new.jpg" alt="Navigation Choice: New Movies" />
```

```
        <img src="images/archives.jpg" alt="Navigation Choice: Movie Archive" />
        <img src="images/submit.jpg" alt="Navigation Choice: Submit Movies" />
        <img src="images/contact.jpg" alt="Navigation Choice: Contact Us" />
        </td>
</tr>
…
```

6. Save the file and refresh your browser.

Add the Contents to Row Two

1. Add the promotional text to the only cell in row two.

```
…
<tr height="115"><!-- Row 2 -->
        <td width="442" colspan="2">
        Nessie's Lost World

        Journey into the depths of Scotland's legendary Loch
        Ness as the infamous Loch Ness Monster, known
        affectionately as "Nessie" swims past our
        cameraman!
        </td>
</tr>
…
```

2. Add the paragraph elements to the text.

```
…
<tr height="115"><!-- Row 2 -->
        <td width="442" colspan="2">
        <p>Nessie's Lost World</p>
        <p>
        Journey into the depths of Scotland's legendary Loch
        Ness as the infamous Loch Ness Monster, known
        affectionately as "Nessie" swims past our
        cameraman!
        </p>
        </td>
</tr>
…
```

A file named copy.txt with the textual contents of this page can be found in the C_Project_HTML folder. You can copy and paste these pieces of text into your document.

3. Mark up the title of the section as a dummy link. (Later we will add JavaScript to this link to open nessie.html in a pop-up window.)

…

```
<tr height="115"><!-- Row 2 -->
        <td width="442" colspan="2">
        <p><a href="#">Nessie's Lost World</a></p>
        <p>
        Journey into the depths of Scotland's legendary Loch
        Ness as the infamous Loch Ness Monster, known
        affectionately as "Nessie" swims past our
        cameraman!
        </p>
        </td>
</tr>
…
```

4. Save the file and refresh your browser.

Add the Contents to Row Three

1. Add the MediEgypt Trailer screenshot and orange arrow image — egypt.jpg and arrow.jpg — to row three.

```
…
<tr height="220"><!-- Row 3 -->
        <td width="175">
        <img src="images/egypt.jpg" alt="Screenshot of Movie: MediEgypt
Trailer" />
        </td>
        <td width="50">
        <img src="images/arrow.jpg" alt="Orange arrow" />
        </td>
        <td width="440" colspan="2"></td>
</tr>
…
```

2. Save the file and refresh your browser.

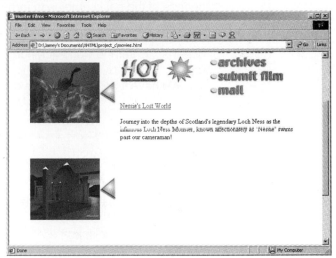

3. Add the promotional text about the MediEgypt movie to row three.

…

```
<tr height="220"><!-- Row 3 -->
        <td width="175">
        <img src="images/egypt.jpg" alt="Screenshot of Movie: MediEgypt Trailer" />
        </td>
        <td width="50">
        <img src="images/arrow.jpg" alt="Orange arrow" />
        </td>
        <td width="440" colspan="2">
        MediEgypt Trailer

        Enter an enchanted world where two legendary
        periods of the past combine to forge a new realm.
        It is a world of ancient magics, superstitions,
        colossal structures and larger-than-life kings and
        queens... Enter the world of MediEgypt.

        We have it and nobody else does!
        </td>
</tr>
…
```

4. Add the paragraph elements to the text.

…

```
<tr height="220"><!-- Row 3 -->
        <td width="175">
        <img src="images/egypt.jpg" alt="Screenshot of Movie: MediEgypt Trailer" />
        </td>
        <td width="50">
        <img src="images/arrow.jpg" alt="Orange arrow" />
        </td>
        <td width="440" colspan="2">
        <p>MediEgypt Trailer</p>
```

```
<p>Enter an enchanted world where two legendary
periods of the past combine to forge a new realm.
It is a world of ancient magics, superstitions,
colossal structures and larger-than-life kings and
queens... Enter the world of MediEgypt.
</p>
<p>We have it and nobody else does!</p>
</td>
</tr>
...
```

5. Mark up the title of the section as a dummy link.

...

```
<img src="images/arrow.jpg" alt="Orange arrow" />
</td>
<td width="440" colspan="2">
<p><a href="#">MediEgypt Trailer</a></p>

<p>Enter an enchanted world where two legendary
```

...

6. Save the file and refresh your browser.

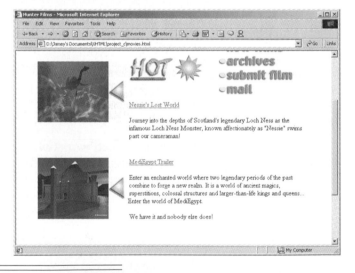

Add the Contents to Row Four

1. Add the 3D logo and arrow images -- logo.jpg and arrow.jpg -- to row four.

...
```
<tr height="220"><!-- Row 4 -->
        <td width="175">
        <img src="images/logo.jpg" alt="Screenshot of 3D Logo" />
        </td>
        <td width="50">
        <img src="images/arrow.jpg" alt="Orange arrow" />
        </td>
        <td width="440" colspan="2"></td>
</tr>
...
```

2. Save the file and refresh your browser.

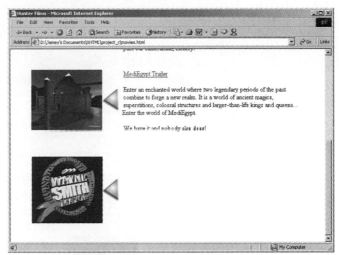

3. Add the promotional text to row four.

```
…
<tr height="220"><!-- Row 4 -->
        <td width="175">
        <img src="images/logo.jpg" alt="Screenshot of 3D Logo" />
        </td>
        <td width="50">
        <img src="images/arrow.jpg" alt="Orange arrow" />
        </td>
        <td width="440" colspan="2">
        USA Logo Competition

        Take a sneak peek at one of the most talked about
        logos in the forthcoming logo competition held each
        year in New York City, USA.

        It's hip, it's cool, and it's patriotic!
        </td>
</tr>
…
```

4. Add the following paragraph elements to the text:

```
…
        <td width="50">
        <img src="images/arrow.jpg" alt="Orange arrow" />
        </td>
        <td width="440" colspan="2">
        <p>USA Logo Competition</p>
        <p>
        Take a sneak peek at one of the most talked about
        logos in the forthcoming logo competition held each
        year in New York City, USA.
        </p>
        <p>It's hip, it's cool, and it's patriotic!</p>
        </td>
…
```

5. Mark up the title of the section as a dummy link.

…

```
<img src="images/arrow.jpg" alt="Orange arrow" />
</td>
<td width="440" colspan="2">
<p><a href="#">USA Logo Competition</a></p>
<p>
Take a sneak peek at one of the most talked about
```

…

6. Save the file and refresh your browser.

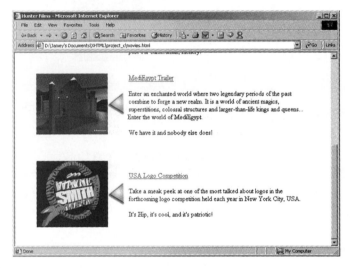

Exercise Setup

We will now add the JavaScript that will enable us to open the movie pages in pop-up windows. We will create a link for each movie that will open the appropriate movie page. Since the code for each of these three pop-up windows will be almost identical, we will use a function to accomplish this task.

Add the Pop-up Window JavaScript

1. Add the javascript element to the page, within the head element.

…
```
<head>
<title>Hunter Films</title>
<script type="text/javascript">
</script>
</head>
<body bgcolor="#ffffff">
```
…

2. Add the variable for the Web page that we want to open and the name of the window in which it will open.

…
```
<head>
<title>Hunter Films</title>
<script type="text/javascript">
```

```
        var fileName;
        var windowName;
</script>
</head>
…
```

3. Insert the following function after the variable declarations:

```
…
<script type="text/javascript">
        var fileName;
        var windowName;
        function openWindow(fileName, windowName) {
        window.open(fileName, windowName, 'height=400, width=400',
        'toolbar=no, resize=no, menubar=no, scrollbars=no');
        }
</script>
…
```

4. Save the file.

Add JavaScript Function Calls

1. Add the following JavaScript to the value of the first movie's link's href attribute:

```
…
<tr height="115"><!-- Row 2 -->
        <td width="442" colspan="2">
        <p><a href='javascript:openWindow('nessie.html', 'nessie'); ">Nessie's Lost
        World</a></p>
        <p>
        Journey into the depths of Scotland's legendary Loch…
…
```

2. Add the following JavaScript to the value of the second movie's link's href attribute:

```
…
<tr height="220"><!-- Row 3 -->
        <td width="175">
        <img src="images/egypt.jpg" alt="Screenshot of Movie: MediEgypt Trailer" />
        </td>
        <td width="50">
        <img src="images/arrow.jpg" alt="Orange arrow" />
        </td>
        <td width="440" colspan="2">
        <p><a href='javascript:openWindow('egypt.html', 'mediegypt'); ">MediEgypt
        Trailer</a></p>
        <p>Enter an enchanted world where two legendary…
…
```

3. Add the following JavaScript to the value of the third movie's link's href attribute:

```
…
<tr height="220"><!-- Row 4 -->
        <td width="175">
```

```
<img src="images/logo.jpg" alt="Screenshot of 3D Logo" />
</td>
<td width="50">
<img src="images/arrow.jpg" alt="Orange arrow" />
</td>
<td width="440" colspan="2">
<p><a href="javascript:openWindow('logo.html', 'logo');">USA Logo Competi-
tion</a></p>
<p>
Take a sneak peek at one of the most talked about
```

…

4. Save the file and refresh the browser.

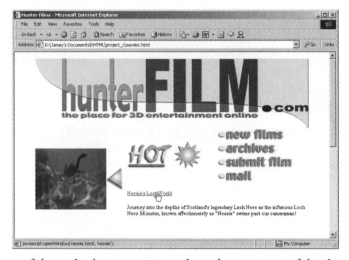

5. Since none of the code changes were made to the structure of the document, there
    should be no visible changes in the browser display.

    Test your three JavaScript links. They should pop up the movie windows created
    earlier. If you haven't done so already, click the Play button to watch the movies.

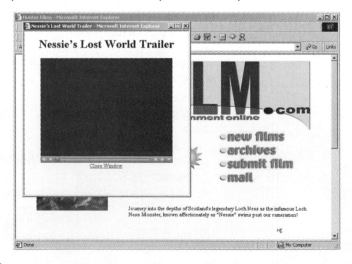

Exercise Setup
Now that the page is completely functional, let's add style information to format the text.

Add the Finishing Touches

1. Add the style element to the document head.

```
…
</script>
<style type="text/css">
</style>
</head>
…
```

2. Insert the following paragraph style declaration:

```
…
</script>
<style type="text/css">
p { font-family: Verdana, Arial, Helvetica, sans-serif;}
</style>
</head>
…
```

3. Insert the following link style declaration:

```
…
</script>
<style type="text/css">
p { font-family: Verdana, Arial, Helvetica, sans-serif;}
a { font-size: large;
     color: #339999 ;
}
</style>
</head>
…
```

4. Save the file and refresh the browser.

Congratulations! Your hunterfilm.com Web site will now display your talents and your products. You have just created an attractive Web page using embedded multimedia and JavaScript and have showcased your Web-design abilities, as well.

Notes:

Project D: North Star Adventure Gear

North Star Adventure Gear (NSAG) has had a Web site for some time. While the site has worked for many users, management has become aware that it is not universally accessible. One senior manager has given up the idea of accessing the site on a PDA after discovering that he couldn't even use it from his laptop because of the screen size. Several employees are colorblind or have limited vision and have complained about the site being hard to read. Some customers have complained about not finding the company through major search engines. Management suspects that they may be losing business because of the site design and want to update the site appropriately.

As a member of the in-house Web team, you have been charged with updating the NSAG site, addressing a variety of usability and accessibility issues without throwing away the present look entirely. You will begin by assessing the site and identifying the issues. Once you have determined the problems, you will redesign the site, using CSS to help separate content from presentation, easing usability and maintenance concerns, and allowing you to build a site that will still be usable even in browsers that do not fully support CSS. You will add <meta /> tags to make the site more accessible to search engines.

Assessing the Usability and Accessibility

1. Navigate to **RF_HTML>D_Project_HTML**, and copy the D_Project_HTML folder to your WIP folder.

2. Open **WIP>D_Project_HTML>before.html** in your browser. Depending on your screen resolution, you will see some differences. For the beginning of this example, we are using 1024 × 768 for our screen resolution.

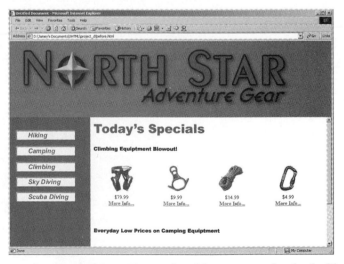

3. If your screen is set to 1024 × 768, you should see a page that looks like the one in the preceding screenshot. If your screen is set to less than 1024 × 768, then you can see a major problem immediately!

To set monitor resolution on a Macintosh system:

- Select Apple (menu)>Control Panels>Monitors.
- Double-click on the desired resolution in the Resolution list on the right side of the window.
  - If the desired resolution is not shown, the combination of the monitor and the computer's video card is not capable of displaying that resolution.
  - Note: if the desired resolution is not visible in the Resolution list and the Show drop-down menu displays Recommended, hold down your mouse button with the cursor over the arrows on the right of the menu to reveal additional options. If available, select All. Once All is selected, additional available-but-not-recommended screen resolutions will show in the list below. Select the desired resolution.

To set monitor resolution on a Windows-based system:

- Right-click the desktop and choose Properties from the pop-up menu.
- Click on the Settings tab.
- Move the Desktop or Screen Area slider to the left or right until the desired resolution shows.
  - If the desired resolution is not shown, the combination of the monitor and the computer's video card is not capable of that resolution.
- Click Apply.

4. Take a few minutes and write down all the accessibility/usability issues that you see with this site. (All of the links are disabled.) After you have finished, proceed to the next step where we will discuss all of the site's problems.

5. Let's begin by looking at this site with a screen resolution that is much more common than 1024 × 768 — 800 × 600. Because the majority of Internet users use this screen resolution, this is how most people will view the site.

6. As you can see, the menu and logo frames scrolling are turned off. Since this Web page was made without regard to screen resolutions other than 1024 × 768, visitors to the site cannot view the entire logo, and more importantly, they cannot successfully navigate through the site.

While turning on scrolling in those frames may alleviate these problems slightly, each frame would have both horizontal and vertical scrollbars at 800 × 600. This makes the content very difficult to read and detracts from usability. The frames also essentially make this site virtually invisible to search engines. This is not favorable for any business!

7. Another problem that you may or may not have noticed is that there is no alt text for any of the images. Because most Web authors check their pages with images turned on, this is a commonly missed problem, but it seriously detracts from the accessibility of the site. This is made much worse because the only text on the page is the prices and links to more information. It would be very unclear to a person using an aural browser to what the prices or links applied.

8. Because the headings are images as well, even if there were alt text, there is no mark up making this text more important. Using <h1> – <h6> enables you to make that information clearly more important to aural browsers, and search engines use this information to help rank your site.

9. The color scheme also needs to be examined. The logo doesn't have much contrast between the foreground and background, which could cause problems for users who are colorblind, have poor vision or are using a poor-quality LCD monitor.

10. The last major usability issue with this site is that the site's title is "Untitled." This is a small, careless mistake that can lead to major problems. Most search engines value the title of the page very highly in their indexing algorithm. This means that you will be that much harder to find using search engines. On the rare chance that someone does find the site and bookmarks it, the bookmark will be read "untitled." The next time that individual cleans out his or her bookmarks, he or she is likely to just delete all untitled bookmarks.

Planning a Better Web Site

Now that we know what is wrong with it, we can plan changes to the site that will make it more user friendly. CSS, tables and frames, when used for layout, can detract from usability and accessibility. A thoughtfully structured page, however, can make use of CSS and tables to create a page that is actually more accessible, as long as it is done carefully.

Our first step is to make a hand-drawn comp of the updated site that we will build.

Carefully planned tables can be used for layout without detracting from accessibility and, in fact, can actually improve accessibility.

Looking at this comp, we have figured out that we will use one containing div to hold all contents. We will also place a div at the top that will have a brown background and a smaller and slightly-reworked version of the old logo. We will have a standard navigational bar and tables to hold our catalog items, which will have text descriptions and alternate text. Below is our comp, annotated with these plans.

Exercise Setup

Now that we have a good idea of what our new Web site will look like and how it will be structured, we can begin to put it together.

Starting the Web Site

1. Open your text editor. Create and save a new file named "after.html" to your **WIP>D_Project_HTML**.

2. Write the basic required XHTML page elements, and entitle the page "North Star Adventure Gear".

```
<!DOCTYPE html PUBLIC "-//W3C//DTD XHTML 1.0 Transitional//EN"
"http://www.w3.org/TR/xhtml1/DTD/xhtml1-transitional.dtd">
<html>
<head>
<title>North Star Adventure Gear</title>
</head>
<body>
</body>
</html>
```

3. Now we want to set the background color for the body. Here we have to be careful. Because of browser differences in setting the background color through Cascading Style Sheets, we could set it to dark green through presentation attributes, then create a white area in which the content will live using CSS.

There's a problem with this, however. An older browser that doesn't understand CSS will get the dark background, but not the white area for text, leaving black text on a dark green background, which is practically invisible.

On the other hand, if we use CSS to set the background color for the page, the problem will be solved, because any browser that doesn't understand how to add the white background won't have added the green one anyway, leaving black text on a white background, which is perfectly acceptable.

Create an internal style sheet for the body tag and set the background color.

```
...
<html>
<head>
<title>North Star Adventure Gear</title>
<style type="text/css">
<!--
body{          background-color: #006633;
}
-->
</style>
</head>
<body>
</body>
</html>
```

4. Save the file.

5. Open **WIP>D_Project_HTML>after.html** in your browser. You should have a plain green page.

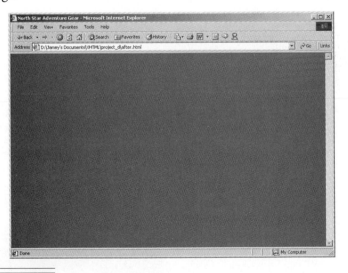

Adding the Main Div

1. Add a div element between the body tags.

```
...
<body>
<div>
</div>
</body>
...
```

2. Make this div 600 pixels wide so that it will fit on most traditional Web-browser windows, including those set as low as 640 × 480. Make the background color white, and add a solid border to it. Set the text color to black. Add the style information to the internal style sheet.

```
...
<title>North Star Adventure Gear</title>
<style type="text/css">
<!--
body{              background-color: #006633;
}

#main{             width: 600px;
                   border: solid 3px black;
                   text-align: left;
                   background-color: #ffffff;
                    color: #000000;
}

-->
</style>
</head>
<body>
...
```

3. Apply the main id style to the div.

```
...
<body>
<div id="main">
</div>
</body>
...
```

4. Save the file and refresh the browser. Because the div has no content, depending on the browser, either we see only the border, or we see a large white box bordered with black. In either case, we will see the background color once we put some contents into it.

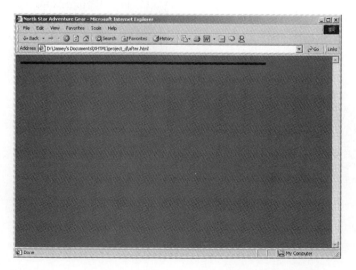

Adding the Logo

1. Add the sm_logo.gif image to the main div. Include an alternate text description as well as the height and width.

```
…
<body>
<div id="main">
        <img src="images/sm_logo.gif" alt="North Star Adventure Gear" border="0"
        width="437" height="97" />
</div>
</body>
…
```

Remember: images are at WIP>D_Project_HTML>images.

2. Save the file and refresh the browser.

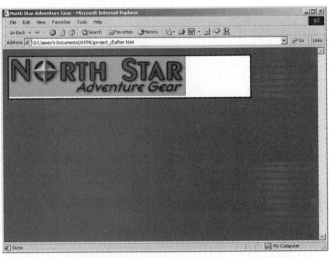

3. Because we want the image centered and we would like to have the brown cover 100% of the width around the image, we will use a div with a background color. Since Netscape will not draw the background color otherwise, add a border to the div. Insert the following style information within the style sheet:

Netscape will not fill a div with background color unless the div has a border.

```
…
#main{          width: 600px;
                border: solid 3px black;
                text-align: left;
                background-color: #ffffff;
                color: #000000;
}

.logo{          width: 100%;
                background-color: #cc9933;
                border:  solid 1px #cc9933;
}
-->
</style>
</head>
…
```

4. Create a div for the image and apply the logo id style to it.

```
...
<body>
<div id="main">
        <div class="logo">
                <img src="images/sm_logo.gif" alt="North Star Adventure Gear"
border="0" width="437" height="97" />
        </div>
</div>
</body>
...
```

5. To center the logo within the div, we have two options. One option is to use the center attribute, but this is deprecated, so for newer browsers the preferred option is to use the style sheet. Cover both bases by adding both.

```
...
.logo{              width: 100%;
                    background-color: #cc9933;
                    border:  solid 1px #cc9933;
                    text-align: center;
}
...
<body>
<div id="main">
        <div class="logo" align="center">
                <img src="images/sm_logo.gif" alt="North Star Adventure Gear"
border="0" width="437" height="97" />
        </div>
</div>
</body>
...
```

6. Save the file and refresh the browser.

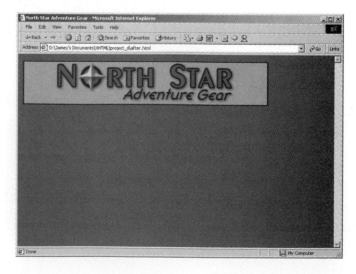

Building the Navigation

1. Now create the navigation bar. Add the following links after the logo div. Notice the addition of the title attribute. This allows us to add more information to our links.

```
...
<div id="main">
        <div class="logo" align="center">
                <img src="images/sm_logo.gif" alt="North Star Adventure Gear" bor-
der="0" width="437" height="97" />
        </div>
        <a href="#" title="Camping Supplies and Equipment">Camping</a> |
        <a href="#" title="Climbing Supplies and Equipment">Climbing</a> |
        <a href="#" title="Hiking Supplies and Equipment">Hiking</a> |
        <a href="#" title="Scuba Diving Supplies and Equipment">Scuba
        Diving</a> |
        <a href="#" title="Sky Diving Supplies and Equipment">Sky Diving</a>
</div>
</body>
...
```

2. Save the file and refresh the browser.

Remember to put a space before and after the pipe symbol (|) so that the links do not run together.

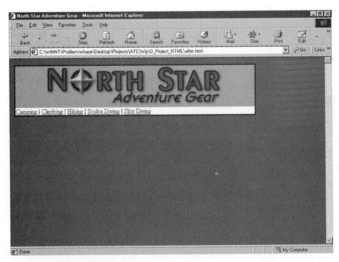

3. To add some visual appeal, add the navigation bar to a div and add a background color and borders to the top and bottom. Insert the following style information within the style sheet:

```
...
.logo{          width: 100%;
                background-color: #cc9933;
                border: solid 1px #cc9933;

}
```

```
.nav{              width: 100%;
                   text-align: center;
                   background-color: #ffffcc;
                   border-bottom: solid 3px black;
                   border-top: solid 3px black;
}
-->
</style>
…
```

4. Now we need to make our links conform to our color scheme. Insert the following style information within the style sheet to make the links the same color as the page background.

```
…
.nav{              width: 100%;
                   text-align:center;
                   background-color: #ffffcc;
                   border-bottom: solid 3px black;
                   border-top: solid 3px black;
}

a{                 font-size: .8em;
                   color: #006633;
                   font-family: arial, helvetica, sans-serif;
                   font-weight: bold;
                   text-decoration: none;
}

a:hover{           color: #ffffcc;
                   background-color: #006633;
}
-->
</style>
…
```

:hover is not supported in Netscape 4.

5. Wrap the links in a div element and apply the nav style to it.

```
…
        <div class="logo" align="center">
                <img src="images/sm_logo.gif" alt="North Star Adventure Gear" bor-
der="0" width="437" height="97" />
        </div>
        <div class="nav">
        <a href="#" title="Camping Supplies and Equipment">Camping</a> |
        <a href="#" title="Climbing Supplies and Equipment">Climbing</a> |
        <a href="#" title="Hiking Supplies and Equipment">Hiking</a> |
        <a href="#" title="Scuba Diving Supplies and Equipment">Scuba Diving</a> |
        <a href="#" title="Sky Diving Supplies and Equipment">Sky Diving</a>
        </div>
</div>
</body>
…
```

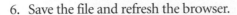

6. Save the file and refresh the browser.

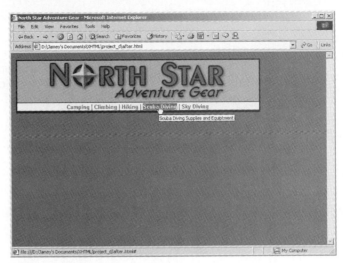

Adding the Main Contents

1. Add the first two headlines and mark them up as level 1 and level 3 headings, respectively.

```
…
<a href="#" title="Sky Diving Supplies and Equipment">Sky Diving</a>
        </div>
<h1>Today's Specials</h1>
<h3>Climbing Equipment Blowout!</h3>
</div>
</body>
…
```

2. Insert a table with four columns, one row and the following attributes:

```
…
<h3>Climbing Equipment Blowout!</h3>
<table align="center" width="100%" border="0" cellpadding="10" cellspacing="0">
        <tr>
        <td></td>
        <td></td>
        <td></td>
        <td></td>
        </tr>
</table>
</div>
</body>
…
```

3. Add the headline after the table, and mark the headline up as a level 3 heading.

```
…
        </tr>
</table>
<h3>Everyday Low Prices on Camping Equipment</h3>
</div>
…
```

4. Copy the entire table into your clipboard, and paste it after the last heading to make a second copy.

```
...
</table>
<h3>Everyday Low Prices on Camping Equipment</h3>
<table align="center" width="100%" border="0" cellpadding="10" cellspacing="0">
        <tr>
        <td></td>
        <td></td>
        <td></td>
        <td></td>
        </tr>
</table>
</div>
</body>
...
```

5. Save the file and refresh the browser. Notice that the tables cannot be seen. This is because the browser collapses all empty table cells.

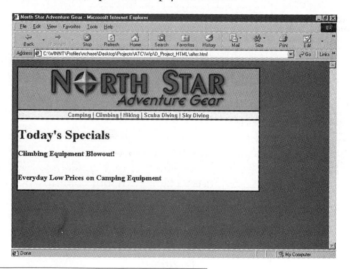

Adding Content to the Main Content Tables

1. Add the product information to each cell in the first table. Notice the use of title and alt attributes to make the links and images more accessible to aural and text-only browsers.

```
...
<table align="center" width="100%" border="0" cellpadding="10" cellspacing="0">
        <tr>
        <td>
        <img src="images/dring.jpg" alt="D-Ring" /><br />
        <b>D-Ring</b><br />
        Standard-sized locking D-Ring.<br />
        <b>Price:</b> $4.99<br />
        <a href="#" title="More information on this D-Ring">More Info...</a>
        </td>
        <td>
```

```
<img src="images/harness.jpg" alt="Climbing Harness" /><br />
<b>Climbing Harness</b><br />
Great harness with comfortable fit.<br />
<b>Price:</b> $79.99<br />
<a href="#" title="More information on this climbing harness">More
Info...</a>
</td>
<td>
<img src="images/ring.jpg" alt="Descent Ring" /><br />
<b>Descent Ring</b><br />
This descent ring prevents slippage<br />
<b>Price:</b> $9.99<br />
<a href="#" title="More information on this descent ring">More Info...</a>
</td>
<td>
<img src="images/rope.jpg" alt="50' of Nylon Rope" /><br />
<b>Nylon Rope</b><br />
50' of heavy duty nylon rope.<br />
<b>Price:</b> $14.99<br />
<a href="#" title="More information on this nylon rope">More Info...</a>
</td>
</tr>
</table>
<h3>Everyday Low Prices on Camping Equipment</h3>
…
```

2. Add the product information to each cell in the second table.

```
…
<h3>Everyday Low Prices on Camping Equipment</h3>
<table align="center" width="100%" border="0" cellpadding="10" cellspacing="0">
<tr>
<td>
<img src="images/tent1.jpg" alt="Two-Person Tent" /><br />
<b>Two-Person Tent</b><br />
Tear and fire resistant. <br />
<b>Price:</b> $139.99<br />
<a href="#" title="More information on this tent">More Info...</a>
</td>
<td>
<img src="images/lantern.jpg" alt="Camping Lantern" /><br />
<b>Camping Lantern</b><br />
Battery-powered and long-lasting<br />
<b>Price:</b> $39.99<br />
<a href="#" title="More information on this lantern">More Info...</a>
</td>
<td>
<img src="images/tent2.jpg" alt="Three-Person Tent" /><br />
<b>Three-Person Tent</b><br />
Tear and fire resistant.<br />
<b>Price:</b> $149.99<br />
<a href="#" title="More information on this tent">More Info...</a>
</td>
```

```
            <td>
            <img src="images/bag.jpg" alt="One-Person Sleeping Bag" /><br />
            <b>Sleeping Bag</b><br />
            Ideal for cold weather. Extra cushioning.<br />
            <b>Price:</b> $69.99<br />
            <a href="#" title="More information on this sleeping bag">More Info...</a>
            </td>
            </tr>
    </table>
    </div>
    </body>
    </html>
```

3. Save the file and refresh the browser.

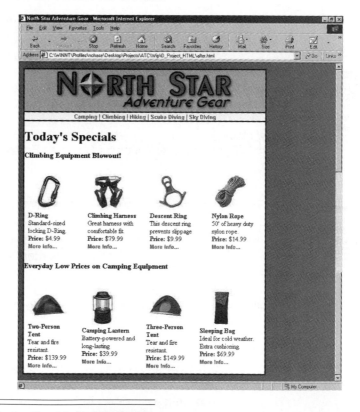

Adding Style to the Main Contents

1. The first style that we need is to help us align all of the contents of each cell to the center. Add the following style information to the style sheet:

```
...
a:hover{color: #ffffcc;
background-color: #006633;
}

td{          text-align: center;
}

-->
```

```
</style>
</head>
<body>
…
```

2. Apply the following styles to the h1 element inside the style sheet:

```
…
td{             text-align: center;
}

h1{             color: #006633;
                font-family: "arial black", helvetica, sans-serif;
                margin-left: 15px;

}
-->
</style>
</head>
<body>
…
```

3. Apply the following styles to the h3 element inside the style sheet.

```
…
h1{             color: #006633;
                font-family: "arial black", helvetica, sans-serif;
                margin-left: 15px;

}

h3{             color: #000000;
                font-family: arial, helvetica, sans-serif;
                margin-left: 25px;

}
-->
</style>
…
```

4. Center the entire contents by setting the text-alignment on the body tag to center. (If you're using Netscape, you won't see this effect, but it doesn't affect the usability or readability of the page. This graceful degradation is your goal. Even if a user can't see everything you intend, he or she should still be able to experience the content fully.)

```
…
body{           background-color: #006633;
                text-align: center;
}…
```

5. Save the file and refresh the browser.

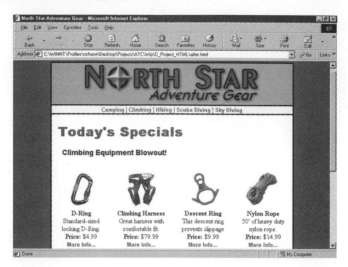

Exercise Setup

While we now have a page that resembles our comp, we must keep the real goal in mind. We want to have a page that is as usable and accessible as possible.

We've covered the main issues, such as alternate text on images and links, but Web Accessibility Initiative Guidelines provide additional suggestions. Because we're using tables for presentation instead of structure, we don't want to add structural information such as headers, but there is more information we can add.

Adding the Finishing Touches

1. Add following summary to the first table:

```
…
<h1>Today's Specials</h1>
<h3>Climbing Equipment Blowout!</h3>
<table align="center" width="100%" border="0" cellpadding="10" cellspacing="0"
summary="This table contains four products that are currently on sale, including a
D-Ring, a Climbing Harness, a Descent Ring, and a 50' Nylon Rope. Contact us at
webmaster@nsag.com for more information.">
        <tr>
        <td>
        <img src="images/dring.jpg" alt="D-Ring" /><br />
…
```

2. Add the following summary to the second table:

```
…
</table>
<h3>Everyday Low Prices on Camping Equipment</h3>
<table align="center" width="100%" border="0" cellpadding="10" cellspacing="0"
summary="This table contains camping equipment at our everyday low prices.
These include two- and three-person tents, a lantern, and a cold-weather sleeping
bag. Contact us at webmaster@nsag.com for more information.">
        <tr>
        <td>
        <img src="images/tent1.jpg" alt="Two-Person Tent" /><br />
…
```

3. Add contact information at the bottom of the page, after the second table. Use the style attribute to center the text.

…
```
</table>
     <p style="text-align:center">
     <a href="mailto:webmaster@nsag.com" title="Contact our webmaster with web-site-related issues">webmaster@nsag.com</a>
     </p>
</div>
</body>
</html>
```

4. Now add the meta information to improve our rating with the search engines.

…
```
<html>
<head>
<title>North Star Adventure Gear</title>
<meta name="author" content="John Smith" />
<meta name="copyright" content = "2001, North Star Adventure Gear Inc." />
<meta name="keywords" content="North Star Adventure Gear, North Star, Adventure, Adventure Equipment, camping, climbing, hiking, scuba diving, skydiving, rappelling" />
<meta name="description" lang="en" content="North Star Adventure Gear is an online dealer of fine adventure gear. We carry equipment for camping, climbing, hiking, scuba diving, and skydiving." />
<style type="text/css">
```
…

5. Save the file and refresh the browser. The only visible difference will be the link at the bottom of the page, but we know that our page is much more accessible and usable.

Congratulations! Your boss and senior management have tried out the new site and are very pleased with the changes that you have made. You have made the site more accessible while retaining some of the previous look and style so that it doesn't seem like a jarring change to users. Now customers can find North Star Adventure Gear in the search engines and can use the site once they find it.

Notes:

INDEX

top
alignment 38
tr 88
transform
text 76
Transitional DTDs 11, 345
vs. Strict DTDs 18
triggering events 234
typesetting
code 9

U

u 64
underline 50, 64
Uniform Resource Locator 6, 46
unintentional returns 54
Unisys Corporation 34
universal selector 68
unlawful content 304
unordered lists 90
uppercase 342
URL 6, 46
relative vs. absolute 54
usability 306
user
control over sound 270
disabled 306
experience customizing 224
information acquiring from forms 134
international 306

V

validation 12
form 251
parser 16
service 16
value=" 141
values
hex 78
RGB 77
variant 75
VBScript 225
vector graphics 353
verifying
a form 236
vertical space 93
video 264
visibility 216
Visual Basic 225
visual flow
of a Web page 195
visual media
and style sheets 73
volume 274
VR QuickTime 271

W

W3C 9
watermark 82
WAVs 266

Web address 46
weight
font 75
white space 20, 54
wide vs. deep 308
width
image 41
table columns 89
table 89, 97
window.open() 262
Windows Media Player 282
Working Draft 352
World Wide Web Consortium 9
wrapping text around an image 38
write() 229
WYSIWYG 74, 197

X

Xanadu 6
XForms 352
XHTML 6, 8, 9
and Cascading Style Sheets 64
XLink 353
XML 10
xml:lang 345

Y

Yahoo 11

Z

z-index 204

NOTES